THE MORMON MIRAGE

LATAYNE C. SCOTT

THE MORMON MIRAGE

ZONDERVAN®

ZONDERVAN.com/
AUTHORTRACKER
follow your favorite authors

ZONDERVAN

The Mormon Mirage

This title is also available as a Zondervan ebook.
Visit www.zondervan.com/ebooks.

Requests for information should be addressed to:

Zondervan, *Grand Rapids, Michigan 49530*

Library of Congress Cataloging-in-Publication Data

Scott, Latayne Colvett, 1952-
The mormon mirage: a former Mormon looks at the Mormon Church today / Latayne C. Scott.—3rd ed.
p. cm.
Includes bibliographical references (p.) and index.
ISBN 978-0-310-29153-4 (softcover)
1. Church of Jesus Christ of Latter-day Saints—Controversial literature. 2. Scott, Latayne Colvett, 1952-. I. Title.
BX8645.S35 2009
230'.9332—dc22 2008045543

All Scripture quotations, unless otherwise indicated, are taken from the *Holy Bible*, King James Version.

Any Internet addresses (websites, blogs, etc.) and telephone numbers printed in this book are offered as a resource. They are not intended in any way to be or imply an endorsement by Zondervan, nor does Zondervan vouch for the content of these sites and numbers for the life of this book.

Published in association with the Books & Such Literary Agency, 52 Mission Circle, Suite 122, PMB 170, Santa Rosa, CA 95407-5370, www.booksandsuch.biz

Interior design by Michelle Espinoza

Printed in the United States of America

---

09 10 11 12 13 14 • 23 22 21 20 19 18 17 16 15 14 13 12 11 10 9 8 7 6 5 4 3 2 1

Thank you, God, for leading me to Dan.
Thank you, Dan, for leading me to God.
Thank you, Ryan and Celeste, for keeping me near him.

CONTENTS

ACKNOWLEDGMENTS

For the two previous editions of this book I gratefully remember the help of Sandra Tanner, Dave Wilkins, David and Donna Lusk, Carol (Allen) Norris, Carol Jantz, Raylie (Lusk) Pribble, Virginia (Lykins) O'Dell, Melissa (Harding) Taylor, Rhonda Varley, and Ray Smith, as well as my patient family.

For this edition, I acknowledge with great gratitude Clodette Woodhouse, Gary and Marie Smith, Steve Cable, John Hunter, Sandra Tanner, Candy Evans, Dennis A. Wright, Janis Hutchinson, John Farkas, Phillip Arnn, Lane Thuet, Celeste Green, and Mike Strawn. Bruce MacArthur went above and beyond the call of dedication and duty to supply suggestions, editing, and research. This book would have been impossible for me to complete without their help.

Two additional chapters, one regarding the LDS version of the story of Joseph Smith, and another entitled "Priesthood, Purse Strings, and Proselyting" are bonus chapters that appear only in the e-book version of this work.

All hyperlinks are operational as of June 2008.

All Bible quotes, unless otherwise indicated, are from the King James Version.

Quotations from the Book of Mormon, Pearl of Great Price, and Doctrine and Covenants, unless otherwise noted, are from the latest editions of these works in print in 2008.

Preface:

FROM MIRAGE TO REALITY

The callow chestnut of Mormonism that says if you want to know about Fords, then you don't ask a Chevrolet dealer, and if you want to know about Mormonism, then don't ask a non-Mormon, is both wrong and lacks critical judgment. Groups like Consumer Reports prove their maxim false. Some of the best information comes from outside investigation (like Ford's exploding Pinto gas tank), which outside information can be life-saving.

—Kurt Van Gorden

In the preface in previous editions of this book I recounted how I once lived Mormonism fully, responsibly, and joyfully. I never was (nor ever will be) perfect, but I was a good, faithful Mormon. Finding out that Mormonism wasn't true was not initially a liberating experience. It was soul ravaging and sickening. I will never completely recover from it.

I am middle aged now. The day approaches when I will go before my God and give account for what I've said, done, and written. I ponder the fact that though the original publishing of this book ceased some years ago, scarcely a week goes by that I don't get requests for copies of it. Many, many other books on the same subject have been published, and to counter them, LDS apologists use sophisticated and complex arguments to support the *Book of Mormon*, Joseph Smith, and the superstructure of a church based on them.

I wrote this book for "regular people," not scholars, and as I have revised it for a new century, I have done so with the first aim of updating my statements about Mormonism that are no longer true—because Mormonism itself has changed.

Part One of this edition is a replication of the reasons why I left Mormonism—with updated sources for the information on which I based that decision, and new resources that validate those original sources and decisions. In some cases I have left in the text some statements that reflect how I felt, just a few years out of Mormonism, even though I might not state it that way now.

We are witnessing the sea change of Mormonism. As a result of doctrinal changes, the LDS Church is in the midst of a significant but invisible split into two camps. One group of both scholars and regular members still believe and treasure the doctrines I loved when I was a Mormon. Many of them see the second group as syncretistic and postmodern, abandoning the uniqueness of a faith that is based on continuous and reliable revelation. Those of the first group are struggling with the Church's new insistence that the prophets of the past should be discounted when their official (even thus-saith-the-Lord) teachings disagree with twenty-first-century pronouncements. The second group looks for acceptance from—and sometimes even fellowship with—Christians, with immunity from questions about the past. Many in the second group refer to criticisms of traditional Mormonism as straw-man arguments that are no longer viable.

Since one sociologist of religion has estimated that "at any given moment, the majority of Latter-day Saints are first-generation converts"[1] (that is, people who would have no ancestral ties to Mormonism and who would see its past quite differently from the descendants of handcart pioneers, for example), these differences are far beyond superficial. I have attempted in this book to provide thoughtful, researchable material for both groups even though they themselves have increasingly less common ground between them.

If at all possible, look up references that are footnoted in this book. I have written this book for the Internet generation (and an expanded-content e-book, with clickable footnotes, is available at www.zondervan.com). If a footnote is too long or complicated to type in, go to Jerald and Sandra Tanner's site, www.utlm.org, and search for the subject matter among the wealth of documents and photographs of documents there. For printed books from which I quote, I have attempted to use only those which are accessible at the time of the writing of this book. I have directed special attention to those written at a layman's level and by both Mormon and ex-Mormon scholars and researchers. I hope to provide updates of information on my website, www.latayne.com.

Part Two of this book is all-new material. With the vantage point of years away from Mormonism—and yet as a more-than-disinterested observer—I have outlined nine issues and challenges the LDS Church currently faces. In a final chapter I provide a personal retrospective that might make Mormons, Christian friends, and even my closest associates a bit uncomfortable, a perspective via representational theology, and some final assessments.

My reasons for leaving the LDS Church were then, and are now, quite simple. They don't really have much to do with archaeological findings (nor with the absence of them). Nor do they have to do, so much, with the false prophecies, suppressed history, and constantly changing doctrine of the Mormonism of the past.

Its claims that it is a gospel different from traditional Christianity remain unchallenged. No matter how you dress it up or water it down, Mormonism is not Christianity. Jesus Christ promised that the gates of hell would not prevail against the church he founded—it could not be taken from the earth for 1,700 years.

The once-human, fleshly god of Mormonism is not the Almighty God of the Bible. And none of us will ever become a god. There is only One.

To him alone, who is worthy, be all praise and glory.

PART ONE

Chapter 1

A GENTLE APOSTASY

Every Mormon, when he or she is about twelve years old, has the opportunity to go before a man of the LDS community who is revered for his wisdom and experience to receive a patriarchal blessing. I was about thirteen when I went before Garland F. Bushman, the patriarch of the stake, or region, in which I lived. Patriarch Bushman placed his hands on my head and said:

> In the preexistence, you were one of the choice souls of heaven noted by Father Abraham. Your ancestors were noble people, of the tribe of Ephraim. You yourself have a great destiny to become a leader of women in the church and in the state where you will reside. You will meet a fine young man, be married in a temple of our Lord, and raise up righteous children. Finally, you will arise in the morning of the first resurrection, surrounded by your family.

These wonderful predictions made me weep for joy. The patriarch warned me, however, that Satan wanted my soul very much—so much, in fact, that he would try hard to deceive me. All the blessings promised me would therefore be conditional upon my resisting Satan, and my obedience to the precepts of Mormonism.

Now, years later, I have left Mormonism and I feel so strongly about it that I am writing a book telling why I have left.

It wasn't easy to leave. I owed, and still owe, the Church of Jesus Christ of Latter-day Saints and its members a great debt of gratitude. But I am regarded by them as a traitor and an apostate. I left Mormonism after tasting some of its sweetest fruits.

Though my parents were Baptists, we did not attend church regularly until my father was converted to Mormonism by missionaries. I gladly received the missionary lessons, and my younger brother and I were baptized into the Mormon Church when I was eleven. My mother, however, never accepted the Joseph Smith Story. Through the tumultuous years of my adolescence, the LDS Church was security. Teachers and counselors in the church were compassionate and truly interested in me. These people were bound together by great love for their families, the Church, and each other.

The excellent youth programs (including track meets, road shows, supervised dances, cookouts, camps, sports activities, firesides, work and service projects, and much more) filled a gap in my life that might otherwise have been filled with early dating and associations in unsavory places. Through the LDS Church, I found a concrete way to express my fervent love for God and my desires to serve him. I gave love freely, and had it returned a hundredfold.

Some of Mormonism's blessings were even more tangible. I received an education of the highest quality at Brigham Young University, and through writing contests I was awarded scholarships that made it easier for me to attend. The part-time jobs I held while in school (dorm resident assistant, staff writer for the university's weekly magazines, translation and public relations work for a professor in the Latin-American Studies department, and counter work at the basketball arena's concession stand) were provided by the BYU board of trustees, who were deeply interested in the welfare of its students.

Once, even the food I ate was provided by the LDS Church. My father had undergone extensive surgery, and when the church officials heard of this, they brought hot meals to our home for several days and assessed our grocery supply to determine what we needed. They returned with sacks and sacks of groceries, and even offered to make car, house, and utility payments if needed.

I loved Mormonism for these things, and in return showed my love by living and serving as a "good Mormon." Each time that I was interviewed by my bishop (ecclesiastical leader of my local ward or congregation) and asked about such things as my attendance at meetings, payment of tithes, observance of the Word of Wisdom (health laws), sexual purity, and support of Church doctrines and leaders, I was awarded a precious "temple recommend."

During my young adulthood, I served as a teacher in Sunday school, Relief Society (a ladies' organization), and Primary (a children's organization). I was active as a speaker in Sacrament meetings and was often called on to prepare programs for the youths' "Mutual Improvement Association" and for special occasions. For a while, I worked as my ward's media aids supervisor, and in various other church "jobs."

I was never lukewarm. What I believed, I lived. I say all this because I believe that someone who has not lived a doctrine has no grounds to criticize it[1]—just as a grade-school science student cannot reasonably speak with authority on nuclear physics. I lived Mormonism; I loved it—and I left it.

My "apostasy" did not happen overnight. Once the process began, however, it moved quickly. The summer after my junior year at BYU, I returned to my home in Albuquerque, New Mexico, to work. I was annoyed when my mother, a lukewarm Baptist who played ragtime piano at a local pizza parlor, suggested that I date non-Mormons that summer. A missionary I was "waiting for" was due to return that fall,[2] and I just wasn't interested in a non-LDS "Gentile." But she introduced me to Dan Scott, the object of her praises, who started off our introductory conversation by saying, "So you're a Mormon. I've read the *Book of Mormon.* It was, uh, interesting."

Immediately I thought to myself, *Maybe he could be converted.* Then, more cautious, I stalled, searching for a reply. Everyone I'd ever known who'd read the whole *Book of Mormon* had become a Mormon. In fact, I reflected, I'd known plenty of faithful Mormons who had never read the whole thing unless and until required to do so in a religion class or while on a mission. Perhaps, I thought, this would be a good time to terminate this discussion, and I left quickly.

A few weeks later, a voice on the phone said, "Hi! Bet you don't know who this is!" His Tennessee accent had betrayed him. I said, "Yes—Dan Scott." He was crushed, his surprise foiled, but not crushed enough to forget to ask me out. I accepted against my better judgment.

Our first date was a disaster. He took me to midweek services at his church where he announced, "She's a Mormon." I was stared at as if I were from another planet. (Mormons get accustomed, to a degree, to such treatment from curious non-Mormons. Once when I was in junior high, a sincere classmate asked me if something her mother told her was true: that Mormons didn't have navels. We quickly went into the girls' room, and I dispelled that myth with a tug of my blouse!)

Nonetheless, I was attracted by Dan's openness and decided to date him again if he asked, and he did.

I soon found Dan to be a true and warm friend with a sense of humor he could aim at himself as well as at others. Our only disagreements came when we discussed religion. He was so transparently shocked when I answered his questions about baptism for the dead, polygamy, treatment of Negroes, and the LDS priesthood that we made an agreement. He would study the *Book of Mormon* and other LDS scripture with me if I would study the Bible with him. I felt this to be a personal triumph, because I'd never studied Mormonism with anyone (except my mother) who did not join the LDS Church.

Soon Dan and I had to admit to ourselves the love that was growing between us. One thing we both agreed on: We could not take the chance of becoming more deeply involved with our hearts so near and our souls so far apart. We both acknowledged that our respective religions weren't just "versions" of each other. They were not just different; they were oppositional.

Our discussions usually put me on the defensive. I was knowledgeable about my religion, and what was more, I was stubborn. Add to that a strong dose of love for the doctrines and people of Mormonism, and you have an idea of the battle Dan had to fight. He didn't fight it alone, though; he had several powerful weapons.

One was his brother-in-law, Charles Williamson, a preacher of great intelligence and patience. One day Charles and I agreed to sit down and talk only about religion. We sat on opposite sides of a table, me with my Bible, *Book of Mormon*, *Doctrine and Covenants*, *Pearl of Great Price*, and *Principles of the Gospel*; he with his Bible. Dan soon left the room, a scene he described as a "verbal ping-pong game." Both Charles and I were exhausted after about two hours of table-slamming debate. I was on the verge of anger. I learned later that Charles told Dan in confidence that I knew more than any Mormon elder he'd ever spoken with, and frankly he didn't know if there was any hope for me.

My recurring headaches signaled tension that had begun to grow as my doubts had. Dan and Charles didn't think their talks had served any purpose. I was filled with a sick dread that I then thought was a godly sorrow for the lost souls of people like Dan and Charles. Actually, I was beginning to fear that *my* soul might be lost, and I dared not voice this fear—not even to myself.

Another of the mighty weapons used by Dan in the battle for my soul was the literature he somehow managed to find. These books dealt objectively and factually with Mormonism, from the view of non-Mormons. I was blessed by the fact that Dan chose the books he did for me to read. Most writings that criticized LDS doctrine that I had previously read had had very little lasting effect on me.

There are many books and magazine articles written to convince Mormons of their doctrinal errors. Many of these, however, make at least one of two major mistakes. One is underestimating the intelligence, integrity, or character of the LDS people. Many times when I was a Mormon, I had read some otherwise factual literature against Mormonism which by its bitter or berating tone turned me off. The doctrinal point the writer was making never sank in. Such literature implies that Mormons believe as they do because they are stupid, narrow-minded, or satanic. Since I considered other Mormon friends and myself to be intelligent, open-minded children of God seeking to do his will, I would toss such offensive literature into the nearest trash can. Then I would offer a prayer to God for the soul of anyone who would tell such lies in print where they might be accepted as fact by someone who'd never met a good Latter-day Saint.

The other great error committed by many writers on Mormonism is that of not checking their facts. Like the mother of the girl who asked me about my navel, such writers discredit themselves with inaccuracies. Some writers, carried away in their enthusiasm, embellish facts—it's easy to do—but when I would run into such stretching or bending of the truth in writings critical of Mormonism, I would dismiss as also erroneous anything else I read there that didn't agree with LDS doctrines I had been taught.

When you confront many Mormons with, for example, copies of the original 1830 edition of the *Book of Mormon*, or strange prophecies made by Joseph Smith which never came true, some will be dumbfounded. Often such things are unavailable to them through regular Church channels. If, therefore, a book errs when covering things they *do* know about, how can they trust new information on things they have never heard of?

The most effective weapon of all in Dan's armory was three-pronged. First was his overwhelming faith and confidence in the Word of God, the Bible. Second was the prayer that he continually offered for my soul's enlightenment. Third, and most penetrating, was the love he had for me. Had we not loved each other, I don't believe I would have had the courage to leave the comfortable LDS way of life. Had he ceased loving me before my conversion was completed, I fear I would have returned to the womb of Mormonism and lived ever an infant, frightened and dependent, but secure in my deliberate ignorance.

I finally came to an impasse in my spiritual progress. I was struggling against the bonds of Mormonism—tradition and heritage, doctrinal comfort and love. Yet I felt that something was terribly wrong there—why did my teachings and background in Mormonism conflict so sharply with my new knowledge of the Bible? Why the inconsistencies in LDS historical accounts and early documents?

One final acid test remained at the end of the summer. Since I had a scholarship and a writing job waiting for me at BYU, I decided to return, promising Dan that we would marry—if I came back in December feeling about Mormonism as I did then in August. As I was packing, I felt as if the summer had been a dream. Or was it the real part, and the rest of my past life the illusion? I was unhappy about leaving Dan, but I knew I must make my decision alone. No matter how much I loved him, my eternal soul and my relationship with God were more important to me.

I was putting my books into boxes when, tired, I sat down with my *Doctrine and Covenants.* Always it had been my favorite book of scripture because of its practical commandments, like the Word of Wisdom, which had purified and uplifted the lives of millions of Latter-day Saints. Also commonly bound in the same volume with the *Doctrine and Covenants* is another book of scripture called the *Pearl of Great Price*, which includes two books that Mormons believe were written by Moses and Abraham. These scriptures are unique in that they have what purport to be illustrations by Abraham himself. These illustrations, reproduced by woodcuts, are in the ancient Egyptian style. I have always loved Egyptology, though I have no more than an avid layperson's knowledge of the subject.

I was looking idly through these familiar woodcuts when I was struck by an incongruity that upset me. Two of the women in the woodcut known as "Facsimile 3" had been labeled by Joseph Smith as men! Egyptian women are easily recognized in ancient documents by their distinctive strapped, ankle-length dresses.

Why I had never noticed this before, I do not know. I had looked at these woodcuts for years. I knew from reading authoritative experts on Egyptology that Egyptian women in history had dressed as men and acted as Pharaoh (Queen Hatshepsut, for example), but no Egyptian man would have been caught dead in a woman's clothing, especially to be preserved for posterity on a papyrus roll!

It was with this discovery that my most concrete doubts about Mormonism began to multiply. No "anti-Mormon" writer had pointed this out; no hater of the LDS Church could have falsified or altered these prints; they were in my own personal copy of scripture. I found myself crushed and exultant, all at the same time.

On the plane trip to Utah, I was shaken and lonely. I had left Dan behind; he was my bulwark of support and I was conscious that the events of the next few months would change my life. I brooded over this frightening thought (for who truly welcomes change?) and tried to keep my mind occupied by reading a paperback book on Mormonism that Dan had given me. I was so absorbed in reading that I hardly noticed a young woman sit down in the seat next to mine. She had a clean-scrubbed, open, friendly face. She smiled and began our conversation by asking about the book I was reading.

I could hardly formulate my thoughts; first, because of the fear that she might be a fellow Mormon who might question my motives in reading such literature; and second, because I didn't quite know how to explain my situation.

"It's about Mormonism," I finally blurted out, pointing to the book.

She smiled. "Are you thinking about becoming a Mormon?" she asked.

"No. I mean—I am one. I mean, I was—I'm thinking about leaving it ..." On the verge of tears, I was helpless to finish.

She gave me a look of soul-searching compassion. "How hard it must be to make that decision," she said.

And so I told her of my background in the LDS Church, and my love for it. Then I explained what had happened when I met Dan, and what I'd learned through reading and prayer, and how confused and muddled and lost I felt. Before I knew it, we had touched down in Grand Junction, Colorado, which was her destination.

As she prepared to leave, she leaned over and touched my arm. "I'll pray for you," she said. "God knows what is in your heart, and he will guide you to make the right decision."

She arose and walked out of my life as quickly as she had entered it, and I was left with a greater peace in my soul than I'd known for many months. She had touched my life with the bare wire of love, and peace had passed from her soul to mine like a transfusion. Then she was gone.

When I arrived in Provo, I set about making myself as busy as possible. Soon old friends began to arrive for the new school year, and I fooled myself by thinking they wouldn't notice the difference in me. I registered for classes, reported for work, and caught up on all the news of who had married whom, who had gone on missions, and what missionaries had returned.

But I have never been a good deceiver, and soon my feelings about the Church began to surface. Close friends made no secret of the fact that they thought I'd gone crazy. Some attributed my change of heart about Mormonism to a broken relationship with a missionary. Many of my LDS friends, to this day, assume that I wanted to leave the LDS Church because of that missionary. An unhappy bargain that would be—to trade my soul's salvation for revenge!

I became even more upset each time I attended church services. My branch (congregation) hadn't really changed. There were new faces, but it contained the same back-to-school jokes about snoring roommates and the excitement of worshiping together with maybe-your-future-spouse. Nothing had changed as much as I had, and I was sick at heart. In a letter to Dan in late September, I said,

> I can't explain the feelings I had in church today. I was looking at Mormonism through new eyes. In Sunday school class I listened to a discussion on the Holy Ghost and silently refuted almost everything that was said—by looking in the Bible. Things I've accepted for years seem suddenly strange. I experienced in part the pity that you felt for Mormons. Dan, I don't know what I'm going to do when they call me to a church position—and they surely will. I simply cannot stand up in front of people and teach from the *Book of Mormon* the way I feel now.

The dreaded call came late one afternoon when I was asked to meet with my branch president. Newly appointed to this job, he was nervous and unsure of himself. Everyone in his BYU student branch was to be interviewed and assigned a church job—teaching, visitation, social activity planning—and he seemed anxious to get these assignments over.

He began by congratulating me on my past service in the Church (he had my records before him) and asked me about the kind of job I'd be willing to do.

"I'd like to work on an activities committee," I said, "or work on cleanups—I'm really good at that, and honestly, I don't mind. In fact, I'd love it."

He looked at me, confused. What did someone with teaching and leadership experience want with a cleanup job? Then a smile broke across his face. He had solved the puzzle—I was trying to be modest! He laughed, relieved, and then asked a question he thought would put us on common ground.

"Well, Latayne," he said, leaning back in his chair, "how do you feel about the Prophet?"

Just that week, Harold B. Lee, the "Prophet, Seer, and Revelator of the Church," had come to BYU. When I had seen twenty-five thousand students rise to their feet and sing through tear-choked throats the song "We Thank Thee, Oh God, for a Prophet," I had felt faint and ill. How could I now tell this branch president of my feelings?

I looked away and said, "I don't think he *is* a prophet."

The young president sat up so suddenly that the back of his chair snapped forward. He acted as if he had had a bad day and I was pulling a very, very poor joke on him. I tried to explain that I hadn't come to a decision about the Church, that I wanted to avoid talking about it publicly, but still wanted to attend services and work in the Church.

He only shook his head, his disbelief turning to anger. "How can you think such things?" he asked. "Don't you know that if you leave the Church, you'll never be able to reach the Celestial Kingdom? *You will never be happy again!*"

Never to be happy again! What a load to put upon a young mind already troubled with uncertainty and fear of displeasing God! I left that interview with a dread in my soul. I went back to my apartment. That night I called Dan, and the next day disenrolled from Brigham Young University, telling only a few of my decision. My roommates were incredulous, my landlady tearful and reproachful, and all but one school official unsympathetic. A similar conflict, this registrar told me, had faced him when he was young. He had taken the part of Mormonism with few regrets, but his experience made him understanding, and concerned with my best interests.

When I arrived back in Albuquerque, little of the pressure was relieved. I received many letters, most anonymous and many cruel, which persuaded and threatened, pleaded and rejected. All had one object in mind—my return to Mormonism. Many pleaded, saying that my leaving would affect those I had taught and helped to convert, or those weak in the faith. (I pray to God it may be so!) Some of the letters told of the punishments awaiting apostates, and one ended by saying, "Don't you realize that you'll *never see the inside of a temple again?*"

Phone calls, too, didn't diminish for several months. Most were from friends who had "heard and just couldn't believe it." Close friends called one night and said several dozen other friends would be fasting and praying together the next day for me. On that day, I too fasted and prayed for my soul; for though I felt that I should leave Mormonism, I wasn't sure that Dan's teachings were any more reliable. Once you've found the tenets you most trusted and believed in to be false, you are not anxious to embrace a substitute.

Of only one thing was I certain: However I might begin to comprehend God, I knew that he loved me and knew my anguish, and would show me the way through his Son. This—and no more—could I be sure of.

Even Dan, much as I loved him, could not be the basis of my faith. I knew that if a group of people as dedicated and as sincere as most Mormons are could be so very wrong, then so could Dan, and his teachings. I have never felt more alone in my life.

I labored in agony with the great questions that left me sick at heart and spiritually weakened. I pulled this burden along behind me, pushed it before me, and tried to take it upon my shoulders. When I found that I *could not* move it alone—it was too heavy—I gave up and did what I should have done long before. I put it in God's hands, and wondered why I had taken so long to make that wisest of decisions in my life.

I spent a lot of time reading everything I could get my hands on that dealt objectively with Mormonism, especially the densely printed double-columned books first published by Jerald and Sandra Tanner, which included reprints of early Mormon documents. They, like I, had tried to prove Joseph Smith and the *Book of Mormon* true, and finally were overwhelmed with the information they decided to print for others.

I was both fascinated and repelled the more I realized my errors. A near-physical sickness would engulf me when I stopped to realize how I had flirted with hell while thinking I was courting heaven. Only a few doubts (those last barriers to real repentance) remained, and I took my questions to Lon Elkins, Dan's minister. I had grown to admire this man's vast knowledge of the Scriptures and of archaeology.

How simply he answered those questions I had been hiding so deep in my heart for so many months! I hadn't dared to ask anyone who it was Christ spoke of when he said, "Other sheep I have, which are not of this fold: them also I must bring, and they shall hear my voice" (John 10:16). The Mormons identify those "other sheep" as the Nephites, that is, the people the *Book of Mormon* teaches were the ancient inhabitants of the Americas who lived at the same time Christ did. The LDS Church teaches that Christ spent part of the time between his death and resurrection here in America, teaching those Nephites. Could a Christian offer as reasonable an explanation?

Thank God, Lon both could and did. After he had explained this and answered many other questions, I realized how it is that any religious group teaching false doctrine can so easily misrepresent the Scriptures to someone who is unfamiliar with them. The greatest battles a cult can wage over the soul of the ignorant person, I believe, are already won when the proselyte is too lazy, or afraid, or unwilling to seek a more correct interpretation of a Scripture passage that is presented to teach a supposedly "new" doctrine. We have nothing to fear *but ourselves* when we ignore the admonition to "search the Scriptures."

I had realized this too late to undo my years in the Church of Jesus Christ of Latter-day Saints. I cannot say that I wish I had never been a Mormon. God richly blessed me during those years. Perhaps they were a preparation for my Christian life. I do not question or doubt the wisdom of God, even though I still sorrow for the wrong things I did and taught.

I knew then as now that I must recommit myself to God—I must become a new creature, as different from my LDS self as a butterfly is from a caterpillar. I had so many doubts—not knowing for certain what to trust, or what doctrine was true. I decided on a course of action that included two things: I would be baptized for the remission of my many sins, and I would depend wholly on the Bible as my spiritual guide.

Dan was a little apprehensive as we prepared for my baptism. He was anxious and happy to baptize me, as I had requested. But he was afraid because he'd never baptized anyone before, and he feared he would let me slip into the water or choke. I could only laugh—I knew I could take care of myself in that situation, because I once had been baptized thirty consecutive times (all within a matter of minutes) while doing proxy ordinances for the dead in the Manti, Utah, LDS temple!

This baptism was different, though. From that still September night to this very day, I feel a great sense of the majesty of God, and of his mercy so undeserved by me, a sinner. Mormons may regard a book showing the errors of Mormonism as a strange way to repay a debt of gratitude. I only wish that when I was a Mormon someone had told me the things of which I write.

Chapter 2

THE JOSEPH SMITH STORY

I was left to all kinds of temptations; and, mingling with all kinds of society, I frequently fell into many foolish errors, and displayed the weakness of youth, and the foibles of human nature.

—Joseph Smith, *Pearl of Great Price*, History 1:28

God is in the still small voice. In all these affidavits, indictments, it is all of the devil—all corruption. Come on! ye prosecutors! ye false swearers! All hell, boil over! Ye burning mountains, roll down your lava! for I will come out on the top at last. I have more to boast of than ever any man had. I am the only man that has ever been able to keep a whole church together since the days of Adam. A large majority of the whole have stood by me. Neither Paul, John, Peter, nor Jesus ever did it. I boast that no man ever did such a work as I. The followers of Jesus ran away from Him; but the Latter-day Saints never ran away from me yet.

—Joseph Smith, *History of the Church*, 6:408–9

An LDS song entitled "Praise to the Man"[1] deals with Joseph Smith in a way that exemplifies the LDS attitude toward him. That he was a martyr to his cause is history, and the testament of his blood to the things he taught charges that history with emotion. Mormons from earliest childhood are taught stories about Joseph Smith interspersed with, and undifferentiated from, stories of Bible characters like Daniel and David and Timothy, and characters from the *Book of Mormon* such as Alma and Nephi, and LDS leaders such as Hyrum Smith and David O. McKay. To them, all were great men, all prophets, and all equal. Only two stand above the rest: Christ, and just below him, Joseph Smith.

Brigham Young once stated that Joseph's consent was required for a person to be able to enter into the Celestial Kingdom of heaven, because Joseph was now reigning there, like God.[2] He also said that Joseph "was a god to us"[3] and that he himself was "an apostle of Joseph Smith,"[4] saying that "every spirit that does not confess that God sent Joseph Smith and revealed the everlasting gospel to and through him, is of Anti-christ."[5]

It is clear, therefore, that a casual attitude about Joseph Smith is not possible for a true believer in Christ. Joseph Fielding Smith, a descendant of Joseph's brother Hyrum Smith and who long served as historian and later as president of the LDS Church, once stated that

> Mormonism … must stand or fall on the story of Joseph Smith. He was either a prophet of God, divinely called, properly appointed and commissioned, or he was one of the biggest frauds this world has ever seen. There is no middle ground. If Joseph Smith was a deceiver, who willfully attempted to mislead the people, then he should be exposed; his claims should be refuted, and his doctrines shown to be false.[6]

I take this challenge seriously. After prayer and study, I found that the picture painted of Joseph Smith by his modern-day followers is not a good likeness of the man as he was.

Part of this is due to the overzealous efforts of LDS writers of so-called "faithful history," who present only the good side of Joseph Smith to their people. Unflattering references to him and his lifestyle and role as a prophet don't appear in modern printings of Church documents and most materials written below the scholarly level. Therefore, with the information available through official church channels, the average Mormon has no reason to doubt the Christlike nature and divine calling of Joseph Smith. When I was a Mormon, nothing to the contrary was found in my LDS books about the first Mormon prophet, even in university-level classes.

Have non-Mormon writers simply fabricated the stories they tell of Joseph Smith's dishonesty and carnality? No, for the most part these stories have come directly from unexpurgated early editions of books written by faithful Mormons, or at least from firsthand witnesses to the events they describe. I learned of these changes largely through the efforts of two ex-Mormons, Jerald and Sandra Tanner, who began a printing company in

Salt Lake City to produce photographic-type copies of original Mormon documents. For decades their printed documents were the only source of controversial documents that the LDS Church withheld, in many cases from their own scholars.

Jerald is now with the Lord, but even in death he, along with his still-living wife, Sandra, are despised as troublemakers by most Mormons who know of their work. Once, while I was a faithful Mormon, I found some of their literature that had been left at the door of my apartment, two blocks from the BYU campus. A bishop's wife told me not to read the literature; the Tanners were infamous for their sexual immorality (practicing polygamy) and the lies they propagated with forged documents that made the Mormon Church look bad (both false charges). But I believed this bishop's wife and threw the pamphlet away.

My attitude was, I think, typical of the average Mormon. I didn't want to associate with such people or to further their cause by letting them plant seeds of doubt about Mormonism in my mind. (In fact, I would later learn, association with ex-Mormons could keep a faithful Mormon from being able to attend temple ordinances or attain leadership positions.)

With the advent of the Internet and the availability of free resources about Mormonism, an increasing number of LDS people are caught in this same dilemma, a cognitive dissonance between what the LDS Church wants them to believe, and what history shows. (Google "Joseph Smith" and "polygamy" in the same search, for example.) Such a struggle has been mirrored most recently in the life of a Mormon man named Grant H. Palmer. He painstakingly presents an abundance of documentation about the questionable claims of Joseph Smith in his book *An Insider's View of Mormon Origins.*[7] Palmer, a three-time director of the LDS Institutes of Religion in California and Utah, and high priest instructor in his own local LDS ward, tried to reconcile all the inconsistencies in Joseph Smith's story and was disfellowshipped after his book was published.

Typical LDS history books are not unique in what they *tell* about Joseph Smith (they leave in just enough references to his humanity to make him believable), but in what they *don't* tell. And what they don't tell is what has shown me, Jerald and Sandra Tanner, Grant Palmer, and other seeking, faithful Latter-day Saints that Joseph Smith could not possibly have been the prophet of God that he and his followers have claimed him to be.

CHILDHOOD AND THE FIRST VISION

Many who examine the life and influence of Joseph Smith search for explanations for the strange doctrines of his adulthood by looking in his childhood and youth. Mormons would say that his "first vision" was the most significant event of his young life, but—aside from the dynamics of the personalities of his parents and the supercharged atmosphere of religious fervor of upper New York State in the early 1800s—one traumatic, formational event may provide some explanation. When Joseph was about seven years old he became very ill with typhoid fever and underwent three horrific surgeries without anesthesia. According to all accounts the child suffered bravely the gruesome extraction of a significant section of his left leg bone while he was awake and screaming in agony.[8] According to Dr. William D. Morain, a physician who called on his experience in treating children who have undergone similarly traumatic medical experiences, such a nightmarish event would have consequences: "I soon began to ask myself what adult behavior patterns might be expected in such an individual whose brutal childhood trauma held themes of dismemberment, punishment, and worse. Would there be allusions to this incident in his writings? In his religious rituals?"[9]

Smith himself rarely ever mentioned the event that caused his lifelong limp. Instead, the foundational event he later in life canonized was his account of how he had been motivated in his youth to seek God's counsel on which church to join because of the religious turmoil around him. This, he said, was due to the many great religious revivals in his area in 1820.[10]

The revivals in the Palmyra area in 1820, unfortunately, existed only in the mind of Joseph Smith. Wesley P. Walters, in his pamphlet *New Light on Mormon Origins*,[11] elucidates this. Mr. Walters did extensive research in the records of the Methodist, Presbyterian, and Baptist churches of the 1820s in the Palmyra area, and discovered that the only revivals mentioned by the leaders of these churches occurred in 1817, 1824, and 1829. (Walters' conclusions have been since confirmed by many others.)[12] Since a revival is something to be proud of, it is not likely that these church leaders of the time would have had any reason to suppress information about a revival in 1820, had there been any.

Even Joseph's own accounts of the first vision must be viewed with some reservations. No mention of his first vision—which supposedly took place in 1820—was ever made in print, until twenty years later when Orson Pratt, a longtime friend of Joseph Smith, published an account of the vision in a book called *Remarkable Visions.* Then in 1842 Joseph himself published an account of the two gods who appeared to him in a grove and told him not to join any existing church.

Why no hint of any kind concerning this first vision is found in any Mormon (or non-Mormon) literature published prior to 1840, I cannot understand. After all, this was supposedly a major event in human history! By comparison, look at the way that Peter and John were absolutely irrepressible in speaking about their experiences with a risen Savior. Even the threats of powerful officials had no effect on them, and they said, "For we cannot but speak the things which we have seen and heard" (Acts 4:20).

Joseph Smith said in his "official" account of the first vision (found in the *Pearl of Great Price*) that when he told others immediately afterwards of what he had seen and heard in the grove, he was greatly persecuted.[13] But the evidence (or lack of it!) shows that no one even knew about it until twenty years later. It certainly was not the source of doctrine or testimonies until that time.

In 1831 or 1832, however, Joseph Smith did write an unpublished account of a vision.[14] If this document records the first vision Mormons are familiar with, then somewhere Joseph had gotten his details mixed up. This record of a vision does not mention the revivals that reportedly caused Joseph to seek divine aid, nor the evil force he said overpowered him. It also fails to mention the appearance of God the Father—it speaks only of Christ.

Another version of the first vision has been identified by a professor of history at BYU as a previously unpublished record of how Joseph Smith told the story of his decision to join no existing church. This account, however, identifies Joseph as being fourteen at the time of the vision, and mentions "many angels," which are absent in the official 1842 version. The "pillar of light" was in this version a "pillar of fire." There were two distinct personages mentioned in this version, but they are in no way identified as God and Jesus Christ.

Confused by all the details? At the Nauvoo Christian Visitors Center in Nauvoo, Illinois, a nine-square quilt hangs that depicts each of nine different versions of that first vision.[15] Edmond C. Gruss and Lane A. Thuet have identified eleven versions.[16] Richard Abanes, in his comprehensive book, *One Nation Under Gods: A History of the Mormon Church*, has provided two clear and helpful charts comparing the details of various versions of the visions.[17]

Even if this first vision—in whatever form it had—had really taken place, I think Joseph Smith as a prophet on whom doctrine depended should have been impressed enough with such an earth-shattering experience to remember the main details. Could he have made the whole thing up? LDS leaders deny it when they say he was only a teenager and incapable of fabricating such a thing. I'm sorry, but these LDS leaders need only look into the many juvenile detention centers throughout our country to discover just *how* fertile a teenager's imagination can be in inventing excuses for erratic or antisocial behavior.

Nor is a young active imagination exclusive to our century. In 1837 an illiterate youth named James Colin Brewster said that at age ten, he, like Joseph Smith, had been in direct communication with the angel Moroni. Brewster began "translating" nonexistent records that he said were the lost books of Esdras, and had published numerous extracts from his work, as well as supposed translations of ancient inscriptions, all before he was twenty-one years of age. Many former Mormons, seeing similarities between Joseph Smith and this young man (who was also a visionary and money digger), actually joined the church that Brewster founded in 1848.[18]

Thus confusion has always surrounded the story of the visions. My own conclusion is that Joseph Smith did not put his story of his first vision together until he was pressed for evidence to substantiate his "many gods" theory, about 1838. He could then say, "Why, I knew that God and Jesus were separate, distinct personages with flesh and bone bodies way back in 1820, when they appeared to me." This, surely, lent credibility to his teachings on the plurality of gods and at the same time gave him a retrofit divine stamp of approval early in his life.

TRANSLATING AND TREASURE SEEKING

And surely he needed heavenly approval, for his younger years had many things to be ashamed of. But his followers were credulous enough to believe almost anything, it seems. An adoring public which believed indiscriminately in witches, warlocks, fortune telling, and angelic visitations (all at the same time)[19] could hardly be expected to disbelieve Joseph's story of his vision.

But even their "willing suspension of disbelief" could have been easily snapped had they realized the nature and extent of the "weakness of youth and the foibles of human nature" in which Joseph Smith participated in the early 1820s. In 1822, about two years after he supposedly received the first vision, Joseph Smith found what he called a "seer stone" in a well. According to Martin Harris, one of the witnesses to the *Book of Mormon*, this stone was used to see things like the location of the hidden gold plates and other lost or hidden objects.

Joseph would place this seer stone in a hat, then close the hat tight around his face. The location of whatever he was looking for would then appear to him. He soon acquired quite a reputation as what his nineteenth-century contemporaries called a "money digger." Mormons might deny the validity of such a statement, but the evidence from sworn witnesses proves overwhelmingly that he was heavily involved in the then-common practice of treasure hunting. Though he never was very good at it—by his own admission he never received more than about fourteen dollars a month for his efforts[20]—he was persistent, and even as long as ten years after he left the town of Palmyra the townspeople remembered his attempts at divining out buried treasure and hidden money with his peepstone.

But the most damaging evidence to prove Joseph Smith's activities with his peepstone is found in the account of a March 20, 1826, trial that was published in *Fraser's* magazine in 1873. Joseph Smith was accused of having used his peepstone for three years to try (usually unsuccessfully) to find such things as hidden treasure, lost property, money, gold, a salt spring, and a buried trunk. He was found guilty of the charges against him and of being "disorderly and an imposter."

The record of this trial and conviction was not published until 1873, which has caused LDS critics to cast doubt on its reliability. They have denied the authenticity of this "Bainbridge record," as it is called, saying there was no proof that the judge mentioned in it (Justice Albert Neely) was really a judge in 1826. Nor, they contend, was there any official court record to corroborate the *Fraser's* account. LDS scholar Hugh Nibley went so far as to say in his 1961 book *The Myth Makers* that if this court record were authentic, it would be the most damning evidence in existence against Joseph Smith.[21]

Joseph's damnation, then, came in 1971 when researcher Wesley P. Walters found, in the cellar of the Chenango County (New York) jail, the official appointment papers of Judge Neely, dated November 16, 1825. Walters also located there the judge's own records[22] of the court costs in the 1826 preliminary hearing regarding "Joseph Smith the Glass-Looker"—all of which corroborated the details mentioned in the "Bainbridge record." This hearing occurred within about eighteen months of the date Joseph was supposed to have received the golden plates.

LDS writers often mention Joseph Smith "helping to find a silver mine," or his powers of discernment in finding things "invisible to the naked eye." But few speak of the extent of his deceptions, with his stones and "powers," which he inflicted on innocent and gullible country folk.[23] One LDS scholar (later excommunicated) who documented the connection between early LDS history and magic is D. Michael Quinn. His book *Early Mormonism and the Magic World View* gives a jaw-dropping, detailed look at the role of the occult in Joseph Smith's life.

Nor are magic elements only in the past for the Mormon Church. LDS historians today affirm the existence of Joseph's seer stone. As late as 1956, one of the presidents of the Church, Joseph Fielding Smith, stated in his book *Doctrines of Salvation* that "this seer stone is now in the possession of the Church."[24] No wonder then, that few "faithful history" biographies of Joseph Smith published by the LDS Church mention his activities as a treasure hunter, charlatan, and self-avowed divine.[25]

Even Joseph Smith himself must have realized eventually that he wasn't going to become rich or famous in that line of work. He had to come up with something more unique than his small-change (and unsuccessful) business of trying to find lost objects.

I haven't wanted to believe that Joseph Smith was evil or diabolical; rather that he was simply possessed of a great drive for power and fame, coupled with a vivid imagination and personal charisma. "There was something compelling in what he said and the way that he said it that riveted his listeners to his every word," reported biographer Robert V. Remini, in his biography of Smith.[26]

Smith's wife Emma once said that she believed God dictated the *Book of Mormon* because her husband could hardly speak clearly nor compose a clearly written letter.[27] The speeches and writings we have of him contradict this assessment. In addition, others described Smith as articulate and descriptive from his youth on. Joseph's mother, Lucy Mack Smith, wrote that when he was eighteen years old he used to amuse his family by describing

> the ancient inhabitants of this continent, their dress, mode of travelling, and the animals upon which they rode; their cities, their buildings, with every particular; their mode of warfare; and also their religious worship. This he would do with as much ease, seemingly, as if he had spent his whole life with them.[28]

Imagination was something Joseph Smith had in abundance. However, one problem with such a fertile mind was that sometimes he didn't keep details straight. An example of this is the "official" version of the story that he was given the golden plates by an angel named Moroni—well known to every Mormon child. However, numerous early and (at the time equally "official") versions of this story identified the being who delivered the plates as being Nephi.

POSSIBLE ORIGINS OF THE *BOOK OF MORMON* THEME

However, the "Indian" stories were eagerly accepted by his family, because it was the current and popular belief among even scholars of that day that the American Indians were descended from the "lost" Ten Tribes of Israel. *The Wayne Sentinel*, the local newspaper to which the Smith family subscribed, carried articles that supported this idea. A book called *View of the Hebrews; or the Ten Tribes of Israel in America* by Ethan Smith (no relation to Joseph) was published in 1823, and it mentioned the author's theories that Indians were wicked Israelites who had killed off their more civilized relatives in America and were left in their barbarous state until the coming of the white man. (That, of course, is exactly the plotline of the *Book of Mormon*.) The noted LDS historian B. H. Roberts began late in life to ask pointed questions about whether Joseph Smith had "followed the course" of Ethan Smith, noting that the *View of the Hebrews* was published five to seven years before the *Book of Mormon*.[29]

Other pre-Mormon books could also have furnished structural or background information used in the writing of the *Book of Mormon*. Among them were James Adair's *History of the American Indian* (London, 1775), Charles Crawford's *Essay upon the Propagation of the Gospel, in which there are facts to prove that many of the Indians in America are descended from the Ten Tribes* (Philadelphia, 1799), Elias Boudinot's *A Star in the West; or, a Humble Attempt to Discover the Long Lost Ten Tribes of Israel* (Trenton, N.J., 1816), and Josiah Priest's *The Wonders of Nature and Providence Displayed* (Albany, 1825).

Priest's book, like the others, advanced the Hebrew-Indian theory and in addition told some "new" stories about the plague of darkness in Egypt (Exod. 10:21–23)—details of which are mentioned almost verbatim in the *Book of Mormon* but are conspicuously absent in any Bible manuscript. In fact, virtually every nonbiblical idea presented in the *Book of Mormon* has its roots in one of these books, which represent only a small portion of their kind!

Some researchers have seen the stamp of another set of personalities on the *Book of Mormon*. In a book called *Who Really Wrote the Book of Mormon? The Spaulding Enigma*, three authors[30] formulated an interesting theory documenting interconnections of early LDS leaders with the author of a now-lost manuscript that contained references to persons named Nephi and Lehi, and told of the Jewish origins of the American Indian and of great battles between the Nephites and the Lamanites, the latter of which finally triumphed.

TRANSLATING THE INSCRIPTIONS

Everyone is fascinated with the story of the gold plates. But Joseph Smith kept them hidden from even his family, especially his wife and mother, who never laid eyes on them. Once when Emma, his wife, touched the cloth-covered bundle that Joseph said contained the plates, she felt a metallic rustling, but she never saw the plates. Joseph, she said, *didn't even unwrap them to translate them*; he just peered into the Urim and Thummim, or his seer stone.[31]

When a farmer named Martin Harris took over Emma's job as scribe, he did indeed as Mormons claim take a copy of some of the characters from the plates to Dr. Charles Anthon at Columbia University in New York City. But there truth and LDS fiction part paths. Harris claimed that Professor Anthon said that the characters Harris brought were authentic ancient Egyptian, and were translated correctly. The other untranslated characters, said Harris, were declared by Anthon to be "Egyptian, Chaldaic, Assyriac, and Arabic."

However, in two separate letters he wrote later, Professor Anthon substantiated Harris's claim that he had brought the characters to Anthon, but the professor vehemently denied that he had ever given the impression that the squiggles on Harris's paper were ancient Egyptian—or ancient anything, for that matter. Anthon regarded the whole thing as "a trick."[32]

But what if, as Mormons claim, Professor Anthon had indeed endorsed the translation and hieroglyphics, and then just denied it for some capricious reason of his own? Then Anthon himself would have been a fraud. In 1828, when the Anthon interview took place, the translations of Egyptian hieroglyphics were not yet published by Champollion, that great linguistics pioneer who unlocked the padlock of the ancient Egyptian language with the Rosetta Stone's key. If Anthon *had* said that the Egyptian hieroglyphics were truly translated, then he would have been whistling in the wind, for no man in America at that time (including Joseph Smith) was capable of translating ancient Egyptian—much less the "reformed Egyptian" of the *Book of Mormon.*

If the only existing copy of the inscriptions from which Joseph Smith supposedly translated can be held in such doubt, how much more the conflicting stories of the mechanics of *how* Joseph Smith performed the translations. Emma Smith, as well as "witnesses" David Whitmer and Martin Harris, said that Joseph translated by putting the previously mentioned "seer stone" into his hat. He would peer into the hat, and a line of script from the plates would appear in his field of vision. Underneath it, he said, the English translation of that line would appear. Joseph would read the English to his scribe, and the scribe would write it down and then repeat it to Joseph. If it was correctly written, that line of script would disappear and a new one would appear.

But other Mormons claim that the *Book of Mormon* was translated by means of the Urim and Thummim, which was a combination of a breastplate and attached spectacles that was given to Joseph by the angel, along with the plates, specifically for translation purposes. Mormons explain the conflict by saying that the seer stone was sometimes called the Urim and Thummim. Or sometimes they claim that Emma said that the first 116 pages of manuscript (later lost by Martin Harris) were translated by using the Urim and Thummim, and the rest with the seer stone. Some other LDS thinkers, facing all the contradictions, have come to agree with Grant H. Palmer, who concluded that perhaps it was just a kind of stream-of-consciousness in which God cooperated with Joseph's mind. Most fascinating of all is the explanation that the *Book of Mormon* is an example of automatic writing.[33]

If this sounds confusing, consider the plight of the poor Mormons who are asked to believe it without ever understanding it. I remember sitting in a class at BYU where the methods of translating the *Book of Mormon* were being discussed. I didn't understand, and resolved the difficulty by returning to my prior opinions on the translation technique: I didn't know and didn't care. It was enough for me to *trust* that the *Book of Mormon* was true and correct. This I know to be the position of most Mormons—they shut their eyes to what is confusing or conflicting. I'll wager that not one Mormon in a thousand can explain how the *Book of Mormon* was translated. This, indeed, is blind faith; and many will pay the price of their souls for their comfortable ignorance.

THE WITNESSES

Many seek solace in the thought that there were enough reliable witnesses to substantiate the *Book of Mormon*'s validity and justify their own faith in it. But just how reliable were these witnesses? Mormons often claim that none of them ever denied their testimony of the *Book of Mormon.* However, Brigham Young in the LDS *Journal of Discourses* says that "some of the witnesses of the *Book of Mormon* who handled the plates and conversed with the angels of God, were afterwards left to doubt and to disbelieve that they had ever seen an angel."[34] This must refer to Oliver Cowdrey, David Whitmer, and/or Martin Harris, who alone in their written testimonies (printed in the front of each copy of the *Book of Mormon*) claimed to have both handled the plates and seen an angel. The *Journal of Discourses'* use of the plural ("some of the witnesses") indicates at least two of them doubted, though one in this passage was identified as a member of the Quorum of the Twelve Apostles who fell away.[35]

Most of the witnesses to the *Book of Mormon* did indeed fall into apostasy, and far from having the "spotless reputations" claimed for them by present-day Mormons, they were a disreputable band if we take the word of their LDS contemporaries. Consider this:

> "Such characters as McLellin, John Whitmer, David Whitmer, Oliver Cowdrey, and Martin Harris are too mean to mention, and we had liked to have forgotten them."[36]
>
> "Hiram Page (1800–1852), appears to have been somewhat fanatical. He found a stone through which he claimed to receive revelations, often contrary to those received by Joseph Smith. For this he was reprimanded."[37]
>
> Oliver Cowdrey left Mormonism, became a Methodist, and "admitted his error and implored forgiveness and said he was sorry and ashamed of his connection with Mormonism."[38]
>
> Martin Harris was referred to twice in the *Doctrine and Covenants*, which purports to be a series of revelations from God, as "a wicked man."[39] The LDS magazine *The Improvement Era* of March 1969 admitted that Martin Harris "changed his religious position eight times," including his conversion to Quakerism from Mormonism and back again during his stay in Kirtland, Ohio.

Now, does this sound like testimonies of stable, respected men of spotless reputations?

One LDS author stated: "Given the fact that the three witnesses saw a vision and that the experience of the eight witnesses seems to have been similarly visionary, there is no compelling evidence that Joseph Smith actually possessed anciently constructed plates."[40] Perhaps we could at most give the witnesses credit for being gullible. Jerald and Sandra Tanner have explored the possibility that Joseph Smith, with the aid of Oliver Cowdrey (another of Smith's scribes, who had been a blacksmith when young), had made some sort of metal plates which they covered up and presented to the witnesses to touch as "proof" of Joseph Smith's golden plates theory. Richard Abanes, in *One Nation Under Gods: A History of the Mormon Church*, demonstrates conclusively that all eleven "witness" accounts boil down to either visions or the experience of hefting a heavy object under a cloth.[41] Biographer Remini offers a more secular explanation of the witnesses' "testimony": They can be attributed to Joseph's documented ability to "mesmerize" audiences, or to the mass hysteria characteristic of other Great Awakening religious groups, or even to a conspiracy of fraud to profit from the *Book of Mormon*.[42]

Not even the testimony of Joseph Smith himself is infallible. On June 15, 1828—years after his supposed visit from God, who told him that all churches on earth were corrupt—he tried to join the Methodist Church but was asked to leave because of his alleged involvement with necromancy.[43] The Tanners have concluded that Joseph's membership in the Methodist church "occurred eight years after he was supposed to have received his first vision and at the very time he was translating the *Book of Mormon*!"[44]

If the testimonies of such men concerning the *Book of Mormon* were proven unreliable by their unreliable characters, then how much more can we doubt what they said about other things!

When Oliver Cowdery became Joseph's scribe, the work of "translating" the *Book of Mormon* progressed very rapidly. Whereas the first 116 pages had taken Joseph Smith two months to "translate" with Harris as a scribe, the rest of the 275,000 words were finished in about three months when Cowdery began helping Joseph. Part of this is no doubt due to Joseph's improvement with practice in dictation (and the fact that when his well of inspiration ran dry he simply quoted long passages from the Bible, practically verbatim). But some of this was undoubtedly due to the influence of former schoolteacher Cowdery, who, as Fawn Brodie noted, had "a certain talent for writing."[45]

BUILDING THE MORMON KINGDOM

Then, as today, the first hurdle to be crossed by a prospective Mormon was belief in the *Book of Mormon.* This must have been very difficult for those early converts. The book's first edition was filled with grammatical, punctuation, and spelling errors that necessitated more than four thousand changes to bring it to its present, slightly more readable condition. This was explained to me as the result of the book having been printed by someone who hated the Mormons and wanted to make them look bad.

Even LDS historians, though, say most of the errors couldn't be blamed on the printer or typesetter, because they weren't typographical errors.[46] But Joseph Smith boldly stated that the first edition of the *Book of Mormon* was "the most correct of any book on earth."[47]

Apparently the poor quality of the book's language didn't seriously dampen its effect on the often semiliterate converts it won. Some of its first converts, who were to remain faithful for life, were Joseph's father, Joseph Smith Sr., and his brother, Hyrum. Emma, Joseph's wife, also joined the Church, though she was not so tractable and believing as the others.

Joseph began handing out revelations directed at anyone he thought needed encouragement or rebuke with the authoritative clout of "thus saith the Lord" to back it up. One of the most amazing (and least-noticed) revelations he gave out is that found in *Doctrine and Covenants* section 15. The heading to the revelation states: "The message is intimately and impressively personal in that the Lord tells of what was known only to John Whitmer and Himself." What is that personal matter the Lord had in mind? Starting in verse 3, we read,

> And I will tell you that which no man knoweth save me and thee alone—For many times you have desired of me to know that which would be of the most worth unto you.... And now, behold, I say unto you, that the thing that will be of the most worth unto you will be to declare repentance unto this people.

And what is so amazing about this revelation? The fact that it is repeated word for word in the next section, a revelation given to a man named Peter Whitmer. Only the names have been changed. That is how "intimately and impressively personal" the revelation to John Whitmer was!

Perhaps this was a time-saving device. Joseph was busy organizing God's kingdom on earth. On April 6, 1830, the Church was organized under the name of The Church of Christ (later changed because other churches also claimed that name). LDS history records that Joseph laid hands on Oliver Cowdery, confirming him an elder in the Lord's Church, and Oliver did the same to Joseph. This all makes sense to Mormons because they believe that you cannot give an office to someone without having it yourself—and the "authority" to back it. Supposedly this authority was given to Oliver and Joseph in late 1829 or early 1830. This, though, is admittedly sheer supposition on the part of LDS theologians.

LaMar Petersen, in his book *Creation of the Book of Mormon*, has noted that the 1833 equivalent of what is now *Doctrine and Covenants* section 27 (dated August 1830) did not mention heavenly visitors and two separate ordinations of priesthood. These references were added later. Petersen notes that in this collection of the first sixty-five revelations the absence of such details is suspicious.[48]

I see the invention of the stories about holy ordinations as evidence that Joseph Smith often resorted to "divine revelations" to reaffirm his leadership and beat back doubters within the Church.[49] Because there were always some people who remembered the past "revelations" and ill-advised conjurings of his youth, he was always on his guard, to protect both his reputation as a prophet and holy man, and also to safeguard his creation and passport to fame, the *Book of Mormon.*

I have often wondered how I would have responded, had I been an adult in New England in the early 1830s. Part of me wants to believe that Bible knowledge would have kept me from believing the story of the gold plates. The New Testament warned against people who claimed visits from angels with a different gospel (Gal. 1:6–9; Col. 2:18–19). Both the Old and New Testaments told of a God who was spirit, and said that the next time Jesus returned to earth to establish his end-time kingdom it would be a very public event that everyone would see. I would have understood, if I had studied the Bible, that it claimed its words would never pass away, and that the church Jesus founded was likewise a type of spiritual protectorate under the wing of a divine kingship. Such an eternal entity would not be subject to anything resembling a complete apostasy.

But then again, I'm a woman, and many women seemed absolutely unable to resist Joseph Smith. Diaries, journals, and other personal records of people who knew Joseph Smith described him as a charismatic, nearly irresistible character. General Moses Wilson transported Smith in his custody to Independence and observed, "I carried him in my house a prisoner in chains, and in less than two hours my wife loved him better than she loved me."[50]

PROBLEMS IN KIRTLAND

More trouble was brewing in Smith's assistant Sidney Rigdon's newly established Mormon colony in Kirtland, Ohio. Here there were few people who had known Joseph in his treasure-hunting days, so the threat of exposure from that faction was minimized. Even more dangerous, however, were new converts who took the prophet's teachings about prophesying and spiritual gifts so seriously that instead of saying that Joseph Smith had no rights to revelation, they asked the logical question, "If Joseph can do these things, then why not us?" Here, probably, the doctrine of the necessity of authority in order to receive revelation got its start. Joseph continually had to remind his followers that he alone, as God's chosen leader, had the right to revelation concerning the whole Church. Others had only the right to revelation for themselves and those under them in the Church hierarchy. Thus, today, any young Mormon who would come before his bishop or stake president and announce any change in church policy because he'd received a revelation to that effect would be first counseled, then reprimanded, and finally excommunicated if he persisted in his story of such a vision. He is not entitled to any such revelation—therefore, either he is lying, or the source of that revelation was not God, but Satan. Case closed.

The same was true in the formative years of the LDS Church, and any revelation received by Church members was only considered valid if it was approved by Joseph Smith, because any revelation that contradicted Joseph's just couldn't be true. It pains me to think how the Spirit of God was stifled in the hearts of those who thought they had found truth in Mormonism, and were taught to reject all feelings of doubt and disbelief because those feelings must be from the devil.

There were other problems in Kirtland too. The idea of communal living, having all things in common, was not a new one to the American scene of Joseph Smith's time. It was the former follower of Alexander Campbell, Sidney Rigdon, who, after seeing the success of colonies like Robert Owen's New Harmony, persuaded Joseph to start one like it. Dubbed "The United Order of Enoch," it was patterned loosely like other communal ventures, and, like them, it was a good idea at heart. A Church member would deed all his personal property and belongings to the Church permanently, and would in turn be given "stewardship" over enough to make a living for his family, as well as enough to purchase necessary clothing and modest personal belongings. Any profit made from a man's stewardship went back to the Church as a whole under the direction of Bishop Edward Partridge, who distributed surplus as he saw fit. However, Mormons in the early 1830s were in the middle of industrial and cultural changes sparked by and sustained by the free enterprise, capitalist ideal. In other words, the spirit was willing, but the flesh was weak, and the United Order failed.

While at Kirtland, Joseph made a prophecy that is unfamiliar to most Mormons. Just before the first general Church conference, he predicted that "not three days should pass away before some should see the Savior face to face."[51] At this conference a man seemed to have been suddenly stricken deaf and dumb, so Joseph exorcised the devil from him. Then Joseph tried unsuccessfully to heal a crippled man's hand, and another's lame leg, and finally to raise a lifeless child from the dead. This spiritual debacle, along with news that the Mormons were soon to be legally ejected from Ohio, spurred Joseph to leave quickly with thirty other men and go to Jackson County, Missouri. Cheered by the glorious vision of a perfect place where they could worship unmolested, the Mormon people began to blame the unspiritual atmosphere in Ohio for Joseph's failures, and they were soon forgotten by most.

Joseph Smith electrified his followers when he announced a revelation that identified Missouri as the promised land. When he and a number of others traveled to the area near Independence, Missouri, they chose a site for a new temple to be built there. This was to be a special place, this "New

Jerusalem," as Joseph called it—he even prophesied that its inhabitants would be "the only people that shall not be at war one with another."[52]

The hopeful tone of his prophecy, however, was soon marred by the tragedy and bloodshed that would eventually mark the end of Mormon life there. But for the time being, Joseph had planned his choice of the Zion of America well.

CONTINUING REVELATIONS

Joseph Smith returned to Ohio after Mormon settlers from New York relocated to Missouri and were established in the area that is now Kansas City. These settlers began to live the United Order, though in extreme poverty. In Ohio, Joseph started his own version of the Bible. The idea that the King James Version (though better than all other non-LDS versions) is in some places erroneous and incomplete is essential to LDS doctrine. (Why else would there be a need for additional revelation such as the *Book of Mormon*?) Thus it was only logical that Joseph Smith should put the Bible back into its original divinely correct form. This included inserting in his version of Genesis a prophecy concerning his own coming as a great prophet. While in Ohio, also, he developed the doctrine of the three degrees of heaven—the celestial, the terrestrial, and the telestial—where all people on earth would eventually dwell after death. All, that is, except for a very few "sons of perdition" who would end up in hell.

In 1832 Joseph issued one of his most famous prophecies—that which supposedly predicted the outbreak of the Civil War. Though his revelations were often personal in tone and aimed at particular individuals and their problems, rarely did he seek inspiration for problems as sweeping as the Civil War. Mormons today regard this prophecy as sure proof to us Gentiles of Joseph Smith's divine powers of prophecy, that he could foretell events which did not happen until much later. But a careful reading of the entire passage shows problems. First of all, Smith predicted a war caused by a slave uprising (*Doctrine and Covenants* 87:4). And the timing is all out of sync—most Mormons don't realize that in 1832, when Joseph said he received this "revelation," secular periodicals in his area were predicting the same thing: imminent civil war because of South Carolina's threats to secede. But the newspapers and magazines were as wrong as Joseph Smith: the Civil War didn't occur until many years later. Mormons assume too that Joseph Smith prophesied the 1832 rebellion of South Carolina when in fact *it had already occurred* at the time Joseph said he received the revelation.

Part of the revelation reads,

> For behold, the Southern States shall be divided against the Northern States, and the Southern States will call on other nations, even the nation of Great Britain, as it is called, and they shall also call upon other nations, in order to defend themselves against other nations; and then war shall be poured out upon all nations.[53]

This certainly gives the impression that the American Civil War would involve the whole world when Great Britain called on other nations, which of course it did not. But that is what the contemporaries of Joseph Smith expected. Orson Pratt, one of Joseph Smith's twelve apostles, prophesied in all seriousness in 1861 that some in his listening audience would see New York City and other great cities completely ruined and "desolate, without inhabitants," saying of the Civil War, "This great war is only a small degree of chastisement, just the beginning."[54]

Unless some of his listeners are still alive, both Pratt and Joseph Smith were dead wrong about the results of the Civil War.[55]

False prophecy became a habit for Joseph Smith. Most estimates of the number of recorded false prophecies that Smith made range from fifty to sixty. Edmond Gruss and Lane Thuet have documented the fact that Smith made at least one false prophecy per year from 1829 until the year of his death.[56]

This is easy to see in hindsight, but the Mormons of 1832 were full of rejoicing over a prophet who could produce such important predictions. Caught up in all this excitement was burly, youthful Brigham Young, who eagerly joined the inhabitants of Kirtland in beginning one of Joseph's greatest projects—the building of the first Latter-day temple.

The next year some of this enthusiasm was channeled into helping out the Missouri Mormons, who, in one of the blackest pages of anti-Mormon history, were savagely treated and turned out of their homes in the dead of winter. There were reasons why people were so threatened by them, according to LDS writer Richard L. Bushman: "The Missourians believed that Mormons thought Joseph's revelations put them beyond the law. Since the word of God outranked the law of the land, Mormons were suspected of breaking the law whenever the Prophet required it."[57]

I agree with the non-LDS Missourians of that time that the LDS Church was (and is) built on false revelation, but the treatment the Mormons received cannot ever be justified. Of course the Ohio Mormons were enraged at the insensitivity of Missouri law officials, but Joseph Smith made one of the greatest mistakes of his life when he announced that the Lord had said that Zion (Jackson County, Missouri) could be regained by force.[58]

When he and his pitiful two-hundred-man force returned from Missouri, ravaged by cholera and discouraged, the best he could do was promise that Zion's redemption lay still in the future. This Mormons sincerely believe today, confident that Jackson County, Missouri, will be the site of the New Jerusalem, where all the lost tribes of Israel[59] will gather at some future date.

In 1833 Joseph Smith announced the famous health-law revelation, called the Word of Wisdom (*Doctrine and Covenants*, section 89). Undoubtedly this revelation was a natural outgrowth of the nineteenth-century temperance movement. Since, though, this was supposedly a divine commandment, one could expect complete obedience to it from men like Joseph Smith. Such, unfortunately, was not the case.

Mormons are taught that abstinence from tea, coffee, alcohol, and tobacco is essential for entrance into the celestial kingdom. If this is true, Joseph Smith must be a candidate for the terrestrial or telestial kingdom, because he repeatedly violated the Word of Wisdom. An examination of early church sources in the original editions compared to the corresponding modern-day versions shows that the references to the drinking habits of early Mormon leaders have been purged from the original records. In other words, a great cover-up has been effected.

This is hard to prove to Mormons unless they see with their own eyes the original documents, or photos of them, which of course aren't usually available. In Jerald and Sandra Tanner's book, *Mormonism—Shadow or Reality?* they say,

> The Mormon leaders have made three important changes concerning the Word of Wisdom in Joseph Smith's *History of the Church*.... In one instance, Joseph Smith asked "Brother Markam" to get "a pipe and some tobacco" for the Apostle Willard Richards. These words have been replaced with the word "medicine" in recent editions of the *History of the Church*. At another time Joseph Smith related that he gave some of the "brethren" a "couple of dollars with directions to replenish" their supply of "whiskey." In modern editions of the *History of the Church*, 23 words have been deleted from this reference to cover up the fact that Joseph Smith encouraged the "brethren" to disobey the Word of Wisdom. In the third instance, Joseph Smith frankly admitted that he had "drank a glass of beer at Moessers." These words have been omitted in recent editions of *History of the Church*.[60]

Now, this is not to say that Joseph Smith was a drunkard. I don't think anyone believes that. But the fact that he compromised on one of his own rules compromises him. Add to this evidence that for a short while he kept a well-stocked bar in his own home in Nauvoo (ostensibly for entertaining visitors from out of town) that he removed only when his wife threatened to move out of the house—does this look like a defender of truth and temperance?

Any Mormon who might "lose his testimony" of Joseph Smith after hearing of these things can find comfort in knowing that he is not the first to be so bitterly disappointed. A whole family once apostatized when Joseph Smith's wife offered them tea and coffee while entertaining them at the Smith's home.[61]

About this time, in the mid-1830s, Joseph began another, darker, secret practice—that of polygamy. His first plural wife was Fanny Alger, according to LDS writer Todd Compton. "Her marriage to him in Kirtland, Ohio, established a pattern that was repeated in Nauvoo, Illinois: Smith secretly marries a teenage servant or family friend living in his home, and his first wife Emma forces the young woman from the premises when she discovers the relationship."[62]

JOSEPH THE TRANSLATOR, TEMPLE BUILDER, FINANCIER

Intoxicated by the slavish way that many of his followers adored him, Joseph was pushing the envelope in many different areas of his life. Probably Joseph's intemperate use of alcohol and tobacco (he openly smoked cigars while in Nauvoo) are not as embarrassing to modern Mormons as his boasts of knowing many languages. On one occasion he quoted from seventeen different languages (not always accurately). At another time he claimed, "I know more than all the world put together" and went on to discuss the meaning of various Hebrew, Latin, German, and Greek versions of the Bible.[63]

Joseph Smith's self-avowed abilities as a great linguist have been shown to be fraudulent by scholars studying the LDS scripture called the *Pearl of Great Price.* Joseph Smith supposedly "translated" a part of this book—the "Book of Abraham"—from some ancient Egyptian papyri. Until the late 1960s, his translations could not be challenged with certainty because the papyri were thought to have been destroyed in the great 1871 Chicago fire. But in 1967 the original papyri were rediscovered in a research room of the Metropolitan Museum of Art in New York City. They had been stored away and mostly forgotten for years.

The science of Egyptology has been greatly refined since 1835, and modern archaeological linguists (even the braver Mormon ones) agree that the writing on the scrolls has *nothing* whatsoever to do with Abraham, Moses, Joseph, or anything else even remotely Judaic or Christian. (The fact that this book contains the basis for the Mormons' former anti-Negro policies is another source of friction that Mormons hoped would go away.) But with the "translation" of Joseph's scrolls, the Mormons of 1835 rejoiced, happy that another new scripture had been given to them.

In 1836 the first LDS temple was officially dedicated. In an all-male gathering inside the temple, the ordinances of foot washing and anointing with oil were instituted. Joseph encouraged the many men present to prophesy, promising that the first one who would do so would be endued with the spirit of prophecy. Anxious to outdo each other, the men began to predict marvelous events of the future. This, it must be noted, occurred after a twenty-four-hour fast had been broken by drinking wine and eating bread. This could explain the "visions" some of the men saw, and their boldness in prophesying and cursing their enemies.

Part of the prosperity in Kirtland was due to Joseph's ingenuous issuing of bank bills which paid everyone's debts off, until it came to light that they weren't backed by gold, silver, or anything of value. When local merchants refused to trade with the Mormon currency, the Mormons were incredulous. Many apostatized, including Warren Parrish, an apostle and bank officer, because they had been taught that this divinely inspired banking institution was incapable of financial failure. Joseph Smith resigned from the bank, claiming that the debacle of the "Kirtland Anti-Banking Society," as the bank was called, was due not to its own faults but to the "age of darkness, speculation, and wickedness"[64] in which it was operating.

The blame was largely put on the apostates such as Warren Parrish, who was accused of stealing $25,000—to which Fawn Brodie has pointed out, "If he took the sum it must have been in worthless bank notes, since that amount of specie in the vaults would have saved the bank, at least during Joseph's term as cashier."[65]

Joseph's resignation from the bank didn't keep his angered creditors from besieging him with warrants for his arrest. Even Parley P. Pratt, an apostle, threatened to sue him. But as other banks around the country began to fail during this time of general financial instability, the Mormons regained faith in their leader. He sent many on missions to England where they could forget their financial woes in the fervor of proselyting. Joseph himself went on a short missionary journey to Canada, but was aghast when he returned to find the church split.

The three witnesses to the *Book of Mormon*—David Whitmer, Martin Harris, and Oliver Cowdery—along with many others had fallen in behind the leadership of a Shakerlike dancing prophetess, a young girl who used a seer stone to foretell the future. All three witnesses were severely rebuked, but Martin Harris was finally excommunicated when he refused to repent to Joseph's satisfaction.

MISSOURI

Dissension continued, and finally Joseph Smith himself left Kirtland in the dead of night to escape two things: a warrant for his arrest for banking fraud, and the scores of men who took over the temple, Joseph's pride and joy, and cursed his influence in Kirtland.

By the time Joseph reached Far West, Missouri, he had turned the financial and spiritual ruin in Kirtland into a sign of God's providence in sending the cream of Mormonism to the promised land. If Joseph Smith thought he could leave all his problems behind in Ohio, he must have been sorely disappointed. Here in Missouri his woes were not only financial but political. Since most of his converts were Northerners opposed to slavery, Missouri was a tinderbox and they the insuppressible sparks.

Soon the Mormons' basically neutral political position was undermined by the organization of the Church-sanctioned group called the Danites. Though Joseph Smith alternately denied and affirmed the existence of such a group, numerous testimonies exist describing the operations and purposes of this murderous clandestine organization. Though the names of this group changed, it had several distinguishing characteristics: the use of secret signs and passwords among members (both of which are strictly forbidden by the *Book of Mormon*), oaths to preserve the secret nature of the group, instructions to members to lie to protect and defend each other and to "waste away the Gentiles by robbing and plundering them of their property,"[66] and the commitment to carrying out the aims of the Danite band *without regard to personal feelings of conscience.*

If this sounds like something the present-day Mormons should be ashamed of, it is! Many modern Mormons have never heard of the Danites, because most popular LDS writers either ignore their existence or soft-pedal their activities. But there are notable exceptions: Bushman's book, the earlier *The Story of the Latter-Day Saints* by James B. Allen and Glen M. Leonard, and a book by William E. Berrett called *The Restored Church*. Not only did

Berrett, for instance, have the courage to admit that the Danite organization did exist, he further asserted that "the organization had been for the purpose of plundering and murdering enemies of the Saints."[67]

The most embarrassing fact about the Danite persecution was not their treatment (though deplorable) of non-Mormons, but their secondary duties: sacking of the homes of dissident *Church members*. Perhaps in an attempt to divert attention from the underground activities of the Danites, Joseph Smith tried unsuccessfully to reinstate the United Order among Church members. But they were suspicious after the recent financial problems in Kirtland, and the plan was modified into work-produce cooperatives. This, and the fervor exhibited by the cornerstone-laying ceremonies for the (never-completed) Far West temple frightened the Missouri natives, for Sidney Rigdon whipped a listening crowd into a frenzy with a speech that advocated "a war of extermination" between the Mormons and the Gentiles.

Just over a month later a fracas between a small group of Mormons and some Missourians over voting privileges on Election Day was amplified by word of mouth until half the county believed that there had been a full-scale battle. A warrant was issued for Joseph's arrest, and though he was bound over on bond to avoid a showdown, it was the average Mormon who suffered. Non-Mormon businessmen, especially millers, refused to trade with them, and when flour ran out in Far West, there was no more to be had. Mobs of Missourians plundered Mormon property throughout the state, and the Danite band grew to include all healthy Mormon men. Now it was called "The Army of Israel."

THE MORMON MOHAMMED

Joseph Smith likened himself to a Mohammed for that army, saying,

> If the people will let us alone, we will preach the gospel in peace. But if they come on us to molest us, we will establish our religion by the sword. We will trample down our enemies and make it one gore of blood from the Rocky Mountains to the Atlantic Ocean. I will be to this generation a second Mohammed, whose motto in treating for peace was, "the Alcoran or the Sword." So shall it eventually be with us—"Joseph Smith or the Sword!"[68]

For all the bloodiness of this speech, it still reflects the basic feelings of Joseph and his followers at this time. They wanted peace badly—but not at the expense of their homes, their personal safety, and their human dignity.

And these things were exactly what the Missourians most wanted to take from them.

This, and prophecies made by the Mormon leaders regarding the invincibility of the Army of Israel, spurred the Missourians to the offensive. When they began to return like for like, many Mormons, including two apostles, left Far West.

The Missourians stepped up their plundering activities. News of actual and imaginary Mormon raids so alarmed the governor, Lilburn Boggs, that he issued his infamous "extermination order." One of the results of this order was the massacre of eighteen Mormons, including a young boy, at an outlying settlement called Haun's Mill. Secretly Joseph Smith sent word to the military leaders of Missouri that the Mormons wanted peace—at any cost. The price General Lucas demanded was high: a complete exodus from Missouri by all Mormons, after surrender of their arms and confiscation and sale of their property to pay "damages," punitive and actual. The only ones excepted were the church leaders who were to stay in Missouri to stand trial for treason.

Far West was the scene of rapes, pillaging, starvation, and humiliation for the Mormons, who were forced to stay there under Missouri militia rule. Joseph Smith and others were imprisoned in the jail at Richmond. When they were arraigned, one of the star witnesses for the prosecution was an apostate who spilled the beans about his own involvement in the Danite activities.

Joseph and five others were indicted without bail and spent the next four months in Liberty Jail. While here, Joseph began canonizing the doctrine he then called "the patriarchal order of marriage," or polygamy—a practice he had been engaged in for years.

Meanwhile the belongings of his people were auctioned off. Brigham Young, who had somehow escaped indictment, was the leader to whom the homeless Mormons turned for guidance. They left Missouri, crossing the Mississippi River into Illinois, where they were treated kindly by most people but exploited by the land speculators. Joseph was returned meanwhile to Daviess County, where, since no impartial jurymen could be found, he argued and won a change of venue into another, less prejudiced, county.

On the way, however, he bribed his guard and escaped with his fellow prisoners to the Mississippi River that marked his freedom. In Illinois, Joseph founded a city that he called Nauvoo. He said this name meant "beautiful plantation" in Hebrew, but the word never existed except in his mind. From his mind, too, sprang this lovely, well-ordered city, and it took shape through the hard work of his followers. What most popular LDS histories do not record, in recounting the virtues of Nauvoo, though, is the brewery authorized by Joseph Smith, nor the bar he had in his own house, nor the short-lived Nauvoo whorehouse, nor the Masonic temple where Joseph himself "became a first-degree Mason on the night of the installation, and the next night rose to the sublime degree."[69] Though the Mormonism-Masonry connection was flatly denied when I was a Mormon, LDS scholars now not only acknowledge the connection but have written quite extensively on it in recent years.[70]

It is impossible to overestimate the power and influence of Joseph Smith in Nauvoo. What he wanted, he got—either by exercising his civic powers (he was mayor) or by revealing a "revelation," as in the case of the "Lord" awarding Joseph's family and posterity five rooms and free board in the town hotel.[71] It is impossible, too, to overestimate the size of this man's ego. A visitor to Nauvoo in 1843 characterized him as "the greatest egotist I ever met."[72] Supposedly to test his people's faith, Joseph once preached a sermon and then rode through the streets of the city smoking a big cigar.[73]

Another element of Joseph's character that often goes unmentioned or unknown by Mormons was his hot temper and physical violence.[74] He was persuasive and vain, boasting to visitors of his intelligence and good looks. He persuaded many church leaders, among them Brigham Young, to leave their families practically destitute and go on missions to England. Success there was phenomenal, and many converts came to Nauvoo. Meanwhile Joseph reigned supreme and unrivaled in his beautiful city.

If *reigned* seems too presumptuous a word, it is substantiated by evidence that Joseph Smith actually had himself ordained a king, according to LDS author Klaus Hansen.[75] Because this was kept very secret, even from most Mormons of that time, the non-Mormons who lived around Nauvoo were not alarmed by Joseph's aspirations to royalty denied him by blood. The residents of Illinois did, however, resent the pious attitude reflected by town regulations forbidding swearing and vagrancy inside the Nauvoo town limits. The new Mormon temple there became a symbol of the "clannishness" and secretiveness they claimed was characteristic of the Mormons. In this temple, unspeakable (or at least unmentionable) rites were performed, strange garments worn, and terrible oaths of vengeance sworn.

Non-Mormons also chafed when the "Nauvoo Legion" of four thousand men was hastily chartered by an Illinois legislature anxious to corner the numerous Mormon votes before the coming election. What this charter gave the Mormons, as they saw it, was independence from Illinois law and great military power in its own right. Joseph Smith embraced the role of military leader with as much gusto as he wore his role of spiritual leader, and preferred the title of Lieutenant General (given to him by Illinois Governor Carlin) above even the title of president of the Church. He was proud of his snappy uniform and his troops, which represented to him a defense against his constant fear of extradition to Missouri. He even had a menacing personal bodyguard of twelve devoted and physically powerful men, most former Danites.

All of these things brought to the minds of the people of Illinois the troubles their neighbors in Missouri had experienced with the Mormons, and they waited uneasily as the Mormons grew in numbers, prosperity, and visible military strength. This feeling of uneasiness grew greater when it became common knowledge that Orrin Porter Rockwell, Joseph's blindly faithful and immensely strong bodyguard companion, had been in Missouri at about the same time the hated Missouri official Boggs had been shot three times in the head. When Rockwell returned from what he admitted was a trip to Missouri, his pockets full of much more money than he'd had when he left Illinois, people began to remember a prophecy made by Joseph the year before. This prophecy stated that Boggs would die violently. Most assumed that Rockwell had merely expedited the prophecy, and he and Joseph Smith were served a writ of extradition from the governor of Missouri. Stalling for time, both Joseph and Rockwell escaped into hiding after they were released on a writ of habeas corpus.

Joseph feared the improbable conviction on charges of accessory to the attempted murder of Boggs (who miraculously recovered) not so much as he feared the atmosphere of rekindled hatred toward Mormons that he was sure he would find in Missouri after the Boggs shooting. Missouri wanted blood—and Joseph wanted to make sure they got none of his.

He was in hiding in and around Nauvoo for almost four months. During this time more and more stories and gossip surfaced about polygamy. For a long time Joseph had been angrily denying the recurrent rumors that Emma was not the only woman with whom he shared matrimonial vows and privileges.

Joseph Smith was always "a great favorite with the ladies."[76] He once said publicly that he had to "pray for grace" whenever he saw a pretty woman. But he had a reputation to protect, and he resolved the conflict between his rakish tendencies and the teachings of the Bible and the *Book of Mormon* on monogamy in the same way that had always worked before. He got a "revelation" permitting him and other faithful Mormon men to have as many wives as they pleased.

Many Mormons believe that though Joseph Smith believed in polygamy, he never practiced it. This attitude is the result of two things: first, their own ignorance of their history; and second, the LDS Church's practice of just "not talking" about issues that would tend to confuse the average member—or cause him or her to think deeply. After all, the Church has had to reconcile Joseph's statements about the vital necessity of polygamy with the Church's modern abhorrence of the practice.

Joseph Smith had formulated the concept of a man's privilege of having more than one wife here on earth, as well as in heaven, but it was a theory that had to be advanced slowly. He first tried it out on men he most trusted after he himself had tested the waters, so to speak. Eventually it became a kind of litmus test of loyalty to his leadership. By the time he died, he had at least twenty-seven wives (as documented by LDS Church historian Andrew Jenson) and perhaps as many as forty-eight (the number documented by Fawn Brodie).

LDS historian Todd Compton, in his book *In Sacred Loneliness*, provides biographies of thirty-three plural wives—not counting Emma. Eleven of those were aged fourteen to twenty. Says Compton,

> The teenage representation is the largest, though the twenty-year and thirty-year groups are comparable, which contradicts the Mormon folk-wisdom that sees the beginnings of polygamy as an attempt to care for older, unattached women. These data suggest that sexual attraction was an important part of the motivation for Smith's polygamy.[77]

Fully one-third of Smith's wives were legally married to other men when he married them, which logically means of course that Smith also introduced polyandry.[78]

As a Mormon I regarded Emma with a mixture of respect and pity. I respected her because she was the Prophet's beloved wife, and was witness to a glorious age in the restoration of the gospel. The pity I felt for her, though, has greatly increased since I left Mormonism. She apparently was never really convinced in her heart of hearts concerning Joseph's spiritual authority, and this must have caused her great emotional turmoil. (Or worse: Brigham Young, in the annual Conference address in October of 1866, claimed that Emma actually tried twice to poison her husband.)[79]

In section 25 of *Doctrine and Covenants*, Joseph exercised all the authority he could summon in the name of God to try to shake Emma into being the obedient, dutiful wife he needed. Apparently he never ceased to love her for her free and independent spirit. She, indeed, is to me the true martyr of the LDS religion—a woman torn between love for a marvelous and imaginative man and the haunting doubt that his inspiration was simply his own mind or something worse. Perhaps it was this love, and pride, that prevented her from exposing Joseph early in his career; for twenty-five years later, after his death, his legend would be one so great that even his wife could not discredit it.

Surely Emma Smith was one of the most patient women alive. (A good, recent biography of her is *Mormon Enigma: Emma Hale Smith* by Linda King Newell and Valeen Tippetts Avery.) When I was a Mormon I used to wonder what I would do if polygamy were reinstated as a commandment and I were asked to give my permission to my husband to take another wife. I was taught that a first wife's permission was necessary, but history shows that Emma never knew about many of her husband's other wives. The humiliation of giving permission for another wife (surely a symbol to her of Joseph's view of her own inadequacy) was enough to encourage Joseph to keep many of his newer wives under cover. No pun intended—but it is a fact that some of Joseph's plural wives claimed privately that they had consummated their marriages to him.[80] One plural wife, Eliza R. Snow, who wrote the lyrics to some of Mormonism's most famous hymns, reportedly miscarried Joseph's child when she fell down a flight of stairs after having been beaten violently with a broom by Emma. Emma, it seems, had come upon Eliza and Joseph embracing in the hallway of the Smith home, and for once could not contain her rage.

This vignette alone should be enough to dispel the popular LDS myth that plural wives lived together amicably as sisters. Perhaps some did, but many experienced natural jealousies and rivalries.

At any rate, polygamy wasn't very popular at all in its early years.[81] Church leaders fought it, but soon succumbed to "reason" when they saw a young new wife could be justified—even commanded—by God's laws. Gentiles found repugnant the fact that Joseph Smith had married women whose husbands were still living. If only they'd known the whole story—Joseph's many wives ranged in age from fifteen to fifty-nine. He married five pairs of sisters, and one mother and daughter.[82]

Many of the marriages were performed before the release of the official "revelation" on polygamy, dated August 12, 1843. This revelation contained a threat that Emma (poor Emma) would be "destroyed" if she didn't submit to the results of polygamy. (However, he had at least sixteen wives before Emma began giving her "approval" for polygamy.[83] And, according to Emma's biographers Linda King Newell and Valeen Tippetts Avery, "by late summer 1843, most of Emma's friends had either married Joseph or had given their daughters to him."[84])

Meanwhile, Joseph excommunicated anyone else who taught or practiced polygamy without his express permission and approval.

In 1843 there occurred another incident most Mormons would rather forget. Joseph had been released in January of that year when, after the four months of hiding, he had given himself up to Illinois officials. The Missouri writ of extradition (regarding involvement in the Boggs shooting) he had so feared was declared in court to be invalid. Rockwell too was cleared after some months, though in later years he boasted of having shot Boggs. It was with an air of renewed confidence, then, that Joseph Smith faced the world in the spring of 1843. He was so confident of himself and his powers that when six inscribed metal plates were brought to him by men who had dug them out of the ground, he was reported to have said,

> Monday, May, 1 ... I insert facsimiles of the six brass plates found near Kinderhook ... I have translated a portion of them, and find they contain the history of the person with whom they were found. He was a descendant of Ham, through the loins of Pharaoh, king of Egypt, and that he received his kingdom from the Ruler of heaven and earth.[85]

Unfortunately for Joseph's future reputation as a translator, one of the men who claimed to have "found" the plates also confessed to having helped "engrave" them with acid, using as a model for the hieroglyphics the characters on the lid of a Chinese tea box. He and some friends then "aged" the plates with rust, concocted the story of a dream revealing their whereabouts, and pretended to discover them in the presence of a Mormon elder.

The Mormon community was overjoyed at the prospect of a sequel to the *Book of Mormon* that would verify Apostle Pratt's prophecy that more revelation would come from the ground as did the golden plates. When Joseph let it be published that he was working on a translation, the conspirators too were overjoyed at the prospect of a new "scripture" from their forged plates. But Joseph died before the translation apparently was finished. Since one of the plates is still in existence, though, modern scientists have inspected it and agreed: (1) Its composition and construction are compatible with the theory that they were forged in a blacksmith's shop of the Midwest in the 1840s, (2) the inscriptions could indeed have been made with acid, and finally (3) the inscription is in the Lo language of China. All of this agrees with the men's story of forging, aging, and inscribing the plates with symbols from a Chinese box.

So what do the "Kinderhook Plates" (which I never heard of while a Mormon) prove about Joseph Smith? No one said it better than Charles Shook, who put it succinctly: "Only a bogus prophet translates bogus plates."[86]

MORE LEGAL PROBLEMS

John Cook Bennett, who in his apostasy had developed a hatred for Joseph Smith that bordered on rabidness, pressured Missouri governor Reynolds in June of 1843 to try once more to extradite Joseph to Missouri, where he could be tried on the old treason charge. A Missouri posse ambushed and kidnapped Joseph and took him to Dixon, Illinois. On the way to Quincy, they were joined by a 140-man armed escort from the Nauvoo Legion, who feared a second kidnapping. Instead of going to Quincy, they rode on into Nauvoo, where Joseph won his freedom by claiming that he was not the Joseph Smith Jr. named in the Missouri writ, but Joseph Smith Sr. (This was at best a half-truth, as both his son and his father were named Joseph Smith; therefore he was *both* Sr. and Jr.) He also denied having committed treason, or ever having been a fugitive from justice (both of which denials depend for their truthfulness on how he defined "treason" and "justice") and claimed that his Nauvoo court had the right to issue a writ of habeas corpus (a legally untenable provision of the city's special charter).

He was aided in his legal battle for his life by Cyrus Walker, the influential head of the Illinois Whig Party, to whom he pledged his vote and that of his people in the upcoming election. Joseph won his case, but infuriated the Whigs by indirectly endorsing Walker's Democratic opponent a few days before the election. Hyrum Smith, Joseph's brother (who had been promised a seat in the state legislature if the Mormons voted as Democrats), conveniently received a "revelation" telling the Mormons to vote Democratic, and publicized his revelation widely. Torn between conflicting loyalties, Joseph proved the old adage about the thickness of blood over water. After the election, the defeated Whigs thirsted for Joseph's traitorous blood.

Joseph saw as a solution to this dilemma the endowment of Nauvoo with legal rights that ignored the laws of the state and county in which it lay. Thus he could make and enforce laws without interference from civic officials. He wanted Nauvoo to be declared an independent federal territory whose mayor (himself) could call out troops (the Nauvoo Legion) whenever he saw fit (such as when he thought a writ of extradition was about to be served on him). The most flagrant of his proposed laws called for life imprisonment in the Nauvoo jail for anyone who entered the town bearing a writ for the old treason charge. The criminal's only recourse for mercy? A pardon from Joseph himself.

For Joseph, being commander-in-chief of the powerful Nauvoo Legion was not enough. Being mayor of a city or the governor of the federal territory of Nauvoo was not enough. Being prophet, seer, and revelator was not enough. Being "king of God's kingdom on earth" was not enough. Joseph Smith wanted to be president of the United States of America.

In truth, I don't think he ever really expected to win the 1844 national election. But like many one-cause-oriented candidates of today's politics, he knew that the publicity he would receive from just entering the race would focus national attention on his cause. And he knew well from his experience in state politics (however unwisely he had gained that experience) that a bloc of voters as large as the Mormons could well decide an election and make their good graces a commodity to be desired by other candidates.

The "theodemocracy" he advocated was not really that, for in its ultimate state it would have been a one-party system. As Mormons would say, "the right party," meaning the Mormon party. Joseph also advocated abolition of slavery, annexation of Texas, and drastic penal reform.

While Joseph was riding the crest of a wave of confidence that seemed would never break on the shores of reality, some of his closest counselors and friends stood on the sand watching bitterly. Some he had alienated by approaching their wives, trying to fatten his polygamous harem. Others he had denounced publicly for crimes of which they felt themselves innocent. Still others were disgusted by Joseph's use of Church money to buy property that he sold at a profit to new converts, while the workers on the Nauvoo temple were ill-fed and lived in shacks. Some still believed in the doctrines of early Mormonism, but felt that Joseph had fallen from the favor of God by abusing his authority.

Some of these men brought suit against Joseph for slander, false swearing, adultery, and polygamy. Their charges were countered by claims in the Nauvoo Mormon newspapers that the accusers were sexual profligates who had seduced many innocent women. In May Joseph himself denied publicly that he had *ever* had more than one wife. This may have satisfied those who were ignorant of his scores of wives, but what soul searching it must have caused those who knew the truth, and heard such a monstrous lie coming from the lips of God's mouthpiece!

But the press begun by the Mormon dissidents, *The Nauvoo Expositor*, printed details of the involvement of high Church officials with polygamy.

To spare humiliation to the "spiritual wives," many of whom had been bullied, seduced, or tricked into accepting their polygamous unions, *The Nauvoo Expositor* mentioned no names. But the readers of the newspaper recognized in its stories the situations of many friends and loved ones. They were torn with mistrust of the prophet's vehement denials of the existence of polygamy and the extent to which it was practiced.

Joseph's solution to this challenge to his authority was simple. The staff members of the *Nauvoo Expositor* were "tried" without judge, jury, or witness for their own defense, accused by members of the city council, and declared to be operating a public nuisance. Part of the Nauvoo Legion was dispatched to destroy the presses and all existing copies of the publication, and in its smoking ruins Joseph thought he saw a return to peace in Nauvoo.

When news reached the shocked outside world, though, the flame of Joseph's life flickered on a shrinking wick. Perhaps Joseph realized it, for more and more of his public statements and prophecies referred to his imminent death.

The people of Illinois were aghast to learn of the destruction of the *Expositor* press. Some local militia from surrounding towns were ready to attack Nauvoo at a moment's notice, but to prevent mob invasion Governor Ford ordered Joseph and his co-conspirators to appear in Carthage, Illinois, for trial. Joseph and his brother Hyrum, along with Willard Richards and Orrin Porter Rockwell, escaped into Iowa Territory across the flood-swollen Mississippi River.

The leaderless Mormon people, under imminent attack from all sides, felt betrayed by Joseph's flight. Word was sent to the fugitives, imploring them to return. Joseph, upon hearing the urgent message, was shamed into action, saying, "If my life is of no value to my friends, it is of no value to myself." He and the others returned to Nauvoo, where Joseph prepared his legal defense, and then rode on into Carthage. He and Hyrum were jailed on charges of rioting and put into the two-story Carthage jail. Joseph sent for the Nauvoo Legion with a message that entreated them to break him out of the jail, for he feared for his life.

Time ran out for Joseph and Hyrum and their two visitors, Willard Richards and John Taylor. As they sat sipping wine, a commotion outside made them jump for their two smuggled guns. When the door was breached, they fired back—hardly the defenseless sacrificial lambs described to me when I was a Mormon. When the smoke cleared, Taylor was slightly wounded, and Richards untouched. Joseph and Hyrum were shot dead by the mob.

In the final analysis, the Smith brothers didn't die as victims of religious persecution. According to author Robert V. Remini, Smith's standing army of five thousand heavily armed men, his posturing as the head not just of a religious group but of a separate nation, and the "last straw" of his desires to run for the presidency of the United States were too much for his neighbors. "His murder," said Remini, in his biography of Smith, "was a political act of assassination."[87]

Those who hoped Mormonism would die with Joseph were disappointed. Had his desire that his son succeed him been realized, perhaps Mormonism would not be so powerful today. That son, Joseph Smith III, and his mother, Emma, eventually allied themselves with a dissident group that renounced the doctrine of plural marriage and others of Joseph's teachings, saying that these were perversions of truth, and that Joseph Smith had "fallen" in his later years.

What Mormonism did need, and got, was the strong leadership of a man like Brigham Young. Mormons are taught that he was a gruff, plainspoken man. What they fail to appreciate is how power affected that man. The triumph of leading his people in the trek across the American Plains never wore off. When he arrived in Utah, he became a despot who controlled with a grasping hand the economy, religion, and morals of the people of the Salt Lake Valley. His legendary scores of wives, his excesses of rage, his amazing (and now repudiated) teachings on blood atonement and the identification of Adam as God—all are unknown or unnoticed by most Mormons of today who admire in him the ideal of work and fortitude.

Perhaps the LDS people, for survival as a people, needed a prophet like that. Perhaps they needed a Joseph Smith.

But a Christian needs only Christ.

Chapter 3

THE *BOOK OF MORMON*: "THE MOST CORRECT OF ANY BOOK"?

I told the brethren that the Book of Mormon *was the most correct of any book on earth, and the keystone of our religion, and a man would get nearer to God by abiding by its precepts, than by any other book.*

—Joseph Smith[1]

One purpose of the LDS missionary lessons is to convince a prospect that God did not protect his church after the death of the last apostle, and that he did not protect his Word, the Bible. The devaluation of Holy Writ is accomplished in two ways. First, Mormons point to works by Hebrew writers, such as the "Book of the Wars of Israel" and the "Book of the Covenant" mentioned by Moses, the "Book of Jasher" mentioned by Joshua, the "Book of the Acts of Solomon" mentioned in First Kings, the "Book of Jehu" and "Acts of Uzziah" by Isaiah, the "Sayings of the Seers," and other "lost" books we might title "Third Corinthians," "Second Ephesians," and the "Epistle to the Laodiceans" referred to in the New Testament. Mormons say, "See—these books are missing from the Bible. It is incomplete and thus unreliable."

Bible students, however, know that many obviously uninspired literary works are likewise mentioned in the Bible. In the New Testament, for instance, the apostle Paul quoted from pagan Greek writers (Acts 17:28; Titus 1:12). No one, including LDS apologists, would assert that the complete works from which these quotations were taken should be regarded by us as Scripture, nor that the Bible is incomplete without those complete works.

An argument citing the "incompleteness" of the Bible is indeed a weak crutch upon which to lean the plea for the necessity of "more scripture." If these "missing" books of the Bible were necessary for our salvation, why didn't Mormonism just *restore* them? This same argument equating "incompleteness" with invalidity must hold true also for Mormons when they consider that the writings of characters like Zenos, Zenock, Neum, and Ezias are all mentioned in the *Book of Mormon.*[2] What must they assume, knowing that these works don't appear there (or anywhere else), except in partial form or passing reference?

Of course, we know that the works mentioned in the Bible which do not appear there in their completeness are not necessary for our salvation. John 20:30–31 clearly tells the believer that not every detail regarding the life of Christ was written down by his gospel biographers. (Perhaps an important part of divine inspiration was selectivity!) At any rate, this Scripture passage teaches us that what *was* written was for the express purpose of saving our souls. Dare we ask more of a generous God?

The Mormons do so dare. They claim that not only are there parts of the Bible missing which are mentioned in Holy Scripture, but that many "plain and precious parts" were edited out of the Bible we have.[3] In a notebook given to me for use in a seminary class, there was a page that was intended to teach the young LDS student exactly how these "plain and precious parts" found their way out of the Bible. On this page was a drawing of a medieval-era priest, brows knit together and smirking wickedly, who was furtively scratching out lines written on a scroll. This was intended to show how wicked monks just blotted out the parts of the Bible with which they did not agree.

Now, anyone who has ever studied about Bible manuscripts knows that those manuscripts that are now in existence, from the earliest to the later ones, are a striking testimony to the divine protection of God over his holy records. Over one hundred years ago R. A. Torrey noted,

> We now possess so many good copies [of the Bible] that by comparing one with another we can tell with great precision just what the original text was. Indeed, for all practical purposes the original text is now settled. There is not one important doctrine that hangs upon any doubtful reading of the text.[4]

It is interesting to note that Torrey penned these words almost fifty years before the discovery of the Dead Sea Scrolls, which substantiated everything Christians had been saying all along about the reliability of our copies of Old Testament Scriptures, at least. In addition, F. F. Bruce, in his classic book *New Testament Documents: Are They Reliable?* noted that we have over five thousand Greek manuscripts containing part or all of the New Testament. We have some manuscripts that are only removed in time a few years from their inspired authors. The older the manuscripts discovered, the narrower the time period in which such falsification claimed by Mormons would have to have happened. Perhaps someday Christians will be blessed with the discovery of part of a Bible manuscript contemporaneous with its author; and faith tells us that it will not differ substantially, if indeed at all, from the Bible versions we read today.

THE RESTORATION OF THE "PLAIN AND PRECIOUS" GOSPEL

A claim made proudly by Mormons is that they practice Christianity in its pure first-century form.[5] However, LDS doctrine of the past and present has commanded polygamy, "endowment" temple rites, the potential for humans to become gods, and other strange doctrines. Since these are the "extras" we don't find in traditional Christianity, we can only assume that these are included in the "plain and precious parts" the *Book of Mormon* needed to restore. But why is there no mention of such things being both advocated and practiced by early Christians,[6] even in the writings of secular historians who surely would have noted such deviations from the Jewish norm?

Even more to the point, does the *Book of Mormon* itself restore—or even mention—any of these doctrines? In fact, the theology of the *Book of Mormon* isn't Mormon—at least, not twenty-first century Mormonism. Latter-day Saints quote *Doctrine and Covenants* 20:9, 42:12, and 135:3, which claim that the *Book of Mormon* has "the fullness" of the everlasting gospel. But as ex-Mormon writer Bob Witte has pointed out, most of the elements that make modern Mormonism distinctive aren't in that book. In addition to temple worship, plural marriage, and the Negro-priesthood issue, Witte notes that the *Book of Mormon* also *does not teach* the following recently advocated LDS doctrines:

- God has a body of flesh and bones
- God is an exalted man
- God is a product of eternal progression
- There is a plurality of gods (polytheism)
- Men may become gods
- The Trinity consists of three separate Gods

- There is no eternal hell and punishment
- "Intelligences"[7] are eternal
- The preexistence of humans as spirits
- Marriage for eternity
- Three degrees of glory[8]
- A Mother in heaven
- A New Testament–era "Melchizidek Priesthood" with the offices and functions of elder, high priest, seventy, patriarch, and apostle
- A New Testament–era "Aaronic Priesthood" with the offices and functions of deacon, teacher, priest, and bishop
- The functions and offices of evangelists, bishoprics, stake presidencies, apostles, a first presidency, and president of the Church
- Baptism for the dead and "second-chance salvation"[9]

Authors Gruss and Thuet add to this list the requirements for LDS exaltation (that is, entrance into the Celestial Kingdom) that aren't commanded in the *Book of Mormon*: LDS baptism and confirmation, paying of tithes, priesthood ordinances, and eternal polygamy, among other doctrines.[10]

This matter of "plain and precious parts," that the *Book of Mormon* supposedly restored, has puzzled Christians since 1830. A kind way to put it is to say that it is certainly no easier to understand than the Bible. Nor does it explain in any greater detail any biblical tenet. Though the *Book of Mormon* does go off on tangents like Christ's visit to the Americas and Lehi's vision of the world, these and other stories don't explain—or make plainer—any ideas found in the Bible. In fact, in many cases they are barefaced contradictions of the Bible.

The Bible-believing Christian does not have to search the Scriptures for long to effectively refute the claim that our Bible is incomplete. First Peter 1:25 says that the word of the Lord—the gospel—will endure forever. Second Timothy 3:16–17 says that the Bible ("all Scripture") will completely equip the man of God. Contrast this to 2 Nephi 29:3–6, which bluntly asserts that only a "fool" would accept the Bible as God's only Scripture. So the supplement offered by Mormonism is their *Book of Mormon.*

Joseph Fielding Smith, president of the LDS Church from 1970 to 1972 and one of its most prolific modern-day theologians, said that there are many as yet unexplained principles relating to the Celestial Kingdom and to exaltation, but that "the Lord has revealed in the *Book of Mormon* all that is needful to direct people who are willing to hearken to its precepts to a fullness of the blessings of the Kingdom of God."[11] If this be true, that the *Book of Mormon* can guide people to salvation where no other book could, then we could certainly expect its predecessor, the Bible—though seen by Latter-day Saints as incomplete—to point us toward such an essential scripture. In support of this theory we are offered many passages from the Bible that supposedly herald the advent of Mormonism.

It must be noted parenthetically here that those Scripture references which will follow are taken from the King James Version of the Bible,[12] which Mormons claim is the most correct one (aside from the standard German translation which Joseph Smith lauded as a nearly perfect rendering of God's Word).[13] Anyone who reads the *Book of Mormon*'s often bumbling attempts at imitating seventeenth-century English, however, would be hard pressed to understand why Mormons are so anxious to constantly invite such a comparison.

WRESTING OF BIBLE SCRIPTURES

One of the first Bible Scriptures with which every LDS student becomes familiar is found in Ezekiel 37:15–20.

> The word of the LORD came again unto me, saying, Moreover, thou son of man, take thee one stick, and write upon it, For Judah, and for the children of Israel his companions: then take another stick, and write upon it, For Joseph, the stick of Ephraim, and for all the house of Israel his companions: And join them one to another into one stick; and they shall become one in thine hand. And when the children of thy people shall speak unto thee, saying, Wilt thou not shew us what thou meanest by these? Say unto them, Thus saith the Lord GOD; Behold, I will take the stick of Joseph, which is in the hand of Ephraim, and the tribes of Israel his fellows, and will put them with him, even with the stick of Judah, and make them one stick, and they shall be one in mine hand. And the sticks whereon thou writest shall be in thine hand before their eyes.

The late LDS apologist Dr. Hugh Nibley put forth the standard Mormon explanation that the "stick of Judah" here mentioned is the Bible, because it was written by Judah's descendants, the Jews; and that the "stick of Ephraim" is the *Book of Mormon*, written by the Nephites, who were supposedly descended from Ephraim. Everyone knows, say the Mormons, that old-time scrolls were rolled up on sticks, and from this the conclusion is drawn that the Ezekiel passage refers to two books of scripture that would be of equal importance and united in purpose in the hand of the Lord.[14]

There are several serious flaws in this interpretation of this section of Ezekiel's writings. First of all, the Hebrew word for "stick" used here is found in other places in the Bible (Num. 15:32; 1 Kings 17:10; 2 Kings 6:6), but in every instance where it is used, it means a piece of wood. Another, different word is used in the Bible for the word *scroll.* I think that if God had meant *scroll* in Ezekiel 37, he would have said it.

Even if the word *stick* were meant to signify a scroll, we are left with a dilemma: It is true that the Bible was recorded on scrolls, but what about the supposed source of the *Book of Mormon*—its fabled golden plates?

Any serious Bible student would agree that Ezekiel himself ("thou son of man") was told to inscribe the two sticks. Always in Ezekiel's prophecy the phrase "son of man" (used ninety-one times) refers specifically to the man Ezekiel. Thus if the prophet Ezekiel was to *write* on these two sticks, we can either accept the fact that he was told to inscribe a few words on two pieces of wood, or follow the LDS argument to its logical conclusion: Ezekiel must have written both the Bible and the *Book of Mormon.*

Finally, God himself gave the interpretation of the meaning of the two sticks in verses 18 through 23: the unification of people, not records.

The second Scripture used by Mormons to show a biblical foreshadowing of the coming of the *Book of Mormon* is found in Isaiah 29:1–4.

> Woe to Ariel, to Ariel, the city where David dwelt! add ye year to year; let them kill sacrifices. Yet I will distress Ariel, and there shall be heaviness and sorrow: and it shall be unto me as Ariel. And I will camp against thee round about, and will lay siege against thee with a mount, and I will raise forts against thee. And thou shalt be brought down, and shalt speak out of the ground, and thy speech shall be low out of the dust, and thy voice shall be, as of one that hath a familiar spirit, out of the ground, and thy speech shall whisper out of the dust.

Mormons say that the voice from the dust with a familiar spirit is the *Book of Mormon* which was buried in the ground and which contained some of the teachings of the old Jewish prophets such as Isaiah.[15] With this interpretation Mormons have violated one of the most valuable principles of responsible Bible study: They have taken the idea of "voices from the dust with a familiar spirit" entirely out of context.

The careful reader will note that Ariel, or Jerusalem, is in this passage *rebuked* for its spiritual debauchery, which is exemplified by her intimacy with "familiar spirits"—or the practice of the black arts. The Hebrew word used here for "familiar spirit"—*ob*—means demon. In other words, the Jews were practicing witchcraft. Do the Mormons really want to use these verses to support their own scriptures?[16]

Mormons also use 2 Corinthians 13:1 to show the necessity for scripture such as the *Book of Mormon.* The latter part of this verse states, "In the mouth of two or three witnesses shall every word be established." The Bible, say the Mormons, is only one witness and alone it is unsubstantiated without the corroboration of another book. However, if I regarded the Bible as fallible and thus imperfect, I wouldn't think that another book of scripture could corroborate it—you can't build successfully upon a faulty foundation! Our gracious and generous God has already given us two witnesses, the Old and the New Testaments (actually a total of sixty-six literary witnesses), and added to these the confirming witness of the Holy Ghost (Heb. 10:15).

LDS missionaries often combine two Scriptures, one from the gospel of John and one from the gospel of Matthew, to raise questions in the mind of a Christian.

> And other sheep I have, which are not of this fold: them also I must bring, and they shall hear my voice; and there shall be one fold, and one shepherd. (John 10:16)
>
> But he answered and said, I am not sent but unto the lost sheep of the house of Israel. (Matt. 15:24)

If, Mormons say, Jesus was to go to other sheep, and if the other sheep were only of the house of Israel, then the other sheep must be displaced Jews—displaced in, say, America. They assert that the other sheep could not possibly be Gentiles because of what Matthew 15:24 says. Again, this is a problem caused by taking Scripture out of context. (When we read the entire "lost sheep" passage in Matthew 15:21–28, we find that at least one time Jesus did indeed minister to a non-Jew who heard his voice.) But this is only a peripheral issue. What is important is that Christians of today are certainly Christ's sheep, though many have no traceable Jewish heritage. Christ promised to *bring us*, which (praise his name) he has done—not to visit us as the Mormons claim he did to the Nephites; not to watch us receive the Holy Spirit in his presence (compare John 16:7 to 3 Nephi 19:20–22); and certainly not to endorse a gospel so foreign to his own!

PRODUCING THE *BOOK OF MORMON*

One such matter that is very hard for the non-Mormon to understand is the process of translation used in the production of the *Book of Mormon.* Accounts from eyewitnesses vary greatly, but according to Joseph Smith (who, if anyone, should have known), much of the translation was accomplished with the aid of the Urim and Thummim. Just what these were is a mystery to Mormon and non-Mormon alike. They were mentioned in Exodus 28:30, Leviticus 8:8, Numbers 27:21, Deuteronomy 33:8, and 1 Samuel 28:6; and from these references we infer that they were treasured objects used by the high priest to inquire of the Lord. According to Joseph Smith, God prepared them for the express purpose of translating the gold plates, and they were used also by the Nephite prophet Mosiah[17] and subsequently buried with the gold plates.

(One might wonder how they got from the possession of the Jewish high priest into the hands of the Nephites. Supposedly God gave them to the Jaredite party before they left the Old World at the time of the building of the Tower of Babel, and they brought them to the Americas, according to LDS writers Reynolds and Sjodahl.[18] This argument breaks down because of 1 Samuel's mention of the Urim's existence during the reign of King Saul.)

As described by Joseph, the Urim and Thummim were two stones fastened in silver bows and attached to a breastplate.[19] One early Mormon drawing of them suggests that they were mounted on the breastplate to form spectacles for the wearer. In spite of such a marvelous tool for translation, even modern editions of the *Book of Mormon* show evidence of where Joseph "slipped" in dictating and had to backtrack. Consider the following:

> Now behold, the people who were in the land Bountiful, *or rather Moroni,* feared that they would hearken to the words of Morianton and unite with his people, and thus he would obtain possession of those parts of the land, which would lay a foundation for serious consequences among the people of Nephi, yea, which consequences would lead to the overthrow of their liberty [italics mine]. (Alma 50:32; see also Alma 24:19; Mosiah 7:8; Helaman 3:33)

Mormons explain that such errors existed before the translation—they were on the plates themselves when the Nephite writers etched them into the metal; and because of the time and trouble involved in scratching out mistakes, the Nephite prophets just corrected their mistakes as they went along. But behind this careful backtracking to correct obvious mistakes, I see not the efforts of a prophet to preserve a record from error, but the efforts of a deceiver to protect himself from exposure.

This point of criticism is mild compared to the self-evident grammatical errors of the *Book of Mormon*'s first edition. Jerald and Sandra Tanner have compiled in *Mormonism—Shadow or Reality?* an astounding list of grammatical errors of early editions of the *Book of Mormon.* Some examples of the later-corrected grammar of the 1830 edition include its use of "wrecked" for *racked* (as with pain), "was" for *were,* "is" for *are,* "much" for *many,* "had not" for *ought not,* "arrest" for *wrest,* "arriven" for *arrived,* "wrote" for *written,* "done" for *did,* "exceeding fraid" for *exceedingly afraid,* "began" for *begun,* "took" for *taken,* "gave" for *given,* "no" for *any,* and many other errors involving double negatives. Mormons try to brush off criticisms of the first edition of the *Book of Mormon* by saying that the translation was not as automatic as some early church leaders described it (i.e., the mechanical writing), or that many of these errors were due to scribes' incorrect hearing of what Smith dictated. At least this new explanation absolves God of having the bad grammar! But saying that Joseph Smith just used his own manner of speaking leads one to the logical conclusion that Joseph Smith spoke in a kind of Elizabethan English—surely a strange dialect for a nineteenth-century New Englander!

Then too the *Book of Mormon* (and any reader of it) is cursed with the clumsy, repetitive phrase "it came to pass" that appears hundreds of times in the book, on almost every page. When the *Book of Mormon* was translated into German, those lucky people were spared having to read and reread that phrase, because it is not translatable into their tongue. Therefore, in every German edition of the *Book of Mormon,* this phrase was replaced by closed brackets, [ ], and an explanatory note on the first page of the text; all of which makes the reading of the book in German a whole lot smoother.

Recent LDS apologists' efforts are focused on pointing out linguistic features that they say are distinctly Hebraic and whose presence therefore in the *Book of Mormon* would validate the Hebraic origins of its Nephite authors.[20] Such features include poetic forms and chiasmus.[21] However, such features would be logical to—and perhaps even subconsciously inherent to—a writer like Joseph Smith, who was trying to write a "Hebrew" book. Furthermore these features and others appear all over books like Solomon Spaulding's *Manuscript Story,*[22] a book contemporaneous to Smith and which many people believe was one of the primary sources that Joseph Smith consulted in writing the *Book of Mormon.*[23]

DOES CHIASMUS VERIFY THE *BOOK OF MORMON*?

I remember the day that a fellow student at BYU told me he had some exciting news. "We finally have proof that the *Book of Mormon* is an ancient book," he told me, and began to tell me about a literary structure, a feature of Hebrew poetry in the Bible. The last great hope of saving the *Book of Mormon* was a language device hidden deep within its sentence structures, something Joseph Smith couldn't have known about, he said.

The language structure of which he spoke is chiasmus. Basically it is three or more successive word groups, a "pivotal" phrase or word, and then the first three are repeated in reverse order: as in ABCDCBA. A contemporary example might be:

My cat,
awesome in power,
chased down the mouse;
he killed it.
The mouse lost the race,
because of the speed of his pursuer,
my beloved feline.

Biblical scholars document this structure—which is often much looser and not nearly so symmetrically balanced as my pedantic example—throughout poetic books of Scripture.

It is true that this structure can be found in the *Book of Mormon*. Does this prove that it is an ancient Hebrew document like the Bible? Perhaps not. Consider that chiasmus is also found in the *Doctrine and Covenants*[24] (which *makes no claim to antiquity*), in the Koran,[25] and reportedly in *Science and Health with Key to the Scriptures*, the handbook of Christian Scientists. Knowing that, I have come to two conclusions. First, apparently there is something satisfying about chiasmus, and perhaps it is even inherent in many of the world's language patterns. Second, anyone familiar with the Holy Bible can imitate that structure as loosely as it is seen in the *Book of Mormon*. If you have heard the "Holy Hand Grenade of Antioch" speech in the movie *Monty Python and the Holy Grail* (I recently realized with delight), you have heard chiasmus as pseudo-scripture.

REFORMED EGYPTIAN

Also questionable is the form of Egyptian some Mormons say was utilized on the gold plates. Even LDS writer Hugh Nibley admitted that demotic (the form of ancient Egyptian he theorized was used by Nephi) was one of the most unwieldy and impractical systems of writing in history. If we look at the America of Joseph Smith's day, however, it is easier to understand why he claimed that the plates were inscribed in a type of Egyptian. In the early nineteenth century, the entire United States was caught up in an antiquities craze. Joseph Smith merely cashed in on this and at the same time gambled on the likelihood that Egyptian would never be deciphered. Indeed, were it not for the discovery and translation of the Rosetta Stone, Joseph Smith might to this day have gotten away with more of his claims for the *Book of Mormon* and the Book of Abraham in the *Pearl of Great Price.*

Some LDS experts say that the original plates written by Nephi (the earliest *Book of Mormon* writer), as well as the brass plates of Old Testament scripture brought from Jerusalem, were in pure Egyptian; but by the time that Moroni, the compiler of the book, wrote one thousand years later, the language had been altered to "reformed Egyptian."[26] One LDS apologist, Sidney P. Sperry, claimed that Nephi wrote Hebrew characters (the "learning of the Jews and the language of the Egyptians," as described in 1 Nephi 1:2), which he compares to writing English in Gregg shorthand.[27] Aside from the obvious flaw in this comparison that ignores the fact that Gregg shorthand was invented specifically for writing English, a devout Jew such as Nephi should have been horrified at writing scripture only in a foreign tongue. To the Jew, the Hebrew language is sacred, and recording its *sole official copy* in the pagan Egyptian language would be an unthinkable sacrilege.

Again, the claim of Joseph Smith that Professor Anthon had endorsed Smith's translation of the reformed Egyptian is shown to be a false one: If only the Nephites (and Joseph Smith) could read this special form of Egyptian, that leaves out Anthon as an authority either way.

Whatever the languages of the ancient Americans about whom Joseph Smith wrote, it can be safely assumed that they knew no Greek. But Greek words and names are used in the *Book of Mormon: Alpha* and *Omega* (3 Nephi 9:18), the Greek name *Timothy* (3 Nephi 19:4), and the New Testament version of the name *Jonah*, which is the Greek *Jonas* (3 Nephi 19:4). This is despite the blanket statement of the LDS Church that no Greek words appear in the *Book of Mormon.*[28]

Although some names are thus of Greek origin, others are lifted from the King James Version with spelling idiosyncrasies intact, some are a hodgepodge of miscellaneous Hebrew syllables, and many others have solely Indo-Aryan roots that cannot be justified as coming from an ancient Jewish culture. Many other names unfamiliar to non-Mormons which are found in the *Book of Mormon* can be formed by combining parts of Bible or Apocrypha names (for example, Sariah is a combination of Sarah and Saria, both Bible names); or by altering such names slightly by simple means such as the transposition of letters. Joseph Smith's personal Bible contained an Apocrypha and a list of all the names of the Bible alphabetically arranged.[29] Give me the same materials, and I guarantee you that I or almost anyone else could come up with 180 "new" names like those found in the *Book of Mormon*.[30]

THE HISTORY OF THE ANCIENT AMERICAS

Dr. Ross T. Christianson of Brigham Young University, in speaking of the *Book of Mormon*, once made the statement that "if the book's history is fallacious, its doctrine cannot be genuine."[31] Taking up that challenge, let us consider: Just what *is* the story told by the *Book of Mormon*?

It ambitiously covers a time period of some 2,600 years—from about 2200 BC to AD 421. Much time is spent in recounting events in the lives of the heroes of the book, perhaps to keep the reader from noticing the introduction of strange doctrinal material along the way. For instance, the detailed accounts of Lehi and Nephi sugarcoat the idea of Adam's "fall upward," and the story of the great faith of the brother of Jared is to prepare us for the idea that someone could see and talk to God, literally face-to-face.

The *Book of Mormon* skims over vast years of history in little books like those of Jarom and Omni, using the "smallness of the plates" (Jarom v. 14) and the wickedness of the record keepers as an excuse, but quotes extensively from Isaiah. It drags the reader through rivers of blood recounting battles and wars, recording details that interest no one but Mormonism's critics, then plays catch-up in the final book of Moroni—filling in the reader on the divine truth about infant baptism, the sacrament (what Christians refer to as the Lord's Supper or Communion), and other doctrinal matters all squeezed compactly into a few short chapters.[32]

Basically the book follows the histories of three groups of people who migrated from the Holy Land to the Americas. The first group to migrate was the Jaredites, who were named after their leader, Jared. As recorded in the *Book of Mormon* in the book of Ether, they left the Old World about the time of the Tower of Babel, escaping the confusion of tongues and thus, according to Joseph Fielding Smith, they spoke and wrote the pure Adamic language of God.[33] Jared's brother, who was identified in later "revelation" as having the name Mahonri Moriancumer, was a man so full of faith that the premortal Jesus was unable to prevent him from seeing his physical body in its entirety.[34] God instructed the Jaredites in how to build eight small, light, airtight, seaworthy vessels in which to cross the Atlantic to the New

World. About fifty Jaredites made the journey in the eight boats in 344 days. Also on board these boats were a divine source of light, a food supply, flocks, herds, fowl, fish (and, we would assume, a food supply for the beasts), bees, seeds, tools, and personal possessions.[35] Then they established themselves and anointed a king who reigned righteously, but soon wars and contentions broke out among the people. As in the Bible, the people went through cycles of righteousness and peace, then apostasy and "secret combinations."[36] A great prophet named Ether arose in the Jaredite nation's blackest period, predicting the coming of Christ and the fall of the Jaredite people if they did not repent. A great battle between the righteous and unrighteous factions ensued at the Hill Cumorah, and all of the more than two million people of the Jaredite nation were destroyed except Ether (whose fate is unknown) and a warrior named Coriantumr.

The least significant migration to the Americas occurred much later—at about the time of the Babylonian captivity (c. 589 BC), when Mulek, the son[37] of Zedekiah king of Judah, came over with another group of refugees. These Mulekites or "people of Zarahemla" brought with them none of the sacred Scriptures of the Jewish faith, and thus their descendants soon fell into apostasy and moral decay—even their language became corrupted. In about 189 BC they discovered the aforementioned Coriantumr, who lived with them about nine months and left with them a written account of the history of his now-extinct people, the Jaredites.

By far the most important migration to America recorded by the *Book of Mormon* occurred in about 600 BC when a holy man of Jerusalem, Lehi by name, took his wife (Sariah—one of only three women mentioned by name in the *Book of Mormon*), his daughters, and his sons (Laman, Lemuel, Nephi, and Sam) out of the land of his forebears, where his life had been threatened by those who ignored his urgings to repent. Lehi's family was joined by two other extended families who would intermarry, all of whom traveled down the western edge of the Arabian Peninsula with the aid of the Liahona, a divine "director" ball that guided them. Contentions soon developed between the wicked sons of Lehi (Laman and Lemuel) and the righteous ones (Nephi and Sam). After much difficulty, they all built a ship and in about 589 BC the group, numbering at least twenty-four, arrived in the promised land of America. There they soon separated into two distinct groups, the wicked Lamanites and the good Nephites. The bulk of the *Book of Mormon* is taken up with the struggles between these two factions.[38]

The Lamanites, though, were always depicted as the aggressors in warfare, for the Nephites believed in fighting only to protect themselves. The wicked Lamanites were punished for their rebellion when God turned their skins dark, and they continued in their savage and warlike ways. Meanwhile, the Nephites lived upright lives, keeping records of their history and theology on plates of gold, and built temples, like that of Solomon, to their God.

In about 200 BC the Nephites anointed their first king, Mosiah, who discovered the people of Zarahemla (the Mulekites), who then united themselves with the Nephites from that day forward. Many other kings followed, both good and wicked. Then from about 91 BC to the coming of Christ, the Nephites were governed by at least thirteen judges. During this time many of the Nephites had become wicked, while many Lamanites were converted and lived righteous lives. After being smitten with a pestilence, the Nephites returned to God. Great prophecies of the coming of Christ were relayed by prophets to the people, and the day Christ was born, great signs appeared in the New World. However, many hardened their hearts and were led to disbelieve, but those Lamanites who remained faithful became "white and delightsome"[39] again, and were from then on numbered as Nephites. However, the Church itself was rent by dissension between the times of Christ's birth and death.

In America, the *Book of Mormon* tells us, great signs accompanied the crucifixion of Christ. There were tempests, earthquakes, whirlwinds, fires, three days of total darkness, a great voice from heaven, and the complete destruction of every wicked person in the land. The people who remained alive gathered at a temple where Jesus Christ appeared to them, teaching and healing and blessing them. The Holy Ghost was bestowed and twelve Nephite disciples chosen—all of whom were granted their hearts' desires. Three of them desired never to die and were granted the privilege of staying on earth until the second coming of Christ (3 Nephi 28:6–7).

For almost two centuries after Christ's return to heaven, the American Church flourished in righteousness. But soon many dissented and began to call themselves by the name of Lamanites and to practice the unregenerate ways of their namesakes. They began to outnumber the righteous people and went to war with them. The final battle at the Hill Cumorah (where the Jaredites also exterminated themselves) saw 230,000 men die. The holy records on the golden plates were completed by Mormon and Moroni, who like their brethren also perished, and the history—or at least, the story—of the *Book of Mormon* came to an end.

THE CURSE OF THE DARK SKIN

The Lamanites of course continued in their lawless and wicked state, and so have remained. Nephi referred to them as "the seed of my brethren" (to distinguish them from his own descendants, the Nephites); and in 1 Nephi 12:23, they are characterized as "dark and loathsome and a filthy people, full of idleness and all manner of abominations." This dark skin, according to 2 Nephi 5:21–23, had four characteristics. First, it was black; second, it marked the curse indelibly upon them; third, it made them loathsome to righteous people; so that, fourth, it would prevent the Nephites from intermarrying with them, thus mixing their blood and marking their children to share in the curse. Much confusion is due to the fact that the *Book of Mormon* identifies the Lamanites' skin as being black. Some Mormons have justified this, saying that the words *dark* and *black* are interchangeable in the Hebrew language.[40] This argument hinges on the assumption that the golden plates were written in Hebrew, not in the reformed Egyptian of Joseph Smith's claims.

It has long been an established scientific fact that Native American Indians are not Semitic but rather Mongoloid/Asian, as evidenced by sparse facial and body hair; head hair that is coarse in texture, black, and straight; a reddish skin; a wide-shaped head with prominent cheekbones; and two distinctive features that are characteristic of the Mongoloid/Asian only: the epicanthic eyefold and the "mongolian spot" that appears on the backs of their newborn children.

However, up until late 2007 the *Book of Mormon* contained an official introduction stating that most Native American Indians were of Jewish/Israelite origin. Prior to 2007, this statement appeared: "After thousands of years, all [Jaredites, Nephites, and Lamanites] were destroyed except the Lamanites, and they are the *principal ancestors* of the American Indians" (italics added). It now reads, "they are *among* the ancestors of the American Indians" (italics added).

However, many early LDS prophets such as Brigham Young clearly stated that Native American Indians were Lamanites.[41] This was openly taught in *Book of Mormon* classes and, in practice, universally understood when I was at Brigham Young University, where Native American Mormons were referred to as "our Lamanite brethren."[42]

In 2004 Simon G. Southerton, an Australian molecular biologist and former LDS bishop, published *Losing a Lost Tribe: Native Americans, DNA, and the Mormon Church.* This book dealt a devastating blow to *Book of Mormon* doctrine, and Southerton's findings ultimately caused him to leave the LDS Church.[43] The book demonstrates unequivocally through DNA testing that Native American Indians (and the Polynesians that Mormons have long called Lamanites as well) have no Jewish/Israelite ancestry. None. They are, as their bodily characteristics have always demonstrated, Mongoloid/Asian.

The *Book of Mormon*'s account of the arrival of Lehi in the Americas does not include any record of any non-Jewish predecessors, and 2 Nephi 1:8 specifically states that "it is wisdom that this land should be kept as yet from the knowledge of other nations." If the *Book of Mormon* is taken at face value in its statements about the pure Hebrew origins of the people it chronicles, then there could be only three logical explanations of how the Native American Indian became predominately Mongoloid/Asian.

First, they must have come from some other place and intermarried with the Jewish Lamanites. Any such intermarrying would have taken place between AD 400 (the close of the *Book of Mormon*) and AD 1000 (when the first recorded western explorers came to the Americas), and have been by such an overwhelmingly large number of Mongoloids that the Semitic characteristics of the Lamanites were *completely bred out* in just six hundred years!

A second possibility is suggested by LDS apologists such as Daniel Petersen, professor of Near Eastern Studies at Brigham Young University. Instead of holding to the traditional view of all Native Americans being Lamanites, such apologists suggest that the history depicted in the *Book of Mormon* occurred only in a small section of Central America. Here, they say, the Hebrew Lamanites who survived the great wars were so small in number that their DNA was "swamped" by the larger, Asian-heritage tribes.[44] This explanation, however, contradicts the implicit teachings of the *Book of Mormon* that there were no other inhabitants.

The third explanation from LDS apologists suggests that when God cursed the Lamanites and changed their skin color, perhaps he also changed their DNA to an Asian DNA. Southerton responded: "If so, why would God change the DNA so it matched Asian DNA? As Latter-day Saints, we have already offended Blacks and the Indians. Are we going to offend Asians now, as well?"[45]

According to Alma 3:6, the dark skin was a curse levied on the Lamanites for their transgressions, but it was to be taken away when the Lamanites accepted Christ. In the *Book of Mormon* such a skin-color change was accomplished in a single year when converted Lamanites "became white like unto the Nephites."[46] Of course, there are Native American Mormons who are third and fourth generation members of the LDS Church who still have their lovely brown skin color. The ever-resourceful LDS Church constantly reinvents itself, and in 1981 changed the text of 2 Nephi 30:6, which had previously promised that they would become "white and delightsome," to read "pure and delightsome." However, by so doing they only dodged a bullet that now seems quite insignificant compared to the atomic bomb that Southerton's book has discharged.

THE CHALLENGE OF THE *BOOK OF MORMON*

Mark Twain once described the *Book of Mormon* as "chloroform in print."[47] To the non-Mormon Christian, the claims and doctrines which are truly sacred to the faithful Mormon often appear ludicrous, and we must be cautious in criticizing them. After all, just because something seems humorous to us, it does not necessarily follow that it is wrong; that is, in conflict with the Scriptures. The Bible is the only reliable yardstick against which to measure seemingly false doctrine. In fact, we have been challenged by God, who has commanded us to try every spirit because of the many false prophets who will try to deceive us (1 John 4:1).

THE PLOTLINE OF THE *BOOK OF MORMON*

The first few chapters set a scene that the writer hoped would put the reader into a receptive mood. By telling about Lehi, and tying the beginning of the story in with a period with which most Christians are familiar, he hoped to establish early the authenticity of this book. The first book division of this work is entitled 1 Nephi, and it is laden with prophetic dreams and visions designed to awe the reader so that reality and dream, truth and falsehood blend together in a dizzying swirl. We sympathize with the gentle protagonist, Nephi, and are led to mentally boo and hiss the wicked Laman and Lemuel, those embodiments of evil. We, with Nephi, are encouraged to rationalize his own cold-blooded murder of a man to steal scripture from him—"better that one man should perish than that a nation should dwindle and perish in unbelief."[48] We become so involved that we do not even question why such a wicked man had the holy scriptures, and why a great prophet such as Lehi could not by more honorable means obtain even scrolls containing the Word of God (which would certainly be less bulky than the brass plates he took on their transatlantic voyage). We are caught up with the building of the ship, and in the glorious arrival in the "promised land." Just like in the Bible, we think.

Longstanding theological mysteries are explained in this *Book of Mormon*—the circumstances of the fall of Adam, for instance, and man's right to choose good from evil, details of the resurrection, and the reason for the multiplicity of religious denominations in our world. Then the book seems to get down to serious history. This is the point at which most readers, Mormon and non-Mormon alike, will put the book down with a yawn. Wars and bloodshed spatter the pages as Nephites rise in righteousness, and then go through cycles of prosperity, indifference, apostasy, and defeat by their enemies. Just like the Bible. All along too the Nephites are tantalized by the promise of a savior, but—will they be destroyed by the Lamanites, or persevere and live to see his face?

A man is raised from the dead; a beautiful young woman dances so seductively that she is rewarded with the head of her enemy; and a persecutor of the church is struck dumb by the Lord and asked, "Why persecutest thou the church of God?" Kings are deposed and judges appointed. Just like the Bible.

Then Christ comes to the Nephites—and he teaches them the same things that he taught the Jews, with a few important additions. The Nephites are righteous after his ascension, and live in peace for 150 years. Mormon and Moroni, though, record the evil that creeps into their society, and as Moroni starts to finalize the Nephite record before his death, he suddenly remembers a few little details that really ought to be in the writings. And so the *Book of Mormon* closes with a tidying up of several doctrinal points: how to ordain priests and teachers; the manner of administering the bread and wine; and teachings on baptism, faith, hope, and charity. Just like the Bible.

GODLY AND UNGODLY TENETS

But an examination of the doctrines of the *Book of Mormon* in a little more depth shows that these teachings often add to those of the Bible, or worse yet, contradict it. One of the most basic tenets of Mormonism involves the fall of Adam, the necessity of opposition in all things, and the resulting free agency of man.

The *Book of Mormon* view of the fall of Adam leaves the Bible reader thoroughly confused with the definition of sin. According to 2 Nephi, chapter 2, Adam *needed* to sin for his and our own good. Without his eating of the forbidden fruit, we would never have been born. Eve would have grown old and died while he lived forever, alone. In the words of LDS writer Sterling W. Sill, who was an Assistant to the Council of the Twelve Apostles, "Adam fell, but he fell upward."[49] This concept is based on the LDS premise that God put Adam in a dilemma that was literally unresolvable. He forbade Adam to eat of the fruit of the Tree of the Knowledge of Good and Evil, but he also commanded him to have children. Therefore Adam had to break one law in order to fulfill another. By implication, we in like manner should look forward to opposition in our own lives, that righteousness might come to pass.

The God of Mormonism, thus, is an inexplicably vindictive one who makes pleasing him impossible, giving commandments he knows to be impossible to keep. How different this is from the God of Christianity! "Let no man say when he is tempted, I am tempted of God: for God cannot be tempted with evil, neither tempteth he any man: But every man is tempted, when he is drawn away of his own lust, and enticed" (James 1:13–14).

If the *Book of Mormon* disagrees here with the Bible, it is surprisingly orthodox regarding its teachings on the Trinity. Anyone who is familiar with the modern LDS concept of the separate, anthropomorphic natures of God, Jesus, and the Holy Ghost is very surprised when he reads from the *Book of Mormon.* That's because it was written long before Joseph Smith formulated in detail his story about his first vision and the resulting doctrines on the three separate personages of the Godhead—for the *Book of Mormon* clearly teaches the unity of the Godhead.[50] In fact, the *Book of Mormon* might be thought of as Trinitarian or even modalistic (quite in contrast to twenty-first century LDS doctrine). In 3 Nephi chapter 12, for example, the resurrected Christ appearing to the Nephites affirms over and over again that he, the Father, and the Holy Spirit are one. Of course modern LDS teachings make light of this glaring discrepancy by saying that the oneness of the Godhead is only in purpose.

Another teaching that appears in the *Book of Mormon* is the prohibition of infant baptism. This was a very hot theological issue in Joseph Smith's time, and it is obvious that he could not resist resolving the controversy. In Moroni chapter 8 the writer not only condemns infant baptism as a "solemn mockery before God" (v. 9), but also condemns to hell its advocates (v. 14). In like manner the *Book of Mormon* has the "definitive answer" on adult baptism. According to 3 Nephi 11:21–34, proper baptism has five features: (1) it is to be done for the remission of sins; (2) it is only for those of accountable age (who are capable of truly repenting of their sins); (3) it is to be accomplished by a single immersion; (4) it is to be performed only by one who has the proper authority; and (5) specific words are to be said at the time of the baptism ("Having authority given me of Jesus Christ, I baptize you in the name of the Father, and of the Son, and of the Holy Ghost"—v. 25).

These instructions, as mentioned before, are found in the latter part of the *Book of Mormon*, supposedly given by the resurrected Christ. They aren't nearly so hard for a Christian to consider as the teachings of Nephi, who in about 550 *BC*—that's *Before Christ*—commanded his people to be baptized.[51] This amazing commandment is another of the startling evidences of the false nature of the *Book of Mormon* and its teachings—here Christ is consistently spoken of *in the past tense!*

Another procedure for an important ordinance of the Church is found in 3 Nephi 18:5–29. Here we find the proper mode of administering the sacrament, as the Mormons refer to the Lord's Supper. Its outstanding features are: (1) it is only to be partaken of by baptized believers; (2) it is to be in remembrance of Christ; (3) it seals a covenant by the believer to do God's will; (4) it is to be partaken of often; (5) it is not to be partaken of unworthily; (6) it must be administered by someone holding the proper priesthood authority; and (7) it is to consist of bread and wine (in contrast to water, which is used in LDS services today). These were the instructions given to the Nephites by the resurrected Christ himself, but Moroni (supposedly writing four hundred years later) decided that Christ had left out an essential part of the instructions. So this Nephite prophet in Moroni chapters 4 and 5 gives the exact wording of the prayers to be said over the bread and wine (which no doubt gave Joseph Smith some problems in late 1830 when he received a revelation telling him to use water in the sacrament instead of wine).

The *Book of Mormon* also presents some amazing doctrines regarding the state of the soul after death. There's nothing surprising about Alma's teachings on the impossibility of repentance after death.[52] What is surprising is how today's Mormons get around this scripture and justify their baptism for the dead by saying that the "night of darkness" mentioned is not death, but a spiritual state wherein one loses the will to repent.[53]

The resurrection, according to Alma, will be a reuniting of the soul and body, and a restoration of that body to a perfect state, according to Alma chapter 40. The LDS missionaries who baptized me said that this meant that every person would be resurrected with his body in the prime of life (as it was somewhere around the age of twenty-five, with no physical imperfections).

Alexander Campbell once noted that the *Book of Mormon* managed to comment on a surprisingly large percentage of the religious issues of their time.[54] In addition to infant baptism, authority and ordination, the nature of the Trinity, free agency of man, the fall, and the resurrection, here is a more complete listing: freemasonry (Helaman 6:21–29; 3 Nephi 4:7), spiritual regeneration (Alma 5:14–21), rights and responsibilities of civil governments (Mosiah 29:11–17), church government (Moroni 4:6–9), the atonement (2 Nephi chapter 9), eternal reward and punishment (Alma 41:3–7), Catholicism (1 Nephi chapters 13 and 14), fasting (Alma 17:3), repentance (Alma 5:49), "religious experience" (Mosiah 27:24–29), and transubstantiation (3 Nephi 18:28–30).

In the *Book of Mormon* too we can see evidence of misconceptions that Joseph Smith had regarding the Native American Indians of his day. Indians were thought of as "painted savages" who ate the flesh and drank the blood of their enemies, so it is only natural that we should find references to such things—war paint in Alma 3:4, and cannibalism in Moroni 9:10.

It also seems that when Joseph Smith ran out of such stories in his own head, he went to convenient source books,[55] lifted a few stories, then embroidered them with extra details and changed or omitted other details. Probably his most convenient source book was the Bible, as is evident when we read in the *Book of Mormon* stories that mirror the Bible accounts of Salome, the raising of Lazarus, the conversion of Saul, and the allegory of the tame and the wild olive trees found in Romans 11. This last example is turned around by LDS apologists, who explain that Paul quoted from the Nephite prophet Zenos, instead of the obvious truth—Joseph Smith copied from Paul.

Jerald and Sandra Tanner in their research found hundreds of parallels between the *Book of Mormon* and the New Testament, documenting in *Mormonism—Shadow or Reality?* four and one-half large two-columned pages of these parallels. In addition, in 1998 they published *Joseph Smith's Plagiarism of the Bible*, which lists almost four thousand examples.

THE THREE NEPHITES

Sometimes the *Book of Mormon* seems to want to be just one up on the Bible. An example of this is in the story of the three Nephites (found in 3 Nephi 28). Since some people have taken John 21:22–23 to mean that Christ promised John that that apostle would never die (in spite of even Christ's denial of such a thing), the *Book of Mormon* teaches that Christ promised *three* of his American apostles that they would never taste of death. These three Nephites, who are unnamed in the *Book of Mormon*, were among the twelve disciples chosen by Christ in America. When asked by him their hearts' desires, nine of the twelve asked to die quickly when their days of life and ministry were ended (at the age of seventy-two), that they might rejoin Christ without delay. The other three, however, asked never to die but to stay on earth until Christ should return in his glory. Their bodies underwent a miraculous transformation that not only gave them immortality, but also immunity from pain and all sorrow except sorrow for the sins of the world. From that day forth they went out preaching and baptizing, and even though imprisoned and thrown into pits, dens of wild beasts, and furnaces, they escaped unscathed each time.

According to the legend, these three Nephites, along with the apostle John, are still alive today and ministering to the faithful, unbeknownst to most of the recipients of their good deeds. Many a Mormon has a story of how a mysterious stranger helped a friend or relative, and they attribute many inexplicable good deeds to these three immortals. An LDS researcher, Hector Lee, catalogued the different Nephite legends in his fascinating book *The Three Nephites: The Substance and Significance of the Legend in Folklore.*[56] In addition, scores of references to the legends can be read online. Most Mormons will not claim to have seen an angel, but almost all have heard a "true" anecdote about contact with one or all of the three Nephites. These stories are warp and woof of the fabric of Mormon life. Some claim that the three Nephites, who were translated beings, greeted the sailors on Columbus's ships when he arrived in America, and helped to design the American flag.[57] So much has been ascribed to them that researcher Hector Lee reported: "The tendency on the part of some members of the Church to attribute any unusual happening to the three Nephites led to an alleged assertion by Dr. James E. Talmadge, of the Quorum of the Twelve Apostles, to the effect that the three Nephites 'are the most overworked of all individuals.' "[58]

If the *Book of Mormon* be true, where were these three Nephites during the time that the Church (and its divine authority) supposedly disappeared from earth as Mormons claim it did at the death of John, the last apostle? The mission of the three Nephites was to convert souls to the truth. If they were immune to death and suffering, they should have been fearless and unsilenceable proclaimers of the gospel. Where are records of such men? Mormons claim that authority to baptize and confirm was taken from the earth. Didn't the three Nephites and John have this authority? Why weren't the three Nephites, instead of the resurrected beings John the Baptist, Moroni, Peter, and James (along with John) chosen to "restore" the gospel ordinances? Indeed, why a need to *restore* such things at all, if they were in the possession of living men?

ARCHAEOLOGY AND THE *BOOK OF MORMON*[59]

Sometimes in speaking to people who want to know why I believe that the *Book of Mormon* is not of God, I find that the spurious nature of the ideas and the theology of the book are more slippery than the solidity of such things as archaeology. Had the plot of the *Book of Mormon* been placed by its author in a more nebulous time period, and located more indefinitely as to setting, perhaps using archaeology as a tool to disprove it would not be so feasible. But Joseph Smith reasoned, and rightly so, that his nineteenth-century audience would want dates and times and places to authenticate the book in their minds. It is precisely this exact dating that makes disproving the *Book of Mormon* easier. Time in the *Book of Mormon* is figured from either the Tower of Babel, the time of the departure of Lehi from the Old World, or the birth or death of Christ. In addition, the book's geographical landmarks such as the Hill Cumorah,[60] the "narrow neck of land," and the "land northward," and so forth, give the modern non-Mormon archaeologists a basis for prospective sites. Such specifics have caused non-Mormons and many Mormons as well to conclude that there is simply no such thing as *Book of Mormon* archaeology.[61]

Mormons claim that after the death of the last righteous Nephite in AD 421, the only inhabitants left in the Western Hemisphere were wicked, filthy, and ignorant (just the way the nineteenth-century reader viewed the Indians of his day). However, archaeology has shown that, far from being the *complete end* of a period of great culture, this date marked the beginning of the emergence of some of the greatest pre-Columbian civilizations of the Americas.

Mormons take the great buildings and skilled artwork of these cultures as proof of the Nephite theory. In the front of older clothbound editions of the *Book of Mormon* (once commonly given to proselytes by LDS missionaries), there are many beautiful color pictures of examples of the skilled craftsmanship of old American cultures. A picture of some gold tablets is inscribed with writing. The tablets were found in Persia, but no picture of such plates from either North or South America is offered. A picture is shown of bronze and copper tools that are mentioned in the *Book of Mormon*, but no tools of iron and steel as such are also described. A photograph of some small gold "plates" depicts objects obviously used for decoration and not communication. A great Mexican mural is described as "Egyptian-like," but so are those of many artistic early cultures. And there is an abundance of carefully selected pictures of buildings whose cultural dates *do* fit in the *Book of Mormon* period—even though the buildings themselves are obviously not the work of any Christian civilization.

Must the faithful Mormon, though, identify the cultural achievements of American Indians before the fifth century AD as the work of Nephites exclusively? Yes, unless he would deny the *Book of Mormon*. While the Nephites were an industrious and creative people, the Lamanites were depicted by their biographers as being interested only in making trouble and war. Since these savages became expert at the art of killing, they managed to destroy the more peaceable Nephites and thus outlive them. This creates a dilemma.

If they were by nature lazy and ignorant, they could never have achieved the high level of civilization of the Nephites. But how does one explain, for example, the advanced culture of the people of Montezuma?

Often Mormons look to their leaders for guidance in these puzzling matters. (I say puzzling with absolutely no sarcasm—imagine the plight of the poor Mormon who is asked to believe in something that has been the laughingstock of the archaeological community for years. We Christians know our anti-evolutionist teachings to be unpopular, but at least there *are* reputable non-Christian scientists who side with us, and a united front of archaeologists who can point with confidence and unanimity to the artifacts of the cultures chronicled in the Bible.) Since the late 1990s several LDS parachurch "research" organizations have published books and posted articles on the Internet in an attempt to give Latter-day Saints access to materials to bolster the claims of the *Book of Mormon* with obscure archaeological findings. Quite starkly in contrast to the evidence-rich field of biblical archaeology, even in this advanced age conclusive scientific proof of the validity of the *Book of Mormon* is utterly lacking.

Not only that, these "research organizations" depend upon the redefinition of English words to support their claims. If the *Book of Mormon* mentions horses and pigs, they suggest that tapirs or deer could be what was meant. If it talks of silk, they offer that rabbit hair garments noted by the conquistadors looked like silk. Metals like the gold of golden plates or the steel of weapons, they say, were of the North and South American varieties. This explanation will not hold up if Joseph Smith was given by God the English words to write the *Book of Mormon.* If an appropriate English word like *tapir* existed at the time, God knew that. Not only that, but those supposed things for which there were no English terms (*curelom* and *cumom*, for instance) appear on the plates—negating the necessity for an inaccurate English term.

Just how far Mormons will go to try to grasp at archaeological support for the *Book of Mormon* is demonstrated in the fact that they have found great comfort in what even they admit is the "first" archaeological find that *might* be tied to the book. In the book of 1 Nephi which begins with the journey of the mythical Nephites across the Arabian Peninsula, a burial place called "Nahom" was described by Joseph Smith. The discovery of an altar on that peninsula with the letters NHM (both ancient Arabic and Hebrew are written usually without vowels) has been seized on by Mormons to "prove" that their Nahom existed. In fact, three Bible names (to which Joseph Smith had access) include those consonants: Naham, Nahum, and Nehum. The fact that the three consonants would comprise an ancient name in that part of the world is not surprising. I think that almost two hundred years of desperate searching for something that would tie the *Book of Mormon* to reality allows for at least a few coincidences.

But no proof. Even the outspoken LDS apologist Dr. Daniel C. Peterson is reduced to defending Joseph Smith's opus with "seminal studies" that he says establish "a highly plausible ancient American setting for the *Book of Mormon*," and "believable Lehite locations on the Arabian peninsula." *Plausible, believable—but no proof.* Peterson suggests that Smith's golden plates "can be persuasively argued to represent an authentically ancient alloy known as tumbaga,"[62] but he can produce no ancient writings upon such an alloy. Though LDS archaeologists search for Nephite cities and artifacts, they will not find them, for they never existed.

Book of Mormon geography will always be a problem. Though it is as fairly detailed as Middle Earth, and as in Tolkien,[63] traveling distances are often mentioned, it is as fictional. Currently LDS apologists who operate online "information" sites such as FARMS and FAIRLDS point to the studies of a Mormon scholar, John L. Sorenson, for support and clarification. However, to make Mesoamerican geography fit the *Book of Mormon* account requires more contortions than a Twister game, and many LDS scholars have repeatedly discredited the findings of Sorenson.[64] In contrast, archaeologists both secular and Christian acknowledge biblical archaeology: the presence of Hezekiah's tunnel, ancient Jericho (2 Kings 20:20, 2 Chron. 32:3–4), and Egyptian inscriptions of the "Habiru," or Hebrew people.

Two of the LDS Church's staunchest supporters who were historians came to lose all confidence in the *Book of Mormon* by the time they died. One, Brigham Henry Roberts (1857–1933), "sorrowfully" concluded that the *Book of Mormon* was the creation of the mind of Joseph Smith.[65] The other, Thomas Stuart Ferguson (1914–83), one of the most noted defenders of the *Book of Mormon* in the 1950–60s, was also finally forced to conclude it was fictional.[66]

Perhaps the most significant recent writer to address the problems with the Joseph Smith story and the events and contents of the *Book of Mormon* is Grant H. Palmer, who was a three-time director of LDS Institutes of Religion in California and Utah. His book *An Insider's View of Mormon Origins* (Signature Books, 2002) shows the earnest attempts of a Mormon historian and educator to come to grips with his conclusion that the "religious allegories" of the *Book of Mormon* should not be viewed as literal history.[67]

Writers who "stayed the course" to support the LDS Church included the formidable late Dr. Hugh Nibley, for decades the intellectual "go-to" scholar of the LDS Church. Hemmed in on one side by the facts of archaeology which even his considerable charm and verbal acrobatics could not stretch to fit the *Book of Mormon*, and on the other side by his stubborn support of Mormonism, he resorted many times to what might be termed "negative evidence" to support the *Book of Mormon*. A considerable number of his successors have followed his lead.

CITIES OF THE *BOOK OF MORMON*

For instance, Nibley claimed that there is no way of telling if any of the cities of the Nephites have been found in routine archaeological excavations. "We have no description of any *Book of Mormon* city to compare with Homer's description of Troy. How shall we recognize a Nephite city when we find it?"[68] While it is true that no city as such has been described in Mormon writ, much appears in the *Book of Mormon* regarding Nephite, Jaredite, and Mulekite culture. Of course all the pagan cultures of Mesoamerica could fit the description of Lamanites, but Nephites were described as the industrious builders. Here is a checklist of what even the most faithful Mormon would agree should be evident in a Nephite *Book of Mormon* city,[69] even if we confine a search to Mesoamerica, the area most twenty-first century LDS scholars believe to be the site of the events of Joseph Smith's book.

1. It should, by accepted archaeological standards, fit in the time period covered by the *Book of Mormon* (circa 2200 BC to circa AD 425).
2. Its artwork will not be totally pagan in nature (although some non-Jewish or non-Christian artwork could be present due to some foreign inhabitants or trade with such people). However, the longevity and high level of culture ascribed to the Nephites should have left copious evidence.
3. At least a few metal coins—the "pieces" mentioned in the *Book of Mormon* which the dictionary defines as a coin as in "pieces of eight"—would be found in any Nephite city dated after the time of Alma (82 BC—see Alma chapter 11).
4. Some evidence of "reformed Egyptian" writing, such as that of which Joseph Smith left examples, should be evident.
5. Some trace of sheep, cattle, horses—domesticated animals—could be found.

6. We should see chariots as well as the remains of roads for them.
7. The advanced technology of smelted iron, and weapons and tools made from it which are mentioned in the *Book of Mormon*, should surely have withstood the ravages of time.
8. Some evidence of the Jewish-based culture of the Nephites should exist.

SEARCH FOR THE CITIES

LDS apologists must admit that no such city has ever been found. To find out why, let's examine the points on the checklist individually.

1. Though some ancient American cultures, such as the Tlatilcos and the Ticomans, have left artwork and other evidences that indicate their civilized state, there is absolutely no evidence that they ever reached the level of civilization ascribed to the Jaredites, who supposedly lived in the Americas from about 2200 BC to about 200 BC. The Olmec civilization is dated as 1200 BC to 300 BC, but they had little in common with either the Nephites or Jaredites of the same time period. Apparently they had no written language, quite unlike the Nephites. Not only that, the representations they left of themselves are of people with decidedly non-Jewish facial features.[70] The Mayans, of whom we have thousands of translated inscriptions and documents, have no apparent linguistic ties to Egyptian or Hebrew, and do not record anything about Nephite culture. The Teotihuacan people of central Mexico flourished at the apex of their civilization in the third and fourth centuries after Christ, but they too were patently pagan. Any of the other, later civilizations after the Teotihuacans were of course later than the *Book of Mormon* time period.

2. Nowhere is there the slightest clue as to a Christian (or Jewish) background in any artwork. (Bear in mind that 2 Nephi 25:29, 26:12, 30:2, and 31:17, supposedly written in 545 BC, speak of the Messiah and the "gospel"; and Alma 46:15, supposedly written a hundred years before the death of Jesus, called Nephites "Christians.") Even the "tree of life stela,"[71] a carving found in Chiapas, Mexico, which was given a loud (but short-lived) heralding by Mormons as "proof" of *Book of Mormon* teachings, has been shown to have none of the connections to Mormonism once claimed for it, nor does the Dresden Codex's illustration of a tree coming from the chest of a man have anything to do with *Book of Mormon* stories.

3. The matter of Nephite coinage consistently poses a dilemma for LDS scholars. According to the *Book of Mormon*, the Nephites' monetary system

was on a barley standard (that is, it was determined by barley, just as our paper money was once backed by gold reserves). The money itself was in the form of coins ("pieces") made of silver and gold.[72] However, archaeologists tell us that no native gold or silver coins have been found in American excavation. The current LDS explanation is that "pieces" had some other meaning than the traditional monetary one (as in "pieces of eight"), which explains why no coins have been found. In other words, to get around the problem, LDS archaeologists have to redefine English terms.

4. To date, we have no evidence of an Olmec writing system. Some Mormons see similarities between Mayan hieroglyphics and the reformed Egyptian scribbles of Joseph Smith (which author Charles Shook called "deformed English"). Most archaeologists see few such similarities. Furthermore, Mayan hieroglyphics developed independently about the time the *Book of Mormon* was drawing to a close, and had no apparent traceable etymological origins. Add to this the fact that Mayan was always inscribed on rocks (never on metal plates), even the earliest of which dates only from about the fourth century AD. In fact, there is no example I have ever seen of any writing on metal plates by Native Americans during any time period covered by the *Book of Mormon.*

5. The *Book of Mormon* repeatedly refers to domesticated animals, such as cattle, oxen, sheep, swine, and goats. These supposedly were brought over on the ships with the Jaredites and the Nephites, but there is no definitive archaeological evidence that they existed here during the indicated time period, nor is there definitive evidence of horses, which played an important part in *Book of Mormon* lore.[73] It mentions elephants that, too, were long extinct by the time period under consideration. (Or are we expected to believe that they came over on the ships also?) The *Book of Mormon* lists two other animals whose existence no one can prove or disprove. They were called cureloms and cumoms, and what they were is anyone's guess—except that the *Book of Mormon* says that they, along with the elephants, were especially useful.[74]

6. Ancient Americans used rollers to move large stones, and they used spindle whorls in textile crafts, and very rarely they used a solid disc on toys. However, even LDS apologists agree there is no archaeological evidence for anything remotely like a spoked wheel nor a single chariot. The great Yucatan highways many Mormons think were used for the nonexistent chariots were only for pedestrians—and they were built long after the *Book of Mormon* time period. LDS apologists suggest that perhaps the "chariots" of the *Book of Mormon* were either discontinued or deteriorated and thus

we have no evidence of them; and one particularly inventive LDS apologist described litterlike chariots that don't use wheels.[75] All such explanations ignore a central issue: Joseph Smith spoke English and wrote the text of the *Book of Mormon* in English. If there was not an appropriate word for such a device, why call it a chariot (which is, by definition, a wheeled vehicle)?

7. Another defeat for the *Book of Mormon* comes when we examine its accounts of warfare. Where is evidence of the *great mounds* of weapons, the steel-smelting operations necessary for their production, and the warfare technologies described in this book? LDS apologists grasp at straws with their allusions to things that could "possibly" support its scenarios. (One apologist suggested that the steel mentioned in the *Book of Mormon* could have been from another metal than iron, for instance—another example of redefining the English terms that were the "correct" translation. Other apologists suggest that perhaps the swords were made of really hard wood with obsidian edges.) But no reputable non-LDS scholar has ever even hinted that there is archaeological evidence of Nephite/Lamanite warfare with the weapons and the scope that the *Book of Mormon* depict.

8. The last question is really the crux of the whole question about the authenticity of the *Book of Mormon.* There is no non-LDS archaeologist who would ever assert that the culture of any civilization anywhere on the two American continents before Columbus resembles as a whole the culture presented in the *Book of Mormon.*

In addition to the checklist points I mentioned that should be common to every Nephite city, the *Book of Mormon* also tells of several other features of *Book of Mormon* geography that should be traceable by archaeologists. But neither Mormons nor non-Mormons can pinpoint with any security any single site mentioned in the *Book of Mormon.* The geographical descriptions, though vague, have caused LDS geologists and archaeologists to identify the "narrow neck of land,"[76] the Hill Cumorah,[77] and the River Sidon[78] as being either in the Mexico City valley, or in Costa Rica. These are the places where they could logically exist geographically according to their descriptions (and the travel distances noted through the book).

But LDS proponents of these theories were blasted by Joseph Fielding Smith,[79] who maintained to his death that the Hill Cumorah was in New York State, where Joseph Smith found the golden plates that had been deposited there by Moroni, and that the narrow neck of land is Panama. The seminary notebooks given to me contained maps which were a bit more cautious: *Book of Mormon* cities and landmarks were "tentatively" identified on two rather amorphous land bodies connected by a narrow isthmus that resembled the Americas only enough to tantalize the imagination.

The matter of the location of Cumorah is of no slight importance. According to the *Book of Mormon* over 230,000 persons lost their lives in the final battle at this hill only 1,600 years ago. Why are their bones not found all over the Cumorah, New York, area? Mormons might say that Mormon 6:15 states that their bones mouldered and returned to the earth. All right, but what of their metal weapons? What of their chariots? If Cumorah in New York State was indeed the site of so much history, the LDS Church could certainly vindicate itself and the claims of its scripture by excavating part of it. Surely BYU's Archaeology Department could be trusted to be respectful and thorough in their excavations—for they, most of all, have so much at stake.

Instead, the current LDS explanation for the lack of *Book of Mormon* artifacts in upper New York State is that there must have been two Cumorahs—the one where Joseph Smith found the gold plates, and another, as yet undiscovered site, probably in Central America, where the final battle took place. Then, say apologists of this theory, Moroni somehow made his way thousands of miles to what is now New York State to bury the plates in the other Hill Cumorah.

OWNING UP TO THE TRUTH

Why can't the Mormons own up to the fact that the *Book of Mormon* is a fraud? The historical picture painted by the LDS epic is totally unlike the world of ancient Americans as they have found it in extensive excavations. Mormons have in the past claimed that many other records or inscriptions "proved" the *Book of Mormon.* Among these records were the Bat Creek Stone, the Newark Stones, and the "Phoenician Ten Commandments" found in Los Lunas, New Mexico. And let's not forget the Kinderhook plates, which even Mormons admitted were contemporary forgeries, intended to entrap Joseph Smith as he translated them.[80] All were highly touted, but all were forgeries. Why not place the *Book of Mormon* with them?

The answer is, of course, obvious. If the *Book of Mormon* falls, so does the entire Mormon structure. Surely the evidences presented thus far in this chapter should be sufficient to show any open-minded person the false nature of this book. But let's assume, for the sake of argument, that we must not pass judgment on this book because of outside evidences offered in fields such as anthropology, archaeology, or geography. Let's look at the book alone, and with the Scripture it was supposed to complement, the Bible; for it is really not fair to judge a book of scripture on a set of secular scales only.

It must be admitted that many, many of the doctrines taught in the *Book of Mormon* would be welcome and familiar doctrine in even a conservative Christian church. Some doctrines, in fact, are exactly the same, even to the wording that matches sections of the King James Version of the Bible. The *Book of Mormon* urges people to be righteous, to fear and honor God, and to live harmoniously with their fellow men and women.

CONTRADICTING THE BIBLE

But sadly, in its efforts to supplement the Bible, the *Book of Mormon* often contradicts it. One good example of such contradiction occurs in Alma 13, where the prophet Alma describes the priesthood. Even Mormons will admit that this chapter is one of the hardest of their scriptures to understand because of the confusing changes of tenses, and its referral to the atonement of Christ and the Holy Ghost in the past tense (even though Alma supposedly lived one hundred years before the birth of our Savior). Alma got into even deeper trouble in speaking about Melchizidek whom he said "reigned under his father" (v. 18), in spite of the fact that the Bible characterizes Melchizidek and his reign as being "without father" (Heb. 7:3). This chapter of Hebrews, in fact, completely negates the need for any such priesthood as is described by Alma, and says further that Christ *alone* is worthy of holding the higher priesthood—he did away with the need of sacrifice for sin with the offering of his own sinless life. Finally, the Old Testament priesthood was held only by descendants of Levi (Num. 3:9–10), yet in the *Book of Mormon* Nephi consecrated two descendants of Manasseh to be priests (Alma 10:3).

Another example of the *Book of Mormon* differing radically from the Bible is found in Alma 45:19, where it states that when Alma died "he was taken up by the Spirit, or buried by the hand of the Lord, even as Moses." At first glance it seems that the *Book of Mormon* writer was offering the reader a choice of believing *either* that Alma was taken up, or that he was buried like Moses. Not so, said Joseph Fielding Smith, who *equated* being "taken up" (or in LDS language, "translated") with being buried by the Lord. In Smith's book *Doctrines of Salvation*, he said that "Moses, like Elijah, was taken up without tasting death."[81] Contrast this to Deuteronomy 34:5–6, which states clearly that Moses died, and God buried him. Any other explanation makes mockery of God's promise to Moses that he would never enter the Promised Land. Surely God would not rebuke Moses by translating him!

Alma 30:3 states that Nephites, who were Jews, "were strict in observing the ordinances of God, according to the Law of Moses." Yet conspicuously absent from the *Book of Mormon* is any mention of the essentiality of the Passover, nor the specific wave, peace, or other types of offerings, nor altars in the New World. In the *Book of Mormon* there was no ark of the covenant, no mercy seat, no Day of Atonement, no incense, no lavers. In fact, all that made Jews distinctive—Sabbath keeping, circumcision, feasts and festivals, and a specific set of laws to delineate the concept of clean and unclean—these things are foreign, literally, to the *Book of Mormon.*

A serious error in the *Book of Mormon* appears in Alma 7:10. Here the prophet Alma in about 83 BC is supposedly prophesying the birth of the savior, but he predicts that the savior will be born "at Jerusalem." LDS commentaries gloss over this, saying that the whole area around Jerusalem, including Bethlehem, was called Jerusalem. But if the Nephites had, as they claimed, brought over their Jewish Scriptures with them on the brass plates, they would immediately have exposed Alma as a false prophet. Inscribed on those plates would have been the prophecy of Micah, which told of the future birth of the Savior in Bethlehem (Mic. 5:2–5).

The signs which accompanied the death of Christ differ too when seen from the viewpoints of the Bible and the *Book of Mormon.* According to the Bible, there were three hours of darkness on "the whole land" (Mark 15:33; Luke 23:44) before the death of our Lord. Immediately after his death, there were earthquakes, and many saints were raised from the opened tombs. How different from the account in the *Book of Mormon*! The best that can be said for the signs supposedly seen by the Nephites is that they were only similar. The darkness they experienced there lasted three days, and was described as being a thick vapor that even prevented the kindling of light.[82] Instead of being followed by the earthquakes described in the Bible, this darkness came after the earthquakes, which were also accompanied by torrential storms, the sinking of great cities, whirlwinds, and fires.[83]

In the Bible, the result of the signs at the time of the death of Christ was new life for some who had been dead. Contrast this concept with the actions of the vengeful god of the Nephites who destroyed—killed—every man, woman, and child whose wicked iniquities he wanted to hide from his face.[84]

> The whole argument of the New Testament is that men are not judged because of their acts of sin but because they will not receive Christ as their Savior. To destroy the wicked at the time of the performance of the act of redemption is to violate all the principles of the Christian Gospel.[85]

Another principle of the gospel violated by the *Book of Mormon* is its teachings on the establishment of Christ's church. In the Bible, Christ spoke of the establishment of his church always in the future tense, because it could not be established until after his death (see Heb. 9:15–16). For instance, Christ said to Peter, "Upon this rock I *will* build my church" (Matt. 16:18). But in the *Book of Mormon*, we are told that the Church was established in 147 BC.[86] In 73 BC, believers in the New World were called Christians, according to Alma 46:15, in spite of what the Bible says about believers first being called Christians at Antioch (Acts 11:26). A critic of Mormonism, George W. DeHoff, once asked the question, "Who is silly enough to believe there were Christians before Christ?" In addition, 2 Nephi 31:12–13 (supposedly written in 545 BC), speaks of the baptism of fire and the reception of the Holy Spirit (for which the apostles in Jerusalem waited in Luke 24:49 and received in Acts 2:1–4).

A similar error occurs in Mosiah 16:6–7, where the birth and resurrection of Christ is referred to in the past tense by a prophet who lived in 148 BC. Apparently the writer of the *Book of Mormon* realized the incongruity of this, for he attempted to explain this confusion by adding that the prophet was "speaking of things to come as if they had already come" (v. 6).

Some people who read about these blunders wonder how they could have slipped under the noses of Mormons for so long. The truth is, as I will say many times, that most Mormons are like many Christians: they simply don't bother to sit down and read their scriptures often enough ever to be accused of being familiar with them. But some of the errors in the *Book of Mormon* were so obvious and so embarrassing that they were amended after the book's first edition. On page 236 of this edition, for example, Christ was referred to as the "son of the only begotten of the Father," which of course makes Christ God's grandson. Christ was also referred to as the "Eternal Father" (later changed to the "Son of the Eternal Father"—1 Nephi 11:21), and Mary was called "the mother of God" (which now reads in 1 Nephi 11:18 as "the mother of the Son of God").

Probably one of the hottest areas of controversy rages around the *Book of Mormon*'s teachings on polygamy. Those unfamiliar with the teachings of this book might be surprised to learn that polygamy was flatly condemned in the book of Jacob. Jacob was a Nephite prophet who said polygamy was abominable (2:24) and equated the practice with whoredoms (2:28). Modern Mormons, though, twist verse 30 of this same chapter—"For if I will, saith the Lord of Hosts, raise up seed unto me, I will command my people, otherwise they shall hearken unto these things"—to provide for possible future endorsement of the practice God considered so abhorrent.

The earlier Jaredites, however, had no teachings we know of on polygamy, but several things indicate that perhaps they could have practiced polygamy. The brother of Jared (the one who was so holy that he could behold the entire body of the Lord) had twenty-two children (Ether 6:20), and another Jaredite, Orihah, had thirty-one (Ether 7:2). In addition, Ether 14:2 states that in a time of warfare "every man kept the hilt of his sword in his right hand, in defense of his property and his own life and of his *wives* and children" [italics mine], which certainly implies the practice of polygamy. Thus the teaching of the *Book of Mormon* on polygamy seems to be this: God permitted the Jaredites to practice it without comment; he allowed it but condemned it in the Israelites; and he forbade it to the Nephites, while saying that it might be all right some time in the future.

The writer of the *Book of Mormon* really got himself into trouble when he put Bible Scriptures into the mouths of *Book of Mormon* prophets *before* the Bible passages were written or spoken. In 1 Nephi 22:15 (written in 585–45 BC) the words of Malachi are quoted. Somebody should have told Malachi 150 years later that he was plagiarizing and that he should give the Nephites credit for what he was saying. But then in 3 Nephi 23:6, Jesus supposedly announced to the Nephite people that he was going to give them scriptures which he said "ye have not." What follows is a quote of the third and fourth chapters of Malachi. This is a paradox hard to resolve: the Nephites in 1 Nephi 22:15 quoted from the works of a prophet who was not yet alive, and then 585 years later are given part of this same prophet's writings because they left Jerusalem before he wrote them.

Even Nephite prophecy is suspect. Nephi predicted that the Lamanites would dwindle (1 Nephi 12:22). Did they dwindle? Then why are so many of them still around, and where are all the good Nephites? A lot of good their righteous behavior and white skin did them. If it were all a question of survival as a reward for choosing righteousness, then the *Book of Mormon is* a very convincing argument for a life of sin!

PRAYING ABOUT THE *BOOK OF MORMON*

In the end, though, Mormons urge proselytes to "prove" the *Book of Mormon* by prayer. The *Book of Mormon* itself in Moroni 10:3–5 asks readers to test it by first reading and pondering it in their hearts, and then by asking God to manifest its truth (in other words, to give the reader personal revelation).

How different from the Bible! We are not told to pray about it. It never suggests that it needs our corroboration for validity. Christ never commanded us to pray about his messiahship. His fulfillment of prophecy and the manifestations of his divine power, culminating in his glorious resurrection, negated any need to *pray about* his divinity.

Shall God, who has given his only Son to die for us, be called upon to follow us around confirming or disproving every crackpot religious theory we contact? How much better would our time be spent in studying God's sweet Word, which would eliminate any doubts in our minds regarding the need for "further revelation"! Nor can we rely on our consciences—"feelings"—to guide us. Who can say that our consciences are a reliable guide?[87] The Bible is replete with examples of consciences seared by sin. And we all sin.

God has given us several tools with which to fashion our spiritual lives. He has given us the master plan, the Bible. He has given us the confirming and guiding influence of the Holy Spirit. And last he has given us intelligence, the ability to perceive truth and evaluate falsehood. We do ourselves a disservice and render ingratitude to God if we neglect any of these. A Mormon who is unsure about how he views the Bible, and afraid he might confuse his own selfish desires with the prompting of the Spirit *can* use his intelligence. I challenge any LDS reader to look up all the scriptures in context that I have used in this chapter. Write the BYU Department of Archaeology and ask if there is any evidence of such things as iron, gold and silver coins, domesticated animals—any of the things the *Book of Mormon* mentions that I said didn't exist in America from 2200 BC to AD 600. And pray—not demanding that God will "reveal" truth to you, but searching the Holy Bible and casting yourself upon the mercy of a just and loving God. Believe that the Bible in and of itself is a sure guide. Read it without LDS commentaries.

A FINAL LOOK

The *Book of Mormon* has affected millions of lives, many of them for the better. The same claim, however, is made by adherents of the Qur'an, *Science and Health with Key to the Scriptures*, and the teachings of Buddha. But the *Book of Mormon* is a unique scripture which its adherents can change (and have changed) at will to suit their own purposes. Without the valuable checks-and-balances system of the many manuscripts and papyri available to the Bible scholar, the various editors of the *Book of Mormon* have through the years made additions, deletions, and corrections to their own holy writ which are much more significant in terms of doctrine than those they claim to have been perpetrated on the Bible. Even so, the inconsistencies which remain mark this book as being from a source other than God.

The *Book of Mormon* was a pioneer in the field of LDS doctrine, the first of many scriptures that formed Mormonism as we know it today. But what is its place in modern LDS thought? Surprisingly, it is not as important today as many of its critics think it is. In fact, most of the careful coaching that LDS youth undergo in learning about it is for the exclusive purpose of answering the objections of those who might perceive its imperfections and contradictions. For all the turmoil it has created, it contains no real earth-shaking doctrines other than its basic premises that ancient Israelites saw Christ in this hemisphere and that Joseph Smith was a prophet who brought this record to the modern world because the Bible was corrupted. Beyond this, all the "good stuff" of Mormonism is found in other "scriptures," where the reading is easier, the historical anachronisms less obvious, and the doctrine more personally applicable and exciting. At least that is how I saw it when I was a Mormon, and I know that my views were not uncommon.

Many people say that the proof of the *Book of Mormon*'s non-divine origin is in the fact that it is not beautiful in a literary sense. As a poet, I must disagree—in some places Joseph Smith rose above his fumbling of grammar and syntax, and in his fervor achieved a raw, wild sort of poetry. In fact, I think he himself realized the power he had with words, even early in life. In the twelfth chapter of Ether, he had one of the Nephite prophets apologize for the poor quality of his speech, but then in a burst of lyrical strength, Joseph put these words into the mouth of the Lord:

> Fools mock, but they shall mourn; and my grace is sufficient for the meek, that they shall take no advantage of your weakness; And if men come unto me I will show unto them their weakness. I give unto men weakness that they may be humble; and my grace is sufficient for all men that humble themselves before me; for if they humble themselves before me, and have faith in me, then will I make weak things become strong unto them.[88]

Joseph Smith was no John Milton, but this passage could be compared to Milton's sonnet XIX, on his blindness, which concludes:

> *God doth not need*
> *Either man's work or his own gifts; who best*
> *Bear his mild yoke, they serve him best. His state*
> *Is kingly: thousands at his bidding speed,*
> *And post o'er land and ocean without rest;*
> *They also serve who only stand and wait.*

Both passages, diverse as they are in time and purpose, are "inspired" in the loose sense of the word: they are uplifting. Both strike a responsive chord in us because they provoke thought on an eternal truth. But is the *Book of Mormon* as a whole any more inspired—any more "God-breathed-into," to translate the word *inspired*—than the works of Milton? Which is more acceptable to a just God, the words of a humble man praising his Creator for his wisdom, or the words of a book that flouts God's Word and ascribes to *itself* his wisdom?

> Let no man deceive you with vain words: for because of these things cometh the wrath of God upon the children of disobedience. Be not ye therefore partakers with them. For ye were sometimes darkness, but now are ye light in the Lord: walk as children of light: (For the fruit of the Spirit is in all goodness and righteousness and truth;) Proving what is acceptable unto the Lord. (Eph. 5:6–10)

Chapter 4

ONE BIBLE, TWO BOOKS OF COMMANDMENTS, AND UNLIMITED WIVES

For behold, I reveal unto you a new and an everlasting covenant; and if ye abide not that covenant, then are ye damned; for no one can reject this covenant and be permitted to enter into my glory.

—*Doctrine and Covenants* 132:4

It was still warm at the end of August—my last semester at Brigham Young University. I sat in the crowded classroom and looked at the other students who surrounded me. I hoped no one would talk to me. I was only taking this religion class because each full-time student at BYU was required to take at least one per semester. It was hard enough for me to return to BYU with a tentative decision that Mormonism was wrong. But I thought I had made a wise decision in taking a New Testament class to fulfill that requirement. I hoped thereby to avoid the issues that would arise in other classes, such as *Pearl of Great Price* or "Teachings of the Living Prophets."

When I saw the teacher enter, I began to relax. He introduced himself, recognizing by name former students and smiling. "Welcome to class," he said. "In this course we'll study the first four books of the New Testament. Our text for the class will be *Jesus the Christ* by James E. Talmadge. Of course, you'll need your *Book of Mormon*, *Pearl of Great Price*, and Bible as supplementary texts."

HOW MORMONS VIEW THE BIBLE

Nowhere else could you expect to find the Bible used as a "supplementary text" for a New Testament class. This incident is indicative of the way Mormons regard God's Word, the Bible. In looking back at the instructions I received in seminary classes on the Bible, the emphasis was on LDS concepts, for which we were given passages to memorize and mark in our Bibles. I see now that many of the Bible passages were taken out of context. We were taught unrelated verses to support erroneous doctrines. Sometimes I think it might have been better never to have opened the Bible at all.

When I was a Mormon, the Bible wasn't my favorite book of Scripture. It wasn't very definitive on LDS doctrine, but it was often useful as a backup. Though LDS television ads now offer free Bibles, our Holy Book is not the source of their unique doctrines. However, I never reached the mental depths of the young LDS missionary who, after a long discussion, threw a Bible across a table to an ex-Mormon friend of mine and screamed at him, "Well, you can just *have* that stinking book!"

This missionary's point of view, though unfortunate, isn't too hard for a reader of the *Book of Mormon* to understand. Second Nephi 29:3 mocks the trust of the Bible believer by having him say mindlessly, "A Bible! A Bible! We have got a Bible, and there cannot be any more Bible," with the Lord responding by calling such a man a "fool" (v. 6). Actually, says the *Book of Mormon*, the Bible is so imperfect that, instead of leading men to God, *it actually causes them to stumble and gives Satan power over them.*[1]

The Eighth Article of Faith formulated by Joseph Smith states that the Bible is the Word of God as far as it is translated correctly. To this might be added, "And as far as it seems to agree with current LDS theology." In my experience, there are only two places where the LDS Church will directly say that the Bible is mistranslated. The first is found at the end of Deuteronomy where the death and burial of Moses is recorded. This doesn't fit with LDS doctrine that states that Moses never died, but was taken to heaven as was Elijah.[2] Second, the words of John 4:24, where Jesus declares that "God is a Spirit: and they that worship him must worship him in spirit and in truth" (KJV) appears in the Joseph Smith translation as "For unto such hath God promised his Spirit. And they who worship him, must worship him in spirit and in truth," supporting the LDS contention that God the Father has a physical body.

Here's a rule of thumb: Wherever God's Word can be twisted to seem to prophesy the coming forth of Mormonism, or to support its doctrines such as those concerning the "great apostasy," then Mormons accept the Bible as true.[3] Usually any Bible statement that flatly contradicts the ideals of their faith has either been publicly "explained away" by an LDS leader or flatly changed or deleted in their other scriptures.

Mormons say that the many variations in different Bible manuscripts "prove" that Holy Writ is not above being corrupted. Such variations in Bible manuscript readings involve only one one-thousandth of the entire text, if we discount variations in spelling, punctuation, etc. And of this one one-thousandth disputed part, there is no real doctrinal question left unresolved. As Luther A. Weigle said in *An Introduction to the Revised Standard Version of the New Testament*, "No doctrine of the Christian faith has been affected by the revision for the simple reason that, out of the thousands of variant readings in the manuscripts, none has turned up thus far that requires a revision of Christian doctrine."

LDS defenders compare the Bible to a car that is started up and just aimed in a certain direction—such a venture will, without supervision and correction, veer off course. However, the Bible is not an unattended, mindless vehicle. Jesus promised that the gates of hell would not prevail against his church (Matt. 16:18). And the basis of all his church's teaching is the Bible—an extraordinary book like none other, divinely protected throughout the ages. Surely the God of the universe who can raise the dead can keep his Book from error.

Actually, as I have studied textual criticism and have investigated for myself some of the documents from which the New Testament was translated, I am awed at how God has protected his Word. However, when I was in LDS seminary, teachers compared textual transmission to the child's game of "gossip"—in which a line of people whisper a message from person to person and see how, at the end of the line, a message can be changed beyond recognition. However, such analogies do not apply to the history of Bible transmission. There are "families" of papyrus documents from all over the Eastern world—some of which date to within years of the death of the last apostle. Comparison between them has operated as a checks-and-balances system to ensure that no essential information was lost, and no heretical information was inserted, in the hundreds of years since the close of the New Testament. In addition, the discovery of the Dead Sea Scrolls has provided proof positive that the passage of time and multiple scribes had minimal effect on manuscript transmission of the Word of God.[4]

The LDS Church looks at the denominationalism and religious division of the last few hundred years and says, "Your mistranslated Bible has caused all this. You took out important parts of the gospel, and have no prophets to give them back. You poor fools!"

Unfortunately, even living prophets do not guarantee religious unity. In First Kings 19 Elijah cried to the Lord that of all the children of Israel, he alone was left to serve God. (Of course he learned later that actually seven thousand Israelites remained faithful, but even at that the number represented only a small part of the Israelite nation.) Let's face it, religious division has always existed—even when true living prophets headed Israel. And no Mormon with his eyes open can deny the divisions over doctrine that exist in his own "prophet-guided" church.

Furthermore, as Dr. James D. Bales has noted, "The majority of believers are not divided over what the Bible says, but they are divided over what the Bible does not say."[5] Both Mormons and Christians would agree that the Bible does not say anything about what formulates distinctively LDS doctrine. The casual observer might wonder if the Mormons use the Bible at all. They do, but in my experience it was used more in debating with Christians than in searching for doctrinal truth.[6]

BIBLE VERSIONS USED BY MORMONS

Mormons are limited to a single "official" version of the Bible, one that is based on the so-called King James Version.[7] There are numerous reasons for this. First, many doctrinal tenets of Mormonism are built upon the foundation of the Mormons' peculiar affinity for and interpretation of Elizabethan English. For years LDS missionaries were sent out with instructions to use only the King James Version when quoting from the Bible: the "common ground for proselyting purposes."[8] Another reason Mormons cling to the King James language so tenaciously is that it is quoted verbatim in many LDS scriptures, especially in the *Book of Mormon*. In addition, the angel Moroni who supposedly spoke to young Joseph Smith as recorded in *Joseph Smith—History* used the language of the King James Version.

The official title of Smith's own "translation" of the Bible is *The Holy Scriptures Translated and Corrected by the Spirit of Revelation by Joseph Smith the Seer.* For years Mormons called it "the Inspired Revision," but today refer to it as the "Joseph Smith Translation" (JST). These titles bring up many questions in the mind of an observer. If the Scriptures were corrupted, were they still "holy"? From what language did Joseph "translate" them?[9] And if they were in such need of being corrected, why didn't Joseph just do that to begin with, without bringing in the complicating factors of the *Book of Mormon*?

It seems that the *Book of Mormon* had pretty well served its purpose in Joseph Smith's doctrinal plans up until late 1830. But at that time Joseph felt that he needed some biblical authentication for the ideas on priesthood that he and Sidney Rigdon were in the process of formulating. His "inspired" Bible was the perfect vehicle. The book of Genesis, with its familiar stories of the patriarchs and their open communication with God, was the section of the Bible most mutilated by Joseph Smith. The *Book of Mormon* concept that the fall of Adam was good and necessary (2 Nephi 2:15ff) was expanded upon, and the concept of a preexistent state of all men and women was forced upon the creation story. Adam was identified as a great priest, and the story of Enoch was stretched out into an entire chapter which would later provide the basis for "the United Order of Enoch," the LDS Church's unsuccessful attempt at communal living.

The idea of the Melchizidek Priesthood was validated by Joseph Smith's padding of the story of Melchizidek in both Genesis and Hebrews, to produce a supposed priesthood succession from Melchizidek through Christ to modern man—totally destroying the original intention of both Bible passages. And in Genesis 50, Joseph Smith could not resist the temptation of adding a "prophecy" foretelling that a descendant of the biblical patriarch Joseph would arise in the last days. He would be named Joseph, and would be the son of a man named Joseph ... just like Joseph Smith.[10]

The mainstream Latter-day Saint Church did not in the past officially recognize the "Inspired Version" as doctrine, claiming that it was never completed by Joseph Smith, and that what was finished was later corrupted by uninspired persons. In recent years, the influence of the JST has grown in LDS scholarship and layperson's thinking alike. Both the Utah LDS Church and the Community of Christ (formerly known as the Reorganized LDS Church) print the JST, and a significant number of footnotes to the LDS printings of the KJV reference Smith's "translation" as well. Nevertheless, the Bible that most Mormons have bound in their "Quad" or "Quadruple Combination" (along with the *Book of Mormon*, *Pearl of Great Price*, and *Doctrine and Covenants*) is still a King James Version, cross-referenced to the other three books.

According to Joseph Smith's own statement in the *History of the Church*, he did indeed complete his translation.[11] *Doctrine and Covenants* 124:89, in fact, commands that the translation be printed. I knew several faithful Mormons at BYU who read the Inspired Version to the complete exclusion of the King James Version, reasoning that the Old and New Testaments had been corrupted for thousands of years, whereas the enemies of Joseph Smith had only a short time in which to do their damage.

Since at any rate the LDS Church is—by its own admission—left without a completely reliable, stand-alone Bible, surely one of the most pressing needs of the Church would be to correct the errors in that Book. The job of course would ascribe itself to the present-day "prophet, seer, and revelator" of the Church. Is there a need for true Scripture? Does the LDS prophet have the power to so correct and translate?[12] If he does, why have he and past presidents of the LDS Church deprived their people of truth?

Many LDS apologists try to erode confidence in the Bible by pointing to the period of time before the official canon of the Bible was established. But the qualifications for inclusion in the holy canon were ones that LDS "scriptures" could never fulfill. For instance, all Old Testament and New Testament books had a history of acceptance and established origin—in the mouth of two or three witnesses, every word was established (Matt. 18:16). However, neither the *Book of Mormon* nor the *Pearl of Great Price* had such provenance. Another qualifying requirement for books of the Bible were that they must harmonize with other Scripture. As already noted, the *Book of Mormon* calls the Bible an instrument of Satan. So much for harmony.

Even after he completed his Inspired Version, Joseph Smith himself continued to quote almost exclusively from the King James Version. Even when it differed from the King James Version, he did not quote from his own translation. Those Latter-day Saints today who have characterized the JST as "inspired commentary" have acknowledged that it often contradicts the best ancient manuscripts of the Bible. Yet, Robert Millet, dean of the Department of Religion at BYU, pushes aside the implications: "If we find that the prophet's Bible translation does not fit with extant Hebrew or Greek manuscripts, we must still receive his work with all patience and faith."[13] I study from a Greek New Testament, and I have seen that Greek manuscripts do not support LDS claims. (One glaring example is Joseph Smith's misuse of the King James words *celestial* and *terrestrial* in 1 Corinthians.)

Psalm 119:160 tells us that God's Word is true from the beginning, and verse 140 tells us to love it because of its inherent purity. Jesus himself said that even though heaven and earth pass away, God's Word would not (Mark 13:31) and said of Scripture that it could not be broken (John 10:35). But Mormons call the Bible corrupted and misleading. In fact, as LDS apologist Millet points out, the most primitive foundations of Mormonism rest upon biblical insufficiency: Joseph Smith believed he could not find answers within its pages but only by asking God.[14] Millet gives a succinct, twenty-first century LDS assessment of the Bible: "We love the Bible and cherish its messages. But the Bible is not the source of our doctrine or authority, nor is much to be gained through trying to 'prove' the truthfulness of the restored gospel [i.e., Mormonism] from the Bible. Ours is an independent revelation."[15] In such a statement Millet shows himself to be a true spiritual heir of Joseph Smith, who began his "ministry" by teaching that all Christians were corrupt and their doctrines were equally devoid of truth.[16]

Can we depend upon the Bible of our Christian heritage? Common sense alone tells us that God would not leave humankind with an unreliable guide upon which to base both our faith and our judgment of future revelations, should there be any. A just storekeeper would not punish his clerks for selling underweight produce when he himself had provided them with an inaccurate set of scales. In the same way, our God is just and wise; he has not left us without inspired Scripture to teach us doctrine, to rebuke and correct us, and to teach us righteousness unto perfection (2 Tim. 3:16–17). We cannot blame the religious conflicts of the world on God's Word, but on the conflicts that exist within the darkened heart of man. Nowhere in the Bible is a reader told to verify its teachings by their own feelings.[17] God's Word doesn't have to prove itself to anyone—it is inherently true. It is not the cloth to be measured—it is the unerring, finely wrought yardstick of truth itself.

HISTORY OF THE *DOCTRINE AND COVENANTS*

I often remarked to friends and roommates that the *Doctrine and Covenants* was my favorite book of scripture. It was so practical, so contemporary. Indeed, it is the only "standard work" which the LDS Church claims was written in modern times.[18] Mormons cherish the *Doctrine and Covenants*, regarding it as an accurate, nearly chronological record of the adding of revelation upon revelation for the formulating and perfecting of the young Mormon Church.

The first edition of the *Doctrine and Covenants* was published in 1833 under the title *Book of Commandments*. This little volume, containing sixty-five revelations, is today a rarity, since most of the copies of it were destroyed when a mob burned the printing office where they were stored. Ten thousand copies were originally intended for publication, but obviously only a small fraction of this number was actually printed. It was printed again in 1835 under the title *Doctrine and Covenants of the Church of Latter-day Saints*. This change of name was a great surprise to many members of the Church, who maintained that God had himself named the collection of revelations *Book of Commandments* in its original chapter 1:2. Church leaders justified changing the name by putting the former title in lowercase letters in later editions, making it seem like a description rather than a title.[19]

The book was printed again in 1844, 1876, and 1921. Today's edition is basically the same as the 1921 edition (with a few significant additions), but differs *radically* from the *Book of Commandments.* An LDS commentator on the *Doctrine and Covenants* says euphemistically of the *Book of Commandments* that it was "not complete, and its readings frequently differ from corresponding sections in later editions."[20] It would be more accurate to say that the *Book of Commandments*—supposedly God's Word to his infant church—was so changed, added to, and mutilated as to be almost unrecognizable when compared to today's *Doctrine and Covenants,* which in its first section claimed that its own words would never "pass away." Melvin J. Petersen documented no fewer than 2,643 changes in the 1835 edition of the *Doctrine and Covenants* as compared to the 1833 *Book of Commandments.*[21] Writer Charles Crane went so far as to characterize the *Doctrine and Covenants* as the religious text holding the record for "the most changed book ever to have claimed to be scripture."[22]

In the early 1960s, LDS researcher Wilford Wood republished the 1830 edition of the *Book of Mormon* (as Volume I), the 1833 *Book of Commandments,* the 1835 edition of the *Doctrine and Covenants, The Lectures on Faith,* and the "Fourteen Articles of Faith" (as Volume II) under the title *Joseph Smith Begins His Work.* At first the LDS Church both printed and actively promoted these books. However, as Mormons compared the early documents with their present forms, many began to apostatize—and the LDS Church began to suppress the books. Even today, the LDS Church is still afraid of the contrast between the *Book of Commandments* and the modern *Doctrine and Covenants.* They claim that additions to the *Book of Commandments* were due to Joseph Smith's adding of explanatory material to the revelations, and that the deletions were those of non-essential parts. But contact with a *Book of Commandments* is bound to raise questions in the mind of a Mormon. Who gave Joseph Smith the right to add to God's Word, even if only to make it easier to understand? Or how could he cut out parts of Scripture, calling them "non-essential"? It is a variable god, indeed, who gives a revelation that needs major revision only two years after its publication.[23]

Although much material has been added to the *Doctrine and Covenants* since its inception, seventy-five pages of material were deleted from the 1921 and all subsequent editions. This material was known as the "Lectures on Faith" and is now published in a separate volume with the explanation that it was never accepted as doctrine equal with the revelations in the *Doctrine and Covenants,* though they are "profitable for doctrine."[24] (Second Timothy

3:16 uses the phrase "profitable for doctrine" as a definition of Scripture, but Mormons apparently see a difference in the two.) At any rate, many Mormons breathed a sigh of relief when the "Lectures on Faith" were removed from the *Doctrine and Covenants*, for they are surely some of the most tedious reading ever produced by Joseph Smith.

CONTENTS OF THE *DOCTRINE AND COVENANTS*

More of today's practices and doctrines within Mormonism arise from the teachings of the *Doctrine and Covenants* than from either the *Book of Mormon* or the *Pearl of Great Price.* Ask the average Mormon to tell you the outstanding doctrines of the *Book of Mormon*, and he'll get to "opposition in all things" and stop. Ask him the same about the *Pearl of Great Price*, and he'll probably be stumped after the Joseph Smith story and the concept of the preexistence. But every LDS child knows the *Doctrine and Covenants* to be the source of such teachings as the Word of Wisdom, the three degrees of heaven, revelations on polygamy, baptism for the dead, priesthood ordination, how to tell a good angel from a bad one, etc.

But the truth is, much of the *Doctrine and Covenants* is just plain uninteresting. Early sections especially seem like a hodgepodge of Bible verses picked indiscriminately from the Old and New Testaments, interlaced with commands, cajolings, and scathing rebukes, all aimed at anyone who crossed the path of Joseph Smith. Overall, the *Doctrine and Covenants* covers a wide assortment of subjects, ranging from personal instructions to doctrinal teachings on the Holy Ghost, the fall, the atonement, salvation for the dead, eternal marriage, repentance, baptism, the priesthoods, other scriptures, the economic status of man, and our final destiny. It is a book of instructions and invectives, of pleas and unbelievable promises.

The revelations in the *Doctrine and Covenants* supposedly were given in four different manners. One way that Joseph Smith said he received revelation was directly: that is, the Lord spoke directly to him. He also claimed that some of the revelations came through the Urim and Thummim. A notable example of this is his use of the magic spectacles to translate an original document written by John the Beloved (recorded in section 7). The Urim and Thummim, however, was not used after 1829 when Joseph Smith claimed to have received the Melchizidek, or higher, Priesthood. Joseph Smith also said some of the revelations came through visions. Another method for receiving revelations was through direct conversation and visual contact with a heavenly, formerly dead messenger such as Peter or Moroni.

WHAT THE *DOCTRINE AND COVENANTS* TEACHES

It is very difficult to provide a simple "overview" of a book as complex as the *Doctrine and Covenants.* What follows here is a roughly chronological outline of the high points of this book. The *Doctrine and Covenants* is divided not into chapters, but into "sections." Each section is numbered and divided into verses, and has a short heading that describes briefly the circumstances surrounding the receipt of the revelation, including the date and a synopsis of its contents. The *Doctrine and Covenants* has a short concordance, a chronology of the revelations, and introductory material attesting to their validity.

It is obvious to even the most casual reader of the book that its first sections—notably 3, 5, 10, and 17—have as their outstanding purpose the *validation of the Book of Mormon*, and through it, the standing of Joseph Smith as a prophet. Other introductory sections—2, 13, and 27—purport to be the *words of angels.* In section 2 Moroni spoke concerning the (Aaronic) Priesthood, and in section 13 John the Baptist ordained Joseph and Oliver Cowdery to that Priesthood. In section 27 Joseph was told by another angel that he was not to use wine (except that made by Mormons) in the Church's sacrament services. This prohibition led to the now universal practice among Mormons of using water as the only liquid served in sacrament.

The parchment record supposedly written by the apostle John the Beloved and translated via the Urim and Thummim as section 7 has already been mentioned. Later, in section 93, verses 16–18, it says that "the fulness of the record of John" is yet to be revealed. Just what was this record and where is it now? The *Doctrine and Covenants Compendium* gives the reader two options. Either God actually gave John's parchment to Joseph Smith to translate; or Joseph Smith simply looked into the Urim and Thummim, and the parchment and its words became visible there. The *Compendium*'s author speculated, "It would seem natural ... to assume that the parchment was still hidden in a safe place possibly somewhere in the Near East."[25] Of course, it is obvious why Joseph Smith never produced John's parchment. Its authenticity could have been immediately ascertained by the Greek scholars of his day. Whereas Joseph could be a little more daring with Egyptian (which at that time was untranslatable) and with "reformed Egyptian" (which everyone knows to be untranslatable), he couldn't afford to try to fake ancient Greek. So it stayed "hidden away," and the supposedly translated portion tells us that Christ did indeed promise John eternal life, and that he, like the three Nephites, is alive and well among the Jews, preparing them for the great "gathering" when they shall regain their fatherland.[26]

Of more than passing interest is section 13, which contains the words of the ordination of Joseph Smith and Oliver Cowdery to the Aaronic Priesthood, and sections 65 and 109 which are *prayers*. The last two illustrate especially well Joseph's gift with words, and his use of "revelation" to jab at his enemies (see 109:29).

A great many of the revelations of the *Doctrine and Covenants* are *addressed to certain individuals*, some of whom went on to be leaders of the Church, and some of whom left it completely. Mormons see these revelations as great examples of a personalized gospel from a God who knows men's hearts and gives specific instructions to each one who needed it. To a non-Mormon they come across as tongue-lashings backed up by threats of divine and eternal punishment. An example of this is found in section 10, wherein *Book of Mormon* witness Martin Harris, who lost a part of the "translation" of the Nephite manuscript, was called "wicked," and later, by implication, a liar (vv. 1, 28).

Did Joseph Smith *use the revelations he received to exalt himself*? Section 21 ordered him to keep a record naming him "translator, a prophet, an apostle of Jesus Christ, an elder of the church" (v. 1). (A Christian might compare such gasconade with the modest statements of Paul about himself, and that apostle's reluctance to boast.) Joseph Smith even used the revelations of the *Doctrine and Covenants* to command a house to be built for himself (41:7).

Joseph Smith also *used the revelations to "answer" questions* about the Bible. Section 77 purports to be no more and no less than a question-and-answer quiz of God. Joseph asked questions about the meanings of several of the symbols of the book of Revelation. The literal interpretations he ascribed to many of these symbols betray his lack of understanding of figurative language as used by John. Sections 74, 86, and 113 also claim to be explanations of Bible verses. The question of just how an unbelieving spouse is sanctified by the believing one, and how their children are made holy is dealt with in section 74. In section 86 the parable of the wheat and the tares is made to apply to priesthood holders (wheat) and the blessings promised to them. Section 113 also forces the concept of priesthood onto several unsuspecting, isolated verses from Isaiah.

The *mechanics of how to run a church* is the subject of many sections of the *Doctrine and Covenants*. Section 20, for example, speaks definitively on baptism, how to administer the sacrament, the duties of elders, priests, teachers, deacons, and members; the function and timing of conferences, and the blessing of children. Section 27, as we've already seen, forbids "Gentile" wine in the sacrament. Section 42 deals with church discipline, and 107 with priesthood offices and duties.

Four of the sections of the *Doctrine and Covenants* are *records of visions*. Section 76 is perhaps one of the most basic in LDS theological teachings on Satan, hell, and heaven, and must be read if one is to understand the official LDS belief on these subjects. The vision in section 110 records the appearance of Christ, Moses, Elias, and Elijah in the Kirtland temple.

Sections 137 and 138 were added to the *Doctrine and Covenants* after I left the LDS Church in 1973, even though both were "received as revelations" long before I was born. Little in either of these two "revelations" held any surprises for the Mormon of 1976, for they were already the basis of much doctrine about the dead. Each of these sections was printed as part of the *Pearl of Great Price* during a three-year period from 1976 to 1979, then transferred to the *Doctrine and Covenants* where they more logically belong.

Section 137, Joseph Smith's "Vision of the Celestial Kingdom," is regarded by some Mormons as a "new" revelation, but it can hardly be regarded as such since the event supposedly occurred in the 1830s. This short, ten-verse section assured Joseph Smith that he was not to worry about people who died without hearing the LDS gospel, because God would judge their hearts, and if he knew they would have accepted it had they the chance, then they would be "heirs of the celestial kingdom" (v. 7). The same would apply to people living in the future, and to children who died before reaching the "years of accountability"—age eight.

Section 138, the "Vision of the Redemption of the Dead," supposedly received in 1918 by Joseph F. Smith (sixth president of the Church), was also canonized as part of the standard works in 1976. This long passage tells of how Christ went into the spirit world after his death, and with the help of certain righteous men, preached "faith in God, repentance from sin, vicarious baptism for the remission of sins, the gift of the Holy Ghost by the laying on of hands" (v. 33). Those who were dead had the option of accepting these principles and paying the penalty of their transgressions (v. 59). Then they were treated just like those who had accepted the LDS gospel on earth. In addition, righteous Mormons of today will have the opportunity after death of preaching to heathen peoples.

When I was a Mormon, section 78 contained some strange foreign-sounding names which were assigned to the persons mentioned in this section (such names were also used as aliases for church leaders in sections 82, 92, 96, 103, 104, and 105 as well). Such names as "Baurak Ale" for Joseph Smith ostensibly prevented the Church's enemies from knowing the intentions of plans such as section 103 detailed—the recovery by force of the land they'd left in Missouri. However, uses of names like "Enoch" also led ordinary church members of the time to think the "revelations" were about ancient personages, thus concealing plans that Church leadership kept from its own members as well.[27] Since 1981, the code names are no longer printed in modern editions of the *Doctrine and Covenants*, another example of how the LDS Church can and does change the words of its own scripture, even if they are the words of its god.

The famous Civil War prophecy of section 87 has for years been touted by Mormons as proof positive of Joseph's powers as a prophet. However, the force of this assertion is lessened considerably when one considers that "the rebellion of South Carolina" mentioned had occurred at least two weeks before it is claimed that Joseph Smith received a revelation concerning it. Even Mormons admit the "prophecy" was not put into print until 1851. Besides, a careful and objective reading of the entire "prophecy" would lead one to believe that the coming Civil War would mark the beginning of an era of continuous war on "all nations"—which has certainly not proven to be the case. (Not even by a great stretch can it be said that "the Northern states" and "the Southern states" had anything to do with the Spanish American War or World War I, for instance.)

HEALTH, INTELLIGENCE, AND OTHER MATTERS

Section 89 records probably the most famous and far-reaching command, the Word of Wisdom, or health law. It professes that it was not originally given as a commandment (v. 2), but was "given for a principle with promise" (v. 3)—a sort of bargain with God for health. Because of the restrained language of the section, many Latter-day Saints have regarded it as optional. However, any modern-day Mormon who wants to enter a temple must consistently practice its principles. The LDS Church for decades barred from temple attendance its members who drank liquor, coffee, tea, or caffeinated drinks, or who smoked or otherwise used tobacco. In other words, disobedience to the Word of Wisdom meant that they could not marry for eternity, do proxy baptisms, attend the temple weddings of their more-faithful children or other relatives, or do any of the other things that would put them on the coveted path to godhood or save their dead non-Mormon friends and kin.

Read literally, the Word of Wisdom forbids the use of "wine or strong drink" for any purpose other than in the sacrament or for washing one's body; it forbids tobacco for any purpose other than as a poultice for bruises, and for "all sick cattle"; and it says that "hot drinks" are neither for the body nor the belly. It encourages the use of fruits and herbs in season, but cautions man to use meat sparingly. It says that wheat is for humankind, corn is for oxen, oats are for horses, rye is for swine and birds, and barley is for "all useful animals." Those who keep the Word of Wisdom are promised many things: health, wisdom, knowledge, freedom from fatigue, and protection from the destroying angel.

The background for this revelation is an interesting one. Brigham Young said that it was precipitated by Emma Smith's complaining about the mess she had to clean up after Joseph's friends got together and spat tobacco all over the floor.[28] Joseph too was disgusted by the clouds of smoke from the men's pipes, so he "inquired of the Lord" as to the use of tobacco. In 1842 Hyrum Smith defined the "hot drinks" mentioned in section 89 as coffee and tea. Thus, today, the average Mormon's concept of the substances forbidden by the Word of Wisdom is limited to liquor, tobacco, coffee, and tea.

The Word of Wisdom has become the badge of faithful Mormons of all ages, and it is not merely coincidental that Mormons often live longer, healthier lives than their non-LDS counterparts. I thank God for their health, and fervently desire that Christians would become as sensitive to the care of their "temples" (1 Cor. 3:16) as our LDS friends. Too often, though, the emphasis in observing the Word of Wisdom is focused on the "four forbiddens." The definition of "hot drinks" as coffee and tea in particular opens several questions.

Can one drink iced coffee and iced tea? The answer is no. In addition, Apostle George Q. Cannon advised against the use of another hot drink, cocoa.[29] Some Mormons do not use chocolate in any form. I did not use it for eight of the ten years I was a Mormon, though it was served freely in the dormitory cafeterias at Brigham Young University. On the other hand, all caffeinated sodas were forbidden when I was a Mormon. However, the Church has relaxed its stance on such sodas, though many faithful Mormons still do not drink them.

No one would argue with the Word of Wisdom's condemnation of the addictive substance, alcohol. But in the Word of Wisdom its use is encouraged as an agent in washing the body. I am as much puzzled by this as by the Word of Wisdom's advocating the use of tobacco on bruises, and for all the diseases of cattle. A great emphasis is placed on what Mormons should *not* eat or drink, but the profitable use of these substances as advised in the *Doctrine and Covenants* is virtually ignored (maybe because they don't work?). Also often passed over is the Word of Wisdom's warning against the overuse of meat. As a Mormon, I would eat meat at only one meal a day, but of all my many acquaintances in the densely LDS population of Brigham Young University, there were only a few who said they consciously limited the use of meat because of the Word of Wisdom. In addition, I knew of no Mormons who limited their intake of corn, rye, barley, and oats.

Past Church leaders were adamant in their condemnation of the liquor and tobacco industries. The Word of Wisdom, according to its own admission, was given "in consequence of evils and designs which do and will exist in the minds of conspiring men" (89:4). Dr. Sperry, in his *Doctrine and Covenants Compendium*, characterized the directors of the tobacco industry as "men without conscience ... moral cowards," and mentioned the "lack of ethics and morality"[30] of the liquor industry. But it is a documented fact that Joseph Smith sold liquor in Nauvoo, and Brigham Young in Utah built a distillery and sold alcoholic beverages[31]—both instances occurring after the Word of Wisdom "revelation." At one time, the largest liquor business in the state of Utah was run by the LDS Church-owned department store, Zion's Cooperative Mercantile Institution (ZCMI).[32] Joseph F. Smith confirmed the fact that ZCMI sold liquors but excused it by saying that if any unfortunate who depended upon liquor didn't buy it at ZCMI, he would just go somewhere else.[33] So much for being your brother's keeper!

Section 93 is perhaps the most definitive in LDS scripture on the relationship of truth, knowledge, and intelligence; and the source of the famous LDS assertion that "the glory of God is intelligence" (v. 36). It is also one of the few stand-alone statements by Joseph Smith on philosophical tenets that makes any sense at all to a non-Mormon.

A revelation of unusual form is found in section 102. This consists of the minutes of a meeting. Unlike other revelations which say, "thus saith the Lord," this section's only pretension to inspiration is the fact that it is included in the *Doctrine and Covenants*, and is thus scripture. It is signed by two clerks, and deals with the organization of a high council, and discipline therein.

Another distinctive organization spoken of in the *Doctrine and Covenants* is the United Order. Also known as the Order of Enoch, the United Order was an altruistic, communal venture in which all participants were "to have equal claim upon properties, for the benefit of managing the concerns of your stewardship" (82:17). It was patterned after the LDS concept of the people of Enoch, who with him were taken up to heaven without tasting death because they all shared equally amongst themselves. The United Order was described in section 78 verses 8–16 as an "everlasting" covenant that could never be broken. However, history shows it was a considerable failure for the many causes previously discussed in the chapter about Joseph Smith.

Much of the *Doctrine and Covenants* is devoted to the concept of a New Jerusalem. In section 57, Missouri is designated as "the land which I have appointed and consecrated for the gathering of the saints ... the land of promise, and the place for the city of Zion" (vv. 1 and 2). Mormons were encouraged to buy all the land they could around Independence ("the center place"). Section 84 prophesied (with two "verilies") that a temple would be built there "in this generation" (vv. 4 and 5). In spite of the obvious failure of this prophecy, Mormons still look to Missouri as the site of the New Jerusalem, even with the knowledge that the site dedicated for the temple by Joseph Smith is now tenaciously owned by an LDS splinter group known as the Church of Christ—Temple Lot.

An area in Daviess County, Missouri, is identified in section 116 as "Adam-ondi-Ahman," the site where Adam supposedly built the first altar after the expulsion from Eden, and where he blessed his children before his death (107:53). This will also be the place where a great council meeting will be held just before the second coming of Christ, which will be attended by Michael, Gabriel, and other holders of the priesthood keys who will relinquish those keys to Christ.

CONFLICTS

One thread that runs consistently through the *Doctrine and Covenants* is the theme of persecution and the LDS response to it. The beginning of section 98 commands courage and patience in regard to their enemies. Section 122, which is surely one of the classic examples of Joseph Smith's artistry with words, advises him that persecution is for the good of the one persecuted, for it always results in valuable experience.

Two sections of the *Doctrine and Covenants,* 127 and 128, are in the form of *letters* from Joseph Smith to the Church at large. In section 127 verse 2 he comments that "deep water is what I am wont to swim in," and then he plunges into the doctrine of baptism for the dead. He details the need for witnesses and recorders of such baptisms, and even gives instructions for the location of the fonts in the temples.[34] The remainder of sections 127 and 128 are taken up with Joseph Smith's twisting of Bible verses to make them seem to support baptism for the dead, and is an excellent example of the unfettered magniloquence of the literary prophet. These two "epistles" certainly belie Emma Smith's assertion that her husband couldn't compose a letter.

Since most of the *Doctrine and Covenants* was composed during the time that Mormons were experiencing *conflicts with the state and federal governments,* it is interesting to note sections 98 and 134. Section 101 states that God himself established the American Constitution (v. 80), and the people of the Church were encouraged in section 98 to uphold it. A more detailed statement on the Church's beliefs regarding its responsibilities to the government and the government's duties to the Church is found in section 134, which was composed by Oliver Cowdery.

Sections 129, 130, and 131 spell out some specifics of LDS doctrine. Section 129 gives the vision-prone LDS people a test to know if a supernatural being who appears to them is from God or from Satan. (Offer such a being your hand. If he takes it, and you don't feel anything, you're in trouble.) Section 130 deals with the dwelling place of God and the angels, identifying it as a faraway planet, and speaks of the importance of gaining knowledge. It also deals with the physical nature of the bodies of God and Christ, and other matters. Section 131 describes the three degrees of glory in heaven, and defines spirit as a kind of refined matter. It also deals with a little-understood (even by Mormons) doctrine known elsewhere as "having one's calling and election made sure," as a result of what is here called "the more sure word of prophecy." This is an absolute assurance by God of one's personal salvation, and guarantees that one's soul cannot be lost.

Section 135 was written by John Taylor (third president of the LDS Church), and is a narration of the events surrounding the deaths of Joseph Smith and his brother Hyrum. The bitterness and loss felt by Joseph's bereaved followers can be read even between the lines, and no one, no matter how little divinity he might impute to the life and works of Joseph Smith, can read this moving account without wishing that Joseph Smith had died a more peaceful death.

Section 136 was written by Brigham Young and is his only contribution to the book. It contains instructions for the trek westward and definitely reflects the personality of Young, even though it is supposedly the Word of the Lord. It gives practical, definitive directions for the organization of the traveling companies, with a minimum of the scripturalistic verbiage that characterizes Joseph's writings tucked in at the end so that no one would mistake it for anything less than a revelation.

Also added after I left Mormonism is "Official Declaration—2," which announced in 1978 that men of all races were, from that point forward, allowed to hold the LDS priesthood—which had been denied to people of color during the first century and a half of LDS history.

POLYGAMY

I have saved until last the most controversial section of the *Doctrine and Covenants* because its culmination comes near the end of the volume. Section 132 purports to be God's explanation of why ancient prophets were allowed to have multiple wives and concubines. The revelation is in the form of an answer to Joseph's question. Verse 1 sets the tone for the entire section by assuming that God approved heartily of the "doctrine" of polygamy:

> Verily, thus saith the Lord unto you my servant Joseph, that inasmuch as you have inquired of my hand to know and understand wherein I, the Lord, *justified* my servants Abraham, Isaac, and Jacob, as also Moses, David, and Solomon, my servants, as touching the principle and doctrine of their having many wives and concubines. [italics mine]

Thus, with no prefatory argument, Joseph Smith resolved for the LDS mind the question of whether or not God approved of the Old Testament practice of plurality of wives. Joseph bypassed the whole issue by saying that not only did God tolerate it, he actually *required* it.

This argument is suspended (securely, some Mormons think) from Joseph Smith's version of the story of Abraham. According to section 132 verse 35, God *commanded* that Old Testament prophet to take Hagar the handmaid of his wife as a concubine so that he could have the seed that God had promised him. But anyone who reads Genesis 16 can see the holes in this argument. God didn't tell Abraham to take Hagar, Sarai did; and in verse 5 of Genesis 16 she admits that this, in hindsight, wasn't a very good idea. (In fact, today's bloody conflict in the Middle East shows the outcome of the rivalry between those who claim to be descended from Abraham's two sons.)

The *Doctrine and Covenants* says that the plural wives of Isaac, Jacob, Moses, and Solomon were also commanded of God (vv. 37–38), and that all of David's wives except the wife of Uriah were given to him by God. But in no modern translation of the Bible can we find an example of where God commanded a man to take more than one wife. (There is a possible exception to this in the case of a levirate marriage, wherein the next of kin of a man who died childless would marry his kinsman's widow [Deut. 25:5–6; see also Gen. 38:1–26 for the history of Tamar]).

No matter how plural marriages were tolerated by God in Old Testament times, Jesus himself made it clear that under the new kingdom of heaven that he instituted, practices once overlooked in Old Testament times were no longer tolerated (see Jesus' teachings on divorce in Matthew 19:1–9). By the time that divinely revealed standards for the New Testament church were delineated, all married leaders were limited to a single wife (1 Tim. 3:2, Titus 1:6).

Section 132 does not make polygamy an optional marital relationship. It is called a "new and everlasting covenant" in verse 4, which states that "if ye abide not that covenant, then ye are damned, for no one can reject this covenant and be permitted to enter into my glory." (Researcher Bruce MacArthur has aptly pointed out the contradiction in LDS claims that polygamy is an ancient command of God—instituted, as verse 5 says, "from before the foundation of the world"—immediately after the nineteenth-century *Doctrine and Covenant* definition of plural marriage as a "a new and an everlasting covenant" in 132:4). The earthly marriage union, which we Christians regard as blessed and approved of by God, says this section, is "of no efficacy, virtue or force in and after the resurrection of the dead; for all contracts that are not made unto this end have an end when men are dead" (v. 7).

One underlying principle of LDS polygamy is that anyone who refuses it will receive an inferior inheritance in heaven and will be appointed to be servant of those who did accept it (vv. 16 and 17). Polygamous saints are promised great blessings. In verses 19 and 20 we learn that if "sealed" Mormons shed no innocent blood, they will be raised in the first resurrection, or shortly thereafter, inheriting thrones, kingdoms, principalities, powers, dominions, and all heights and depths. They will be able to pass unscathed by angels and gods, and their family relationships (marital, parental, and filial) will be eternal. Finally, they are promised that "then they shall be gods, because they have all power, and the angels are subject unto them" (v. 20).

The crux of the *Doctrine and Covenants* section on polygamy is that no one can be exalted without it, and that only Joseph and his successors have the "keys" to this ordinance. Anyone who rejects it is damned; as is any man or woman who commits "adultery" by having marital relations outside the covenant having once entered into it. The wife of such an adulterous man would be given to another, faithful man, who will "be made ruler over many" (v. 44).

The last dozen or so verses of the revelation are transparently aimed at those who would oppose these teachings, most specifically at Joseph's wife, Emma. It is obvious that this revelation, like the Word of Wisdom, was written with her in mind. She is told to accept all of Joseph's plural wives (v. 52), and she is threatened with destruction (v. 54) if she cannot "abide this commandment." Furthermore, she is told that Joseph will be given even more wives if she fights against the revelation (v. 55). Poor Emma! Damned if she did, and humiliated if she didn't! Joseph tried to soften all this by saying in verse 61 that a first wife would have to give permission for her husband to take a second one, but he himself repeatedly took wives without Emma's knowledge or consent, claiming that he was exempt from this provision of the commandment (v. 65).

Apparently polygamy as a whole never went much more smoothly than what we see in the *Doctrine and Covenants*. LDS lore is full of stories of childless "aunts" who lived with Grandmother and Grandfather in uneasy cohabitation. Emma Smith fought the doctrine of plural wives with every psychological weapon at her disposal, but lost. Brigham Young had dozens of wives, one of whom rebelled so expressively against the slavery of polygamy that her book, *Wife Number 19*, is a classic among books about polygamy. Some highly recommended books published more recently on the subject of polygamy as practiced by Joseph Smith, Brigham Young, and other LDS leaders include *Mormon Enigma: Emma Hale Smith* (Linda King Newell and Valeen Tippetts Avery) and *Mormon Polygamy: A History* (Richard S. Van Wagoner).

Many people have wondered why a man would want more than one wife anyway. One LDS writer, Todd Compton, theorized that Joseph Smith took to heart Matthew 22:30, in which Jesus said of people in the resurrection, "they neither marry, nor are given in marriage." Says Compton, "Smith apparently interpreted this to mean that one had to create one's 'extended family,' one's kingdom, by marriage while on earth. Orson Pratt, in a discourse given in 1859, taught this explicitly."[35]

The first man mentioned in the Bible who had more than one wife, Lamech, is remembered for the fact that he was also a murderer (see what two wives can drive you to!). We're all familiar with the contentions between Abraham's wife, Sarah, and his concubine Hagar. In addition, the Bible recounts Jacob's problems with Leah, Rachel, Bilhah, and Zilpah, and the mess that King David's household was always in. Solomon's one thousand foreign wives leeched Israel's money from him to build altars to their heathen idols; and his son Rehoboam (also a polygamist) let pagan worship prevail in the by then divided Israel. In short, far from being a symbol of kingly power, polygamy in the Old Testament usually signaled moral decay.

The revelation commanding polygamy was not announced to the LDS Church as a whole until 1852, eight years after the death of Joseph Smith. It was not until 1876 that it was added to the *Doctrine and Covenants* and assigned the section number 132. Up until that time, though, there was another revelation (numbered 101 in the 1835 edition and 109 in the 1854 edition) which flatly denied that polygamy was practiced among Mormons, stating:

> Inasmuch as this church of Christ has been reproached with the crime of fornication and polygamy; we declare that we believe that one man should have one wife; and one woman but one husband, except in the case of death, when either is at liberty to marry again.[36]

This revelation was dropped from the *Doctrine and Covenants* when the section commanding polygamy was added. Therefore, there existed a forty-five year gap between the receipt of the polygamy revelation and its inclusion in the doctrinal canon. During twenty-one years of that time, too, the Church was denying publicly that they had anything to do with the practice of polygamy.

It is easy to see why many Mormons don't delve too deeply into the history of section 132, and if they do, why they want to avoid the issue altogether. Utah Mormons maintain that Joseph Smith introduced the doctrine of polygamy before his death, which doctrine was brought to fruition under the auspices of his successor, Brigham Young. The average member of the Community of Christ (formerly known as the Reorganized Church) would deny that the Prophet Joseph ever even thought of the doctrine, because he denied it so vehemently before his death. Others, like Isaac Sheen, said that Joseph did indeed preach and practice polygamy, but that he "repented of his connection" with it, claiming that it was of the devil.[37]

Probably Sheen was closest to the truth. By the time he died, Joseph probably wished he'd never mentioned the word *polygamy*. Just when he first formulated the doctrine will probably never be known. But it is obvious that by the time he got around to asking God about it (remember, section 132 is supposed to be God's answer on the matter), he already had multiple wives. In verse 52, God told Emma to "receive all those who *have been given* unto my servant Joseph" (italics mine). Mormons say that a certain number of women were promised, or "given," to Joseph before he actually married them. But history tells us that Joseph was married to at least twelve women before July 12, 1843, the date of the "recording" of section 132.[38]

In addition, Joseph Fielding Smith, a former president of the LDS Church, in his book *Blood Atonement and the Origin of Plural Marriage*, quoted an affidavit which verified that not only did Joseph have plural wives, but that he "cohabited with them as wives."[39] His oldest wife was fifty-six years old, his youngest a child of fourteen years of age.[40] Worst of all was the fact that Joseph Smith married women who were already married to other men: Besides committing adultery himself, he used his power and influence as a supposed prophet to coerce other men's wives to join him in sin and to commit the crime of polyandry.

Joseph Smith claimed that he did not introduce polygamy to God's people, but that he merely restored it. But the Nephites of the *Book of Mormon* are represented as abhorring the idea of plural wives.[41] Early Christians didn't practice it, either. Even if Joseph Smith claimed to be living Old Testament polygamy, he didn't do a very good job of it. An Old Testament polygamist couldn't marry his wife's sister (Lev. 18:18—bear in mind that Abraham, Isaac, and Jacob lived before this law was given). Nor could he have two wives who were mother and daughter (Lev. 20:14). Yet Joseph Smith married five pairs of sisters, as well as a mother and her daughter.[42]

When polygamy was first introduced, many men were appalled when commanded to take an additional wife (or in the case of Heber C. Kimball, commanded to *surrender his own first wife* to Joseph Smith in marriage).[43] Most either accepted the doctrine or left the Church. The doctrine of polygamy had as one virtue its ability to separate believers from unbelievers, and left few fence-sitters in its tumultuous wake.

In fact, some of its adherents actually claimed the practice was vastly superior to monogamous marriage. George Q. Cannon, an early apostle, said that the children of patriarchal (that is, polygamous) marriages were healthier and more vigorous and intelligent than others.[44] Brigham Young put the blame for civilization's problems with prostitution and adultery squarely on the shoulders of monogamy, saying that polygamous societies had no place for such sins.[45] He regarded extra wives as a sort of escape valve for the poor suppressed monogamous man who could not otherwise control his passions.

Some LDS apologists shrug off polygamy by claiming, as I did while I was a Mormon, that less than 3 percent of the Mormon men ever practiced polygamy. But other Mormons have admitted that the real figure might have been well above 10 percent.[46] Non-Mormons have estimated an accurate figure to be as much as 20 percent. A standard LDS explanation of the necessity for polygamy is that there were many more women than men in the early Church and that plural marriage was a good way to absorb the surplus women of the population. I grew up thinking that polygamous men married old or homely women just to give them a home and (if they weren't past childbearing age) a family. But John A. Widtsoe, an LDS writer, affirmed that "there seems always to have been more males than females in the Church."[47] Furthermore, apparently the LDS leadership wanted first choice of incoming female converts brought to Utah.[48]

The "new and everlasting covenant" as practiced by Mormons proved to be far from everlasting: Polygamy as an officially approved and practiced tenet of the Utah LDS Church came to a halt in 1890, when the president of the LDS Church, Wilford Woodruff, issued a document that appears near the end of the *Doctrine and Covenants*, titled "Official Declaration—1." Whereas for thirty years LDS leaders told members they would be cursed by God if they didn't practice polygamy,[49] now Woodruff cited the constitutionality of the 1862 federal laws against polygamy, and said, "I hereby declare my intention to submit to those laws, and to use my influence with the members of the Church over which I preside to have them do likewise."[50]

How could this be? How could an "eternal" principle, essential to salvation, be suddenly revoked? Many Mormons thought Wilford Woodruff had lost his mind or his priesthood authority, and continued living in polygamy. Some went to court for their right to practice the doctrine. Many went to prison. A number took their wives and went "underground," or to Mexico where sanctions against polygamy existed but were rarely enforced. Still others left the Church and tried as best they could to undo the damage done in their lives by polygamy.

Many a polygamous wife claimed that her marriage was never happy after the coming of other wives, even according to Brigham Young.[51] But the situation was even worse for plural wives when polygamy was declared by the Church to be wrong.[52] What did a man do with his other wives, if cohabitation with them was illegal? What of his children by them? Many bitterly blamed the US government for its "cruel" treatment of such marriages. But was it really the fault of the government?

The laws prohibiting polygamy only voiced the views of Christians who, from New Testament teachings, *knew* polygamy to be wrong. If the revelation were as irrevocably true as Brigham Young said it was,[53] and as divine as Apostle Orson Pratt said it was,[54] and as necessary as Apostle George Teasdale said it was,[55] then a person would have to be crazy to abandon it!

This is precisely the view of "Fundamentalist" Mormons who even today live in polygamy, both outside the United States and inside our borders. They had their beginnings when Wilford Woodruff issued the "Manifesto" (as "Official Declaration—1" has traditionally been called). They claim that the "everlasting" covenant of plural marriage is just that, and feel that they would rather face imprisonment and fines from the government than abandon their families and face God after rejecting one of his commandments. They claim, and quite correctly so, that Wilford Woodruff "sold out" to the federal government on the matter of polygamy.

Utah, at the time polygamy was at its apex, desired to become a state of the Union. With this as a lever, the government exerted such financial and legal strictures on the LDS Church that its very being was threatened. Mormon author John J. Stewart wrote that "due to the extremely bitter persecution against the Church because of it [that is, plural marriage], President Wilford Woodruff issued the manifesto … suspending the general practice of it in the Church, while still retaining it as a doctrine."[56] But whatever the persecution, Mormons can't rightfully lay the blame on others, but only on the formulators and advocates of this doctrine. Their deception and willfulness must be seen behind the tears of every abandoned plural wife and her children.

Even after LDS leaders told their people to abandon polygamy, some of those in high positions continued to practice it. For instance, Joseph F. Smith, sixth president of the Church, fathered no less than eleven children by plural wives *after* the issuing of the Manifesto, according to his own sworn testimony before a federal investigating committee.[57] This behavior exemplifies an issue that still burns in the hearts of Mormons who are courageous enough to ask themselves two questions. *If polygamy was eternal, why was its practice rescinded?* Some Mormons will shrug their shoulders and say that what God gives, he can take away; and perhaps he was just testing his people anyway. But it is a cruel God indeed who would set up a family system and then deprive innocent children of their fathers. *If polygamy was not eternal, why was it called such, and why did LDS leaders continue to practice it while repudiating it?*

In the end, most Mormons would like to see polygamy as a dead issue. Throughout most of the end of the twentieth century, the majority of Mormons knew little about it, and cared less. Their attention was very rarely directed to section 132 or to the Manifesto, and except for an occasional "rude" reference to it by a non-Mormon, they didn't care to think about it. However, ignoring the issue is growing increasingly more difficult as television shows such as the series *Big Love* glamorize the practice, or present it as a vicarious "guilty pleasure." Movies, websites and news stories discuss polygamy and identify it most often with its roots within the early Mormon Church. It is also becoming a charged political issue in the twenty-first century. With the increasing societal acceptance of "non-traditional" marriages that include same-sex partners, some observers are pointing to polygamy (including polygyny and polyandry) among consenting adults as the next civil rights battle.[58]

Twenty-first century apologists for the LDS Church evince a painful schizophrenia in speaking about its history of plural marriage. A good example of this is Robert Millet, who points to examples of Mormon women who he says loved polygamy and protested its demise; and yet portrays the practice as a whole as a difficult "burden" under which his people suffered and from which they were finally released by God.[59]

Just how burdensome polygamy—which adherents call "living the Principle"—can be was demonstrated in the 2008 federal raid on the Fundamentalist Church of Jesus Christ of Latter-Day Saints compound in Eldorado, Texas. Women who were terrified of going to hell if they could not live in polygamy refused to identify their own children because of fear of sending their husbands to jail and nullifying their marriages. The result was a nightmare for government officials as well as for the women and children who were taken into custody.

Irene Spencer, author of *Shattered Dreams: My Life as a Polygamist's Wife*, pointed out that based on the teachings of the *Doctrine and Covenants* 132:62, the current mainstream LDS Church could justify—as have the polygamists—the marrying of ten "virgin" girls by middle-aged men. Spencer in a 2008 radio interview recounted her acquaintance with a polygamous Mormon man who married a previously married woman, and then married her two daughters—ages nine and eleven—and fathered children with all three.

PROBLEMS WITHIN THE *DOCTRINE AND COVENANTS*

Section 27 illustrates the confusion in this book when the reader is introduced to the idea of an office of "Elias." (Of course, Bible students know that Elias is just the Greek form of the name Elijah, but Joseph Smith obviously didn't know it—he claimed in section 110, verses 11–13, that he saw both Elias *and* Elijah.) Joseph Smith also showed his ignorance of Bible language in section 4. In verse 5, he lists the qualifications for service in the kingdom as faith, hope, charity, and love. Joseph would have been better off if he had kept his eye single to a Greek-English Bible. Anyone who reads only the King James Version, as do most Mormons, might accept "charity" and "love" as separate concepts, but modern translations recognize that "charity" is the Elizabethan translators' attempt to find an English word that would approximate the "agape" love Paul spoke of in 1 Corinthians 13.

In *Doctrine and Covenants* 95:7, we have another example of just how little Joseph Smith knew about Hebrew. Here he took the liberty of translating a scriptural phrase, "Lord of Sabaoth." He said it was "by interpretation, the creator of the first day, the beginning and the end." It is apparent that he confused this phrase with the one found in Mark 2:28, where Christ spoke of the "Lord also of the sabbath," which does indeed have reference to a day of the week—the seventh, not the first, day. "Sabaoth," in contrast, refers to God's kingly role as commander in chief of the heavenly host, and of all living things. It cannot reasonably be stretched to refer to the creation of the first day.

Joseph Smith also seemed to have a lot of trouble keeping straight the gods who gave him the revelations of the *Doctrine and Covenants*. In section 29:1, for example, the speaker in the revelation says that he is Jesus Christ, and then later in verse 42 speaks as the Father. In section 49 the reverse occurs: The speaker says that he is the Father of Christ in verse 5, but later in verse 28 identifies himself as Christ. Since the Mormons assert that God and Christ are totally separate personages, they don't even have a Trinity doctrine to fall back on here.

One last section, 19, might pass unnoticed by Mormon and critic alike—in the beginning it seems to have little to offer to distinguish it from others like it. Its introduction affirms that it is "A COMMANDMENT OF GOD, and not of man" (just in case anyone would think otherwise), and the first twenty verses pound that idea point by point into the head of Martin Harris, the hapless object of the revelation. Harris is told to repent lest God punish him endlessly, and humble him with almighty power. But here is where the revelation begins to differ from the norm. It tells Martin to pay all the debts incurred in printing the *Book of Mormon*, to liquidate and give to the Church all his lands and property except that needed to support his family, and finally, to not leave house and home except to visit occasionally with his loved ones. He is told that the blessings he will so obtain will be greater than the "corruptible" riches he will give to the Church.

And then Joseph Smith, masquerading as the god of this revelation, grandly asks the soon-to-be homeless and destitute Martin, "Behold, canst thou read this without rejoicing and lifting up thy heart for gladness?" (v. 39).

Chapter 5

THE PERILS OF THE *PEARL*

There is nothing hidden but what shall be brought to light, and nothing secret but what shall be discovered.

—Parley P. Pratt, LDS leader[1]

For a Mormon, the *Pearl of Great Price* is quoted less than other LDS scripture, and has few exciting stories in it to compare with the adventures of Nephi or Alma in the *Book of Mormon*. In ten years of Mormonism I was never asked to read this, the shortest of all books of LDS scripture. When I did read it, it was on my own initiative. Many of its doctrines were so deep or so controversial that they were rarely discussed in public meetings.

It was this book, which I was looking at in the fall of 1973, that rocked my foundations as a Mormon. Its woodcuts—pictures copied from the papyrus scrolls that were supposedly the source of the text of the Book of Abraham—stopped me cold, shocking me into the recognition that Joseph Smith was no translator of Egyptian. It was not until much later, though, that I went back and more thoroughly and objectively examined the *Pearl of Great Price*.

THE CONTENTS OF THE *PEARL OF GREAT PRICE*

It is not easy to talk about the *Pearl of Great Price* as an entity because its contents, even more than those of the *Doctrine and Covenants*, are so divergent. Whereas the *Book of Mormon* purports to be the records of the ancient Americans, and the *Doctrine and Covenants* the revelations given to early LDS church leaders, no such blanket statement of contents will suffice for the *Pearl of Great Price.* This short volume contains various short writings. Briefest of all is a listing of the LDS "Articles of Faith," a creed upon which LDS doctrine is loosely based, formulated by Joseph Smith. The *Pearl of Great Price* also contains other writings of the prophet, including a book called "Joseph Smith—History." This tells of his first vision, the coming forth of the *Book of Mormon*, a visit of John the Baptist, and the rise of the Church. There is also an extract from his Inspired Version of the Bible, a passage from Matthew (called "Joseph Smith—Matthew").

The other two-thirds of the *Pearl of Great Price* are supposed to be from the writings of two Old Testament patriarchs, Abraham and Moses. Abraham's writings purport to provide details of that prophet's life not found in the Bible, as well as information about the preexistence, the council in heaven, and divine principles of astronomy. Moses' writings supposedly clarify the events that led to the creation and humankind's history from Adam to Noah.

This anthology of sorts was first compiled by Franklin D. Richards of the Council of the Twelve. He published it under the title *Pearl of Great Price* in Liverpool, England, in 1851. It underwent various adjustments before being canonized as scripture in 1880. It was revised again in 1902 when all the material incorporated into the 1876 *Doctrine and Covenants* was dropped from its contents so as to avoid duplication.[2] Then too it was divided into chapters and verses with references. In its revised form in 1902 it was accepted as a "standard work," joining the Bible, the *Book of Mormon*, and the *Doctrine and Covenants*. But all in all, this little book has undergone thousands of word changes since its 1851 edition.

THE WRITINGS OF JOSEPH SMITH

One of the most oft-quoted elements of the *Pearl of Great Price* is known as the Articles of Faith. These thirteen doctrinal statements were composed by Joseph Smith after John Wentworth, editor of the *Chicago Democrat*, wrote to Joseph Smith in Nauvoo, asking for a brief statement of the doctrinal beliefs of the Latter-day Saints. They are considered to be scripture. A Christian casually observing the Articles of Faith would find few quarrels there. But as we shall see in later chapters, the distinctively LDS doctrines hinge upon the meanings that Mormons assign to the Christian-type terminology of the Articles of Faith. For instance, such concepts as being "saved" or "punished," and the idea of "authority," are uniquely Mormon as Latter-day Saints interpret these words.

The inclusion in the *Pearl of Great Price* of Joseph Smith's own "inspired" translation of Matthew 23:39 and all of Matthew chapter 24 has raised questions in the minds of Mormons and non-Mormons alike. Joseph Smith considered this passage important, and for years it was the only New Testament part of his Inspired Version to be singled out as scripture by the Utah church. (The "Community of Christ," previously known as the Reorganized LDS Church, of course, has always accepted the whole Inspired Version as scripture.) This brief passage is a mysterious monument to Smith's ability to conglomerate scriptures for his desired effect, and its name, *Joseph Smith—Matthew,* is fitting.

Also included is *Joseph Smith—History,* a short autobiography of his early life and the history of the young Church. Of particular interest is *Joseph Smith—History* 1:14–20, which details the appearance of God and Christ to the boy Joseph. This is the most relied upon passage by which Mormons justify their doctrine that God and Christ possess separate physical bodies.

THE BOOK OF MOSES

These writings of Joseph Smith—the Articles of Faith, the Matthew "translation," and Joseph Smith's early history—make up a little over one-fourth of the *Pearl of Great Price.* The rest of this book deals with what Mormons believe to be the writings of Moses and Abraham. Moses' writings were "revealed" to Joseph Smith in 1830 when he was working on his translation of the Old Testament. This "Book of Moses" is supposedly the unabridged story upon which they believe our "incomplete" Genesis account was based. It was first published in six installments printed at irregular intervals from August 1832 until January 1844. Basically the Book of Moses is a revision of the Genesis account that includes a heavy injection of "Christian-type" doctrines into the old-covenant writings. It teaches:

1. Man can talk to God literally face-to-face (1:1; 7:4) and see him with spiritual eyes (1:11).
2. This record of Moses is not included in our Bible because of the wickedness of men (1:23) and is to be shown only to those who believe (1:42).
3. There are many "earths" that God has created (1:29, 33).
4. Joseph Smith is considered by God to be one "like Moses" (1:41).
5. The speaker, God (Elohim) himself alone created everything but man (2:1–25), but he was helped in man's creation by his Only Begotten (2:26).
6. All living things were first created spiritually before being created physically (3:7).

7. Trees are living souls (3:9); thus, by implication, all living things have souls.
8. Satan was a son of God (5:13), brother to Christ and to all humankind. He rebelled when his plan promising compulsory, universal salvation was rejected by God (4:1–4).
9. Adam received the Holy Ghost (5:9).
10. Adam rejoiced after and as a result of his transgression (5:10–11; versus Gen. 3:10).
11. Cain was cursed because he made a secret pact with Satan for gain (5:29–33; note that priesthood is not mentioned).
12. The first polygamist, Lamech, covenanted with Satan (5:49), and kept not God's command (5:52).
13. The "Gospel" was preached in antediluvian days, and was confirmed by the Holy Ghost (5:58–59).
14. The priesthood is said to have originated with Adam (6:7).
15. Genealogies were kept in Adam's day as they should be kept now (6:8).
16. Christ atoned for original sin (6:54).
17. Adam was given the Comforter (6:61).
18. After receiving the Holy Ghost, Adam was baptized—with water (6:64) and with fire and the Holy Ghost (6:66).
19. Canaanites were cursed with a blackness of skin that caused them to be despised by all people (7:8).
20. Enoch built a city called Zion (7:18–22), which was taken up to heaven with him (7:69).
21. The seed of Cain was a race with black skin (7:22).
22. A purgatorial prison was built for those who perished in the flood (7:38).
23. The earth is female in gender, and has a soul and a voice (7:48).
24. An actual thousand-year millennial reign by Christ upon this earth is promised (7:65).
25. Noah taught repentance and baptism for the gift of the Holy Ghost (8:24).
26. Noah, not God, was sorry that man had been created (8:25–26; versus Gen. 6:6–7).

It is interesting to know that this section of the *Pearl of Great Price* has undergone 1,195 word changes since first being published in 1851. How this can be justified is beyond my understanding, in view of the fact that

Mormons claim Joseph Smith received this by direct revelation from God. I can see the LDS point of view when they say that God can give modern-day revelations to individuals, which need to be revised or revoked as situations change. (I can see it, though I don't agree with it.) I *cannot* see why their deity could not accurately relay to Joseph Smith the contents of a record supposedly written by Moses thousands of years ago.

HISTORY OF THE BOOK OF ABRAHAM

Since the original record does not exist, we cannot check Joseph Smith's version of the Book of Moses except against the Genesis account. But the remainder of the *Pearl of Great Price*, the Book of Abraham, *can* be checked, for the original records are available today. The LDS Church possesses several papyrus fragments, from one of which the Book of Abraham was *translated* by Joseph Smith, according to the prefatory passage in the *Pearl of Great Price*: "A Translation of some ancient Records, that have fallen into our hands from the catacombs of Egypt.—The writings of Abraham while he was in Egypt, called the Book of Abraham, written by his own hand, upon papyrus."

Here is another tribute to the resourcefulness of Joseph Smith, who could use anything that came his way to further his own purposes. Early in his life Joseph found a smooth rock that became a "seer stone." Later he used a workman's carving on one of his temples to show what the face of God looked like—except, he observed, the nose was just a *little* too broad. And when a man traveled to him with mummies and papyrus, Joseph couldn't resist building some of his most fantastic doctrines around the history and contents of those scrolls.

To understand the situation in which Joseph Smith thus found himself, we must consider the end of the eighteenth century—the era of Napoleon's visits to Egypt. Everyone in those days knew something about Egyptian art and mummies, but its mysterious ancient hieroglyphic language was a locked door. Then, just six years before the unheralded birth of one Joseph Smith in Vermont in 1805, an equally unappreciated stone was discovered. But when someone noticed that this two-thousand-year-old black rock contained three passages in three different languages—Greek, hieroglyphics, and demotic (a simplified hieroglyphic writing)—then the Rosetta Stone, as it was named, began to receive the notice it deserved.

During the time that Joseph Smith was supposedly receiving the first vision, a young man named Jean Francois Champollion theorized that if the names in all three passages on the Rosetta Stone were equivalent, then the other information probably was. The Greek could be used to decipher the Egyptian, Champollion rightly concluded. In America, Joseph Smith began writing the *Book of Mormon*. At the same time as the organization and early years of the LDS Church, many scholars pored over the Rosetta Stone, painstakingly wresting from this basalt slab the possibility of reading all the silent writings on the walls of tombs and temples.

In the same year, 1832, that Brigham Young became a Mormon, Champollion died, and it wasn't until after his death that the scholarly world truly capitalized on his groundbreaking work. In 1837 the Herculean task of assembling the first ancient Egyptian dictionary was completed. No one had ever supposed that such a thing could be done—least of all, Joseph Smith.

In June of 1835 a frustrated young man by the name of Michael H. Chandler sought out the famed LDS prophet. Chandler had acquired eleven Egyptian mummies. His disappointment at finding that the bodies carried no jewels was barely compensated for by the fact that there was a papyrus roll on the breast of one of the mummies, and a few scraps of papyrus on the others. Chandler had earned a little money traveling around the country exhibiting the curiosities. When he met Benjamin Bullock III, a relative of Joseph Smith's friend Heber C. Kimball, he was told that the "Mormon prophet" could translate anything. As soon as Joseph laid eyes upon the papyrus fragments that Chandler had had examined by other "experts," the Mormon sage asked to be excused, and retired into his "translating room." When he returned a short while later, he carried a written translation in English of the fragment's writing. What the "translation" said, we may never know, but it so impressed Chandler that he presented Joseph with a certificate stating:

> Kirtland, July 6, 1835
>
> This is to make known to all who may be desirous, concerning the knowledge of Mr. Joseph Smith, Jun., in deciphering the ancient Egyptian hieroglyphic characters in my possession, which I have, in many eminent cities, showed to the most learned; and from the information that I could ever learn, or meet with, I find that of Mr. Joseph Smith, Jun., to correspond in the most minute matters.
>
> —(signed) Michael H. Chandler
> Traveling with, and proprietor of, Egyptian mummies[3]

Soon afterwards, Joseph Smith offered to buy the papyri, but Chandler refused to sell them without their owners, the mummies. The sale was consummated to the tune of $2,400. Joseph identified one of the mummies as King Necho,[4] and another time he said one of the mummies was that of a king's daughter. But the mummies were of only peripheral interest to Joseph Smith—the scrolls were what fascinated him. He said that one scroll had on it the "autograph of Moses" and additional writings by his brother Aaron.[5] (Unfortunately we do not have Joseph Smith's "translation" of this latter record.)

There is no question that Joseph Smith claimed that he could translate ancient languages. "I can read all writing," he once boasted.[6] Another time he claimed when discussing his idiosyncratic translation of the Hebrew in Genesis 1:1 (which he said told of a council of gods), "But I am learned, and know more than all the world put together."[7]

Nor do we have the translation of what Joseph Smith in his journal called "the writings of Joseph of Egypt." Joseph Smith, speaking as Nephi in the *Book of Mormon*, mentioned the prophecies of Joseph of Egypt, or the Joseph of the Bible (2 Nephi 4:2). Though some LDS authorities say that Joseph Smith *did* translate the Chandler papyri (as writings Smith attributed to Joseph of Egypt),[8] the translation has never been published, supposedly because its prophecies were " 'too great' for the people of this day."[9]

However, there is proof that Joseph Smith did indeed translate and publish a portion of the scrolls he bought from Chandler. Joseph said that one portion of the papyrus was written in the handwriting of Abraham himself—which made it much older than the Bible account of Genesis which was recorded long after the fact by Moses. Dr. Sidney Sperry, an LDS authority, has even gone so far as to say that the Book of Abraham (like the Book of Moses) was an original document upon which Genesis was based.[10]

The translation was completed in 1842 and published in the Nauvoo, Illinois, *Times and Seasons* between March 1 and May 16, 1842. Joseph Smith oversaw the printing and commissioned a young woodcarver, Reuben Hedlock, to reproduce sections of the scrolls' illustrations for printing to accompany the translations.

Joseph Smith promised further extracts from the Book of Abraham (indicating that what he had published hardly covered the entire document), but was killed in the Carthage jail before doing so. After his death, Joseph's mother, Lucy Mack Smith, took over the scrolls and mummies, exhibiting them to curious visitors who were fascinated by her colorful descriptions of them. Until her death in 1855, Lucy lived with Joseph's widow, Emma, and her second husband, Charles Bidamon. One year later Emma and her son Joseph III sold the Egyptian artifacts to a Mr. A. Combs. The sales receipt of this transaction is still in existence. Evidently some of these artifacts were given to Combs's housekeeper. By 1859 at least part of the scrolls and mummies had been loaned or donated to the St. Louis Museum. In 1863 they were on catalog in the Chicago Museum. It was long assumed that the entire collection burned in the Great Chicago Fire of 1871 that destroyed a great deal of the Chicago Museum.

DOCTRINES OF THE BOOK OF ABRAHAM

That part of the *Pearl of Great Price* which is known as the Book of Abraham was translated from these scrolls, and is the basis for many unique doctrines of Mormonism. If we were to scan it we would find it teaching that:

1. The LDS priesthood was first held by Adam and passed down to Abraham, the writer of this record (1:3).
2. Pharaoh's wicked priest tried to sacrifice Abraham (1:6–15).
3. The land of Egypt was settled by the descendants of Ham (1:23–24).
4. Pharaoh did not hold the priesthood because he was "cursed ... as pertaining to the priesthood" (1:26–27).
5. The priesthood was promised to Abraham's seed (2:9).
6. The "gospel" was preached in Abraham's time (2:10).
7. God commanded Abraham to lie about Sarah's marital relationship to him (2:22–25).
8. Abraham possessed the Urim and Thummim (3:1).
9. The star named Kolob is near to God's throne (3:2–3).
10. Since Kolob revolves once in each one thousand years, one of its days is equal to one thousand of our years in God's perspective (3:4).
11. All spirits are eternal and incapable of being created (3:18–19).
12. Certain persons were forechosen by God, before the world was formed, to be his rulers (3:23–24).
13. Satan rebelled when he was not chosen to accomplish God's aims (3:27–28).
14. "The Gods" organized and formed the heavens and the earth (4:1), as well as collectively carrying out the entire creation process as outlined in Genesis 1 and 2.
15. When the Gods decreed that Adam would die the same day that he ate of the forbidden fruit, they were speaking of the one-thousand-year days of God (5:13).

The record of Abraham was by Smith's own admission incomplete. LDS leaders have theorized that on the basis of some of the Book of Abraham's illustrations, subsequent translation would have told about Abraham's further adventures in Egypt.

THE BOOK OF ABRAHAM UNDER FIRE

While most Mormons of the last half of the nineteenth century and the first half of the twentieth century speculated on what Joseph Smith would have written if he had lived longer, the experts of the Egyptian language scoffed at Joseph's translating abilities. The certificate that Mr. Chandler had given Joseph attesting to his abilities as a translator of ancient Egyptian was worthless because neither Chandler nor the other men he had consulted (like Dr. Anthon, who refused to certify Smith's translations of "reformed Egyptian") could read enough ancient Egyptian to certify *anyone's* translations.

The first proofs of the fraudulent nature of the Book of Abraham began in 1860 when Louvre expert M. Theodule Deveria examined the facsimiles which were printed in the *Pearl of Great Price.* Since Joseph Smith had claimed to translate several names and some of the information on the scrolls from which the woodcuts were copied, Deveria was able to make his own translations and then compare them to those of Joseph Smith. Though hindered in several places by the poor quality of the woodcut reproductions and by untranslatable sections, Deveria was nonetheless able to ascertain categorically that not only were Joseph Smith's translations incorrect, but also that Joseph Smith had apparently altered the original documents themselves. Of course Deveria based his opinions on the facsimiles printed in the *Pearl of Great Price*, but these were also the facsimiles Joseph Smith presented as part of the Word of God.

The flame of controversy was fanned again in 1912 when Franklin S. Spaulding, the Episcopal bishop of Utah, published a book called *Joseph Smith Jr. as a Translator.* In researching his book, Spaulding approached several of the most eminent authorities of the science of Egyptology and asked them their opinions of the woodcuts of the *Pearl of Great Price* and Joseph Smith's interpretations of those woodcuts. The list of experts consulted by Spaulding reads like an honor roll of the best Egyptologists, and included Drs. W. M. Flinders Petrie and James H. Breasted. Every expert had the same thing to say: Joseph Smith had no idea of even the basics of translating ancient Egyptian. A sampling of their comments on Joseph's translations: "an impudent fraud," "pure fabrication," "the work of pure imagination."

The LDS Church was stunned by this publication, and lost no time in coming out with a reply to it. They chose a man to write their "answer" who worked as a professional writer and who at one time in his career wrote a book defending the liquor industry. This man, J. C. Homans, wrote under the pen name of Robert C. Webb, and gave himself the title of PhD—an honor never bestowed upon him by any university. His book was a confusing mass of circumlocution that alternated between generalizations about the culture of ancient Egypt and attacks on the credentials of the experts quoted by Spaulding.

In 1965, Modern Microfilm Company (now known as Utah Lighthouse Ministry or UTLM) operated by Jerald and Sandra Tanner of Salt Lake City, reprinted Spaulding's work,[11] which was by then out of print. This reprinting could have caused as big a stir as its first, but an event of much greater importance intervened.

ATIYA'S "DISCOVERY" OF THE SCROLLS

A professor of Middle Eastern studies at the University of Utah was visiting the New York Metropolitan Museum in the early spring of 1966, doing research for a book he was writing about Eastern Christianity. This man, Dr. Aziz S. Atiya, an Egyptian by birth and Coptic by faith, worked at a university in the middle of Mormon country, and thus was familiar with Latter-day Saint doctrine and scriptures. As he was looking through a large box of Egyptian documents brought to him by a museum attendant, one particular piece of papyrus attracted his attention. Upon closer examination, he saw that the papyrus, which had some parts missing, had been glued onto a piece of more modern paper, and the missing parts drawn in pencil onto the newer paper. Whoever had drawn in the missing sections had done so in a very peculiar manner—and the completed vignette looked just like Facsimile 1 in the LDS *Pearl of Great Price.* Atiya's suspicions were confirmed when he found ten more pieces of papyrus along with the bill of sale signed by Emma Smith Bidamon and her son Joseph Smith III in a storage file.

The history of the scrolls soon came to light. Apparently the Mr. Combs who bought the scrolls from Emma had given them to his housekeeper. The housekeeper's son-in-law sold the scrolls to the New York museum in 1947. There they had been ever since, with the full knowledge of the museum officials. It is not therefore strictly accurate to say that Atiya "discovered" the scrolls, since the museum knew of their whereabouts and significance for almost twenty years. Nor could it be said that Atiya was the first to tell members of the LDS Church of the scrolls' location. One Mormon later coauthored a book, *From the Dust of Decades*, about the "discovery" of the papyri. This man, Walter Whipple, said he himself knew of the location of the papyri and actually had photographs of them back in 1962. There is also evidence that the LDS Church actually leaked to Atiya the existence and location of the scrolls.[12]

I am not implying that Dr. Atiya cooperated with the LDS Church in faking the find. But one must wonder why the Metropolitan Museum did not notify the Mormons about it earlier. (An official of the museum said tactfully, "Frankly, we didn't know what the LDS Church's wishes were.")[13] It wasn't because the papyri weren't genuine. Atiya and other qualified experts have not argued with the fact that the scrolls are uncontested examples of ancient Egyptian papyri. When Atiya found the scrolls and notified the LDS Church, they expressed great appreciation. The New York Metropolitan Museum, realizing the importance of the scrolls to the Mormons, presented them to LDS officials in a formal ceremony on November 27, 1967. But the LDS Church, I am sure, wishes it had never seen those scrolls again.

Why? Because in 1967, the Egyptian language was no longer the barrier it was in Joseph Smith's day. Today a competent Egyptologist can read the *Pearl of Great Price* papyri (formally known as "Joseph Smith Papyri I through XI") and accurately tell you the one thing that Mormons don't want to hear: The papyri say absolutely *nothing* about Abraham, or Joseph, or God, or anything even remotely related to Mormonism.

TRANSLATING THE SCROLLS

As soon as the news of the scrolls came to light, some Mormons began to rejoice that here, finally, could Joseph Smith be vindicated as a translator. But the Church warned members that, pending a new translation by an LDS Egyptologist, no one should depend upon the scrolls to "prove" Joseph Smith's abilities as a translator. Hugh Nibley, the LDS Church's go-to expert on ancient history, had no comforting words. "LDS scholars are caught flat-footed by this discovery," he confessed in Brigham Young University's newspaper.[14] Many Mormons felt confident that the president of the Church, the "prophet, seer, and revelator," would be able to translate the papyri.[15] These were surprised when the documents were given to Hugh Nibley, who kept them for a long time and only translated *one* word from them—and that incorrectly.[16]

Nibley began writing a series of articles for the Church's periodical, *The Improvement Era*, which stretched over a two-year period from January 1968 until May 1970. He used over two thousand footnotes and quoted from such sources as old rabbinical writings to try to find parallels between ancient Egyptian culture and that portrayed in Joseph Smith's translation of the Book of Abraham. Even though at the time I was very interested in the whole issue, Nibley's ponderous display of unrelated facts was impenetrable.[17] I decided that the whole matter was too deep for anyone without a doctorate in ancient languages. In retrospect, that was probably the express purpose of Nibley's writings, for I know that he was more capable of coming to the point than he showed himself there. Once waist-deep in his circumlocution, I, like most other Mormons, forgot to ask the cogent question of the whole issue: What do the papyri *say*?

WERE THESE THE JOSEPH SMITH PAPYRI?

All subsequent research by qualified Egyptologists outside the LDS Church has shown that those eleven papyrus fragments made up the following elements:

1. Part of a "Book of the Dead"—an ancient funerary text—for a deceased woman by the name of Ta-Shere-Min.
2. An illustration of a judgment scene from another "Book of the Dead" made for a female musician named Amon-Re Neferinub.
3. A "Book of Breathings" (a late Ptolemaic Period version of the "Book of the Dead"), also called "Sen Sen" because of the repetition of this word throughout the text—made for a deceased man named Hor.

Of course, some LDS who heard of the undeniably pagan nature of the texts of the papyri thought that perhaps a mistake had been made; perhaps these weren't the same papyri once owned by Joseph Smith. With some of the papyri there was no question—Reuben Hedlock had copied their illustrations—even preserving the ancient Egyptian scribe's misspellings intact in the *Pearl of Great Price* woodcuts. (The LDS Church agreed from the beginning that the papyri were the source of at least one of the *Pearl of Great Price* woodcuts.) Part of the Metropolitan Museum papyri hadn't been used as a basis for the woodcuts, it is true, but they fit exactly the descriptions given by contemporaries of Joseph Smith who had seen and described the scrolls. The Reverend Henry Caswell, for instance, visited Nauvoo and was shown the papyri by Joseph Smith.[18]

A recent book by LDS apologist Robert L. Millet, *Getting at the Truth: Responding to Difficult Questions about LDS Beliefs*, however, refutes these claims by quoting the late H. Donl Peterson, professor of ancient scriptures at BYU, who said, "The Book of Abraham and Joseph papyri were described as 'Beautifully written on papyrus, with black, and a small part red, ink or paint, in perfect preservation.'" Peterson claimed there was no red ink on these papyri, and therefore concluded that the Metropolitan Museum fragments only comprised Facsimile 1 and "some other fragments unrelated to the published account of the present Book of Abraham." Thus, said Peterson, dodging the whole controversy, the papyri now owned by the LDS Church could not be the source of their scriptures.[19] Two problems exist with this explanation. First, photographs do show red ink.[20] Second, we *do have* the Egyptian translations of the identifications of people in the woodcut pictures (again, the LDS Church doesn't deny that the papyri now in their hands is the source)—translations which Joseph Smith undeniably botched. Researchers have also noted that some of the papyri fragments are glued to heavy paper with handwritten references linking them to Joseph Smith.[21]

In addition, Joseph Smith and/or a scribe copied hieroglyphs from the scroll into three handwritten notebooks. These notebooks lie at the crux of the whole LDS dilemma of the relationship between the papyri and the Book of Abraham. These notebooks show, beyond any doubt, that Joseph Smith went through the motions of a deciphering process so that his people would think that he had actually translated the hieratic characters.

Joseph Smith began these notebooks, which are referred to by Mormons as "The Kirtland Egyptian Papers" or by their more descriptive title "The Egyptian Alphabet and Grammar," in the year 1835. They are now in the possession of the LDS Church.[22]

"The Egyptian Alphabet and Grammar" consists of sheets divided into columns. They contain characters copied by Joseph Smith or a scribe from the small Sen Sen papyrus, Smith's pronunciations of the characters, and their "translations" with Smith's commentary. One section of the "Egyptian Alphabet and Grammar" shows Book of Abraham 1:4–28 "translated" using this method. A great number of English words were assigned to each Egyptian symbol, which LDS apologists say implied that each hieratic character could be broken down into individual strokes (just as the English letter "A" could be broken down into three strokes). Each stroke was assigned a weird-sounding name and a meaning.

Some Mormons, including Hugh Nibley, have said that the Grammar is just an illustration of how Joseph Smith liked to play around with other languages for his own amusement, citing as evidence the fact that Joseph Smith never publicized the "Egyptian Alphabet and Grammar," but rather kept it to himself.[23] But in considering this explanation, it must be remembered that Joseph Smith didn't think he would ever be found out. Though Champollion at that time was finally getting recognition for his decipherment of hieroglyphics (unfortunately posthumous recognition), the science of Egyptian translation was still relatively unknown. Certainly Joseph Smith had no access to a complete ancient Egyptian dictionary, so he made up his own. The fact that he did not publish it doesn't matter as much as the fact that he went to all the trouble to formulate it at the very time he said he was "translating" the papyri.

PROBLEMS WITH THE PAPYRI

Some Mormons have zealously maintained the veracity of Joseph Smith's bizarre translating methods by means of several complex arguments. Many feel forced to defend his translations because the introduction to the Book of Abraham as printed in the *Pearl of Great Price* does, after all, state that the scripture was "translated from the Papyrus, by Joseph Smith." Also, Joseph Smith actually quoted some of his made-up Egyptian in public.[24] In attempting to clear up this confusion, some Mormons have evolved complicated systems whereby they claim that Joseph Smith used deeper, second-level or third-level meanings of the Egyptian words to find the story of Abraham hidden in the pagan "Book of Breathings." Some claim that the funerary text was a memory-jogging device to help a reader remember the elements of the Abraham story, which one critic compared to memorizing the book of Jonah by tying it to the French national anthem.[25]

In addition to the problem of the papyri not saying what Joseph Smith said they did, there is the additional dilemma of the age of the papyrus which Joseph Smith used. The Sen Sen was a type of funerary text which was not even in use until the seventh century BC.[26] Other experts have dated the particular Shaiten Sen Sen used by Joseph Smith for the Book of Abraham to the Ptolemaic Period of Egypt—after 332 BC. The papyri were supposedly the source of "the Book of Abraham, written by his own hand, upon papyrus"[27] and added to by the Bible's Joseph, Moses, and Aaron.

Even Mormons must now admit, though, that the scrolls do not date from the time of Abraham at all but perhaps nearer to the time of Christ. Mormons generally offer this explanation: Joseph Smith's boast to an observer that the scrolls contained the "signature of the patriarch Abraham"[28] was not accurate, they say—what he meant was that the scroll he had in his possession contained a copy of Abraham's signature. They say that Abraham did indeed write the original papyrus manuscript, but it was passed down and altered by individuals who did not understand it, until it was finally buried with a princess who may or may not have realized its significance. This won't square with Smith's description of the "writings of Abraham" which, remember, he specifically said were "written by his own hand upon papyrus."[29]

TRANSLATIONS OF THE PAPYRI

From the symbols on this papyrus, Joseph Smith fashioned 5,470 words of the text of the Book of Abraham. It seems strange that he could have given Mr. Chandler an immediate "while you wait" translation, but had to go to all the trouble in a busy time of his life to formulate an Egyptian grammar. In fact, Joseph Smith rendered one single symbol[30] (which in Egyptian is *Khon*, the moon god) into the following passage:

> And his voice was unto me: Abraham, Abraham, behold, my name is Jehovah, and I have heard thee, and have come down to deliver thee, and to take thee away from thy father's house, and from all thy kinsfolk, into a strange land which thou knowest not of; And this because they have turned their hearts away from me, to worship the god of Elkenah, and the god of Libnah, and the god of Mahmackrah, and the god of Korash, and the god of Pharaoh, king of Egypt; therefore I have come to visit them, and to destroy him who hath lifted up his hand against thee, Abraham, my son, to take away thy life. Behold, I will lead thee by my hand, and I will take thee, to put upon thee my name, even the Priesthood of thy father, and my power shall be over thee.
>
> As it was with Noah so shall it be with thee; but through thy ministry my name shall be known in the earth forever, for I am thy God. (*Pearl of Great Price*, Abraham 1:16–19)

How Joseph Smith could get all this—with the proper names of Abraham, Jehovah, Elkenah, Libnah, Mahmackrah, Korash, Pharaoh, Egypt, Priesthood, and Noah—out of a one-syllable word is hard to understand. At another point he "translated" the sixty-one words of Abraham 1:11 from the Egyptian symbol meaning "the" or "this,"[31] and Mormons have been elated that this passage contains both words.

"All of the first two rows of characters on the papyrus fragment can be found in the manuscript of the 'Book of Abraham' that is published in Joseph Smith's Egyptian Alphabet and Grammar," noted Jerald and Sandra Tanner. "A careful examination of this manuscript reveals that Joseph Smith used less than four lines from the papyrus to make forty-nine verses in the 'Book of Abraham.' These forty-nine verses are composed of more than 2,000 English words!"[32] The forty-six symbols used by Joseph Smith in a 1,125-word passage from the "Egyptian Alphabet and Grammar" wouldn't even cover the vocables/phonetic entities in the proper names in the passage under investigation, and would have left an additional 1,060 words unaccounted for.

Thus Joseph Smith could not have "translated" the Book of Abraham from the small Sen Sen papyrus, at least not by any process that could properly be called translating. But this just leads Mormons to further speculations—that the Book of Abraham was translated with the Urim and Thummim (in spite of what Joseph Fielding Smith said about that instrument having been returned to the Angel Moroni along with the gold plates[33])—or that the Book of Abraham was translated by means of a seer stone which the Church possesses even today—or that Joseph Smith was simply "inspired" to bring forth the Book of Abraham using the papyri in a manner we cannot understand. (I'm not sure I can understand any of the proposed methods.)

This uncertainty led to caution in some LDS publications. Many Mormons refuse to use the word *translation* in referring to the Book of Abraham anymore. They refer to the Sen Sen as "an aid to inspiration" and some speak of the symbols thereon as "super-cryptograms,"[34] claiming that if Christians can get a spiritual meaning out of the Song of Solomon, then the same should be true of the "Book of the Dead." But Joseph Smith stated that the Book of Abraham was *translated* from the writings of Abraham himself, on the papyrus purchased from Chandler.

What does the small Sen Sen really say? According to an Egyptologist, it reads:

> Osiris shall be conveyed into the Great Pool of Khons—and likewise Osiris Hor, justified, born to Tikhebyt, justified—after his arms have been placed on his heart and the Breathing Permit (which [Isis] made and has writing on its inside and outside) has been wrapped in royal linen and placed under his left arm near his heart; the rest of his mummy-bandages should be wrapped over it. The man for whom this book has been copied will breathe forever and ever as the bas of the gods do.[35]

THE FACSIMILES

The translation done by Joseph Smith must be considered to be printed exactly as he wrote it, because he was the editor of the *Times and Seasons* when the Book of Abraham was printed therein. The woodcuts which were illustrations of some of the pictures on the scrolls must have met with his approval too, for we read in *History of the Church* that Joseph inspected and corrected the work done by the woodcarver Hedlock.[36]

Even LDS scholars, though, admit the quality of the woodcut illustrations has worsened with each printing of the *Pearl of Great Price.* But it is not hard for me to understand why the LDS Church does not publish new editions of the *Pearl of Great Price* with photographs of the papyri illustrations upon which the woodcuts were based. The reason is that the papyri betray even worse than the woodcuts the fact that Joseph Smith was completely unfamiliar with the things the papyri depicted. One LDS apologist, Nephi Jensen, tried in the early 1940s to prove that Joseph Smith had been able to interpret some of the symbols on the facsimiles. But usually the nearest that Joseph Smith could get to a true interpretation of the illustrations was when he labeled a great percentage of the elements as "gods." By the law of averages and considering the fact that papyri depicted obviously fantastic beings, he was right at least part of the time.

There are three facsimiles printed in the *Pearl of Great Price.* The first one was identified by Joseph Smith as a representation of an attempt by a wicked Egyptian priest to sacrifice Abraham on an altar. The only things in the woodcut which look strange—that is, uniquely un-Egyptian—do not appear on the original papyrus. For instance, part of the papyrus where the jackal head of the god of embalming, Anubis, once appeared had flaked away, even in Joseph Smith's day. Some nineteenth-century person, probably Joseph Smith, simply glued the papyrus to a piece of paper and penciled in a new head—that of a human—and labeled it "the idolatrous priest of Elkenah." He also drew a knife into the "priest's" hand to reinforce his assertion that this was a sacrificial scene. Joseph Smith called the representation of the dead man's "ba" or soul, which hovered over his body, the Angel of the Lord—which blows all kinds of holes in the LDS argument that angels don't have wings.

Facsimile 2 is a poor copy of what Egyptologists would call a hypocephalus. This was a disc placed under the head of a mummy. Unfortunately, the original hypocephalus was not in the collection found in the New York Metropolitan Museum, and its whereabouts are unknown. There are enough extant copies of authentic hypocephali, though, to ascertain what one should look like. Egyptologists were puzzled for many years when they tried to determine the translation of the inscription written around the rim of Joseph Smith's copy of his hypocephalus. Then in the late 1960s researcher Grant Heward discovered that some of the hieroglyphic writing had been replaced by a few lines copied from the Hor Sen Sen fragment. This was evidently done by someone who couldn't read Egyptian—which makes Joseph Smith a prime suspect!—because the hieratic (cursive) Sen Sen characters were sketched in upside down, complete with the spelling errors of the scribe who wrote the Sen Sen.[37]

On the inside portion of the hypocephalus, another missing portion was filled in with a boat containing the hawk-headed god Ra. This god was apparently copied from the papyrus fragment commonly known as the "Trinity" fragment because of the three-headed god represented on it. In addition, Joseph Smith identified a pagan god with an obviously erect phallus as "God upon his throne." This is the way it was depicted when first printed in 1842, but by the time I was a Mormon the official depiction of this god had no phallus. It reappeared when the LDS Church printed the *Pearl of Great Price* in its 1979 and later editions.

An additional problem associated with Joseph Smith's identification of a hypocephalus with Abraham is the fact that no such thing existed until late in Egypt's history—at least a thousand years after Abraham. Some Mormons have concluded that Abraham began the hypocephalus drawings, and that later scribes completed them and put them into the form of a hypocephalus. This is stretching the whole issue far too much for comfort.

Facsimile 3 has also been a great problem for Mormons, because the figures that Joseph Smith labeled as (1) Pharaoh; (2) Abraham; (3) a prince; (4) Shulem, a waiter; and (5) a slave have their real names written above them on the papyrus. They are accurately identified as (1) the goddess Isis; (2) the god of the dead, Osiris; (3) the goddess of truth, Maat; (4) a dead man named Hor for whom the scroll was written (obviously the focal point of the whole picture, for all the others are looking at him); and (5) the god Anubis (part of whose head was missing in the original papyrus). This was the facsimile which so disturbed me when I realized that Joseph Smith had identified the two women as men. Critics of Mormonism have also noted that Abraham 1:27 states that Pharaoh was a descendant of Ham (and thus a Negro), yet the figure that Joseph Smith labeled as Pharaoh is white.

BLACKS, THE PRIESTHOOD, AND THE PAPYRI

The whole issue of denying Mormon priesthood to blacks came from this Egyptian "Book of Breathings." Even the verse in the Book of Abraham (1:26), which talked of blacks and the priesthood, came from a *hole in the papyrus*. But in stubbornly defending this impious fraud, the LDS Church for over a hundred years gave blacks a second-class status in their organization.

The *Book of Mormon* was first published in 1830, and in it 2 Nephi 26:33 teaches racial equality. How did the LDS Church make such a complete turnabout in doctrine to arrive at its racist policies that began in the mid-nineteenth century? Wallace Turner, in trying to analyze the developments concerning the anti-Negro policies, noted that the early Mormons were mainly from New England, New York, and Ohio—all abolitionist areas. But when the Mormons moved to Missouri, a slave state, problems began to erupt between them and Missourians, who thought the Mormons wanted free blacks to immigrate to their state. The Missourians got this impression from an imprudently worded editorial printed in the LDS periodical *Evening and Morning Star*, July 1833. Mormons overreacted in trying to remove that impression, and by 1836 the LDS publication *Messenger and Advocate* was saying it was fine to free slaves after purchasing them from their owners—just so you put the freed blacks on another continent.[38]

PAST POLICIES OF THE CHURCH CONCERNING BLACKS

Negroes were defined by Brigham Young as those having a "flat nose and black skin."[39] He enlarged upon this by making a statement which haunted and frustrated Mormons for over a century. He said that no man with even a single drop of Negroid blood in his veins could hold the LDS priesthood.[40]

Of course LDS leaders when I was a Mormon were not willing to bear the entire burden of answering those who would want to know why they denied the priesthood to blacks. After all, even the "prophet" David O. McKay once commented that the whole issue was based upon only the one verse in the Book of Abraham. With such a thin foundation for such a controversial issue of doctrine, Mormons such as Apostle Mark E. Petersen looked to God to show that he is the great Segregator, "for did he not place the first blacks way over there in darkest Africa?"[41]

In Brigham Young's day, anyone of the "chosen seed" who was found mixing his blood with "the seed of Cain" would be subject to an immediate death penalty. Brigham intended this as an eternal principle, for he actually stated that this "law of God" would "always be so."[42]

The LDS historian, B. H. Roberts, said that Cain, because he murdered his brother, was cursed with black skin. His Negro blood was passed down and preserved during the flood through Egyptus, the black wife of Ham.[43] The question might arise as to why God would allow such a cursed race to continue through the flood. Brigham Young taught that Cain recognized that if he killed his brother Abel, all his own posterity would be cursed, but he, and the preexistent spirits who would become his descendants, agreed to share the burden together.[44] (Such premeditation is uncharacteristic of the Cain I read of in Genesis!) LDS President John Taylor said in the *Journal of Discourses* that it was necessary for the posterity of Cain to continue through the flood so that the devil could be represented on the earth through them, and through their influence help provide the "opposition" Mormons believe is so necessary.[45]

According to the *Pearl of Great Price*, Ham and the Negress Egyptus had a daughter whom they also named Egyptus. Her son, Pharaoh, was the first ruler of the land of Egypt, which his mother had discovered. Pharaoh, being of the blood of Egyptus and Ham, was "cursed ... as pertaining to the priesthood" (Abraham 1:26; see also v. 27). Here, then, is the entire scriptural basis[46] upon which Mormons built the anti-Negro teachings they held for so long. You can look through the *Doctrine and Covenants* and the *Book of Mormon* and never find anything else to substantiate this view—and of course, the Bible teaches that the gospel—in its fullness—is for all people with no regard for their race (Gal. 3:28).

As early as 1843 Joseph Smith was advocating "national equalization" for blacks while restricting them by law to marry only those of their own race.[47] Brigham Young went even further with his rabid abhorrence of black-white relations, insisting that Negroes, because of their supposed inherent stupidity, were *meant* to serve whites. He stated: "The Canaanite cannot have wisdom to do things as the white man has."[48] The *Juvenile Instructor*, an LDS publication, spoke of the Negro's intelligence as being "stunted."[49] A president of the LDS Church when I was a member, Joseph Fielding Smith, once spoke of Negroes as being "an inferior race."[50] Smith later tried to soften his hard public stand against Negroes with his remark in *Look* magazine that "'darkies' are wonderful people, and they have their place in our church."[51]

What Joseph Fielding Smith objected so much to, and why he was so adamantly opposed to Negroes, was the thought of white Mormons marrying blacks—Mormon or not. LDS apostle Mark E. Petersen went so far as to say in 1954 that Negroes had as a primary objective in life the mingling of their race with whites through intermarriage.[52]

Again, Mormons were not willing to bear the responsibility for their racial views alone. Whereas they blamed earthly segregation of Negroes on the God who placed Negroes in Africa, they blamed the Negroes themselves for their years without the LDS priesthood. According to Alvin R. Dyer and many other LDS authorities, Negroes before 1978 did not have the priesthood because they themselves *rejected* it in the preexistence. In the time before the world was created, Negroes were: "not faithful,"[53] "less valiant,"[54] "indifferent in their support of the righteous cause,"[55] and "less worthy,"[56] according to LDS teachings of the past.

All these remarks have to do with the old LDS teachings that when Christ and Satan squared off in the preexistence, one-third of the spirits there went with Satan (and were cast down to earth); and of the remainder, some sided enthusiastically with Christ, and the rest just kind of dragged along with the Savior. For this lack of devotion, these last spirits were sent to earth in black bodies that would be a sign to priesthood holders that they should not pass on their priesthood to these sluggish spirits. Negroes could be baptized but could not hold the priesthood.

Now, the implications of being a black LDS man were these: Unlike your white counterparts, you were barred from receiving any vital inspiration for anyone except your wife and children, since you could hold no priesthood authority over anyone else. Your wife and children were yours for life only, because you couldn't be married "for eternity" in an LDS temple. Without such higher ordinances, you had no hope of being exalted in the celestial kingdom as your white brothers were—though you could go there as a servant to them. (In fact, a Negro woman was once formally "sealed" to Joseph Smith as a servant. LDS leaders seemed piqued that this "did not satisfy her, and she pleaded for her endowments.")[57]

A friend of Joseph Smith, a Negro man by the name of Elijah Abel, was ordained an elder, and later a seventy. He served a mission in Canada too before his death in 1884. Mormons said this was done "before the word of the Lord was fully understood," and they considered Abel's ordinations as a fluke in their history. However, Abel's son Enoch and grandson Elijah were ordained to the priesthood—the younger Elijah as late as 1934, in Logan, Utah.[58]

Lester Bush, writing in the liberal publication *Dialogue: A Journal of Mormon Thought*, related that one late-twentieth-century president of the Church, David O. McKay, let a young Negro be ordained to the priesthood because the blessing the young man received from his patriarch said that, despite the outward appearances of the young man and his relatives, he was not of the "cursed" lineage. McKay also authorized the sealing in a temple of two Negro children to the white LDS couple who had adopted them.[59]

David O. McKay also stated privately once that he, unlike most other Mormons, didn't believe that Negroes were under any curse. In fact, he thought the whole Negro issue within Mormonism hinged on a practice, not a doctrine, which he hoped would soon be discontinued.[60] The Negro problem was surely burdensome to Mormons during McKay's presidency, for that was the time that many Western Athletic Conference schools boycotted athletic events with Brigham Young University. Pressure from black organizations was levied on the LDS Church, but to no avail. The Church's stand on Negroes and the priesthood could only be changed, Mormons insisted, by a revelation from God.

The Reorganized Church (known today as The Community of Christ) meanwhile had managed to avoid all these problems almost before they began. Joseph Smith's son, Joseph Smith III, in 1865 announced that he had received a revelation (now in their scriptural canon) which cleared the way for ordination of blacks.

BLACKS IN THE CHURCH

In the absence of a like revelation, the Utah church tried to make visible changes that would appease its critics. In 1970, for instance, the first black singers were admitted to the Mormon Tabernacle Choir. The church openly welcomed blacks who joined the Church too.

Some black Mormons weren't happy without the priesthood, and said so. And non-LDS Negroes living in Utah know how the LDS doctrine has clouded the atmosphere in that state for them. David H. Oliver, a black lawyer, in 1963 wrote a self-published book, *A Negro on Mormonism*, in which he said that Utah was worse than the South for blacks who wanted employment other than menial labor.

Though most Mormons have tried to welcome blacks into their church as members, this has caused considerable cognitive dissonance for those who remember the formerly "eternal" teachings of the LDS Church, recalling situations that existed prior to the proclamation that black men could hold priesthood. For years before that, Polynesian men who had joined the LDS Church were given the priesthood, because they were from the "isles of the sea."[61] (The *Book of Mormon* story forced Mormons into the assumption that the islanders too were Semitic.) Of course, anthropologists know that most people of, say, the Fiji Islands are Negroid. Mormons, then, had been bestowing their priesthood on certain blacks for many years prior to 1978.

In 1963 the LDS Church announced that it would send missionaries to eastern Nigeria. But the Nigerian government refused to give visas to missionaries because of the Church's racist policies. Black Nigerian Mormons continued to write to Salt Lake City for instructions and books on doctrine for their newfound religion. By 1965 *Time* magazine reported a Mormon membership of seven thousand Ibibio, Ibo, and Efik tribesmen in Nigeria.[62] Then the whole LDS African system started to crumble. The Nigerian LDS leader, Anie Dick Obot, set himself up as bishop over a council of seventy-five elders, unaware that the priesthood was "necessary" for such an organizational move. The Utah leaders meanwhile were appalled by this, and by publicity regarding Nigerians' practice of the LDS tenet of polygamy. The Nigerian LDS empire of the 1960s disappeared almost without a trace, like the wicked cities of the Old Testament, when the Nigerians learned of the LDS Church's teachings of the "inferiority" of their race.

THE NEW "REVELATION"

It was about 1963 too that Church leaders began openly discussing a possible change in their Negro policy. Apostle Hugh B. Brown, a general authority and a member of the First Presidency, said that the "problem" was being "considered."[63] Each time an LDS leader was asked when Negroes could receive the priesthood, the reply would be like that given by Apostle Brown—that it would be "in the own due time of the Lord."[64]

As a Mormon, I never thought I'd see the day that a Negro would hold the priesthood. Brigham Young had said many times that God would never allow a black to rule over a white in government or religion. He also said that the seed of Cain (who had supposedly rejected the priesthood in the first place) wouldn't have the priesthood until after death[65] and after *all* of Adam's other children's seed (that is, all non-blacks) "had the privilege of receiving the Priesthood ... and have received their resurrection from the dead."[66] The tenth president of the Church, the late Joseph Fielding Smith, explored the implications of Young's teachings on when Negroes could receive the priesthood and concluded that Abel, Adam's son, must be resurrected, achieve godhood, and raise up posterity "on some other world" before any faithful descendants of his murderer could receive the priesthood.[67]

On June 8, 1978, I heard an announcement from a national news service that the LDS Church had introduced a new policy regarding Negroes and their priesthood: The First Presidency had released a statement saying that "the long-promised day has come."[68] The statement portrayed LDS leadership as intercessors who had begged the Lord to change his mind about blacks, and that the Lord had relented. Unlike the revelations of the nineteenth-century church, the exact text of this revelation was not given.

But I don't think LDS President Spencer W. Kimball received anything more in that upper room than the end result of his realization that the Church had to make a decision between "revelation" and revenue. In the 1970s and 1980s a legal case that eventually was settled by the Supreme Court, *Bob Jones University v. The United States,* threatened the tax-exempt status of organizations that could be seen as discriminating against people of color.[69] The Church must have seen in this the beginning of the kind of pressure that the United States government put on it before the polygamy "manifesto" was issued. It was mirrored in the case of Doug Wallace, a young Mormon who had passed his priesthood on to a black friend. When Wallace came up with what ex-Mormon writer Bob Witte called "an ironclad case" and presented it to a judge, the judge apparently contacted President Kimball and told him that there'd better be a new revelation on the way giving the priesthood to blacks or Wallace would win this new case, with disastrous financial and publicity results for Mormondom.[70]

However, one of the most prominent propelling forces that influenced the Kimball presidency was the explosive growth of the LDS Church in Brazil and the pending temple dedication there. This was a temple in whose ordinances black men—and nearly half of all Brazilians are undeniably of black ancestry[71]—would not be able to participate.

Even decades after the LDS Church began granting priesthood to Negro men, Mormons still squirm trying to explain to outsiders why the ban was there in the first place. Armand L. Mauss, an LDS apologist, suggests that the biblical and *Pearl of Great Price* scriptures always cited as requiring the denial of LDS priesthood to blacks never explicitly said any such thing; thus it can be concluded that Mormonism, like its nineteenth-century American religious counterparts, simply partook of an omnipresent antebellum racist atmosphere of the day and overlaid it onto sacred writ.[72]

Someone might ask if I don't think it good that the LDS Church finally gave its priesthood to blacks. Though I hope that this would be a good beginning to the breakdown of traditional prejudices, I cannot be happy with any cosmetic change that this organization might effect to make itself and its ungodly doctrines more attractive to my black brothers and sisters.

Chapter 6

THE PRECARIOUS SUMMIT OF CONTINUING REVELATION

And whatsoever they shall speak when moved upon by the Holy Ghost shall be scripture, shall be the will of the Lord, shall be the mind of the Lord, shall be the word of the Lord, shall be the voice of the Lord, and the power of God unto salvation.

—*Doctrine and Covenants* 68:4

Whatever its effects upon the religious world, Mormonism has not, as it originally purposed, done away with religious division. Since the death of Joseph Smith, many denominations claiming authority from him have come into being. Some estimates run as high as two hundred such groups;[1] a conservative estimate is about sixty. Some are small, clannish, and secretive. Most of these groups were founded soon after the death of Joseph Smith.

THE COMMUNITY OF CHRIST

The second-largest group is now known as The Community of Christ, sometimes referred to informally as "Missouri Mormons" to distinguish them from their Utah cousins. In times past they were referred to as "Josephites" or "Reorganites"; but up until 2001 they were officially named the Reorganized Church of Jesus Christ of Latter Day Saints. The Community of Christ claims that before Joseph Smith died, he ordained his son Joseph Smith III to be his successor as prophet, seer, and revelator. Evidence shows this to be true, and to have happened on or about April 22, 1839.[2] Brigham Young even claimed that Joseph Smith's sons had a lineal right to head the Church.[3] After being urged by many men to assume his rightful priesthood office, Joseph Smith III finally consented and was ordained President of the Reorganized LDS Church on April 6, 1860.[4] This office continued to be a hereditary one for them up until the retirement of Wallace B. Smith in 1996. When W. Grant McMurray became president, he was the first president not descended from Joseph Smith Jr., and Stephen M. Veazey has served as president since 2005.

Joseph Smith III was only a young boy when his father died, and after such an experience, it is no wonder that it took him so long to be persuaded by his father's friends to accept the responsibilities of the presidency. He and his successors in the Community of Christ claim their authority from Joseph Smith and the Church that he founded in 1830, but they regard Brigham Young and the subsequent LDS presidents as false prophets. They are particularly bitter toward Brigham Young, because they claim that he formulated the doctrine of polygamy and ascribed this doctrine of his own to Joseph Smith to give it validity. To support this, they cite Joseph Smith's public denials of the practice before his death. The Utah LDS doctrine of men progressing to become gods Reorganites also attribute to Brigham Young. They say that he caused the records of the Church to be falsified to make it seem that Joseph Smith had also taught this during his lifetime.

The Community of Christ has its headquarters in Independence, Missouri. Their own editions of the *Book of Mormon* and the *Doctrine and Covenants*, along with Joseph Smith's "Inspired Version" of the Bible, make up their canon of scripture. They deny any revelations of the *Doctrine and Covenants* that they say were written after the death of Joseph Smith (notably the section on polygamy and those writings of Brigham Young and Wilford Woodruff), and continue to add new material to their own *Doctrine and Covenants* and to publish such new revelations as they are "received." Though they do not accept wholesale the Utah LDS *Pearl of Great Price* (in fact, they reject the Book of Abraham), the Book of Moses and Smith's Matthew "translation" are part of their Bible. Their version of the Joseph Smith story, though, is as it appeared in the *Times and Seasons* periodical.

Nonetheless, a wealth of documentation proves to the serious student that Joseph Smith did indeed preach the plurality of gods who were once men, and the doctrine of polygamy—even though he publicly denied the latter. Persons who were appalled by these teachings were attracted to what is now known as the Community of Christ since it maintained the truth of things like the *Book of Mormon* but rejected those doctrines to which they objected, a sort of halfway house between false doctrine and *falser* doctrine.

Since the Community of Christ does not have the elaborate temple rites of the Mormon Church, their temple services are open to the public. They ordain women and maintain a missionary force, but such workers, unlike the LDS missionaries who might come to your door, are salaried. They claim about 250,000 members in fifty countries, and estimate that over half of their active members do not have English as their primary language. Additional information about the group is available at their official website: www.cofchrist.org/.

STRANGITES

Another splinter group is known as the Church of Jesus Christ of Latter Day Saints, Strangite. It is named after James J. Strang, one of the Nauvoo convert followers of Joseph Smith. Strang claimed that the very day that Joseph Smith died an angel appeared to him, Strang, and anointed him to be the successor. Strang also produced a letter from Joseph Smith that supposedly designated him as the next president of the Church in the event of the death of the prophet. A great many of the influential Mormons of the day followed Strang when he went to Wisconsin, including two of the apostles and William Smith, the brother of Joseph. His position was strengthened by his "vision," which had all the hallmarks of divine authority such as Joseph Smith had. He also "found" a clay receptacle buried in the ground which contained brass plates inscribed with strange characters. When he "translated" them with the aid of a Urim and Thummim, they named him as Joseph's true successor. Later, he claimed to receive some plates he called "the plates of Laban," which when translated by him advocated polygamy. Of course he could not be lax in following God's commands, and among the wives he took was one who had toured the East with him disguised as a male secretary until her pregnancy gave her away.

Strang was known to his followers as "King James," and the Strangite group once numbered almost three thousand. They established themselves in the Beaver Island area of Lake Michigan as "The Kingdom of Saint James." Their scriptures include the *Book of Mormon*, the *Doctrine and Covenants*, and the *Law of the Lord* (translated from "the plates of Laban") which Strang claimed he found, and Strang's own "revelations." He died a martyr to his cause, assassinated by some members of the Church he had founded, and left behind five pregnant grieving widows.

The fact that there are very few Strangites today is regarded by Strangites themselves as fulfillment of prophecy that the true church would not have many members. They deny the virgin birth, the atonement of Christ, and the authority of the Utah Mormon prophets. They worship on Saturday, and attempt to keep the Law of Moses by, among other things, circumcising their males and by offering animal sacrifices. Their online presence is at www.strangite.org/.

HEDRICKITES AND FETTINGITES

The Church of Christ, Hedrickite, also known as the Church of Christ, Temple Lot, is centered in Independence, Missouri. They number about 1500. Their most distinguishing feature is the fact that they own the very spot that Joseph Smith dedicated as the site of the New Jerusalem temple to be built in Independence. Despite lawsuits, attractive financial offers, and additional stringent efforts by other LDS groups to take this land from them, they still own it and insist they will not give it up. In 1929 they started construction on a temple but, because of their limited finances, were unable to get any further in the building process than the excavation of a large hole, which the city of Independence finally filled up in the 1960s. This small group does not believe in nor do they practice polygamy nor baptism for the dead, and they reject the Utah Mormon doctrine of men progressing to become gods. Online: www.churchofchrist-tl.org/.

A Hedrickite by the name of Otto Fetting formed another group, known as the Church of Christ, Fettingite, or "Church of Christ (Otto Fetting)." Fetting claimed to have been visited by John the Baptist in 1930. This and subsequent messages from this heavenly being through Fetting had as their prime objective the building of the temple on the two-and-one-half-acre Hedrickite plot. They differ doctrinally very little from their mother church, the Hedrickites. One offshoot of this church, which calls itself "the Church of Christ–'The Church with the Elijah Message,'" claims a membership of about five thousand. Its website is www.elijahmessage.com.

BICKERTONITES

The Church of Jesus Christ, Bickertonite, was founded in 1862 by Sidney Rigdon and one of his ex-Mormon followers. This man, Bickerton, was told by God to center his people in St. John, Kansas, in 1874. Six years later he himself was disfellowshiped from the Church and was succeeded by William Cadman. Dominic R. Thomas is now president of the Bickertonite Church, which has endured four splits in the 150 years of its history. Most of the Church's American adherents live in Monongahela, Pennsylvania. They do claim, however, to have ten thousand members, 3,500 of whom are black Africans. They do not practice polygamy, baptism for the dead, nor eternal progression; nor do they believe in more than one God. Their website: http://thechurchofjesuschrist.com.

FUNDAMENTALISTS

Perhaps the splinter group of Mormonism about which most is rumored and least known is the Fundamentalists. The largest subgroups of these are the Apostolic United Brethren led by J. LaMoine Jenson, with about seven thousand members centered around the area south of Salt Lake City; and the Fundamentalist LDS Church led by various members of the Jeffs clan, with about eight thousand members located mainly in enclaves on the Utah-Arizona border. A branch of this group was the subject of the raid in Eldorado, Texas, in 2008. There are also notable smaller groups of about a thousand or less, including the True and Living Church led by James Harmston, the Kingstonites, and the First Warders.

All are distinguished by their adherence, against all odds, to the doctrine and practice of polygamy. One conservative modern estimate of the number of men, women, and children in polygamous families is forty thousand, according to a recent Reuters article.[5] Journalists Richard N. Ostling and Joan K. Ostling estimated thirty thousand but say the figure could be "several times that."[6]

These groups are hardly harmonious, however. Best-selling author Jon Krakauer's chilling book *Under the Banner of Heaven: A Story of Violent Faith* (2003) documented the murder of a woman and her daughter by close relatives Ron and Dan Lafferty in 1984, reportedly because the woman was opposed to polygamy. Dorothy Allred Solomon's 2003 book, *Predators, Prey, and Other Kinfolk*, chronicles the author's life as the twenty-eighth of forty-eight children sired by her father, who was murdered by a rival polygamous group. She describes how "religious fixation" led not only to the cold-blooded violence of the Lafferty brothers but also that of rival polygamous cultist Ervil LeBaron and his clan—a fixation that, says Solomon, carries its own twisted logic:

> I read the papers and knew why the Lafferty brothers had murdered their sister-in-law and her eighteen-month-old daughter, slitting her throat from ear to ear because she refused to live the Principle [of plural marriage], in a horrible echo of the Blood Atonement rites I'd once heard described following a priesthood

meeting. I lived through the violence of the LeBarons, which didn't stop when Ervil went to prison, didn't stop until his sons were convicted of murdering four "lambs of God" in Texas.[7]

Most descendants of the Mormons who lived from the 1850s to about 1905 have polygamous ancestors in their family tree, which often motivates them to protect those whose actions they cannot condone. Such sometimes find themselves uncomfortably "covering" for polygamous relatives and friends who are breaking state and federal laws. Ironically, they themselves expect to practice plural marriage in eternity.

Most Fundamentalists are among the more committed of all LDS splinter group members because they consider themselves defenders of the true faith, who are willing to suffer any persecution for their beliefs. Some Fundamentalists feel they are actually a part of the mainstream LDS Church, which they think only issued the "Manifesto" (now known as "Official Declaration—1") banning the practice of plural marriage to ease government pressures on the Church. Others have been bitter about the Manifesto literally for generations, feeling that if the Utah church doesn't believe in section 132 of the *Doctrine and Covenants* enough to practice it, they should "tear it out of the book."[8]

Most Fundamentalists live in Salt Lake City and Bountiful, Utah, near the Utah-Arizona border, and in northern and southeastern Arizona. Some live in constant fear of exposure. Others who would escape such pressure have moved to Mexico or Canada, where they live in "colonies" and are often ignored by local law enforcement officials. However, recent years have seen an emboldened attitude as many polygamists appear on television and radio talk shows, allow themselves to be interviewed for print publications, and are highlighted in fictionalized accounts in movies and television shows.

Plural marriages, with the sanction of the Utah church, were performed in Mexico for at least fourteen years after the Manifesto, according to Stanley S. Ivins, the son of Anthony Ivins, who performed such marriages.[9] Many Mormons in Mexico are products of polygamous marriages, and many follow the example of their fathers in taking plural wives. It is the faithful mainstream Mormon, in fact, who would be most tempted to practice polygamy. In his book *I Have Six Wives*, Samuel Woolley Taylor observed, "Modern Mormons believe in plural marriage, but not its practice. The more deeply immersed a Mormon becomes, the thinner the line may become between belief and practice. The threat of Fundamentalist doctrine is to the most devout."[10]

So who—if, indeed, anyone—is right among these sects? All claim authority from Joseph Smith, and all are founded upon "revelation." Who is to say that James Strang's anointing by an angel has less authority than Brigham Young's selection as prophet by his friends? Why should the "Law of the Lord" be less important than *Conference Reports* of last April's general conference of the Utah Church? If John the Baptist told Otto Fetting, who believed in the *Book of Mormon* with all his heart, to build the New Jerusalem temple, why aren't missionaries of all LDS sects doing it?

Now, I was a member of the Utah Mormon Church. What I've written about the other sects I know primarily from what I have read about them. Mormon splinter groups are treated as illegitimate stepchildren who are pushed into closets and forgotten until someone is rude enough to mention their names. The fact that they even exist as descendants of a church founded on "perfect revelation" is a blemish on its own exclusivistic claims.

THE NATURE OF REVELATION

To understand LDS doctrine, you must first grasp the nature of revelation as the Mormons interpret it. I was taught that I must be as active a participant as God in the process. Man's part in revelation is this: (1) he must desire and seek revelation, (2) he must have faith, (3) he must be worthy in character, (4) he must have an objective need or purpose, and (5) usually he must be aware of this need.[11]

Basically, LDS doctrine delineates six basic types of revelation. The first is a direct message from a heavenly being, such as Joseph Smith received when Moroni appeared to him. The second kind is a vision, such as is recorded in *Doctrine and Covenants*, section 110, wherein Joseph Smith and Oliver Cowdery said they saw the Savior standing on the breastwork of the pulpit in the Kirtland Temple. A third type of revelation is that received by means of a physical object, such as a peepstone, or the Urim and Thummim that Joseph Smith used to translate the *Book of Mormon*. Dreams are a fourth type of revelation. They are exemplified by the dream experience Heber C. Kimball reported in his journal, where he saw the soon-to-be opened mission field of England represented by a field of diseased wheat signifying the area's lack of spiritual depth. A fifth type of revelation is inspiration, typified by this story about Joseph Smith: "At times the inspiration of the Holy Ghost came upon him with such force he knew the ideas that had entered his mind were of divine origin."[12] The last and most commonly experienced type of revelation is that which comes through a spiritual confirmation, and was defined in *Doctrine and Covenants* 9:8–9:

> But, behold, I say unto you, that you must study it out in your mind; then you must ask me if it be right, and if it is right I will

> cause that your bosom shall burn within you; therefore, you shall feel that it is right. But if it be not right you shall have no such feelings, but you shall have a stupor of thought that shall cause you to forget the thing which is wrong.

This "burning in the bosom" is the type of revelation relied upon by most Mormons. It is differentiated from the "inspiration" as just described by the fact that this is the confirmation of what could be an otherwise "uninspired" idea or purposed course of action.

The importance of "inspiration" in Mormon life cannot be overestimated. Christians believe the Word of God, the Bible, is revelation to us. But Mormons, who believe that direct revelation is available to them, must of necessity view scripture as "secondhand revelation." This is borne out by an LDS apologist who said, "In spiritual knowledge, I must say that my own experiences with prayer, the Spirit, and revelation are *primary* evidence, whereas the evidence and testimony of the scriptures, of the prophets, and other good, believing people, and of the historical record of mankind are secondary."[13] From this quote it is easy to see that personal revelation is put on the top level, while the scriptures, opinions of sincere persons, and secular history are put below. Mormons are therefore encouraged to seek revelation for themselves.

THE MECHANICS OF REVELATION

LDS revelation is by its very nature iconoclastic. Joseph Smith, in LDS eyes, *had* to receive direct revelation to organize the Church because "the doctrines and disciplines of other churches would not suffice; in effect, new wine could not be put into old bottles."[14]

One of the scriptures on which the LDS doctrine of continuing revelation is based is Matthew 16:13–19:

> When Jesus came into the coasts of Caesarea Philippi, he asked his disciples, saying, Whom do men say that I the Son of man am?
>
> And they said, Some say that thou art John the Baptist: some, Elias; and others, Jeremias, or one of the prophets.
>
> He saith unto them, But whom say ye that I am?
>
> And Simon Peter answered and said, Thou art the Christ, the Son of the living God.
>
> And Jesus answered and said unto him, Blessed art thou, Simon Barjona: for flesh and blood hath not revealed it unto thee, but my Father which is in heaven.

> And I say also unto thee, That thou art Peter, and upon this rock I will build my church; and the gates of hell shall not prevail against it.
>
> And I will give unto thee the keys of the kingdom of heaven: and whatsoever thou shalt bind on earth shall be bound in heaven: and whatsoever thou shalt loose on earth shall be loosed in heaven.

Catholics would say that the rock on which Jesus would build his church is Peter, thus authorizing their apostolic succession. Christians recognize the rock as the confession of a believer like Peter who accepts not the testimony of humanity (flesh and blood), but the divine record by which the Father in heaven reveals his Son.[15] A group of such believers is the church that Jesus bought with his blood and promised to protect: Thus the basis of the historic church of Jesus Christ has always been the Word that testifies of Jesus. Mormons say that the rock is the process of continuing revelation. They have a problem because they say such revelation requires LDS priesthood authority. And they say that was absent from earth for 1,700 years—having been overcome by the gates of hell.[16]

In contrast, Mormon leaders say their own revelation is perfect. Joseph Fielding Smith, the tenth president of the Church, stated categorically that there was "no need for eliminating, changing, or adjusting any part" of revelation to make it harmonize with previous revelations.[17] When I was a Mormon, LDS leaders spoke of how new revelation "dovetails" into old, fitting as exactly as die-cut jigsaw puzzle pieces. There was no "revelation" that was more authoritative than another, because all were the Word of God: Brigham Young once said, "I have never yet preached a sermon and sent it out to the children of men, that they may not call Scripture."[18]

In the "Teachings of the Living Prophets" manual from which I studied in classes at BYU, this quote appeared: "We rely therefore on the teachings of the living oracles of God as of equal validity with the doctrines of the written word."[19] Thus I believed that what the General Authorities of the LDS Church said, specifically in conference and in their Church-approved and published works, was equal to the Standard Works of scripture.

Today the doctrine is well defined which specifies who can receive revelation about what. A member of the LDS Church can receive revelation for himself and his subordinates. Thus, a mother can receive revelation for herself and her children; a man for himself, his wife, and children. A bishop is entitled to revelation for himself, his counselors, his family, and the members of the ward over which he presides.

Only the president/prophet of the Church can receive revelation for the Church or the world at large. In keeping with the "dovetail" idea, any revelation must concur with previous revelation to be acceptable—unless it comes from a prophet who "alone has the right to receive revelations for the Church, either new or amendatory, or to give authoritative interpretations of scriptures that shall be binding on the Church, or change in any way the existing doctrines of the Church."[20]

However, with the increased awareness by LDS members of previous doctrines—such as Brigham Young's doctrines on Adam-God and other so-called "deprecated doctrines"—LDS Church leadership has clamped down on the revelation pipeline. In an attempt to curtail questions about contradictory past statements by LDS prophets, in the twenty-first century nothing is considered doctrine unless it is in current versions of LDS scripture, in current conference teachings or official teaching manuals, or in official statements by the First Presidency.

JOSEPH'S SUCCESSORS

Joseph Smith's death in 1844 marked the end of the age of visions. Subsequent "prophets" never seemed to reach the heights of revelation that Joseph did. *Brigham Young*, the second president of the LDS Church, was no dreamer; he was a doer. His reign over the Church was characterized by marked numerical and financial growth. He is remembered for his gruff manner, his many wives and children, and his hatred for anyone or anything that got into the way of his dreams of Mormon independence. No matter what his faults, he was loyal to his prophet to the end. His dying words were, "Joseph! Joseph!"

John Taylor, the Church's third prophet, had as his hardest task the job of living up to the leadership qualities and force of character of his predecessors. He was present in the Carthage jail when Joseph Smith was killed, and, like Brigham, was loyal to Joseph until his death in exile because of government pressure due to his lifelong defense and practice of polygamy.

His successor, *Wilford Woodruff*, is remembered by Mormons almost solely for the "Manifesto" that brought an end to the LDS Church's official practice of polygamy. But though he was only president of the Church for nine years, under his direction the Salt Lake Temple was completed, Utah achieved statehood, and most important, he was able to hold together the crumbling shambles of a Mormonism shaken by the polygamy issue.

Successor to Woodruff was *Lorenzo Snow*, president from 1898 until 1901. He is remembered by Mormons for his emphasis on tithing whereby "the windows of heaven" were opened—along with members' pocketbooks. (The interpretation of the law of tithing as a strict 10 percent of one's gross income is the reason that the Utah church is so much wealthier than the Community of Christ, which requires 10 percent of one's "increase"—what is left over after living expenses.) Snow was also the originator of the saying, "As man is, God once was; as God is, man may become,"[21] which I and all LDS children learned by heart. Snow was the brother of one of Joseph Smith's plural wives, the poet and lyricist Eliza R. Snow.

The next president of the LDS Church was also the first near relative of Joseph Smith to hold the office in the Utah Church. His name was Joseph Fielding Smith, but because there was a later president (his son) by the same name, he is referred to as *Joseph F. Smith.* The son of Hyrum Smith (brother of Joseph), Joseph F. Smith was only five years old when his father and uncle were killed in Carthage jail. Under the leadership of Joseph F. Smith, the great debts under which the Church had struggled were paid off in 1907, and a new era of prosperity for the Mormons began. During his presidency, however, the Church was shaken by the investigation of an LDS senator. The issue at hand was whether this man, Reed Smoot, could discharge his duties as a US senator with the conflicting demands his religion might make on him. Smoot was granted his seat in the United States Senate, but in the course of the hearings Joseph F. Smith was called as a witness. Here the "prophet" made the amazing admission that during his presidency, "I have never pretended to nor do I profess to have received revelations."[22] According to historian Kathleen Flake in her book *The Politics of American Religious Identity: The Seating of Senator Reed Smoot, Mormon Apostle*, it was Smith's deliberate attempts to turn public attention away from polygamy and back to the earlier days of the LDS Church that allowed the group to transition into the twentieth century.

When Smith died in 1918 he was followed in the presidency by *Heber J. Grant.* Grant had grown up close to Brigham Young, and his own extreme poverty as a boy made him particularly concerned with this problem in the Church. In 1936 he initiated the program instructing every family to maintain a two-year storage of food, and that same year the Church Welfare Plan was organized. Both are today outstanding features of the LDS Church.

George Albert Smith, the eighth president and also a relative of Joseph Smith, served from 1945 until 1951. A scholarly looking man, he encouraged Church involvement in the Boy Scout program and authorized the first printing of the *Book of Mormon* in Braille. He was also known for his wry sense of humor. Once a member wrote to ask him what he thought of two controversial issues, cocoa and cremation. He thought a moment and then replied to his secretary, "Write and tell him that they're both hot."[23]

David O. McKay presided over the Church during a period of unparalleled peace and prosperity (1951 – 70). Problems over the Church's position on Negroes, however, were intensified when the *Pearl of Great Price* Book of Abraham papyri were discovered, casting doubt on the ability of latter-day "prophets" to translate. McKay emphasized missionary work, and one of his favorite sayings was, "Every member a missionary." He encouraged a weekly "Family Home Evening" for members, declaring that "no success can compensate for failure in the home." Many temples were dedicated or begun during his presidency. He was active politically and tried to influence his subordinates to oppose both the repeal of right-to-work laws and liquor by the drink in Utah. He was the first LDS prophet who didn't have a beard.

Much controversy within the Church was stirred up when *Joseph Fielding Smith* became president in 1970. Son of President Joseph F. Smith, he was by far the most authoritative spokesman on Church doctrine. Though his succession to the office of "prophet, seer, and revelator" was nearly inevitable (the president of the Council of the Twelve Apostles traditionally becomes president of the Church upon the death of the previous president), many Mormons were upset when he became Prophet. I was taught that he was a shy, kindly, gentle old man, but truthful persons more in the know described him as narrow-minded and authoritarian.

He was followed after his death in 1972 by *Harold B. Lee*, who was only president for a short time before his own death in 1973, though he was much younger than most of his recent antecedents. A humble man, he worked in the welfare programs of the Church and placed special emphasis on the place of youth in the future of the Church.

Spencer W. Kimball, a descendant of one of Brigham Young's counselors, was the next president of the LDS Church. He assured himself immortality, at least in the annals of religious leaders, by being the LDS president who declared in June of 1978 that blacks are now eligible to receive the LDS priesthood.

After Kimball's death in 1985, he was succeeded by *Ezra Taft Benson*. Benson was familiar to many Americans because he had served as US secretary of agriculture in the Eisenhower cabinet. He was politically an ultraconservative, though his extreme outspokenness seemed to have been tempered by his advanced age (eighty-seven) and by what many saw as the increasing power of the Council of the Twelve Apostles. Part of this transfer of power to the Council was undoubtedly a necessity because of Benson's reported senility during the end of his life. One significant development during Benson's tenure was the institution of the Church's own satellite system by which it now broadcasts its semiannual conferences and other messages. Benson passed away May 30, 1994.

Howard W. Hunter succeeded Benson, serving from 1994 until his death, March 3, 1995. He has the distinction of serving the shortest period of time as president of the Mormon Church (not quite nine months), but he did encourage all Church members to become "temple worthy."

Gordon B. Hinckley became president in 1995. About that time, Church membership in countries other than the US surpassed Church membership domestically. Early in his tenure Hinkley issued a "Proclamation to the Church and to the World," which spelled out the Church's conservative position on man-woman relationships, the eternal nature of the family unit, responsibilities and roles of parents, and the sanctity of life. Perhaps more media conscious than previous LDS presidents, Hinckley appeared on the television shows *60 Minutes* and *Larry King Live* and was interviewed by *Time* magazine. However, on these venues he overtly "hedged" on whether or not the LDS Church has taught and now teaches that there is a Mother in heaven, that God was once a man, and that faithful Mormons expect to become gods themselves—only admitting to these doctrines when pressed by the interviewers.[24]

In 2006 Hinckley surpassed the record set by David O. McKay as the oldest LDS president. He was succeeded in 2008 by *Thomas Monson*. The longevity of recent presidents such as Hinckley, with the attendant health problems of nonagenarians, leads me to believe that the Church will soon change its policies about using seniority of service in the Quorum of the Twelve Apostles[25] as the criterion for an "apostle" to become "the prophet."

CONTINUING REVELATION

All the recent presidents of the LDS Church have had as one of their greatest duties the management and distribution of the millions of nontaxable tithe and investment dollars that pour into the Church's brimming treasury. It is because of this that critics of the Church have charged that the "revelation" received by twentieth-century prophets is more of the "spirit of Dow-Jones" than of God. Indeed, revelation has surely changed since the days of Joseph Smith's bold (and incautious) prophetic utterings. Parley P. Pratt once said that Joseph dictated revelations slowly, never backtracking or correcting. (Why bother when he could get away with wholesale revisions of revelations even after printing them?) The Church turned down a path from which it apparently will never return with the issuing of the Manifesto, which began tepidly, "To Whom It May Concern." Today's prophets issue terse little press releases and meandering conference addresses that refer to past doctrines and glowing principles of righteousness, rarely ever putting the divine stamp of "thus saith the Lord" on them, as Joseph Smith seldom hesitated to do. Or, even worse, Hinckley and others hedged and parried in an attempt to solidify their public image as a Christian church. When I was a Mormon, LDS leaders would have cut off their tongues rather than pretend to be "like other Christian churches."

Previous LDS prophets have promised the Mormon people not only a continuing stream of revelation—from God to prophet to church member—but have for years tantalized their anxious followers with the promise of new scriptures. Part of the plates from which the *Book of Mormon* was translated, for example, was "sealed" and taken back by the angel Moroni. This portion, which amounted to between one-third and two-thirds of the total volume of the plates, is yet to be revealed and given to faithful Mormons as scripture. Mormons also cite 2 Corinthians 13:1, which says that two or three witnesses establish the truth, and say that the Bible (the record of the Jews) and the *Book of Mormon* (the record of the Nephites) will be joined by a third record, that of the Ten Lost Tribes. And then there's the still untranslated Book of Joseph.

These promises thrilled me when I was a Mormon. New scriptures! I could hardly wait. But I know now that such scriptures will never come forth. Why? Because the LDS Church has lost its nerve. Though I anticipate future bows to financial and public pressure like the Manifesto and the black-priesthood announcement, no "new" scriptures will be translated from ancient records. In the early days of the Church, when the sciences of archaeology and linguistics were in their infancies, Joseph could recklessly turn out volume after improbable volume like the *Book of Mormon*, the writings that became the *Pearl of Great Price*, and the records of Ham and Joseph (ancient documents supposedly translated by Joseph Smith but never published). But no LDS "prophet" is that incautious in this modern age. The mythical remainder of the mythical *Book of Mormon* will stay in the safekeeping of the mythical Moroni. The record of the Ten Lost Tribes will stay lost too. Nor will the Church ever bring out of hiding the "records of Ham and Joseph," which are probably gathering dust in a vault in the Church Historian's office, a potential bonfire of controversy and certain embarrassment. Mormons will have to be content with the continuing history of their church in the "Church News" section of the *Deseret News*, in the *Ensign*, and in *Conference Reports.*

The prophet alone can contradict scripture, according to Harold B. Lee.[26] This is, in the eyes of a Christian, a paradoxical statement. But Mormon leaders like Brigham Young have always placed much more emphasis on the teachings of the "living oracles" than on written scripture of any kind. Of course, aberrant behavior in the lives of men like Joseph Smith and Brigham Young have caused a considerable tempering of this position. A Mormon when faced with irrefutable evidence of the moral vices of early Church presidents will have a pat answer: "A prophet is a prophet only when he is acting as such."[27] This provides a convenient "out" when a prophet in speech or in action blunders. But I, as a faithful Mormon, did not believe that a prophet *could* blunder. The teachings I received led me to believe with all my heart that the prophets were nearly perfect, especially in their pronouncements about religious matters.

Of course the higher the man in the LDS hierarchy, the more vocal he will be in supporting and building up Church leaders. The leaders realize that they can only achieve the high offices to which they aspire by continually exalting these positions. It becomes a process of continually scratching the backs of the men whose offices they covet, and waiting patiently until someone dies so that they can move up.

If, therefore, Mormons cannot judge their leaders by how they practice the principles they teach, and if a prophet can change and/or countermand any of their "scriptures" at will, how then can the Mormon ascertain the authority of his prophet-leader? Harold B. Lee said, "There is one safety, and that is that we shall live to have the witness to know."[28] This puts us right back to Moroni's challenge to *Book of Mormon* readers: Our own volatile consciences serve as judge.

The corporate instantiation of the individual's conscience is seen in the fact that LDS doctrine must be approved by the general membership. For instance in 1880, a general authority named George Q. Cannon asked the general conference of the Church to vote on accepting the Standard Works of the Church as being from God and binding upon them. More recently both the Manifesto, which theologically outlawed the practice of polygamy, and the 1978 Official Declaration—2, giving blacks the LDS priesthood, were not officially binding until the membership voted that they were.

Nonetheless, Mormons are told that their prophet must be obeyed, for he can *never* teach false doctrine.[29] Theodore M. Burton, a General Authority, said in the October 1961 conference, "The Lord will never permit the great prophet, our seer and revelator, to fall or lead the people astray. Before this could happen, God must of necessity remove that man from the earth."

THE VOICE OF SENILITY

Sadly, this is not the case. I know personally of one time when this principle proved to be false. In 1971, I was rooming at Brigham Young University with a girl whose uncle worked near the office of President Joseph Fielding Smith. One day this friend came to me to unburden herself of something that was troubling her deeply. She told me, with horror and doubt in her voice, that her uncle described Joseph Fielding Smith as so senile in his last years that "outsiders" who might detect this were kept away from him. His mind wandered so badly that all his speeches had to be prepared for him, and as soon as he finished reading them, he was ushered quickly back to his seat because otherwise he would ramble on aimlessly. Her story troubled me as deeply as it had her. When I told my boyfriend about what my friend had said, he insisted that there had been a mistake made either on the part of my friend or her uncle, because God would take a prophet from the earth before he would allow him to become senile.

Perhaps he was as concerned as we were by the prospects of a leaderless church; but I think what really scared us all was the fact that someone else was preparing speeches that claimed to be the words of God, and putting them before a figurehead prophet who had only to read them aloud to authenticate them. We could not reconcile such a notion to the idea of a prophet who supposedly "cannot fall" and who is bound to the office until separated from it by death.

History seemed to repeat itself in the 1990s with another elderly president of the LDS church. *Time* magazine reported that Ezra Taft Benson did not appear in public for two years before his death and was fed by a nasal tube until his death at ninety-four[30]—in a condition his own grandson described as both senile and incapacitated. This grandson, Steve Benson, Pulizer Prize–winning cartoonist and now ex-Mormon atheist, described his grandfather: "In the name of maintaining faith, church leaders peddled the myth that the Mormon prophet was actively at the helm when, in fact, he was incapacitated. Propping him up for photo sessions as if he were some sort of storefront mannequin was a calculated, conspiring abuse of power, not to mention disrespectful and undignified for a man we love."[31]

If Joseph Fielding Smith and Ezra Taft Benson could suffer "mental failing" covered up by the Church while in office as "prophets," could this not be true of Joseph Smith, or Brigham Young? When does a prophet become less than a prophet—without ceasing to be a prophet?

THE TEST OF A PROPHET

But one would not have to accept anecdotal stories of doddering prophets of Mormonism to be assured that none of them is God's spokesman. In the Bible God gave us the infallible test of a prophet:

> And if thou say in thine heart, How shall we know the word which the LORD hath not spoken? When a prophet speaketh in the name of the LORD, if the thing follow not, nor come to pass, that is the thing which the LORD hath not spoken, but the prophet hath spoken it presumptuously: thou shalt not be afraid of him. (Deut. 18:21–22)

Note that this Scripture doesn't condemn people for questioning the right of any person to speak in the name of God. In 1 Thessalonians 5:20–21 Paul told Christians that they should not despise prophetic utterances, but in the next breath he told them to *prove all things* and to hold fast to those things that are good.

Second, the Deuteronomy passage doesn't allow for just a "good batting average" on prophecies. For instance, it doesn't say that you should accept someone as a prophet if most of what he prophesies comes to pass. This Scripture passage encourages us to look at *each* thing a would-be prophet might say and to reject him if he prophesies falsely.

Last, Deuteronomy 18:22 teaches a truth that it took me a long time to come to, even after my conversion. We are told that a false prophet—one who has failed the test that God outlined—should have no power over us. We should not fear him. When we are afraid of such a person, we are enslaved by our own minds and not by any power the person himself might have.[32]

It is the fulfilled predictions of Mormonism that are touted so much. Surely LDS prophets must be of God, a proselyte might think, if they could prophesy the coming of Columbus to America[33] and the Revolutionary War[34] (both of which, however, were "prophesied" after the fact). Furthermore, what many regard as Joseph Smith's stellar prediction of the outbreak of the Civil War beginning with South Carolina (*Doctrine and Covenants* section 87) has little credibility when one considers the information available to Smith about unrest in South Carolina, and other details of the prophecy that proved false (for instance, Great Britain did not get involved, and the Civil War did not engender all other subsequent world wars).[35]

FALSE PROPHECIES

Much of the prophecy of Joseph Smith's time was centered on Missouri's future as Zion. Almost all these prophecies are easily documented, and most too have proven to be false prophecies. In *Doctrine and Covenants* 90:37, for instance, the Mormons were promised that they would not be removed from Missouri, but they of course were driven from that place, and most never returned to claim the inheritance they were promised there. Except for the Community of Christ group and other smaller splinter groups, even their descendants live elsewhere.

In *Doctrine and Covenants* we read the prophecy of Joseph Smith that a man named David W. Patten would perform a mission the next spring, but Patten died before that happened.[36] Joseph Smith also prophesied in *Doctrine and Covenants* section 84 that a temple would be reared in Jackson County in his own generation. Even the Temple Lot church's efforts beginning in 1929 to make this prophecy come true were frustrated. Excuses for failure abound, but in *Doctrine and Covenants* 124:49–51, Joseph Smith gave his own: He said the enemy was just too strong. (Since when are opposing physical forces strong enough to frustrate *any* prophecy of the living God?)

When the Mormon people were finally ousted from Missouri, Joseph Smith made many foolish and bitter prophecies. Once, when talking to statesman Stephen A. Douglas, he predicted that the United States government would be "utterly overthrown and wasted and there will not be as much as a potscherd [*sic*] left,"[37] unless it redressed the wrongs done to Mormons to their satisfaction.

In several places in the *History of the Church* we read of instances where Joseph Smith promised individuals that they would live to see Christ come in his glory.[38] In 1835, Smith even put a date on when he himself would see Christ, saying that fifty-six years "should wind up this scene."[39]

Though Brigham Young was not as bold as Joseph was in making prophecies, when he did so, they were whoppers. Considering his anti-Negro bent, perhaps it was just his wishful thinking that led him to prophesy that the abolitionist movement would not free the slaves because slavery was "the sentence of the Almighty upon the seed of Ham."[40]

Heber C. Kimball, one of Brigham Young's counselors, had so much faith in Young's powers that he too waxed prophetic in proclaiming that Brigham would serve as president of the United States.[41]

The most amazing "revelation" to come out of Mormonism is also the most ludicrous. Though Mormons of today believe that celestialized beings (such as God) live on burning planets, few would agree that there are inhabitants on the moon. But Joseph Smith, as quoted in the journal of one of his most devoted followers, Oliver B. Huntington, not only said that there were moon dwellers, but went on to describe them as being all about six feet in height, dressing like Quakers, and having a lifespan of one thousand years![42] Brigham Young also described inhabitants of the moon—and even those of the sun.[43]

THE CASE OF KING DAVID

Those who criticize LDS leaders are often taken to task by LDS apologists who say that one cannot condemn a "prophet" because he drank liquor (like Joseph Smith did), or because he was ruthless and ambitious (like Brigham Young). King David and his ungodly murderous affair with Bathsheba is often cited as proof that a prophet can sin in other than doctrinal teachings. The Bible scholar would agree that prophets, whether of the Bible or of any other "scripture," are human beings of whom we have no right to expect perfection. But let's look at David and see why, even in spite of his sin, he deserves the title of prophet.

First, though he sinned, he repented. It was a sin to covet the wife of another and to have her husband killed. But David saw the grave error he had made and begged God for forgiveness. He did not rail against God when his first child by Bathsheba was taken from him in death. He reformed his life and spent the rest of it demonstrating to God that he was truly repentant. We might as well take a parallel example from the life of Joseph Smith. How repentant was he when he took other men's wives? Second, whatever David gave to his people as the Word of the Lord harmonized with what the prophets before him had said. No one ever accused David of being an iconoclast. People of God know that he is consistent, and they can judge new revelation by old (see 2 John 9–10, Gal. 1:6–12, and 2 Tim. 3:14–17). And last, David was a prophet because his words came true! He didn't tell the exact date of the birth of Christ or about dwellers on the stars of his favorite constellation. He listened to what God had to say and then repeated it to his audience.

What a contrast to the revelation of the LDS Church. Warren Parrish, who was once scribe to Joseph Smith, expressed his disillusionment with the results of the teachings and legacy of Joseph Smith and Sidney Rigdon: "[Smith and Rigdon] lie by revelation, swindle by revelation, cheat and defraud by revelation, run away by revelation, and if they do not mend their ways, I fear they will be damned by revelation."[44]

Chapter 7

THE MORMON PANTHEON

How convenient it would be to many of our great men and great families of doubtful origin, could they have the privilege of the heroes of yore who, whenever their origin was involved in obscurity, modestly announced themselves descended from a god.

—Washington Irving, *Knickerbocker's History of New York*

Many Christians embroiled in the creation versus evolution struggle have wondered, "What could be more ungodly than the thought that man has evolved from a lower form of life?" But in 1844, Joseph Smith introduced a doctrine that many Christians have passively ignored for more than 160 years—the idea that our God "evolved" from a lower form of life. This lower form of life, from which the LDS god evolved, was a man.

THE ETERNALITY OF MAN

You cannot understand LDS theology unless you understand what Mormons believe about their own origins. In a nutshell, they believe that all humans pass through various stages of being: from (1) pure, "unorganized" intelligence, to (2) having that intelligence clothed with a spirit body and thus becoming a spirit being, to (3) birth on earth whereby the spirit is clothed with a physical body, to (4) after-earth life, an eternal condition of godhood in a physical body.

Mormons' unique conception of eternity is one that includes the ever-uncreated consciousness or intelligence of every person. In the words of Brigham Young, "There never was a time when man did not exist, and there never will be a time when he will cease to exist."[1] Each of us, says LDS doctrine, has *always* existed, before the creation of the earth, and before our God *was* God. This intelligence had no form and owed no allegiance to a creator, for it had none. At the core of historical LDS anthropology is the teaching that each such intelligence was an individual entity, and was self-existent and coequal with the being who would become our God.[2]

If God did not create man in the way we have always thought, why do we call him our Creator? Mormons teach that God, an exalted man, had sexual intercourse with his wives in eternity long before earth time began, and the spirit bodies that those wives brought forth clothed the "intelligences." This poses an immediate logical problem: If it is true, as Jesus taught in John 3:6, that flesh gives birth to flesh, and spirit gives birth to spirit, how do a flesh and bone god and a flesh and bone goddess give birth to a spirit body to clothe an intelligence?

Nonetheless LDS doctrine says that the invisible part of a human being consists of his inherent *being* or intelligence and the spirit body from his heavenly father and mother. Mormons teach that this spirit body is adult-sized, and looks like we do—thus, Joseph Smith's spirit body (for instance) looks like his mortal body, and being male, has all the appropriate features.[3] This spirit body is made out of a material so "refined" as to be intangible and invisible to mortals; but it nonetheless exists.[4]

In a bit of confusion of terms in LDS doctrine, the union or "organization" of intellect and spirit body is also known as an intelligence, in the same way that we might refer to a living man as a soul, though that is only part of his being. Thus the spirits that Abraham supposedly saw before the creation of the world were referred to by him as intelligences (*Pearl of Great Price*, Abraham chapter 3).

You can't have a father without a mother, say Mormons. The idea of a Heavenly Mother is a logical necessity in LDS theology. The lyrics to a current, popular LDS hymn, "O My Father," affirm the existence of this Mother:

In the heav'ns are parents single?
No, the thought makes reason stare!
Truth is reason, truth eternal,
Tells me I've a Mother there.
When I leave this frail existence,
When I lay this mortal by,
Father, Mother, may I meet you
In your royal courts on high?[5]

Joseph Smith reportedly once saw this "Heavenly Mother" in a vision.[6] LDS leaders, including two who later became "prophets" of the Church, overtly taught the existence of this female deity. Joseph Fielding Smith argued that just because the Standard Works of the Church do not include any references to a Heavenly Mother, "would not good common sense tell us that we must have a mother there also?"[7] Even more recently, in 1975 Spencer W. Kimball rhapsodized about the "the ultimate in maternal modesty... the restrained and queenly elegance of our Heavenly Mother."[8]

However, since LDS theology teaches that God is a polygamist, then supposedly any inhabitant of God's created earths could be descended from any one of several "Heavenly Mothers." This concept was explored by one of Joseph Smith's original twelve Apostles, Orson Pratt;[9] and since 1980, LDS women have publicly speculated about it as well.[10] When I was a Mormon, I was told that we did not know her name or much about her because the leaders of the Church did not want to make her an object of worship such as the Catholic Church had made of Mary. However, since she was always spoken of in the singular, perhaps it might be in harmony with current LDS teachings to assume that only one of God's wives was mother to all earth inhabitants, and perhaps other wives birthed the spirit bodies of other worlds created by the Mormon god. Remarkably, the nonbiblical doctrine of a Heavenly Mother is one of the few distinctives of Mormonism which the Church seems to be less inclined to disavow in the twenty-first century, quite in contrast to other non-Christian doctrines such as the LDS view of the past human condition of God the Father and the future godhood of faithful Mormons.

THE PREEXISTENCE

Thus LDS doctrine says each person was a fully functioning, born entity long before his mortal birth. In an attempt to find Bible justification for this point of view, Mormons quote Jeremiah 1:5: "Before I formed thee in the belly I knew thee; and before thou camest forth out of the womb I sanctified thee, and I ordained thee a prophet unto the nations."

Only a part of the entities born to God were designated for this earth. God created many more worlds, and *Doctrine and Covenants* 76:24 tells us that the inhabitants of these other worlds too were "begotten sons and daughters unto God." This time span between the birth of the spirit, its growth and maturing in the spirit world, and its later infusion into a corporeal body on earth is known by Mormons as "the preexistence," or first estate. In this state the spirits of men and women made preparations for earth life, living with God the Father and "Heavenly Mother" "in his house and dwelt with him year after year," according to Brigham Young.[11] Existing there too were the spirits of every plant, fish, bird, and animal that has ever lived or will ever live on earth.[12] They too had spirit bodies, made up of intangible matter.

When God and his wives had finished with the creation of the spirit bodies of all who would eventually live on this earth, he called a great meeting of the spirits, a "council in heaven." He proposed a plan whereby his children could live on earth and be tested, and yet return to him after death. The spirits divided themselves up into two factions. God's firstborn spirit Son, the premortal Jesus Christ, supported this plan, which was based on the concept of humankind's "free agency" or ability to choose a lifestyle that would either return them to God or separate them from their Father. Christ's endorsement was no small thing, for if a human were given the prerogative of sinning he would surely do so; and Christ's support of this plan required him to sacrifice himself for humankind's sin, while giving the glory to God the Father.

Another highly favored son of God, his second born, Lucifer, also proposed a plan—one that excluded free agency, but *guaranteed* that all God's spirit children would return to him. In return, Lucifer wanted all the glory for himself. All the spirits divided themselves into factions, and one-third of the spirits sided with Lucifer and his plan. God, however, rejected it.

When Lucifer and his followers found they could not have their way, they rebelled against God. Lucifer had wanted God's glory; now he sought his throne. A great battle in heaven ensued. Lucifer and his spirits warred against the armies of heaven who were led by Michael, the preexistent Adam. Lucifer and his followers lost and were cast down from heaven and condemned to be disembodied spirits throughout eternity.

In order to make our "second estate," or experience on earth, a true testing ground, it was necessary that before birth our knowledge of the preexistence be removed. Mormons of today speak figuratively of this forgetting as a "veil" over our memories. Orson Pratt, however, explained that this loss of memory was due to the traumatic experience of the adult-sized spirit body entering the physical body of a tiny baby: "When this spirit was compressed, so as to be wholly enclosed in an infant tabernacle, it had a tendency to suspend the memory."[13]

Of course all of this is incongruent with the Bible. Genesis 1:26 and 2:7 clearly show man to be a created being—far from the independent intelligence that Mormonism says was "organized" into a spirit body. Genesis teaches us that man *became* a living soul when God breathed life into him.

Of all who have lived on this earth, only Jesus Christ existed before the Creation, as John 1 clearly teaches.

Zechariah 12:1 also strikes a blow against the LDS concept of the preexistence of the human soul. Here the Bible states clearly that man's spirit was *formed within him.* How much more clearly could God say it?

Even the Jeremiah 1:5 passage, "Before I formed thee in the belly I knew thee; and before thou camest forth out of the womb I sanctified thee, and I ordained thee a prophet unto the nations," when read carefully shows (1) the foreknowledge of God even before he makes his creations, and (2) his power to foreordain his servants to great works—after they are created in the womb. If this passage in Jeremiah were to be used effectively by Mormons to prove preexistence, it would have to say that *we* knew *God* before birth—which the passage does not say—not he knew us.

Mormons say we are all literal sons and daughters of God, our spirits begotten—through a premortal birth process—by him. But the Bible tells us that we *become* God's children at conversion (John 1:12). In that sense, we are God's sons and daughters, and thanks be to his holy Name that he should adopt any so unworthy as we are into his family.

THE MORMON GOD

With an understanding of LDS doctrine about the preexistence, one can hardly call Mormonism monotheism but rather polytheism in its most replete form. Mormons have historically ridiculed what the Bible teaches about our one triune God. When I was a Mormon at BYU, LeGrand Richards of the Council of the Twelve Apostles called the Christian world's view of God "the best description of nothing that can be written."[14] Richards, in saying this, was following a long-lived Mormon tradition of reviling the God of the Bible. Joseph Smith once scoffed at the idea of God being three Persons in one[15] by saying,

> I have always declared God to be a distinct personage, Jesus Christ a separate and distinct personage from God the Father, and that the Holy Ghost was a distinct personage and a Spirit, and these three constitute three distinct personages and three Gods ... Many men say there is one God; the Father, the Son and the Holy Ghost are only one God! I say that is a strange God anyhow—three in one, and one in three! It is a curious organization ... All are to be crammed into one God, according to sectarianism. It would make the biggest God in all the world. He would be a wonderfully big God—he would be a giant or a monster.[16]

The Bible believer is dismayed by this sort of discussion of God, and would think that surely a direct refutation from the Bible would suffice to show a Mormon where he is wrong. But John 10:30, where Jesus said, "I and my Father are one," is interpreted by Mormons to mean that they are one in purpose only.

In the earliest writings of Joseph Smith, such as the *Book of Mormon*, there is no hint of the concept of many gods that would so preoccupy him later. In his initial written account of his first vision, a so-called "strange account," Joseph did not even mention God the Father appearing to him, only Jesus Christ.[17] The official account, published in the *Pearl of Great Price* as part of the section "Joseph Smith—History," does of course make much of his contention that a corporeal God appeared to him, but this version was not written until almost twenty years after the supposed experience,[18] and after Joseph Smith began formulating his theories of many gods.

The *Book of Mormon* was unabashedly monotheistic (though, as the whole book shows, more modalistic[19] than trinitarian):

> And now, behold, my beloved brethren, this is the way; and there is none other way nor name given under heaven whereby man can be saved in the kingdom of God. And now, behold, this is the doctrine of Christ, and the only and true doctrine of the Father, and of the Son, and of the Holy Ghost, which is one God, without end. Amen. (2 Nephi 31:21)[20]

The *Book of Mormon* also taught that God is a spirit.

> And then Ammon said: Believest thou that there is a Great Spirit?
>
> And he said, Yea.
>
> And Ammon said: This is God. And Ammon said unto him again: Believest thou that this Great Spirit, who is God, created all things which are in heaven and in the earth?
>
> And he said: Yea. (Alma 18:26–29a)

Even as late as 1833 Joseph Smith was teaching in the "Lectures on Faith" that God was a "personage of spirit, glory, and power," while the Son was a "personage of tabernacle."[21] But in Kirtland, Ohio, when Joseph Smith began his study of the Hebrew language, he realized that one of the Hebrew words for Deity, *Elohim*, was in fact a plural word. In his excitement over this discovery, Joseph ignored two facts: This plural word could be used in the singular (like the English word *deer*—you can have one deer or twenty deer); but in the Bible, in speaking of God, it is always used with a singular verb form ("Elohim is," never "Elohim are"). In addition, he ignored the possibility that the "us" and "we" used by God in the first chapters of Genesis could refer to conversations with his creations, the angels, as Hebrews chapter 1 demonstrates.

Nonetheless, the very notion of plural gods set Joseph Smith off on a tangent which revolutionized his religion. Look what sweeping changes Smith made in his theology in just a few brief years, as LDS writer Grant Palmer sums up:

> From 1820 to 1834 he believed that there is one God, as seen in the *Book of Mormon*, the testimony of the three witnesses, the Book of Commandments 24:13–18, the Book of Moses, the JST, and the 1832 account of his first vision. By 1835 he had come to believe that two personages formed the godhead, as taught in the Doctrine and Covenants 20:28 (cf. Book of Commandments 24:18), the Lectures on Faith (5), and the 1835 and 1838 accounts of the first vision. From 1839 on, he preached a plurality of gods, as seen in Abraham 4 and 5 and the LDS temple ceremony.[22]

As a result of Smith's teachings and those of his successor, Mormons now believe that the godhead consists of three totally separate persons. The head of this organization[23] is the Father, the one who procreated our spirit bodies. He has never been coequal with Christ, for he created his Son. He is not coeternal with the Spirit, either, for the same reason. But like their Christ, the LDS God has a body of flesh and bones. Mormons teach that he looks like a man as, indeed, he once was.

We read in Genesis 1:27 that God created man "in his own image." This, Mormons teach, has two meanings. First, since God created humans as males and females, that would imply that there is both a male and a female God.[24] Second, LDS doctrine would say this Genesis passage refers to these gods' physical bodies after which our own are patterned.

Mormons use other Bible passages to substantiate their assertion that God has a physical body: Proverbs 15:3, which speaks of God's eyes; Isaiah 55:11, which mentions his mouth; Isaiah 30:27, which speaks of his lips and tongue; 2 Kings 19:16, which mentions his ear; and so forth. *Doctrine and Covenants* 130:22 presses the point, insisting that the Father and Son have bodies "as tangible as man's."

Thus, when we read that Christ sits at the right hand of God (Heb. 1:3), say Mormons, the Bible is speaking of God's literal right hand. When the Bible mentions God's finger, or his nostrils, or his arm, these refer to an actual physical, space-contained, somatic person. However, verses like Psalm 89:26 demonstrate that just as God is not literally a rock, no less is he not literally our father. And even Mormons would not affirm that God has wings, despite the imagery in Psalm 17:8; 91:4, and elsewhere.

They say that the voice of God heard at the baptism of Jesus, along with the appearance of the Holy Ghost (Matt. 3:16–17) show that the three members of the godhead are separate and distinct from each other. "Joseph Smith—History," 1:18–20, and *Doctrine and Covenants* 76:14, are also used to show that when Joseph Smith wrote that he saw and talked with Christ, he was not the same as God the Father.

It is hard for a Christian to talk to a Mormon about God. You can say the same words but mean entirely different things. A Christian, in speaking of God, would probably be referring to our heavenly Creator (though the Bible does teach that both Jesus and the Holy Spirit are also God); the eternal One is the same in past, present, and future, but certainly never less than he is today. A Mormon, on the other hand, might use the word *God* loosely as a title referring more to an attainment of an office than to the name of a specific being. General LDS usage, though, ascribes the title of "God" to that person who fathered or organized our spirit bodies in the preexistence, the ubiquitously mentioned LDS "Heavenly Father," who himself began as an intelligence, then was birthed as a human, then became a god.

The LDS God has a real flesh and bones body, like yours and mine in many ways. He is "a resurrected Being," according to LDS Apostles Boyd K. Packer[25] and Dallin H. Oaks,[26] interviewed on the 2007 PBS documentary, *The Mormons*. However, his body does not have blood flowing through its veins,[27] for blood is the element of corruption. According to LDS theology, no person can be immortalized or exalted while his blood remains in his veins. Another miraculous substance, often referred to as "spirit," runs through the veins of all gods and their wives. The same is true of resurrected personages.[28] So what do LDS people do with Bible Scriptures like John 4:22–24?

> Ye worship ye know not what: we know what we worship: for salvation is of the Jews. But the hour cometh, and now is, when the true worshippers shall worship the Father in Spirit and in truth: for the Father seeketh such to worship him. God is a Spirit: and they that worship him must worship him in spirit and in truth.

They say that this passage was mistranslated, and that the end of it should read: "For unto such hath God promised his Spirit: And they that worship him must worship him in spirit and in truth." In addition, LDS apologist Robert Millet redefines the word *spirit* in this passage, saying that when it is used in the New Testament, it means "immortal," thus, God is spirit means God is immortal.[29] (This definition of the word *spiritual* poses a problem in other passages such as Galatians 6:1: "Brethren, if a man be overtaken in a fault, ye which are spiritual, restore such an one in the spirit of meekness.")

So where did the Mormon God get this body? This question lies at the heart of the whole LDS concept of God. The answer is that he too began as an intelligence, had two divine parents who clothed his intelligence with a spirit body (Brigham Young, quoting Joseph Smith, spoke of God's father and mother[30]), and then gained this body like you gained yours—by birth from two physical parents—on some faraway planet. This future god lived on an earth, like ours; obeyed the commandments of his god; and after his death he was resurrected with a "celestialized"[31] version of his body. As a reward for his obedience, he was made a god. He took his wives in connubial intercourse and thus created our spirit bodies, as Apostle Orson Pratt explained:

> We were begotten by our Father in Heaven; the person of our Father in Heaven was begotten on a previous heavenly world by his Father; and again, He was begotten by a still more ancient Father and so on, from generation to generation, from one heavenly world to another still more ancient, until our minds are wearied and lost in the multiplicity of generations and successive worlds, and as a last resort, we wonder in our minds, how far back the genealogy extends, and how the first world was formed, and the first father was begotten.[32]

The consummation of Joseph Smith's teachings on the godhead came just a few months before his death. Mormons say that the famous address he gave shortly before his martyrdom, at the funeral of a man named King Follett, was the Prophet's crowning doctrine. In this speech, before twenty thousand persons, Joseph emphasized that not only is our God an exalted man, but all men should have as their ultimate goals the attainment of godhood themselves.

BECOMING A GOD

Once when I was speaking to a group of high school students on the subject of Mormonism, I outlined the central points of doctrine covered by Joseph Smith in his King Follett Address. One of the students raised his hand as I was talking. He seemed a little annoyed. "That was 1844," he said. "Mormons don't teach that stuff about becoming a god today, do they?"

Yes, they do. There is no doctrine, outside that of continuing revelation, that is more integral to the Mormonism of both the past and the present than that of a progressing God. Their tiny children are taught this from infancy; their adolescents learn "scriptures" to support it; and every faithful adult holds godhood as his or her ultimate and rightful destiny. For the last four years that I was a Mormon, I wore a silver charm of the Salt Lake City LDS Temple to remind myself of my commitment to get married in a temple so that I could eventually become a goddess myself. I believed what Spencer W. Kimball said: "We are gods in embryo, and the Lord demands perfection of us."[33]

Recently, LDS apologists have begun to claim that their teaching about man's ability to become a god is actually true, original Christian teaching: that is, what the first-century apostles and their successors themselves believed and taught.[34] Mormons base their assertions on non-scriptural writings from the first centuries after Christ (specifically those of Iraneus of Lyons and Athanasius of Alexandria), and say that these writings of the early Christian age "sound" more like Mormonism than today's mainstream Christianity. (I don't know of a single Christian expert on that period who would agree with the contention that early Christian writers promoted what is now LDS doctrine.) Such writings (of Iraneus and Athanasius) are not in the Bible, and for that very reason a Christian must not rely upon them for doctrine. They were the opinions of men—some good, some bad, and some downright heretical. (One can just as easily "prove" some of the most grievous excesses and cultural superstitions of the Catholic Church, for instance, from those same writings.)

The primary biblical passages that LDS missionaries and other apologists use to "prove" their teachings on multiple gods and the potential godhood of humans are those scriptures which refer to "gods." (In many cases both Mormons and Christians would agree that certain verses refer to idols or false gods.) However, the many verses that refer to the Lord as being above other (false) gods or being "God of gods" (Ps. 136:2) are used by Mormons to supposedly prove a multiplicity of gods.

But Mormons would go a step further. They say that when Jesus quoted Psalm 82:6 in John 10:34–35, he was saying that people were gods (at least, potential gods). The Psalm passage says, "I have said, Ye are gods; and all of you are children of the most High." However, the context of both passages devastates this idea—nobody believed the unrighteous rulers (the Hebrew word from which "gods" is translated is rendered as "judge" in Exodus 21:6, 22 and 22:8) of the Psalm passage were truly eternal deities. That is proved in Psalm 82:7, which says, "Ye shall die like men." Nor can anyone say that Jesus was in any way approving of the spiritual status of the people he was speaking to when he quoted that psalm.[35] (If Mormons want that kind of godhood, they may just get it.)

Other Bible passages that LDS people use to support the idea of people becoming gods in the future are the Transfiguration (in which former human beings are "glorified"), the commands to "be holy" and "be perfect" like God (see Lev. 19:2 and Matt. 5:48), the idea of participating in the divine nature of God (2 Peter 1:4), the dominion of humans over the created order (Ps. 8:4–6), and all the many, many passages that speak of our adoption into the family of God and subsequent status as heirs. In them, God depicts himself as being and having something completely unique. He is willing to share glory, and holiness, and perfection, and his divine nature, and all that he has with us. But everything in the rest of the Bible—the context for all these teachings—tells us that only God is God; and nobody or nothing else will ever be.

When I was a Mormon, I like all other LDS children memorized the couplet attributed to LDS prophet Lorenzo Snow: "As man now is, our God once was; as now God is, so man may be."[36] That couplet and all the implications of it were openly taught from the children's organization, Primary Sunbeams, all the way up to the college course and Relief Society (women's organization) classes in which I participated and taught. In the past few years I have been told by Mormons that this is not (or is no longer considered as) doctrine. I once had an LDS man challenge me on a live, call-in radio program to "prove" that the Church taught as doctrine what Lorenzo Snow stated. Here's a test of that: Ask anyone who was a Mormon before 1970 if he or she was taught it—at church, by leadership—and if they believed it.

Not only that, consider this quote from Kimball in 1975, after he became Prophet of the Church: "Brethren, 225,000 of you are here tonight. I suppose 225,000 of you may become gods. There seems to be plenty of space out there in the universe. And the Lord has proved that he knows how to do it. I think he could make, or probably have us help make, worlds for all of us, for every one of us 225,000."[37]

A PROGRESSING GOD

Mormons regard their gaining of knowledge and experience on this earth as a mirroring of the progression that God is even now making. Wilford

Woodruff, a prophet of the Church, once said, "God himself is increasing and progressing in knowledge, power, and dominion."[38] But a later prophet, Joseph Fielding Smith, refuted this, saying that God could not now increase in knowledge, because that would imply that he was lacking in knowledge in the past.[39] What happens when the LDS "god" learns "new truth"?

As for morality, I have always explained it this way: A god who is progressing will be better—that is, more godly—tomorrow than he is today. *However, that means he was worse yesterday than he is today.*

If God does not progress in knowledge, it doesn't make sense that he could continue progressing in power and dominion. How can the All-Powerful increase in power? As for increasing in dominion—surely that is sticky human desire pressed upon the face of an insufficient deity.

Francis J. Beckwith, in his article "Philosophical Problems with the Mormon Concept of God," says this:

> The [LDS] church currently teaches that God is, in effect, (1) a contingent being, who was at one time not God; (2) finite in *knowledge* (not truly omniscient), *power* (not omnipotent), and *being* (not omnipresent or immutable); (3) one of many gods; (4) a corporeal (bodily) being, who physically dwells at a particular spacio-temporal location and is therefore not omnipresent like the classical God (respecting his intrinsic divine nature—we are not considering the Incarnation of the Son here); and a being who is subject to the laws and principles of a beginningless universe with an infinite number of entities in it.[40]

The laws of gravity and other natural principles rule over the LDS deity. He did not create them any more than he created us. He only "organized" eternal elements according to implacable laws—both of which (elements and laws) were in existence long before he had a soul—and he combined these elements to form the earth and its inhabitants. In comparing our God to him is seen the difference between Michelangelo painting the ceiling of the Sistine Chapel and a child who crayons neatly within the lines of the pictures in his coloring book.

Mormons laugh aloud at the idea of our God who can fill the immensity of space and yet still gently touch the heart of man unto repentance.[41] Silly, they say. Their bodily god, whom we should emulate, can only be in one place at a time. He lives near a burning sphere called Kolob that revolves once every thousand years. He awaits news from his worlds and sends messages via his angels. He is comforted by his wives and continues the ceaseless reproduction expected of them and him—and us, when we become gods.

I'd rather spend eternity in the sweet rest of my invisible God—"Who alone hath immortality, dwelling in the light which no man can approach unto; whom no man hath seen, nor can see: to whom be honour and power everlasting"[42]—than *be* a Mormon god.

THE ADAM-GOD DOCTRINE

Brigham Young taught a concept that has come to be known as the "Adam-God" doctrine. Now, Mormons of today do not worship Adam. They honor "Father" Adam as the greatest figure of the Old Testament. They teach that in the preexistence he was an archangel and prince.[43] But in times past, he was believed to be much more than this. Brigham Young said:

> Now hear it, O inhabitants of the earth, Jew and Gentile, saint and sinner! When our father Adam came into the garden of Eden, he came into it with a *celestial body*, and brought Eve, *one of his wives*, with him. He helped to make and organize this world. He is MICHAEL, the *Archangel*, the ANCIENT OF DAYS! about whom holy men have written and spoken—*HE is our FATHER and our GOD, and the only God with whom WE have to do.* Every man upon the earth, professing Christians or non-professing, must hear it, and *will know it sooner or later.*[44] (Italics and capitalizations appear in original.)

Elaborating upon this, Brigham Young taught that Adam was a part of the Trinity of Elohim (God the Father), Jehovah (Jesus),[45] and Michael. When placed on the earth, Adam-God fulfilled a divine plan by eating of the Tree of the Knowledge of Good and Evil. His body and that of Eve underwent a change because of this, and they were able to conceive children, who were mortal as Adam and Eve now were. Later teachings of Brigham Young indicated that the resurrected Adam was the father of Jesus Christ.[46]

This all raises a lot of questions the LDS Church doesn't want asked. Such as, if Adam were a god before this earth was created, how could he be tested? How could a god "fall" (even if it were a "fall upward")?[47] And how could a god die, as Adam did?

As I said before, Brigham Young's "Adam-God doctrine" is not taught as official doctrine in Mormonism today. In fact, President Spencer W. Kimball has openly refuted the Adam-God doctrine, identifying it as a false teaching.[48] This has left the LDS scholar with two dilemmas. First of all, *Doctrine and Covenants* 27:11 and 138:8 both call Adam the Ancient of Days, and section 116 says that this is the same as the Ancient of Days "spoken of by Daniel the prophet." Daniel 7:9–22 shows unmistakably that the Ancient of Days is divine. Second, if Brigham Young taught the Adam-God doctrine as revelation[49] and it is false (as Christian and Mormon alike would now agree), doesn't that make Brigham Young a false prophet?

LDS leaders of today fall back on the usage of the word *god* to mean an office attained by the righteous and say that thus, Adam is a god. This explanation might satisfy any Mormon who has neither access to the multivolume *Journal of Discourses* nor curiosity to find it,[50] but no one else. Others say that Adam was the god of this world in the same sense that Satan is the god of this world or age (2 Cor. 4:4).[51] But what does it mean, for instance, that Adam is "the only God with whom we have to do"?

More candid LDS scholars, though, like Rodney Turner, have admitted that an honest examination of Church documents "will admit to no other conclusion than that the identification of Adam with God the Father by President Young is an irrefutable fact."[52] And, though Mormons utterly deny the Adam-God theory which has lent so much ammunition to their critics, the secret temple ceremonies of even this day depict the creation of the earth by Elohim, Jehovah, and—who else?—Michael. And all this in spite of abundant scriptural evidence (Gen. 1:27; 2:7; 3:19) that Adam was created, not a creator.

Adam was not the only person upon whom Mormons have graciously bestowed godhood. *Doctrine and Covenants* 132:37 teaches that Abraham, Isaac, and Jacob are already gods. They have joined the innumerable gods throughout the ages, as described by Orson Pratt: "If we should take a million of worlds like this and number their particles, we should find that there are more Gods than there are particles of matter in those worlds."[53]

What does the Bible say about becoming a god?

> But the LORD is the true God, he is the living God, and an everlasting king: at his wrath the earth shall tremble, and the nations shall not be able to abide his indignation. Thus shall ye say unto them, The gods that have not made the heavens and the earth, even they shall perish from the earth, and from under these heavens. (Jer. 10:10–11)
>
> Ye are my witnesses, saith the LORD, and my servant whom I have chosen: that ye may know and believe me, and understand

> that I am he: before me there was no God formed, neither shall there be after me. (Isa. 43:10; see also Isa. 44:8; 45:21–22)

One LDS writer has attempted to explain away the passages in Isaiah about there being only one God. "Isaiah 44:8 is not a statement delineating how many Gods exist in the eternities," says Stephen W. Gibson, "but a statement telling Israel there is no other God over *them*—no pagan or graven god has his power, and that only Jehovah can save them."[54] The problem with this "explanation" is seen in the continuation of the verse, in God's insistence that he himself *knows of no other Gods*: "Is there a God beside me? yea, there is no God; I know not any" (Isa. 44:8). (The problem is compounded by the LDS understanding that it was Jesus who communicated with human beings throughout the Old Testament: Thus he, speaking as God, would be denying his own Father.) Would Mormons like to contend that God is ignorant? Unable to see the future of humans who will become gods? Lying? All of the above?

The New Testament gives additional support. The apostle Paul acknowledges the existence of entities (or concepts) known as "gods," which Paul says are really not gods at all. He affirms in 1 Corinthians 8:4–6:

> As concerning therefore the eating of those things that are offered in sacrifice unto idols, we know that an idol is nothing in the world, and that there is none other God but one. For though there be that are called gods, whether in heaven or in earth, (as there be gods many, and lords many,) But to us there is but one God, the Father, of whom are all things, and we in him; and one Lord Jesus Christ, by whom are all things, and we by him.

THE MORMON CHRIST

Christ, the firstborn son of God in the LDS preexistence, somehow managed to attain Mormon godhood even before he gained a mortal body (which Mormons say is essential to achieving divinity). LDS author Apostle Bruce R. McConkie explained that Jesus achieved this "by obedience and devotion to the truth" while still in the preexistent state.[55] Christ was highly favored of God (the father of his spiritual body) and of all the other preexistent spirits (who were his brothers and sisters). Mormons say that up until the time of his resurrection, our "Elder Brother," Jesus, was subordinate to God, but at that time he was exalted to equality with him.

Contrast this to the teachings of John chapter 1 and Philippians 2:5–11, which clearly teach that Jesus was "in the form of God," yet didn't hold onto his essential and inherent equality with the Father but instead humbly "made himself of no reputation" so as to submit to death on a cross. After that, he *returned* to his former glory.

Even before his mortal life, Son Ahman (according to LDS doctrine, Christ's name in the "pure Adamic language"[56]) carried out many duties essential to our temporal life and eventual salvation. Under the auspices of his Father, Christ created the world we live on by organizing the existing elements of the universe into this terrestrial ball.[57] Because of this, he is called our Father too, in the same sense that Euclid could be called the father of geometry. He is also referred to as the Father of our salvation, because of his atonement,[58] and because of a principle known as "divine investiture of authority"—wherein he can speak as if he were the Father in any given situation.[59]

This heavy emphasis on Christ as "the Father" is confusing to non-Mormons, but is essential to LDS theology. They teach that the Father of our spirits, Elohim or Ahman, never appeared to nor spoke to man after the transgression of Adam. God the Father was seen with Christ only when it was necessary to introduce and bear record of his Son to humankind, as at the baptism of Christ and in the first vision of Joseph Smith. At all other times the being who appeared as God was Jesus, who through divine investiture of authority was acting as his Father.

As a young Mormon I was very confused by this. I remember asking a missionary, whose knowledge of doctrine I admired, why it was that we prayed to God the Father if Jesus were the one doing all the work, and the only one of the Godhead who would actually communicate back to people. This missionary replied that we prayed to the Father because that was the example Jesus gave us when he offered the Lord's Prayer. That answer satisfied me for a while, but then I was left to wonder why it was that Jesus would say he was the Father, and act as the Father, and then instruct us to pray to a being we really knew nothing about.

Christ's dealings with humanity before he took on a mortal body were to sharpen his skills, so to speak, at dealing with this unruly race. In fact, I heard it said many times that of all the earths God organized and peopled, ours was the only one wicked enough to kill its own Redeemer.[60] The atonement of Christ on this earth, therefore, applied to all the others of God's earths: in the words of Apostle Bruce R. McConkie, "The atonement of Christ, being literally and truly infinite, applies to an infinite number of earths."[61]

Mormons also claim that they have knowledge of certain facts about Christ that people who read only the Bible couldn't know. Though they celebrate Christmas as a religious holiday commemorating the mortal birth of the Savior, Joseph Smith said in *Doctrine and Covenants* section 20 that Christ was actually born exactly 1,830 years prior to the organization of the Church on April 6, 1830—which would make Christ's birthday April 6, AD 1.

Mormons believe in, honor, and teach the being they call Christ. I have been quite heartened to see that the LDS Church has begun to emphasize his name in ways beyond the rote ending of prayers, because I believe that increased exposure to the words of the historic Jesus in the New Testament can have a great effect on the hearts of readers. In 2008 the LDS Church launched a new website that focuses just on him (www.jesuschrist.lds.org). They do not, as some suggest, deliberately de-emphasize him in their teaching, but they see him less as our God than as our "elder brother" who set an example for us. In addition, they have so much extra-biblical doctrine to deal with that Christ is minimized by everything else that is taught, and crushed by the sheer volume of it. LDS children are taught to follow the examples of their leaders, and they emulate the young Joseph Smith or the youthful David O. McKay. Jesus Christ just lived too long ago to relate to when you have "living prophets," and the Bible's "Perfect Man" often drags in a poor second to more contemporary heroes from LDS lore.

CONCEPTION AND MARRIAGES OF CHRIST

Probably the one LDS doctrine most offensive to Christians concerns an LDS version of the virgin birth of Christ. Fundamentalist Christians say that Jesus Christ would have to have been born of a virgin (that is, a sexually inexperienced young woman) in order to fulfill Old Testament prophecies. Early Mormon writings, like the *Book of Mormon*, taught the same concept of the virgin birth that Christians believe.[62]

But Brigham Young claimed that the Bible was in error on the "virgin" birth of Christ. He said: "Now, remember from this time forth, and for ever, that Jesus Christ was not begotten by the Holy Ghost."[63] Joseph Fielding Smith, who later became the president of the LDS Church, vehemently denied that either the *Book of Mormon* or the Bible taught that Jesus was begotten of the Holy Ghost.[64] The implications are startling: What LDS leaders have consistently, historically taught is that God the Father, in his glorified, immortal body, came down to earth and approached the young girl Mary. As a result of this carnal union, Mary became pregnant with a child who was both divine and human; and thus the young Christ was truly the *Son* of *God*.[65] Aside from the sheer blasphemy of this position, it also contradicts the Mormons' own teachings, for as was previously mentioned,

God was never supposed to have appeared on earth after the fall except to witness to the divinity and sonship of Christ, and the only ones who could see him were those with the priesthood.

By violating a betrothed woman, too, God would have broken one of his own laws—which required the death of any man who had carnal knowledge of a betrothed woman (Deut. 22:23–24). Also, unless God had married Mary, he would have been committing adultery against his other wives. Therefore, Mormons have reasoned that Mary had two husbands.[66] One LDS writer speculated that she married Joseph for time (though she was, we must conclude, either a fornicator or a polyandrist), and God for eternity.[67] Thus, after the resurrection she will join God as one of his wives—which makes him guilty of incest too. (Was not Mary his spirit daughter?)

Despite this ample history of LDS leaders who claimed direct revelation from God, and who said that Mary became pregnant by God in the same way that any earthly woman becomes pregnant by a mortal man, despite decades of teaching (including during my time in the LDS Church) and assurance that this was so, the official LDS stance of today is that Mary was, nonetheless, a virgin.

The entire issue of the exact agent of that pregnancy is ignored. In fact, most twenty-first century LDS apologists say that former teachings about a physical relationship between God the Father and Mary fits in a category of repudiated older teachings called "deprecated doctrine." Most Mormons today have a vague sense of a "Heavenly Father's" involvement in the conception without the mental image of sexual relations.

There is just too much confusion in the Mormons' account of the conception of Christ for it to be of God. Brigham Young said that Adam begot Christ[68]; Joseph Fielding Smith said God the Father did; Mormons today say God did but we don't know how—but the Bible said that what was conceived in Mary was "of the Holy Ghost" (Matt. 1:20).

Christ also was a polygamist according to Orson Hyde, an early LDS leader. Though the LDS Church of today says it has "no official position"[69] on whether or not Christ married, Hyde implied that Jesus married Mary, Martha, and "the other Mary" at the wedding at Cana.[70] He supposedly also had children by one or more of these women before he died.[71] Jedediah M. Grant, an early LDS leader, identified the Jews' rabid hatred of Jesus and their desire to persecute and crucify him as the direct result of Christ's advocating polygamy.[72]

Nor is a polygamous Christ just an image for nineteenth-century Mormons. A more modern apologist, Darrick T. Evenson, unabashedly contended that Jesus both married and was a polygamist, as evidenced by (1) the fact that the women who surrounded the cross were taking the role of widows; (2) Psalm 45:6–9, which implies polygamy and was quoted by the writer of Hebrews in 1:8 to apply to Jesus; and (3) legends that Jesus married Mary Magdalene and others.[73] Evenson further asserted that Jesus' turning water into wine showed that he was the bridegroom at the marriage at Cana[74]—despite the clear statement in the Bible that Jesus was invited to the feast. (Since when, in Jewish or modern culture, does somebody invite the bridegroom to his own wedding?)[75]

OTHER LDS DOCTRINES OF CHRIST

According to LDS doctrine as seen in Ether chapter 3 of the *Book of Mormon*, the first person to see the premortal Christ in his spirit body was the brother of Jared, Mahonri Moriancumr, who was so full of faith that the Lord Jesus could not withhold himself from him. This contradicts LDS scripture which states that the Lord appeared to Adam and his descendants,[76] and talked "face to face" with Enoch.

The biblical Christ has characteristics and an eternal history very dissimilar to the Mormon messiah. Deuteronomy 6:4, the famous rallying cry of the Hebrew people, shows that even then God's people understood that the names *Elohim* and *Jehovah* referred to the same entity: *Sh'mah Yisroel Adonai Elcheinu Adonai Echod* translates as "The LORD (Jehovah) our God (Elohim) is one LORD (Jehovah)."

In their preoccupation with the physical bodies that they claim that God and Christ possess, Mormons deny their adherents of one of the most precious gifts of God—the indwelling of Jesus himself within a believer. Ephesians 3:17, for instance, promises that Christ dwells in our hearts by faith. But *Doctrine and Covenants* 130:3 says,

> John 14:23 [Jesus answered and said unto him, If a man love me, he will keep my words: and my Father will love him, and we will come unto him, and make our abode with him.]—The appearing of the Father and the Son, in that verse, is a personal appearance; and the idea that the Father and the Son dwell in a man's heart is an old sectarian notion, and is false.

Besides being a perversion of Scripture, the *Doctrine and Covenants* statement also ignores the Bible's further teachings in Romans 8:9–11, 2 Corinthians 13:5, and Colossians 1:27.

When I was a Mormon, I always referred to Jesus as "the Christ" or "the Savior." It was gauche to say his first name, Jesus: an overreaching of familiarity. LDS Apostle Bruce R. McConkie, in fact, adamantly warned Mormons away from thinking they could have a personal relationship with Jesus Christ, teaching that such a notion was part of Lucifer's plan to lead mankind astray.[77] McConkie, like many LDS leaders, also warned people against addressing Jesus in prayer, saying that we should pray to the Father alone.[78] This contrasts sharply with the worship that Jesus accepted throughout his lifetime, and in particular from Thomas who called him, "My LORD and my God" (John 20:28).

If all of this sounds like the LDS Church has historically taught a different Jesus than Christendom, hear the words of the late LDS President Gordon B. Hinckley when he addressed a crowd of European Mormons in 1998. While affirming that he believed in Christ, Hinckley said that people outside the LDS Church say Mormons do not believe in the traditional Christ. "No, I don't," said Hinckley. "The traditional Christ of whom they speak is not the Christ of whom I speak."[79] He went on to define the LDS Christ as one with a different history than the Christ of the Bible, a history that began to diverge and emerge when Joseph Smith said he met a personage in a grove in 1820.

THE MORMON HOLY GHOST

The Holy Ghost, the third member of the godhead, like God the Father and Jesus Christ, is also uniquely characterized by Mormons. He is not known by what the Bible shows to be an interchangeable name, the Holy Spirit (Mormons make distinction between the two despite the fact that both "Ghost" and "Spirit" are translated from a single Greek word *pneuma*). The LDS Holy Ghost is the Comforter, the medium through which both spiritual and secular knowledge are conveyed to man. He has a spirit body that is in appearance like that of a man. (This is despite the fact that the Bible never describes the Holy Spirit in images that suggest a male body—instead, he is pictured as a dove, a fire, or oil. His agency in bringing about the birth of Jesus shows that this was truly a supernatural event.) *Doctrine and Covenants* 130:22 affirms that "the Holy Ghost is a personage of spirit." Because this spirit body of intangible yet real matter can only be in one place at a time,[80] the LDS Holy Ghost is of limited dimensions, and cannot, himself, be everywhere present.

Just how he, like Christ, got to be a god without a physical body is another of the great mysteries of Mormonism. Nineteenth-century LDS

Apostle Heber C. Kimball once said that the Holy Ghost was "one of the sons of our Father and our God."[81] If that were true, he could be properly referred to as our "brother" in the same way that Mormons call Christ "Elder Brother," though I've never heard the Holy Ghost so described.

Mormons regard the Holy Ghost as the most active member of the godhead in human affairs. He is responsible, they say, for carrying out most of the godhead's decisions that would not require a personal appearance by the other gods. Since he is invisible to humans, he can work "behind the scenes" in both spiritual affairs of humans, and in temporal affairs that would eventually have an effect on the kingdom. Being confined to his man-shaped form[82] as a spirit with a finite spirit body, it follows that he cannot indwell any more than Christ or God can. *Doctrine and Covenants* 130:22 says that the Holy Ghost *can* indwell, but Mormon apologists say that this refers only to his influence.

Poor Mormons! What they are missing by not inviting God in all his manifestations to come inside their hearts! If it is not the biblical Holy Spirit that dwells in them, whose spirit is it?

Mormons emphasize the difference between God and Christ, but not their spirits, which they say are the same. The LDS Spirit of God and the LDS Spirit of Christ are identical. This influence is also known as the "spirit of truth" or the "light of Christ," and is that which lights the way of all men who come into the world,[83] before they are baptized. In contrast, the Holy Ghost influences humans through the "gift" of his influence. The Holy Ghost may give a brief, temporary "flash of testimony" to the truth of the LDS gospel before the baptism of a faithful seeker,[84] but the seeker can only receive the right to enjoy the influence of the Holy Ghost on a more permanent basis by having that gift conferred on him by the laying on of hands by one with LDS priesthood authority, in a formal ceremony for that purpose. And that, of course, entitles one just to the LDS Holy Ghost's "gift," not his indwelling.

As in all other matters of doctrine, though, Mormonism betrays its human origins by the confusion that surrounds its precepts. They say that the Holy Ghost is the comforter promised by Christ in John 14:12–27, but Joseph Smith expanded on that passage thus:

> "And I will pray to the Father, and he shall give you another Comforter, that he may abide with you for ever;" now what is this other Comforter? It is no more nor less than the Lord Christ himself, and this is the sum and substance of the whole matter.[85]

If ignoring the Holy Ghost as in this passage isn't denying him, what is? Mormons are caught in a dilemma here—if the "Second Comforter" is the presence of Christ—"forever"—and Christ has a physical body, does that mean the Savior moves into your house with you? He can't, according to Joseph Smith, dwell in your heart. What about the other people who desire the Comforter?

One of the strangest teachings regarding the Mormon Holy Ghost is, as we have previously seen in looking at the "Adam-God doctrine," his identification with Adam or Michael. Brigham Young once stated:

> The earth was organized by three distinct characters, namely, Eloheim, Yahovah, and Michael [i.e., Adam], these three forming a quorum, as in all heavenly bodies, and in organizing element, perfectly represented in the Deity, as Father, Son, and Holy Ghost.[86]

Why Brigham Young was so hung up on Adam—saying he was God, and then the Holy Ghost—we'll probably never know. The doctrines he bestowed have grown up in a thicket of confusion to snare Christian and Mormon alike. He also taught that the Holy Ghost had nothing to do with the conception of Christ:

> If the Son was begotten by the Holy Ghost, it would be very dangerous to baptize and confirm females, and give the Holy Ghost to them, lest he should beget children, to be palmed upon the Elders by the people, bringing the Elders into great difficulties.[87]

To say, then, that the Mormons have a unique concept of the Holy Ghost is no exaggeration. Because of this, Christians cannot communicate with Mormons on the subject of the Holy Ghost any more than they can on the subject of God. Using the same words—*Holy Ghost, Comforter, Spirit*—does not guarantee that you are saying the same thing!

THE MORMON SATAN

As much as any religious group on earth, the Mormons are acutely aware of the reality of the being they refer to as Satan. His prime objective, according to Mormons, is to influence and finally control those souls he didn't win over to his way in the preexistence.

The Mormon Satan was, like Jesus and all other beings who have come to this earth, begotten by God in the preexistence. In fact, Apostle George Q. Cannon stated, "It may be a startling doctrine to many to say this; but Satan is our brother, Jesus is our brother. We are the children of God."[88] *Doc-*

trine and Covenants section 76 teaches that Satan was once an angel named Lucifer ("Bringer of Light") with a position of authority in the presence of God (v. 25). He led a rebellion against Christ (*Pearl of Great Price*, Moses 4:1–4), and was followed by one-third of God's spirit children. Defeated by the hosts of heaven, Satan became Perdition ("Utter Loss"), and was cast down to the earth (Rev. 12:7–9) with his followers.

The Mormon Church teaches that Satan, though his counterfeit plan of salvation was rejected by God the Father in favor of that advanced by Christ, still continues to preach his false program through any godless doctrine, no matter how otherwise uplifting.[89] Unlike us, he has retained his memory of the preexistence and uses it at every opportunity to try to lead us from God. He is wise and cunning, but according to the LDS definition of intelligence ("light and truth"—*Doctrine and Covenants* 93:36), he is completely devoid of that attribute.

Though they are here upon this earth, we cannot see Satan and his hosts because the greatest punishment for their rebellion was the denial of the privilege of physical bodies. (Many Mormons have wondered, if this were a punishment, why the Holy Ghost has no body either.)

The influence of a devil is necessary, said President John Taylor. "Why is it, in fact, that we should have a devil? Why did not the Lord kill him long ago? Because we could not do without him."[90] Unlike the despicable adversary of Christianity, the Mormon devil is thus a necessary cog in the machinery of God, who *needs* even Satan to carry out his eternal purposes. Author LaMar Petersen noted that

> God tolerates his foe, the Devil, who at times is an unwitting ally, as in the tempting of Eve: the Devil enacted the role requisite to the plan of life and salvation, thus preventing the scuttling of the divine program.[91]

According to LDS tradition, Satan has his own priesthood, a parody of true priesthood, and he has been seen in LDS temples.[92] Although God blessed water in the beginning of history, Mormons say he cursed it in the last days, and now the element of water is the domain of Satan (despite what Psalm 29:10 says about God being enthroned there). The day will come, says *Doctrine and Covenants* 61:13–22, that only the upright in heart will be able to travel on the water. The introduction to this same section says that Elder William W. Phelps saw Satan "riding in power upon the face of the waters." That is one of the reasons LDS missionaries may not swim while on their missions, and why many older Mormons will not get near any body of water greater than that contained in a bathtub.[93]

But the LDS Satan's power is only temporary. He is making the best of his influence over people, for at the last resurrection, he and his followers will be cast down to an everlasting hell. Even in eternity he will not have the preeminence he has always sought, for the "sons of perdition" (unregenerate humans who are placed in hell with him and his angels), though having their progression halted, will be able to rule over Satan by virtue of the fact that they will still have their bodies. Satan and his preexistent hosts are doomed never to enjoy a body, and thus, never to progress, never to be gods.

EVIL SPIRITS

Heber C. Kimball and Orson Hyde, early leaders in the LDS Church, once had an experience with demons that Joseph Smith told them was because they had come so near to the Lord that Satan exhibited his greatest power to inhibit their progress. According to Kimball and Hyde, they were confronted by legions of demons who appeared after Kimball had rebuked an evil spirit that had been tormenting a fellow missionary. The demons seemed to be coming out of the wall of the room where the missionaries were and looked like the most malevolent and destructive portrayals of wickedness imaginable. Hyde "fought them and contended against them face to face, until they began to diminish in number and to retreat from the room."[94]

President Wilford Woodruff once estimated that there were one hundred evil spirits roaming the earth to each living person at any given time.[95] These spirits are so jealous of mortals that they will try at any cost to control their bodies—so desperate, in fact, that they often settle for the body of a lower animal, as when Christ cast a legion of devils out of a man (Mark 5:6–9). The evil spirits then entered into a herd of swine, the only available bodies thereabouts.

Parley P. Pratt said that there was a way to detect if a person was possessed by an evil spirit. The individual would, he said, produce a shock to the observer and emit an unpleasant odor.[96] Though Mormons usually will not talk about it to outsiders, exorcisms are not uncommon today. As LDS writer Bruce R. McConkie cautiously observed, "By the power of faith and the authority of the priesthood, devils are frequently cast out of such afflicted persons."[97]

I had two brushes with such experiences while I was a dormitory senior resident in Helaman Halls, Brigham Young University. In a nearby hall a bishop and other elders were called in to cast evil spirits out of a young girl and to in some way cleanse her dormitory room by rebuking the spirit by the power of the priesthood, forbidding it to return. Though unusual and kept a closely guarded secret, such an event was accepted almost passively by those Mormons who heard of it. We had been taught that Satan would try most violently to influence the choicest spirits, who were most logically found in the high spiritual atmosphere of an LDS home, dormitory, or missionary apartment.

That event did not prepare me for what happened a few months later. One evening, as the girls on my floor were just settling down to studies after dinner, two of the most sincere, earnest girls under my responsibility came into my room. Both were pale and frightened. As they began to speak, I could hardly believe my ears. They had been in the dorm room of the normally vivacious redhead who now stood before me, a shaking mass of fear. Her friend, a candid, light-hearted freshman, had stopped by to visit. They were talking—about nothing in particular, they said—in one of the girl's rooms with the door closed. According to the redhead, her friend was interrupted in mid-sentence by an unseen force which picked her up bodily and threw her against the door, then dropped her to the floor. They had stood, stunned, looking at each other for a moment, and then had run down the hall to my room.

I would not ever doubt the integrity of either girl. They were not liars, nor would they joke about or concoct such an experience—faithful Mormon youth like those do not dabble idly in such things.

In *Doctrine and Covenants* section 129, Joseph Smith perhaps set the tone for such an experience. There he gave a test that Mormons memorize in case they are ever confronted by a supernatural being. Spirits from God, said Joseph Smith, fall into two categories: (1) good angels, who are resurrected personages of flesh and bones and (2) the spirits of "just men made perfect," who have glorious (spirit) bodies, but have not yet been resurrected physically. Mormons know that if they are approached by an unearthly being, they are to offer a hand to that personage. If it is a heavenly angel, he will take the hand and the person will be able to feel the flesh and bone of the angel. A spirit of a just person made perfect, though, will not accept the handshake, because the person's spiritual body would not be tangible. A devil, however, in his eagerness to have you mistakenly accept him as an angel from God, will extend his unembodied hand. So Mormons believe that if anyone offers you a handshake you can't feel, you've got a problem on your hands. (I often wondered, though, why the devils were so stupid as not to be able to restrain themselves from offering the hand, and thus pass themselves off unsuspected as the spirits of just men made perfect.) Obscure LDS doctrine also teaches that any supernatural visitor with sandy-colored hair is a "bad angel,"[98] as is any being who is afraid of weapons.[99]

Could it be only coincidental that a human being who might masquerade as a heavenly messenger would have a tangible handshake? That would fit in with the (admittedly anecdotal) story told by an early apostate who said that Joseph Smith had Sidney Rigdon pretend to be an angel. Though I've never seen a description of Rigdon's hair color, I would bet it wasn't "sandy." *Any* mortal would be afraid of a weapon; the only puzzler is why a devil—who has no corporeal body—would be afraid of a gun or bowie knife, as Heber C. Kimball claimed.[100]

All in all, the LDS conception of Satan doesn't make much sense either. Satan, they say, is the brother of Christ, and of us all; and the son of God. The Bible teaches that a good tree (like God) can only bring forth, or reproduce, to make good fruit. Satan is thus *not* God's progeny.[101]

Human beings, too, as *created* by God—not sired by him—are in a natural state of rebellion against their Maker. Only by being born again can we become sons and daughters of God (1 John 4:7; 5:1); and thus logically become the good seed from the Good Tree. This is our purpose on earth: not to work our way into being reaccepted as rightful heirs, but to receive the grace of God who would adopt us and make us his children.

ANGELS—RESURRECTED AND TRANSLATED BEINGS

Throughout biblical history, it has been necessary for God to communicate with people by means of heavenly messengers. Such messengers are described in the book of Hebrews in a sort of hierarchy: God the Father, Jesus Christ as his heir, angels who are subordinate to Jesus, and man—"a little lower than the angels."[102] LDS doctrine denies the biblical understanding that angels were of a different origin or race from humankind. Parley P. Pratt stated:

> Angels are of the same race as men. They are, in fact, men who have passed from the rudimental state to the higher spheres of progressive being. They have died and risen again to life, and are consequently possessed of a divine, human body of flesh and bones, immortal and eternal.[103]

According to LDS doctrine, though, Pratt was speaking of those messengers who have appeared in the years since the death of Christ, since there was no resurrection prior to that time. Those who ministered before that time were either (1) unembodied (as yet unborn) spirits, (2) disembodied spirits (who have lived but are as of yet unresurrected), or (3) translated beings who had a change wrought on their bodies without tasting death

(LDS examples of these are the three Nephites, John the Revelator, Enoch and his people, and Moses).

Translated beings of LDS theology dwell in a terrestrial state, with those like them who minister to other of God's planets, and do not dwell directly in God's presence.[104] All other good angels reside "in the presence of God, on a globe like a sea of glass and fire, where all things for their glory are manifest, past, present and future, and are continually before the Lord."[105]

The Bible shows the fallacy in the Mormons' belief in their "angels." In Hebrews 1:13–14 we read that angels are "ministering spirits."[106] Jesus stated in Luke 24:39 that spirits do *not* have flesh and bone—which disqualifies all the bodily "angels"—Moroni, John the Baptist, Peter, James, and John—who supposedly appeared to Joseph Smith with new revelations and authority to organize his apostate church. In fact, Joseph Smith made the worst possible choice in selecting "angels" to lend credibility to his stories about the *Book of Mormon* and priesthood ordinations. Perhaps Paul, in prophetic warning, was referring directly to Mormonism when he said:

> I marvel that ye are so soon removed from him that called you into the grace of Christ unto another gospel: Which is not another; but there be some that trouble you, and would pervert the gospel of Christ. But though we, or an angel from heaven, preach any other gospel unto you than that which we have preached unto you, let him be accursed. (Gal. 1:6–8)

The gospel is so precious that not even an angel should dissuade us from it![107]

A CONFUSING DEITY

Everything about the Mormon godhead is a confused mess if you accept all the supposedly inspired teachings of LDS leaders. Brigham Young said that *God* was *Adam*.[108] *Adam*, according to LDS theology, was *Michael* in the preexistence.[109] *Michael* was the godhead equivalent of the *Holy Ghost*.[110] The *Holy Ghost*, said Talmadge, is the *Comforter*,[111] and the *Comforter* is the *Spirit of Truth*.[112] *Christ*, though, is also the *Comforter*,[113] and the *Spirit of Truth*.[114] Finally, *Christ* is the *God* of the Old Testament![115]

So it comes full circle—and even through the Mormon perversion of Scripture, truth prevails. There is only *one* God!

In the final view, though, the LDS god is only a means to an end for his adherents. He did not create man's essential being; he only clothed him with a spirit body. Just as earthly parents were obligated to provide food, clothing, and a home, so their heavenly parents owe them life, instruction, and salvation (yes, salvation—for was it not the Mormon god's *plan* that man should fall so that he could be redeemed?).

Nothing in LDS theology is as it should be. Each man has two sets of parents: heavenly and earthly. God has many wives, and man should too. Mary the mother of Christ had two living husbands, without sinning. Their physical god begets spiritual bodied children and infuses them into mortal bodies so they can become gods too. Meanwhile, his copartner, the Holy Ghost, has no body at all and is still a god. Other beings are punished with the devil for their sins, and their sentence: no body, ever.

This Mormon god is surely the author of confusion (1 Cor. 14:33). My God, the triune, self-sufficient, holy I AM, is not! Praise his holy Name![116]

Chapter 8

SALVATION AND EXALTATION

Then shall they be gods, because they have no end; therefore shall they be from everlasting to everlasting, because they continue; then shall they be above all, because all things are subject unto them. Then shall they be gods, because they have all power, and the angels are subject unto them.

—*Doctrine and Covenants* 132:20

While you might see the angel Moroni atop an LDS temple, you'll never see a cross. Nor will you see that bittersweet symbol of Christ's ultimate love for humankind in any Mormon chapel, temple, or tabernacle. They regard the cross only as a torture instrument and would never think of putting it on buildings nor even on jewelry. Truly, the cross itself has become "foolishness" to them, as Paul described in 1 Corinthians 1:17–25. One reason for this de-emphasis of the cross is the traditional LDS teaching that the atonement of Christ took place not on the cross, but in the garden of Gethsemane.[1] Thus has the cross become "emptied of its power" to represent salvation to Mormons.

The word *salvation* itself is a denatured one for LDS people. When I was a young girl, an earnest-faced young woman handed me a pamphlet and asked me what to her was a vital question: "Are you sure you are saved?" I remember the impatience I felt as I answered her, "Well, of course." For me, "salvation" meant merely the ability to have my body resurrected, and since LDS doctrine states that practically every human being will be resurrected, it was like asking if I was breathing. If she had asked me further if I believed that salvation came through the sacrifice of Christ, I would have been again impatient, for I believed that was what his atonement bought: resurrection of the body.[2]

SALVATION VERSUS EXALTATION

When Mormons speak of eternal life, they are referring not just to living forever, but to the reward that God gives to those who are obedient. The word *eternal*, Mormons claim, is an adjective that refers to God and only secondarily to a temporal aspect.[3] Eternal life, as they understand it, is based entirely on works and is tied inextricably to the concept of becoming a god.[4] Those works, it must be understood, are not the "good deeds" of service to others but rather those of LDS baptism, tithing, temple work, adherence to the Word of Wisdom, and full support of LDS leaders.

Immortality, on the other hand, is seen by Mormons to be the free gift of God. Because of the atonement of Christ, all men will be resurrected, no matter what their deeds. As my conversation with the girl with the pamphlet showed, in Mormonism, "salvation" *equals* resurrection. The third LDS Article of Faith states: "We believe that through the Atonement of Christ, all mankind may be saved, by obedience to the laws and ordinances of the Gospel." A close examination of this statement shows what Mormons really believe. The atonement of Christ is like a vehicle which sits practically powerless without the fuel of man's good deeds.

Grace, the word of heavenly music to a Christian's ear, has a different interpretation for Mormons. It is a reward, not a gift. "Grace," said Mormon Apostle Bruce R. McConkie, "is granted to men proportionately as they conform to the standards of personal righteousness that are part of the Gospel plan."[5] On the other hand, Mormons regard salvation and resurrection to be "inalienable rights" that God owes them by virtue of the fact that God sent them to earth. In the words of George Romney, the Mormon former governor of Michigan, "We believe that everyone will be saved. The question is the degree of exaltation that a man may win for himself in his life on earth."[6]

The process that leads to this redemption from personal sins, this *exaltation* is as different from LDS salvation as a paycheck is from an inheritance. An adage commonly heard from Mormons is that "salvation without exaltation is damnation."[7] Again, a conflict of definitions is seen. Mormons regard any cessation in their progress to become gods as damnation, and compare "damning" to "damming," or halting, the progress of a mighty stream.

As is true with so many other LDS doctrines, this idea of universal "salvation" developed gradually in the mind of Joseph Smith. In his early writings, there was no hint of universal salvation. In the *Book of Mormon*, for instance, Joseph Smith penned the story of the wicked preacher Nehor who "testified unto the people that all mankind should be saved at the last day." Nehor was taken to the top of a hill, made to confess that he'd taught false doctrine, then killed.[8]

But before his death, Joseph Smith had already begun to teach that not only would all men be saved, but that those who pleased God would achieve exaltation. He advocated that men by their good deeds literally "work out their own salvation." In *Doctrine and Covenants* 132:32 his god told the Mormon people, "Go ye, therefore, and do the works of Abraham; enter ye into my law and ye shall be saved." Here he was referring specifically to polygamy, but the fact that anyone could teach people both to be Christian and to do the *works* of the Old Testament—which Jesus died to free us from—is illogical. We know that Christ's atoning sacrifice did away with the old law under which Moses and other Old Testament prophets lived. Because it was so demanding a schoolmaster, Christians rejoice that we have been released from its strictures into the liberty of Christ, for as the apostle James pointed out, "For whosoever shall keep the whole law, and yet offend in one point, he is guilty of all" (James 2:10).

All Christians, on the other hand, are promised eternal life by God: "For God so loved the world, that he gave his only begotten Son, that whosoever believeth in him should not perish, but have everlasting life" (John 3:16). This Scripture verse, Mormons should note, does not say that one must be married in the temple, or do genealogical research, or keep the Word of Wisdom. In fact, it doesn't say anything about works at all!

Christians do work out their own salvation, as Philippians 2:12 tells us to do. But we don't work *for* our salvation, we work *because* of it. In response to the fact that we are saved by God's grace, our grateful hearts are pleased to do good works to honor our Father. But poor Mormons: though they take the resurrection of their bodies for granted, they are continually admonished to work for everything else. They are compelled to do more, and more, and more.

The Bible does teach that all human beings will be resurrected:

> Marvel not at this: for the hour is coming, in the which all that are in the graves shall hear his voice, And shall come forth; they that have done good, unto the resurrection of life; and they that have done evil, unto the resurrection of damnation. (John 5:28–29)

And the Christian knows that not everyone will be "saved," in the correct biblical sense of the word:

> For the time is come that judgment must begin at the house of God: and if it first begin at us, what shall the end be of them that obey not the gospel of God? And if the righteous scarcely be saved, where shall the ungodly and the sinner appear? (1 Peter 4:17–18)

But do works matter? Of course they do! We are known by our fruits, and works are a fruit. But we're not dependent upon them for our salvation, for no one knows better than each of us knows, deep in the heart, how feeble and selfishly motivated many of our "good" deeds are. Christians, rejoice! We are free! God will give us every good thing we need, and only because he loves us.

Only recently have LDS apologists turned toward concepts like "imputed" righteousness (a condition of acceptability before God that is unearned but nonetheless granted to us by God).[9] But any Mormon of middle age or older remembers what was common teaching in the LDS Church, as spokesman Wallace Bennett affirmed: "Once we have been resurrected, it will be our own efforts, not Christ's sacrifice, that will be the deciding factor."[10]

BAPTISM

The fourth LDS Article of Faith states:

> We believe that the first principles and ordinances of the Gospel are: first, Faith in the Lord Jesus Christ; second, Repentance; third, Baptism by immersion for the remission of sins; fourth, Laying on of hands for the gift of the Holy Ghost.

This Article of Faith forms a framework of the first duties of a prospective Mormon who would earn his exaltation. By "joining" the LDS Church, a person makes himself eligible for eternal life. Without this Church membership, he would only have the right to resurrection, along with all the rest of the "Gentile" world.

When a person becomes a Mormon, his new brethren believe it is due to the fact that the convert has the "believing blood" of Jacob. All Mormons are pronounced to be of Jacob's lineage, not because of any genealogical findings, but because they believe that God sent his special spirits to earth to be born into the bodies of Jacob's descendants. These spirits in the preexistence supposedly had the special intellectual and spiritual gift of being able to know truth when they saw it. The fact that a person accepts Mormonism is seen as proof positive that he has this ability to recognize truth; and therefore the conclusion is that he *must* be of Israelite descent.

If this were not enough, Joseph Smith taught that after baptism, the blood of a convert was actually changed to make him of this lineage. "The effect of the Holy Ghost upon a Gentile, is to purge out the old blood, and make him actually of the seed of Abraham."[11]

All Mormons therefore consider themselves to be of triply Jewish descent: they are first born into Jacob's line; then at baptism any Gentile blood is flushed out; and finally they are adopted spiritually into the lineage of Abraham, who was promised multitudes of righteous progeny. No wonder they can call the rest of the world (including Jews) Gentiles!

They teach that at birth, a child is born in an innocent state, in spite of what the *Pearl of Great Price* says about children being "conceived in sin."[12] But the world being as wicked as it is, a child soon becomes "natural," an enemy to God,[13] and by the age of eight becomes accountable[14] and in need of having the effects of Adam's sin nullified.

We Christians know that when we first come to Christ, we come repenting of our sinful nature, which has alienated us from our Maker, as well as for specific sins we have committed. We realize that until conversion we are in a state of rebellion (Eph. 2:3) that does not allow us to enter God's kingdom until we repent of our natures, as well as our sins.

Mormons, on the other hand, believe that they are inherently good, even before conversion, because they are children of God. They repent of the things they have done which they know to be wrong as part of putting themselves in line for exaltation. Baptism, according to Mormons, has a fourfold purpose: (1) to remit the sins that hinder a person's progress toward godly perfection, (2) to establish membership in the Church and Kingdom, (3) to provide access to the Celestial Kingdom, and (4) to form the foundation for personal sanctification.

Mormons are only baptized once in life for themselves. If by chance all records of baptism become destroyed or lost (an unlikely eventuality with today's information retrieval systems), then a second baptism is performed. Or, if a person is excommunicated from the Church and then repents fully, that person may be rebaptized. Around the age of eight most LDS children are baptized, by complete immersion, in a ward baptistry by a priesthood holder. These bodies of water are located below the ground level in all LDS meetinghouses, and going down into one is supposed to signify the death and burial that baptism pictures. Just after the baptism, each new member is "confirmed" by the laying on of hands, a separate ceremony which supposedly bestows the gift of the Holy Ghost.

Those baptized into the Mormon Church as adults sometimes become overwhelmed by what is expected of them as far as church work is concerned. (Men in particular are fast-tracked through priesthood offices.) They see others around them pressing sometimes frantically, sometimes complacently, toward the goal of exaltation.

"SAVIORS ON MOUNT ZION"

Joseph Smith once stated in his famous "King Follet Sermon" that a person's greatest responsibility on this earth is to "seek after his dead." A Mormon's hair might still be damp with baptismal water when he may be reminded that now, since he is on the road to exaltation, his dead relatives need the same ordinance. Not only do Mormons believe that their ancestors cannot receive exaltation without vicarious baptisms done for them in a Mormon temple, but they assert also that they *themselves* cannot be exalted if they ignore their responsibility to research their genealogies. The Church maintains over 4,500 "Family History Centers" in seventy countries that connect to the main genealogical library in Salt Lake City, where over two billion names are stored in digital form. The Church intends in the near future to make public on its website, www.familysearch.org, most of its records. As of this writing, the site already gives access to millions of names from over 110 countries and territories.

Mormons emphasize that the family succession of baptized persons must form an unbroken chain back to Adam.[15] I have heard several Mormons claim proudly that a certain line of their ancestry was traced back that far. (This is usually because in their research they were able to find a distant relative who was a king or a nobleman who claimed descent from a biblical character whose genealogy is found in the Bible.)

Since 1965 all members of the LDS Church were asked to fill out a four-generation sheet, a legal-sized sheet with blanks for family members' names, dates of birth, death, and other pertinent information. These were bound in what is called a "Book of Remembrance," a heavy notebook binder. Computer records now substitute for the heavy binders in many cases. When completed with verified information, duplicates of the "pedigree sheets" are sent to the Church's genealogy headquarters, where they are recorded and archived.

More than 2.3 million rolls of microfilm and 180,000 sets of microfiche are stored in great vaults deep in the granite cliffs of Little Cottonwood

Canyon, outside Salt Lake City. Built at a cost of two and one-half million dollars from 1960–66, these vaults make the records stored therein impervious to damage from humidity, dryness, earthquakes, and atomic disasters. Pedigree information to be archived pours in daily, the result of millions of hours of work from church members who believe that their ancestors will be lost without their help.

Mormons believe that all the names that were never written down or that would in some other way be impossible for them to obtain will be revealed during the millennial reign of Christ. Referring to this, Jerald and Sandra Tanner asked: "Since the Mormon leaders believe that the Lord will have to provide many of the names anyway, would it not be better to spend this time and money helping the living instead of searching for the names of the dead?"[16]

Genealogy has become big business with the LDS Church. Many of its members have become fanatical about their duties to their dead. It is hard for a genealogist of any (or no) religion to do research without bumping elbows with research done on his relatives by some distant Mormon kin he didn't know he had.

Mormons see themselves in a very real sense as saviors of the world.[17] John Taylor once boasted, "We are the only people that know how to save our progenitors, how to save ourselves, and how to save our posterity in the celestial kingdom of God ... we are the people that God has chosen by whom to establish his kingdom and introduce correct principles into the world ... we in fact are the saviors of the world, if they ever are saved."[18]

In an effort to secure some favorable publicity, Mormons have given personal genealogies to public figures like celebrities and US presidents in media-heavy presentations. Christian people like Jimmy Carter, however, probably would not have been as thrilled at the Mormons' work at searching out their dead if they knew that all their deceased relatives have already had proxy baptisms performed for them in LDS temples. In fact, anyone reading this book has almost certainly had many or most of his or her deceased relatives researched, documented, and baptized in proxy at an LDS temple.

Doing genealogy work has not always brought the peace and satisfaction to Mormons that they often claim. Many Mormons who feel obligated to search out their ancestors and yet hate sitting in front of computer screens or microfilm readers, or poring over dusty legal records, often take the easier route. If they can possibly afford it, they have their genealogies researched by professionals. The semi-humorous story is told of a man who paid a genealogist a thousand pounds to trace his pedigree—and then later paid the researcher ten thousand more not to tell anyone what he'd found.[19]

BAPTISMS FOR THE DEAD

The doctrine of vicarious baptism as a way to save someone who has already died was introduced in August of 1840 by Joseph Smith. At first, it was apparently just for relatives of Latter-day Saints.[20] By September of 1842, when Joseph Smith penned the letters that appear now as sections 127 and 128 of the *Doctrine and Covenants*, he had worked out the details of this practice well enough to present them to his people.

The principles behind vicarious baptisms are carefully orchestrated so they will not conflict with the LDS emphasis on free will, or "agency." Mormons do not claim that every person for whom a proxy baptism is performed will be exalted. But they assume that most will be, because there are other Mormons who have died who are teaching prospective Mormons in the spirit world. Once a spirit decides to become a Mormon, he merely accepts the baptism which was done in his name on earth, and the end result is the same as if he had been himself baptized while alive. If no proxy baptism has been done, the person must wait for it. If this spirit person, though, led an evil life while on earth, he must suffer in the spirit world until he has paid for his sins—"the uttermost farthing." When he has atoned sufficiently, he can accept a proxy baptism.

Mormons use several Bible references to justify their practice of vicarious baptism. Some of these references have such an obscure supposed connection to the idea of a spirit prison and baptism for the dead that non-Mormons may have trouble seeing it; such as in Zechariah 9:11; 1 Peter 3:18–19; 4:6; and John 5:25–28. Their favorite is: "Else what shall they do which are baptized for the dead, if the dead rise not at all? why are they then baptized for the dead?" (1 Cor. 15:29).

All of these Scriptures lose a lot of their Mormon punch, however, when read in a more modern version than King James, and are practically defused when read in context, keeping in mind the purpose and audience for which they were written. The Corinthian passage, for instance, in context makes the point that it's futile to be baptized in the hope of meeting a Christian loved one in eternity—if, indeed, there's no future resurrection.

No matter how Mormons stretch Bible Scripture, they can find no biblical precedents for actually baptizing one person to bring to pass the salvation of another. Mormons say there is a precedent in principle, if not in deed, citing Levite priests who acted on behalf of the people in ancient ordinances.

Mormons taking on responsibility for others should be reminded that even Christ shuddered to do so (Mark 14:36; *Doctrine and Covenants* 19:18–19). But he did take responsibility for our salvation, and is now the only intercessor we need, as John noted:

> My little children, these things write I unto you, that ye sin not. And if any man sin, we have an advocate with the Father, Jesus Christ the righteous: And he is the propitiation for our sins: and not for ours only, but also for the sins of the whole world. (1 John 2:1–2)

PROXY BAPTISM

I participated two times in proxy baptisms. The first was in the old temple at Manti, Utah. I went with a group of other young people by bus from our home ward in Albuquerque. Before going, each of us had gone through an extensive interview with our bishop, who asked us specific questions about our moral worthiness and loyalty to the LDS Church, questions that have undergone considerable revision since that time. Today's temple-recommend questions include:

1. Do you have faith in and a testimony of God the Eternal Father, his Son Jesus Christ, and the Holy Ghost?
2. Do you have a testimony of the Atonement of Christ and of his role as Savior and Redeemer?
3. Do you have a testimony of the restoration of the gospel in these the latter days?
4. Do you sustain the President of the Church of Jesus Christ of Latter-day Saints as the Prophet, Seer, and Revelator and as the only person on the earth who possesses and is authorized to exercise all priesthood keys? Do you sustain members of the First Presidency and the Quorum of the Twelve Apostles as prophets, seers, and revelators? Do you sustain the other General Authorities and local authorities of the Church?
5. Do you live the law of chastity?
6. Is there anything in your conduct relating to members of your family that is not in harmony with the teachings of the Church?
7. Do you support, affiliate with, or agree with any group or individual whose teachings or practices are contrary to or oppose

those accepted by the Church of Jesus Christ of Latter-day Saints?

8. Do you strive to keep the covenants you have made, to attend your sacrament and other meetings, and to keep your life in harmony with the laws and commandments of the gospel?
9. Are you honest in your dealings with your fellowmen?
10. Are you a full-tithe payer?
11. Do you keep the Word of Wisdom?
12. Do you have financial or other obligations to a former spouse or children? If yes, are you current in meeting those obligations?
13. [If you have previously received your temple endowment] Do you keep the covenants that you made in the temple? Do you wear the garment both night and day as instructed in the endowment and in accordance with the covenant you made in the temple?
14. Have there been any sins or misdeeds in your life that should have been resolved with priesthood authorities but have not been?
15. Do you consider yourself worthy to enter the Lord's house and participate in temple ordinances?

In the Manti Temple I was baptized thirty consecutive times for deceased women. Eight years later at the Provo Temple, several modern conveniences speeded up the process. After presenting our recommends, girls and boys were sent to separate dressing rooms, where we were given amorphous white baptismal garments made of terry cloth. Our street clothing was put into lockers and we went into the underground baptismal room, which held an immense bowl-like metallic font which was supported on the backs of statues of twelve life-sized brass oxen, symbolic of the twelve tribes of Israel. A platform extended along one side of the great bowl, where we all waited, wide-eyed and silent, for the baptisms to begin.

One by one we were called by name to descend into the font. A recorder sat on a high stool, not unlike a lifeguard's stand, at one side of the font, and witnesses watched. An elder stood in the font in garments like ours, and beckoned for each participant as his or her turn came. He spoke the baptismal prayer in a hurried, monotonous voice, stopping only to lower a proxy into the water.

I sat on the platform, looking furtively for the angels or dead persons I had heard often appeared in temples.[21] When my name was called, I went down into the water. The baptizing elder turned me around so that he could see a large screen, something like an electronic football scoreboard, which he looked at over my shoulder. At the top of the screen was my name, and below it a name I don't remember, but which I'll say was Elizabeth Anderson.[22] "Sister Celeste Latayne Colvett," said the baptizing elder, looking at the screen, "having been commissioned of Jesus Christ, I baptize you, for and in behalf of Elizabeth Anderson, who is dead, in the name of the Father, and of the Son, and of the Holy Ghost. Amen." Then he quickly dropped his right arm from the square and lowered me beneath the water. As I was regaining my footing (you learn after the third or fourth time to put one foot slightly behind the other to help you get back out of the water), he had already begun the same prayer, inserting this time the name of another dead woman which had flashed onto the screen behind me. Fifteen consecutive baptisms were performed with me as proxy in a matter of about three minutes. As I left the font, another proxy was preparing to be baptized.

Then I was led into a "confirmation room" where a man sat on a high stool with a chair near his knees. I sat on the chair, my back to him, and he and several other elders placed their hands heavily upon my head while he pronounced this prayer: "Sister Celeste Latayne Colvett, in the name of Jesus Christ, we lay our hands upon your head for and in behalf of Elizabeth Anderson, who is dead, and confirm you a member of the Church of Jesus Christ of Latter-day Saints, and say unto you: Receive the Holy Ghost. Amen."

As soon as he had finished, he lifted his hands off my head for no more than a fraction of a second and then replaced them, beginning the same prayer again, this time with the name of the second person for whom I had been baptized. This continued, and took only a minute or so, because he spoke very quickly.

This sort of mechanical processing of proxies goes on daily in the ever-growing number of temples around the world (128 in 2008). Literally millions of dead persons have had proxy baptisms done for them in this assembly-line fashion. The more converts made to the Church, the more names submitted, and the more proxy ordinances done.

So far, most of the deceased presidents of the United States, and other prominent persons of world history including Catholic popes and saints, have had vicarious ordinances performed in their behalf in Mormon temples. Wilford Woodruff, a president of the LDS Church (1887–98), said that on April 10, 1898, all the signers of the Declaration of Independence, along with George Washington, appeared to him in the St. George Temple two nights in a row, begging that vicarious ordinances be done for them. Woodruff obliged, and also did the proxy work for Christopher Columbus, John Wesley, and other prominent men of the past, one hundred in all.[23]

Christians want to know how Mormons explain Christ's narrative of the rich man and Lazarus as found in Luke 16:19–26. The late President Joseph Fielding Smith, in his book *Way to Perfection*, explained around the great truth of the Bible's teachings on repenting after death by saying that the "great gulf" was only fixed before the death of Christ. After the Savior's resurrection, it no longer existed. Thus the righteous dead can intermingle with and teach those who have not received the LDS gospel in mortal life.

With such official rationalizations, it is no wonder that Mormons continue researching their genealogies at a record-breaking pace. According to journalist Richard N. Ostling and his coauthor and wife, Joan K. Ostling (as of 1999), "The Family History Library based in Salt Lake City has more than 2 billion names on various kinds of records, over 700,000 microfiche files, and nearly 2 million rolls of microfilmed records ... The microfilmed holdings are equivalent to more than 7 million books of 300 pages each. This collection expands by 5,000 microfilm rolls a month."[24]

When asked why there is no biblical endorsement of ordinances for the dead, Mormons claim that New Testament saints were too scattered to understand the necessity for temples and the need for such practices.[25] I have never read of an authenticated ancient (Bible era) record that clearly documented the practice of baptism for the dead as Mormons understand it, and that identified such ordinances as anything but a presumptuous heresy.[26] Even the *Book of Mormon* (which is far from an authenticated ancient document, but the Mormons accept it as such) teaches that if you reject their gospel after hearing it here on earth, there is no second chance,[27] and says that if you die without ever hearing it, you'll be blessed anyway, "for the power of redemption cometh on all them that have no law."[28]

Some people wonder if Mormons work so hard in "saving" their dead because such work salves the consciences of those who didn't effectively witness to others while they were alive. I remember thinking, when I was a Mormon, that it would be better not to tell a hostile Gentile anything about the gospel and wait until he or she died and could hear it preached in the spirit world.

Proxy baptisms were the focus of fierce controversy in the last decade of the twentieth century. Under intense public pressure, the LDS Church signed an agreement in 1995 with major Jewish organizations saying the Church would stop doing ordinances for deceased Jews without the written permission of all their living descendants.[29] The LDS Church reportedly subsequently purged its own records of proxy baptisms and endowments of over 380,000 Holocaust victims. This is little comfort to many Jews whose relatives' "fraudulent" records will reflect that they were Mormons. "The only thing that a family researcher will see—or know, unless they're conversant with the issue—is that their great-grandfather was a Mormon, when we all know the person lived and died as a Jew," said Schelly Talalay Dardashti, genealogy columnist for the *Jerusalem Post*.[30] Another writer, ex-Mormon Martin Wishnatsky, was even more bitter: "The only solace I have in knowing that the Russian Communists obliterated my ancestors' graves in Lemburg, Poland, is that no hungry Mormon name-robber, looking for records of dead persons to feed the ghoulish endowment factories, will ever be able to uncover any trace of them."[31] In addition, researcher Helen Radkey has documented the continuation of proxy baptism of deceased Jews, and the vicarious baptisms of Adolf Hitler and Eva Braun.[32]

ENDOWMENTS FOR EXALTATION

Proxy baptisms are not the only ordinances performed in the LDS temples. They are, however, the most available—any Church member who is an adolescent or older and can pass the temple-recommend questions may participate in baptisms for the dead. A young man, though, will usually receive his own endowments—a higher temple ordinance—just before going on a mission, at about age nineteen. A young woman receives the endowments when she goes on a mission (at age twenty or twenty-one), or (as is more common) just before her marriage—whichever comes first. Converts to the Church who are already married, and thus would not soon be going on missions, are usually required to wait six months to a year after their baptisms to ascertain their worthiness to participate in the secret temple ordinances.

There are basically three main kinds of temple ordinances other than vicarious baptism. First, there are the washings and anointings. The second type of ordinance is the "endowment of the priesthood," wherein those who show themselves to be worthy and humble can symbolically pass through the veil to the highest level of heaven. (The term *endowment*, though, is often used to refer to these ceremonies in conjunction with the washings and anointings.) The third type of ordinance is eternal marriage. It, like the endowment, can be done in proxy for dead persons who have already had vicarious baptisms and endowments done in their behalf. An appendage to this third ordinance is a sealing ceremony, where children born to parents who were not LDS at the time of their children's birth can be sealed to them after all are proven worthy.

Another temple ordinance about which little is known is something called the "Second Anointing." Whereas other temple ordinances have been documented in recent years by persons who have experienced them firsthand, no ex-Mormon I know of has ever described it. Some accounts of nineteenth-century performances of this ordinance exist. According to LDS researcher David Buerger, "Godhood was ... the meaning of this higher ordinance."[33] Participants are invited by church leadership, such as the prophet, to receive the highly secret ordinance. It involves ritual washing of the feet, and anointings of married couples to be kings/queens and priests/priestesses. A later, separate rite follows this (presumably in the couple's home), in which a woman washes her husband's body (in the same manner as is done in the temple) and feet and then anoints him. This is said to be similar to the way that Mary anointed Jesus in John 11. "The ordinance prepares the husband for burial, and in this way she lays claim upon him in the resurrection," according to the only written account of the procedure that I have ever seen.[34]

The ordinances of today's temples were not practiced in the first LDS temple that was built in Kirtland, Ohio. In fact, there were no secret rites conducted behind its doors—all its meetings were open to the public. Its main floor was used for regular worship services, while its upper story served as a classroom for missionaries.

The church's second temple, in Nauvoo, was the first for vicarious rites. Though it was never completed, proxy baptisms were performed there, and endowment ceremonies took place in its attic. It too was abandoned under pressure, and was burned in 1848 by enemies of the Church who were incensed by the secrecy that accompanied what went on inside its walls. In 1850, a tornado struck down the remaining walls of the building. (A new Nauvoo Temple structure was erected and dedicated in 2002.)

However, it was not for another nine years after the destruction of the old Nauvoo Temple that Latter-day Saints had a place in which to receive their endowments, when the Old Endowment House in Salt Lake City was dedicated. Since then many more temples have been built throughout the world. All these have the same purpose, and the ordinances performed in them are uniform except as to the languages spoken.

The number of temples now in operation or planned for the near future (as of 2009) approaches 145 worldwide. Mormons look forward to the day when they will be able to build the temple in Independence, Missouri, as Joseph Smith prophesied—with two exceptions. It will not be within the lifetime of those who heard Joseph Smith's prophecy; they are all dead.

Neither will it be on the site identified by the "revelation"; it is tenaciously owned by the Church of Christ, Temple Lot. Also revealed, he said, were the temple's dimensions (with a capacity of up to fifteen thousand people), including twenty-four rooms whose names were given to Joseph Smith by God. It will be the temple of temples—when and if it is ever built.

Today's temples, old and new alike, are a strange mixture of old traditions and ultramodern conveniences. The newer ones, for instance, are self-contained units that feature cafeterias for the workers and industrial-type laundry facilities so that garments used therein never have to be seen by outsiders.

Since many young Mormons go on "temple excursions" to participate in vicarious baptisms, as I did, this experience usually serves to whet their curiosity to see the other parts of the temple. Every faithful youth looks forward to the day he or she can receive the endowments. Quite often, though, after a first trip to a temple to receive endowments, a young Mormon is confused. He has been told all his life about how sacred and uplifting the endowment ceremony is, and if it hasn't seemed that way to him, he is told that it is only because he didn't understand it. That the proceedings there are disorienting, there can be no doubt; but complicating the issue is that Mormons who have already received their endowments are not allowed to talk about that experience to anyone, even to prepare someone for it.

A trip to a temple may either be a hurried once-a-week affair sandwiched between appointments for someone who lives near a temple and does vicarious work often; or it may be a once-in-a-lifetime event preceded by much planning and expense, as is the case with many Mormons who live a great distance from a temple.

Going for one's own endowments is a milestone in the life of every Mormon, a sort of coming-of-age where young people are introduced to the secrets their parents have kept all their lives, and which they themselves are expected to honor and guard with their lives. The endowment experience has many parallels with initiation ceremonies of primitive cultures. It is secret; the newly initiated is tested to prove worthiness; he is given a badge or token to prove he has passed (in this case, temple garments); and finally (before temple marriage) it signals sexual maturity and encourages virility and fertility.[35]

Since I never went through a temple for endowments or for celestial marriage, I do not know from experience the details of these ceremonies. However, many former Mormons, some of whom worked regularly in the temples, have written about them. These ceremonies (which last upwards to several hours) are often boring, even to Mormons. Christians would probably find them boring too if they weren't so blasphemous, and in places, ludicrous.

TEMPLE CEREMONIES

What follows is a description of what a Mormon would undergo if he or she "took out endowments" in an LDS temple after 2005. This specificity of date is necessary because the temple ceremony underwent enormous changes—specifically, the deletion of many of its unique elements—over the last one hundred years and notably in 1990. (These changes were instigated after a survey taken by the LDS Church showed that a substantial number of people who had taken out endowments were embarrassed, confused, and resentful of many of the oaths and curses, and the intimate and intrusive nature of the washings and anointings in their previous forms.)

A temple session (which may last up to five hours) begins when a Mormon presents his recommend for verification at the officelike annex of a temple. He has registered in advance, and he has submitted earlier the completed pedigree sheets on persons for whom he will do vicarious work, if that is his purpose. Before leaving the annex, he usually leaves a cash contribution in a receptacle prominently displayed for that purpose.

He is shown into a chapel, where he waits until enough others, men and women like himself, have assembled to form a group. A few songs are sung, a prayer is offered, and a short talk on the solemnity of the occasion is presented by a temple worker during this beginning of the segment of the temple ceremony that is commonly referred to as "the initiatory."

Men and women are separated into dressing rooms with lockers from which each emerges wearing only a one-piece "regulation garment" such as he or she will wear under clothing for the rest of his or her life, and over the garment a poncholike "shield" that reaches to the ankle and is closed on the sides.[36] In a small cubicle (about 4 by 4 feet) each man doing vicarious work for the dead is ordained an elder in behalf of the deceased for whom he is taking out endowments. (Additionally, in the washings and anointings that follow, if they are being performed for the dead, a formulaic prayer states that this is being done "for and on behalf of" the deceased's name.) The temple worker who conferred the priesthood and ordination then reads a short passage from Exodus 40:12–13 about the washing and anointing of Aaron and his sons.

Of course, women are undergoing a similar process in small rooms as well, except for the omission of ordination to priesthood, either for themselves or the deceased person for whom they are performing ordinances. Female workers perform the washings and anointings for females, males for males.

At the risk of seeming noninclusive but to prevent pronoun confusion, we will follow a male through the process (and note variations for females). First the worker explains that his washing actions on the man will be only "symbolic," then dips his finger into water and draws a wet line across the initiate's forehead. He lists the head, the nose, the lips, the neck, the shoulders, the back, the breast, the vitals and bowels, the arms and hands, the loins, the legs, and the feet—but these body parts are no longer touched. A second temple worker then comes into the booth and recites a rote "sealing" formula concerning the washing while both workers put their hands on his head. The endowee moves to another booth and sits on a stool. The "sealing" worker then drips just a drop of oil onto his head and recites a list of the same body parts, and then both workers put their hands on his head to seal the anointing with a rote formula.

Stepping into yet another partition, a worker recites a statement that declares that the garment the initiate is wearing is now "authorized" and is to be understood as a representation of the garment given to Adam in the garden of Eden, a "garment of the holy priesthood" that will be a "shield and protection" to the wearer until death.[37]

A "new name" is given to the endowee by the temple worker. He is cautioned never to reveal this name to anyone except later in the temple ceremony. (If receiving vicarious endowments, the endowee receives the "new name" for the deceased.) The name is usually taken from the Bible, and it is common for all men in a session group to have the same name, and all the women another. A man is to remember his name and that of his wife, but a woman is not allowed to know any name but her own.[38]

At this point a man goes back to the segregated dressing area, removes and stows the shield, and puts on a white shirt, trousers, belt, socks, and moccasins. A woman puts on white clothing also: a blouse, skirt, stockings, slip, and soft shoes. Each carries to the "Endowment Room" a bundle which contains a green apron embroidered with nine fig leaves, a cloth cap (which for women has a veil attached, for men something like a baker's hat), a white "robe," and a sashlike "girdle."

Much of the temple ceremony from this point on is a video that is watched, as well as participated in, by the endowees. They are seated in theater-type seats, men on one side, women on the other. In more modern temples they stay in this room and watch scenes projected onto a large screen.

(In the past and in older temples the participants moved from room to room and actors portrayed the drama that is otherwise enacted in a video.)

In this room a temple worker or "officiator" dressed in white addresses the endowees in front of a curtained doorway. He tells them that they have been washed clean of the blood of their generation, anointed in expectation of becoming kings and queens, and priests and priestesses, and each will be given a new name and a garment. He retires behind the curtain, and voices are heard, indicating a conversation between Elohim, Jehovah, and Michael. Jehovah and Michael appear onscreen and act out the six-day creation process. For the representation of the sixth day, the gods plan the future of the first man: He'll have a garden and must replenish the earth, he'll have the Tree of the Knowledge of Good and Evil and Lucifer to tempt him, and if he fails, he'll have the law of sacrifice and a savior so he can return to the gods after resurrection.

At this point Michael falls asleep and the endowees are instructed to close their own eyes as well. He, one of earth's organizers, awakens transformed into Adam, devoid of remembrance of the recent events. A woman appears and is given to Adam. (From this point onward in the ceremony, male participants are to think of themselves as Adam, and female participants as Eve.)

The next scene portrays the garden of Eden. Adam is instructed not to eat one particular fruit, but to enjoy his new home and any other products of it. Then Elohim and Jehovah leave. The next character to appear is dressed in black and red, wearing a square black apron that he says is the symbol of his power and priesthoods. This is Lucifer, and after identifying himself as her brother, he persuades Eve to eat the forbidden fruit after she is reassured that "there is no other way."[39] Adam, when he learns of this, is stubbornly opposed to partaking also until Eve reminds him that she will be cast out of the garden, and without her, Adam cannot replenish the earth. He too then eats the necessary evil of the fruit. The two realize they are naked and make fig leaf aprons. At this point, the endowees put on the aprons they have brought.

When Elohim and Jehovah return, they curse Lucifer, who leaves with a defiant look, saying he only did what he had done in other worlds. When the gods give Adam and Eve clothing, the endowees rise and put on the other clothing they have brought with them. With a representative couple who go to an altar at the front of the room, all endowees, with their right arms to the square, swear to be willing to sacrifice life and goods for the kingdom.[40]

They are then taught (and coached by attendant temple workers) the "First Token of the Aaronic Priesthood." Its grip or handshake is given by clasping right hands and placing the joint of the thumb directly over one's partner's first knuckle. Its name is the "new name" given to the endowee earlier. Its sign is demonstrated by holding the left arm up to the square, palm forward with thumb extended.[41] The endowees all practice these signs and tokens until everyone can do them properly.

The scene changes once again to a barren landscape where Eve is depicted along with Adam, who is standing in front of a stone altar. He chants, "Oh God, hear the words of my mouth. Oh God, hear the words of my mouth. Oh God, hear the words of my mouth."[42] Lucifer appears and Adam does not recognize him but tells him he is looking for a messenger.[43] Elohim then sends down Peter, James, and John to instruct Adam. He tells them to give the humans "the Law of the Gospel" and warn them against light-mindedness, loud laughter, evil speaking of the Lord's anointed [the LDS prophet], taking the Lord's name in vain, and other unholy and impure practices. Peter casts Lucifer out of the world, but not before this being pointedly warns every endowee that if they break their temple covenants, they will be in his power.

Peter then proves his divine authority to Adam by giving him the First Token of the Aaronic Priesthood. The endowees rise and take oaths to keep "the Law of the Gospel," which includes the prohibitions against disparaging the prophet, and behavior which is not sober and befitting. They put their robes on their left shoulders, put on their hats, girdles, and moccasins, and replace their fig-leaf aprons. They are now ready to receive the Second Token of the Aaronic Priesthood, which is given by clasping the right hands together and placing the joint of the thumb between the first and second knuckles of the other's hand. Its name is the given name of the endowee. Its sign is performed by bringing the right hand to the front with the hand cupped, the right hand forming a square, and the left arm raised to the square.[44]

The men turn their caps and sashes to the opposite side; and after putting their robes on their right shoulders, all endowees prepare for a video depicting the Terrrestial World. After taking a vow to have sexual intercourse with their spouses only, they are given the First Token of the Melchizidek Priesthood, or "the Sign of the Nail." The grip for this token is given by placing the thumb on the back of another's hand, and the forefinger on his palm, indicating the piercing of the hand by a nail. Its name is the Son (of God). Its sign is demonstrated by bringing the left hand to the front of the body with the hand cupped, the left arm forming a square, then bringing the right hand forward as well, with the palm down and fingers together and thumb extended.[45]

The Second Token of the Melchizidek Priesthood is taught after all participants rise and, with arms to the square, swear to keep the "Law of Consecration" described in a copy of the *Doctrine and Covenants* that is held up before the group by a temple worker. This is a vow to consecrate time, energy, talents, and material possessions to the Church. The grip or handshake, known as "the Patriarchal Grip," or "the Sure Sign of the Nail," is described as a representation of the belief that those who crucified Jesus feared the nail through his palms would tear through and therefore they put an additional nail into his wrist (the "sure place"). The little fingers are locked, and the index fingers are extended up the other's wrist. The sign is made while reciting the phrase "O God, hear the words of my mouth!" three times while lowering and raising the arms high above the head. There was never a penalty associated with this token, though participants are reminded of the oath of compliance and secrecy for all temple ordinances.

At this time, the endowees who are receiving the endowments for the first time or who are being married that day come forward and form a prayer circle around the altar at the end of this room. After a review of the signs, tokens, and grips, a list of persons requesting prayer for healing and other issues is placed on the altar. All of the women in the room veil their faces and each man takes the woman to his left by the right hand in the "patriarchal grip" and brings his left arm to the square and rests it on the shoulder of the person to his left. The officiator kneels at the altar, intoning phrases of prayer which are repeated in unison by the persons in the circle.

All the women unveil their faces. Then the endowees seat themselves in front of a very wide curtain. Behind it is a wide archway held up by five pillars. When the curtain is drawn, it shows that between the pillars are hung embroidered veils which have on them the same marks as on the garments: a compass (representing the bounds established by God and the course set for eternal life), a square (an exact reminder of the endowment oaths), a navel mark (representing spiritual and physical health), and a knee mark ("every knee shall bow").

Each bedsheetlike veil also has three other larger holes, known as "marks of convenience." Through one hole, a hidden worker representing the Lord gives the grips to test the endowee's knowledge. Through another hole "the Lord" asks questions, and through the third the endowee gives his answers.

To begin the veil session and show endowees what they should do before the veil, the temple worker representing Peter raps on the metal frame supporting the veil with a metal mallet hung there for this purpose.

"The Lord" asks, "What is wanted?" and the response is given, "Adam, having been true and faithful in all things, desires further light and knowledge by conversing with the Lord through the Veil." At that point "Peter" and "the Lord" exchange tokens and names through the holes in the veil. Near the end of this exchange the two put their left arms each on the other's right shoulder[46] through the holes in the veil as the last token's name is whispered: "Health in the navel, marrow in the bones, strength in the loins and in the sinews, power in the Priesthood be upon me and my posterity through all generations of time and throughout all eternity."

Those who are receiving their endowments repeat what "Peter" enacted, one at a time at each set of veil openings. Those doing it for the first time usually need some promptings to help them answer all the questions asked before the veil. A woman is always accompanied to the veil by a man who may be her husband, or if she has none, a perfect stranger—but she cannot pass through the veil without a man.

After all the questions are answered, the endowee passes through the veil to a luxuriously furnished Celestial Room. If this was his first endowment, he will probably sit there and rest for a while. Many first-time endowment recipients have expressed a feeling of being let down—after all, they were promised "further light and knowledge" and all they got was a chant about marrow and sinews.[47] Others who came through the ceremony bearing the name of a dead person are probably old hands at this and usually hurry downstairs to get dressed and go about other business.

Couples who received their endowments prior to marriage that same day are led into a small "sealing" room which has two opposing mirrors and a small kneeling altar in the middle. Here a couple is joined in "eternal" marriage and encouraged to multiply. They are told to look at the infinity of reflections in the mirrors and told that that is a representation of their progeny when they become gods. The ceremony is usually considerably abbreviated if it is just a proxy wedding for the dead.[48] Here too children are sealed to parents in a very brief ceremony that guarantees the children the same blessings as if they had been born into an eternal marriage covenant.

The temple ceremonies have changed considerably over the years. Around the middle of the 1800s, horrific, graphic oaths were sworn by endowees to avenge themselves against the government of the United States, which neglected to protect the Mormons in Illinois and Missouri. Many old oaths, too, referred to polygamy, but were dropped when that practice was discontinued.

I had a married friend at Brigham Young University whose children I often cared for as she went to the Provo Temple for vicarious endowments. Though she never revealed to me any of the oaths or signs (nor did I, being ignorant of them, ask any questions), I remember her reaction once when I asked her if she looked forward to temple work. "Why, of course!" she said, and then a bittersweet look of mixed emotions passed over her face, and she sighed almost inaudibly. She was obedient and willing to do what she was told to do; but I know now that she, and thousands of other Mormons, must go to their graves confused at the relationship of playacting and handshakes to eternal salvation. In fact, according to ex-Mormon Cindy Bauer, there was an "inside joke" that long-term Mormons would cautiously ask someone who'd just gone through the temple for endowments for the first time: "Do you still have your testimony?"[49]

Any Mason who reads even such an abbreviated account of the temple ceremony as I have outlined will be amazed at the similarities between temple ordinances and Masonic lodge ordinances. Joseph Smith claimed that he got much of the substance of the temple ceremony from the Book of Abraham papyri (though there is no evidence of the ceremony in any extant "translations"). The truth is that Joseph Smith was himself a Mason of "the Sublime degree."[50] He joined, he said, just to find out how far Masonry had "degenerated" from the original temple ceremony he said was first practiced in Solomon's temple.

Joseph Smith claimed that some Old Testament rites were the source of both Mormon and Masonic rites. Masonic ceremonies do of course refer to biblical personages and Scriptures, but no Masonic authority would say that they are descended from the Israelite rituals. The Grand Lodge of Utah has in the past refused initiation to known Mormons, and denied admission to any Mormon Mason who was initiated in any other state.[51]

Traditional Masonic symbols are rampant in older LDS temples. Representations of beehives, heavenly bodies, clasped hands, the All Seeing Eye, the square, the compass, and cloud-painted ceilings are abundant in nineteenth-century Utah temples.[52] Many Masonic symbols that were part of LDS temple ceremonies have been dropped since 1990. Even so, Mormon initiates of the twenty-first century, like their Masonic counterparts, wear special garments with symbolic markings on them and soft shoes, hats, and fig-leaf aprons. They give special handshakes, make ritualistic arm motions, whisper passwords into someone's ear, chant, and receive new names. Over both rites hangs a heavy atmosphere of secrecy and fear of retribution for exposure.

Symbolic—and designedly so—of this secret is the "regulation temple garment" that someone who has been through the temple for endowments must wear. These contraptions began in LDS history as something that looked like long johns, for both men and women, and covered them from neck to wrists and ankles. They were later modified to have short sleeves and to reach only to the knees. With advances in modern textiles, they were made out of different kinds of fabrics, but up until the 1980s for both men and women they were one piece, stepped into through the stretchable neck, with a flapped opening for toilet and sex functions. Now temple Mormons can choose a two-piece model that resembles a T-shirt and long Bermuda shorts. Many faithful LDS will not ever let a garment leave their body—dangling a foot or arm outside a shower with a soiled garment and not letting go of it until a clean one is on the other arm, for example. The women I knew wore undergarments such as bra, pantyhose, etc., over the garment which they wore next to their skin, and many did not remove the garment during sex or childbirth. (The only approved exception for removal was for swimming and athletics, as the BYU basketball team has demonstrated for years.) All LDS regulation temple garments, no matter what their configuration, carry the marks of the temple veil—compass, square, navel mark, and knee mark—as small embroidered buttonholelike designs in the garment.

Because the temple ceremony states that the garment will keep them from satanic attacks, they have achieved a significance much like a magic amulet. All Mormon children know stories about someone who was saved from ________ (fill in the blank with bullets, knives, explosions, wild animal attacks, or other danger) by wearing a temple garment.[53]

MYSTERIES

Mormons say that temples exist as a reward for the faithful, who are privileged to learn what they call the "mystery of God." They could save themselves much of the priceless time God has given us here on earth by reading God's Word. The Bible teaches us two important things about the "mystery of God" in Colossians 1:26–27:

> Even the mystery which hath been hid from ages and from generations, but now is made manifest to his saints: To whom God would make known what is the riches of the glory of this mystery among the Gentiles; which is Christ in you, the hope of glory.

First, this mystery is manifested to every person—not just in secret temple ceremonies. The mystery is for the poor, the abused, the sick of soul. And *what is* this mystery? It is the greatest miracle of all! It is Christ in us—which is a logical impossibility according to LDS doctrine. He's the greatest of treasures. No Christian could afford to put this Light under the bushel of a temple roof and bind his testimony with oaths of secrecy—it is for all people.

Temple rites are an essential and distinctive mark of Mormonism. LDS apologists point to the importance Jesus put on going to the temple and the fact that early Christians met at the temple (Acts 2:46; 5:42); as well as to prophecies about God's temple in the future in books like Isaiah and Ezekiel. However, Mormons ignore the meaning of New Testament temple rites: The temple was a place to meet God and offer sacrifices to him. There, priests represented humankind to God (not the other way around). The reason the temple veil was torn in half—significantly, from the top to the bottom—at the death of Jesus is that he himself became the meeting place between humankind and God, and through Jesus we now have access to the Father at all times.

The book of Hebrews makes this very plain—and also shows that the type of temple rites performed in Mormonism bear no resemblance to the new covenant of Christ. The claim that LDS temple ceremonies are patterned after Old Testament temple practices is likewise incorrect. First, the ancient ceremonies were for priests only, those of a particular bloodline, who represented the masses of the other tribes in their sacrifices and ordinances. Faithful people were represented by the priests but did not directly participate. But LDS temple ceremonies are for any qualifying Mormon. Second, ancient temple proceedings were not secret. They are described in minute detail in Deuteronomy and Leviticus—and they don't even faintly resemble the endowments. The only ordinances performed in the Jerusalem temple were (1) the sacrifices offered for the sins of the nation, and (2) a vicarious offering of worship, by one priest, in behalf of all Israel. A quick study of the design of the temple itself as described in the Bible also shows the difference of function as compared to the Mormon temple—no baptisms, no endowments of priesthood, no marriages, no "sealings" of families.

And finally, 1 Corinthians 3:16 indicates where the temple of God is located from New Testament times on: "Know ye not that ye [plural] are the temple of God, and that the Spirit of God dwelleth in you [plural]?" Mormons do not acknowledge Christ's church as the true temple of God in these last days, and spend enormous amounts of time and money on genealogies and repetitive temple ordinances. In one sense, I am relieved—knowing that the faithful LDS who are engaged in those activities are less like to be out proselyting ill-informed Christians and non-believers.

SINS WHICH PREVENT EXALTATION

All the endowment ceremonies have as their ultimate realization the assurance of exaltation. However, the receipt of endowments puts a person in an all-or-nothing situation, for he has thus gained enough knowledge to hang himself, so to speak. One cannot be exalted to godhood without endowments, but neither can one go to hell without them: A non-endowed person simply can't be held accountable for enough knowledge to go to hell.

By receiving endowments, a person gains enough knowledge and independence that the atonement of Christ is actually diminished. Joseph Smith so taught his people, and added that certain sins would actually put an offender outside the pale of the atonement and necessitate the shedding of his or her blood.[54] Brigham Young stated: "There is not a man or woman, who violates the covenants made with their God, that will not be required to pay the debt. The blood of Christ will never wipe that out, your own blood must atone for it; and the judgments of the Almighty will come, sooner or later, and every man and woman will have to atone for breaking their covenants."[55] Young repeatedly elaborated on this concept, called blood atonement, from his pulpit, as documented in *Journal of Discourses*, volumes 4 and 5. In short, blood atonement means that the offender must have his or her blood actually spilled out to atone for certain sins.

What are those sins that Mormons believe make them personally responsible for having their own blood shed? LDS theologian Sidney Sperry said, "The atonement of our Savior will not apply to a man who deliberately refuses to repent of his sins."[56] Another "unpardonable" sin is the sin against the Holy Ghost. This is defined as (1) denying the Holy Spirit after having received it, and denying Christ,[57] and (2) blasphemy against the Holy Ghost, which is identified as the "sin unto death" of shedding innocent blood after having been sealed unto eternal life and married for eternity.[58] Bruce R. McConkie, in *Mormon Doctrine*, stated that any man who accepted Mormonism and received from the Holy Ghost absolute testimony of the divinity of Christ, and then denied the Church, would be committing the unpardonable sin of murder, because by his actions he assented unto the death of Christ.[59]

For persons who have committed the unpardonable sin, the result would be as if there had been no atonement, except that the bodies of such sinners would be resurrected along with everyone else, but never to enter the kingdom of God. Joseph Smith taught that the only way that a person might have atonement for such sins would be through the doctrine of blood atonement, wherein the sinner's blood could be shed to cover the sins which Christ's blood could not.

This doctrine expanded after the death of Joseph Smith, and before long the following were the other crimes that LDS leaders said deserved the shedding of the offender's blood: adultery,[60] stealing,[61] marrying or having sexual intercourse with an African,[62] apostasy,[63] taking the Lord's name in vain,[64] and breaking covenants.[65] Murder was of course the most serious, because of the impossibility of restitution. *Doctrine and Covenants* 132:27 identifies murder, in fact, as the "blasphemy against the Holy Ghost, which shall not be forgiven in the world nor out of the world." Adultery was next in seriousness, and though it could be forgiven once, it was unforgivable on the second offense.[66]

Brigham Young taught that the doctrine had two purposes: (1) to allow a sinner to atone for his own sins and (2) to put fear into the hearts of any who might contemplate such a sin.[67] He taught too that shedding a sinner's blood for him was a way of showing your love for him.[68]

Mormons have gone so far as to say that blood atonement was *never* practiced. That is untrue. The actual practice of shedding the blood of someone who had committed one or more of these grievous sins was never, admittedly, a widespread practice in early Utah, though numerous people did indeed lose their lives as the victims of blood atonement.[69] John D. Lee documented a case where a man, Rosmos Anderson, who was guilty of fornication, allowed his throat to be slit so that his blood ran into an open grave in which he was subsequently buried. This was done by his bishop and two counselors, who hoped thereby to save his soul.[70]

And of course Lee, the "fall guy" for the heinous Mountain Meadows Massacre, was himself executed with a bullet as he sat on the edge of his coffin. Though he was tried and convicted by the US government, he chose a death that could, according to LDS theology, help him atone for at least one of the murders he committed.

These examples could hardly, I grant, be termed proof of a common practice, though its very occurrence is indicative of their values. But the principles of blood atonement were taught when I was a Mormon by LDS President Joseph Fielding Smith, who stated that the only hope of a person who committed the unpardonable sin was to have his blood shed and that Utah provided for this situation by allowing a convicted murderer to choose between hanging or a death that would actually shed his blood.[71] As evidence of this, up until 1987 the state of Utah allowed a condemned killer a choice of death by firing squad to enact blood atonement's efficacy for the sin of murder. In 1997 criminal Gary Gilmore exercised this option in a Utah prison, as did John Albert Taylor in 1996 (though I am not sure if they did it for for religious reasons).

I saw the implications of belief in blood atonement in my own life when I was a Mormon. A few months after I left the LDS Church, a Mormon girlfriend called me long distance to tell me some very distressing news. The younger brother of a mutual friend, she said, had stabbed to death his teen-aged wife in the woods near Provo. My girlfriend was very upset about this (as I was also), but she became even more agitated when she told me that he had also been accused of stabbing to death his premature newborn son.

"He can atone for killing one person by facing a firing squad," she sobbed, "but not two! There's no forgiveness for that!"

I would never disparage the reality of my friend's grief. But as I look back, I feel sadness too for such Mormons who are more concerned about what their own blood *can't* atone for, rather than focusing on what Christ's blood *can* cleanse.

What does the Bible say about murder and atonement? Can one be forgiven without the shedding of the murderer's blood? Moses murdered an Egyptian (Exod. 2:11–12), and yet he appeared in glory on the Mount of Transfiguration (Luke 9:30–31). King David murdered too, but God put away his sin (2 Sam. 12:13). Saul consented unto the death of Stephen (Acts 8:1) and "persecuted ... unto the death" of many others (Acts 22:4). Were these men forgiven?

> But if we walk in the light, as he is in the light, we have fellowship one with another, and the blood of Jesus Christ his Son cleanseth us from all sin. If we say that we have no sin, we deceive ourselves, and the truth is not in us. If we confess our sins, he is faithful and just to forgive us our sins, and to cleanse us from all unrighteousness. (1 John 1:7–9)

The doctrine of blood atonement is wrong. The teaching that Christ's blood cannot atone for sins for which man's blood *can* atone makes mockery of Christ's sacrifice of himself as the unspotted Lamb.

THE MORMON HEREAFTER

By Mormon definition, death is the separation of the spirit body from the physical body. When this happens, the spirit body stays upon this earth, where LDS doctrine says the spirit world exists. When a spirit body is released from the strictures of the physical body through death, it joins the spirits of all the other persons who have died but who have not yet been resurrected. The spirits of the dead, Mormons teach, are all around us, but we cannot discern them because of the refined substance of which the spirit body is made, unless they are made visible. (That is why I could reasonably hope, while doing baptisms for the dead, that I might have my eyes open to this spirit world and see the deceased persons who otherwise invisibly walk amongst us.)

The spirit world has two great divisions: prison and paradise. Good Mormons expect to wake up in paradise after death. In the spirit prison are all others, notably those who rejected the gospel while on earth (who are by definition non-Mormons). These spirits suffer what Mormons call eternal punishment, or endless punishment. This is not to be confused with punishment which will go on forever, or which will never end. (Remember that Mormons teach that two of the names of God are Eternal and Endless,[72] and that when LDS scripture refers to endless or eternal punishment, it is referring only to the fact that God is doing the punishing, and has nothing to do with the *duration* of the punishment.) These spirits in the spirit prison who are suffering endless or eternal punishment, then, are in a temporary state where they are paying the price of their own transgressions. When this price is paid in full, they are given the opportunity to hear the LDS gospel preached by Mormon spirits who serve as missionaries from the spirit paradise, and to accept it.

Those spirits who accept the LDS gospel in the spirit prison may then migrate to the other part of the spirit world, which is paradise. Here, say Mormons, is where the efficacy of vicarious baptisms, endowments, and sealings is realized. Then they can ratify the vicarious work done in their names on earth. The average Mormon's conception of the spirit paradise—that of a great multitude of people impatiently waiting for temple ordinances to be done for them—is undoubtedly an effective goad to their efforts at researching their own genealogies.

Those in the spirit world who had fair and ample opportunity to accept Mormonism in mortal life, but who rejected it, are given a second chance in the spirit world. According to the LDS point of view, they'd be crazy not to accept it this second time, after waking up in a strange shadowy place that looks exactly as the Mormons on earth had described it, and where vicarious baptisms are the only way to be saved. However, there is a price attached to the first rejection: such a second-chancer cannot receive exaltation in the highest level of heaven, as might his more ignorant brethren on earth.

THE RESURRECTIONS

This spirit world is where all the spirits wait for the resurrections, the first of which will occur just before the Millennium. This resurrection, believe Mormons, will be heralded by a great blast on a horn blown by Michael (aka Adam). The proceedings will then be directed by Joseph Smith (which implies he will be resurrected first). According to Brigham Young, the prophet Joseph will hold the keys of the resurrection, and will pass this authority on to other holders of the priesthood as they are resurrected. They will in turn resurrect their wives (as prefigured by the veil ceremony in the temple) and others who had vicarious ordinances done for them.[73]At this time the righteous Mormons who are living on earth will be "translated" into a resurrected state without tasting death. They will join the resurrected Mormons and all the animals, fish, birds, and other creatures which have lived on earth, which will also be resurrected.[74]

After the Millennium begins, the second phase of this first resurrection will occur. Whereas the "morning" of the first resurrection saw the arising of those who would soon become gods, this "afternoon" of the same resurrection involves those who lived disreputably on earth but paid the price for it in the spirit prison.[75]

After the one-thousand-year reign of Christ on earth comes to an end, the second resurrection, or the resurrection of the unjust, will occur. Two classes of people will be resurrected at that time: people who were so wicked on earth that the entire one thousand years of punishment was necessary, and the sons of perdition, those former temple-endowed LDS men who rejected their covenants, and who will be filthy still.

Thus, every person will be resurrected, even the most wicked. The resurrections will also be indicative of a judgment, for the time when one is resurrected determines one's final fate.

Mormons say that the Bible teaches that there are three heavens, and a paradise, because of what Paul said in 2 Corinthians 12:2–4 about "the third heaven" and "paradise." According to LDS doctrine, these three heavens are named the Celestial (highest), the Terrestrial (middle), and Telestial (lowest). (If you have trouble remembering the order of these, use the learning hook employed by Mormon children who think of them as a sandwich where the slices of bread—Celestial and Telestial—rhyme.)

Brigham Young said that the Celestial Kingdom was closed to anyone who did not have the consent of Joseph Smith to enter it.[76] This kingdom is identified as the "administrative" section of heaven, a sort of higher training ground for gods-to-be.

The Celestial Kingdom is in the Mormon mind the enjoyment of exaltation in the most infinite sense. The ultimate fate of all Celestial Kingdomites is continued progression toward godhood, at which point they would be given dominion over worlds and people of their own. In order to begin this progression, a celestial being must have been married in an LDS temple. They will, according to *Doctrine and Covenants* section 76, receive all the things of the Father, and become kings and priests, queens and priestesses.

The Celestial Kingdom will be located on the sanctified earth, which will serve as a great Urim and Thummim—divining device—for its inhabitants.[77] The result of this will be that it will seem to all celestial beings that they are in the presence of God, even though he will be on his own planet, Kolob. Each celestial being, in addition, will receive a white stone as described in Revelation 2:17. This will serve as an individual Urim and Thummim[78] to each owner, revealing things pertaining to the higher priesthood.

The glory of the inhabitants of the Celestial Kingdom will be like the sun's glory, and one of the manifestations of this glory will be their ability, and desire, to procreate and reproduce themselves endlessly. However, there will be people in the Celestial Kingdom who will not have this power. They are those who fulfilled all the necessary entry requirements *except* "the new and everlasting covenant of marriage." In other words, either they refused to be married on earth or to accept proxy marriage in the spirit world; or if married on earth, they refused to accept plural marriage after death. These unlucky souls are designated to be servants to those who did marry and accept plural marriage. They are referred to as "ministering angels."

The middle, or Terrestrial Kingdom, will differ as much from the Celestial, teach Mormons, as the moon does from the sun. One analogy would give the Celestial Kingdom an "A" grade, and the Terrestrial a "B." This kingdom will be the final destiny of those who "died without law" and did not accept Mormonism in the spirit world. There too will be the people who rejected the LDS gospel on earth, but later embraced it in the spirit world. Honorable men, who were blinded by the teachings of other men which prevented their conversion, will also be in this kingdom, as will lukewarm Mormons who weren't valiant in their testimonies.

Unlike the people in the Celestial Kingdom, the inhabitants of this middle kingdom will not be able to enjoy the presence of God the Father, but they will be ministered to by Jesus Christ.

The inhabitants of the lowest kingdom of heaven, the Telestial Kingdom, will arise in the resurrection of the unjust, after the Millennium of suffering required to cleanse them of their sins. Their sins on earth were such that the atonement of Christ extended to them only as far as the resurrection of their bodies. The glory of the Telestial Kingdom, though as different from the Celestial and Terrestrial as the stars are from the sun and moon, is nonetheless so wonderful that I often heard it said that anyone who could conceive of such glory would kill himself immediately so as to sooner partake of it.

The word *telestial* does not appear in 1 Corinthians 15:40, which was the source of the names of the other two kingdoms. This word was added by Joseph Smith to that verse in his Inspired Revision of the Bible. He said that it referred to the lesser glory of this kingdom.

The inhabitants of the Telestial Kingdom will be the dregs of humanity—liars, sorcerers, adulterers, pimps, and prostitutes. Also in this "hell" will be those who swore falsely, mistreated servants, and did wickedness;[79] sex sinners;[80] persecutors of the Church;[81] teachers of infant baptism and other false doctrines;[82] greedy, rich hoarders;[83] and cursers.[84] Even murderers like King David, and others who atoned personally for committing the unforgivable sin, will be in the Telestial Kingdom. People who rejected Mormonism on earth and in the spirit world, but who never denied the Holy Ghost will be there too, as will ex-Mormons who never repented of their apostasy.

Apparently the bulk of the human race will end up in this kingdom. Neither God nor Christ will commune with these people throughout eternity, but they will have the presence of the Holy Spirit. They will also be visited by emissaries from the higher kingdoms. Their greatest punishment will be anguish at the thought of their former unrealizable potential.

Who then among LDS members will go to the LDS hell? Very few. Those who go to the Telestial Kingdom will already have suffered from the time of their deaths until the end of the Millennium in the hell of the spirit prison. Mormons say that their suffering, or self-atonement, in the Millennium, will have been as exquisite as the passion of Christ.

The final hell, or "outer darkness," though, will have a sparse human population. Its inhabitants will be resurrected in the second resurrection, along with the inhabitants of the Telestial Kingdom. At that time, the hell of the spirit prison will be cast into the "lake of fire" (Rev. 20:14). (It was, after all, only "eternal" and "everlasting" in the sense that God instituted it.) The lake of fire is the final hell and the home forever of Satan, his angels, and the sons of perdition—who remained filthy even after a thousand years of detention.

These sons of perdition (literally, "sons of Satan," who is Perdition) will have their bodies restored, but they will not be glorious bodies, they will be shameful. They alone of all humankind will not be released from the control of Satan, but because of their bodies they will have certain powers over Satan. Their eternity will be one of struggle and contention, forever.

The LDS Church teaches that these sons of perdition were those who sought to be a law unto themselves.[85] Very few persons are qualified to be sons of perdition. These were holders of the Melchizidek Priesthood (which by implication would mean that no females will be in hell),[86] and had personal knowledge of the power of God. They performed the sacred temple covenants, had partaken of God's power, and then left the LDS Church. Some shed innocent blood; others sinned in other ways against the Holy Ghost. In this final hell, said Joseph Smith, man will be his own tormentor.

Some LDS authorities say that hell will not end for "those who have wholly given themselves over to satanic purposes ... They go on forever in the hell that is prepared for them."[87] But others, like John A. Widtsoe, taught that the sons of perdition will finally have their spirit bodies disintegrated, and they will revert back to their original condition as intelligences. They would await new spirit bodies from another god, and a chance to start all over again.[88] "In the Church of Jesus Christ of Latter-day Saints," said Widtsoe, "there is no hell. All will find a measure of salvation ... The gospel of Jesus Christ has no hell in the proverbial sense."[89]

THE BIBLE VIEW

The Bible does not teach two hells, nor a temporary state of suffering that can be terminated through self-atonement. Nor does it teach three degrees of heavenly glory. First Corinthians 15:40 does teach two degrees of glory, but they refer to our resurrected and earthly bodies, not to states of residence. The Bible *does*, though, teach three heavens. There is the atmospheric heaven where birds fly, rain falls, and clouds float (Gen. 7:23; 8:2; Dan. 2:38; 7:13). The second heaven is where the sun, moon, and stars are (Gen. 1: 14–17; 22:17; Mark 13:25; Rev. 6:13; 12:4). Finally, there is the heaven of God's residence (Matt. 6:9), where angels dwell and where the saved finally go (Mark 12:25; 1 Peter 1:4).

Mormons say that Christ referred to their three-tiered heaven when he told his apostles of the many mansions awaiting them (John 14:2). Is three "many"? If Christ meant three, why didn't he say so?

What Mormonism teaches about a resurrected body is proven to be false by the Bible too. If it has flesh and bones (Luke 24:36–43), it will not be a densely physical body like the one we now wear, because Christ in his resurrected body could pass through a closed door (John 20:19). The Bible tells us that Christians don't *know* what Christ will be like, but we are given assurance that we will be like him (1 John 3:2). Who could want more?

The Scriptures do put a great deal of emphasis on the body—but not Christ's physical body, and not ours either, here or in eternity. The body Christ is concerned about is his *church.* A careful reading of 1 Corinthians chapter 12 underscores this.

Mormons teach that those who go to hell are burned forever with unquenchable fire.[90] But their heaven isn't much better, for the saved of Mormonism are promised a home with their God who dwells in "everlasting burnings."[91]

The only conclusion I could offer is that Mormons had better reject their gospel—and soon—or be burned forever!

PART TWO

Chapter 9

ISSUES AND CHALLENGES FACING MORMONISM IN THE TWENTY-FIRST CENTURY — PART I

> *I don't think there is one iota of evidence that suggests a lost tribe from Israel made it all the way to the New World. It is a great story, slain by ugly fact.*
>
> —Michael Crawford, biological anthropologist[1]

In the years that have ensued since the original publication of this book in 1979 and its subsequent updated edition in 1988, the amount of information available to the average person has exploded in both data and depth. This and the following chapter will examine nine categories of challenging, high-profile issues facing the Church of Jesus Christ of Latter-day Saints.

ISSUE #1: THE INFLUENCE OF THE INTERNET

Since the days when Joseph Smith bedded women of all ages unbeknownst to his wife Emma, the LDS Church leadership has practiced a kind of schizophrenic public-versus-private balancing act that remained hidden to the average member. The rationale for this continued in the late 1800s with the then-illegal practice of polygamy, as explained by Richard Abanes:

> This same authority [priesthood of the LDS Church] had allowed polygamy to flourish for years in Kirtland, Nauvoo, and Utah, while at the same time the Church as an organization denied and condemned it. In other words, the Church could officially say just about anything as *the Church*, and yet privately, by virtue of each individual's *priesthood authority*, members could engage in practices diametrically opposed to what had been officially stated.[2]

With the recent defection of notable scholars, the inner workings of the LDS Church of the past and present have been irretrievably exposed. This factor, and the increased ability of the non-scholar to compare Mormonism of the past to Mormonism of the present, have provided a new portrait of Mormonism, framed within the borders of a computer monitor.

On the one hand, the Internet has provided a sense of community for LDS members. Dating and marriage sites provide meeting places for those who want relationships only with Mormons. Chat rooms and message boards allow people to poke fun at "Molly Mormons" (straight-laced LDS young women) and discuss the uniqueness of LDS life, in a web-based subculture sometimes described as "the bloggernacle."[3] One can explore such aspects of LDS folklore as Three Nephite legends, do intensive searches in old LDS documents, research genealogy through LDS databases, or go to the official Church site, www.lds.org, which provides Church news, instructional materials, and doctrinal statements.

However, even the youngest Mormon student who sits down at a computer to research an item from LDS history or doctrine will find herself in quite a different world, one where people who have left the Church share painful experiences and scholars quote prophets who describe and demand, paradoxically, adherence to an "everlasting" gospel that today no longer exists.

When I was at BYU, I remember my roommate Carolyn bringing home stacks of punched cards and telling me that she was going to study computer science. I yawned and wondered why she didn't consider a compact way of storing information, like those nifty new eight-track cassettes. Neither of us, I suspect, ever dreamed of what computers and the Internet would do for Mormons and non-Mormons alike.

According to Jason Gallentine, former Mormon and webmaster of MormonInformation.com, the presence of web-based information has led to an intangible split in the LDS Church membership into two groups he calls "Internet Mormons" and "Chapel Mormons." Each group would characterize itself as "true Mormonism." Internet Mormons are those who are aware of dissonant facts about old Mormon history and prior doctrine (which they identify as temporal or cultural differences from today's Mormonism, or the expressions of the individual opinions of men, even "prophets"). A Chapel Mormon—and I would have to say I was definitely one of these, despite the LDS theology classes I took at BYU—believes that the prophets spoke for God and that LDS doctrine of all epochs always "dovetailed" with previous messages from God, and always will.

An Internet Mormon believes that Mormon doctrine is contained within the covers of the four Standard Works (the Holy Bible, the *Book of Mormon*, the *Doctrine and Covenants*, and the *Pearl of Great Price*), and that all else is subject to evaluation. Chapel Mormons believe what I was taught in my "Teachings of the Living Prophets" class at BYU—that what was spoken at the LDS semiannual conference or was printed in official Church publications was doctrine on an equal plane with previously written scriptures. Gallentine continues:

- Internet Mormons tend to want to "filter" a prophet's words through both his likely cultural influences and his limited sphere of knowledge. Chapel Mormons tend to take a prophet's words at face value.
- Internet Mormons believe that the scriptures supersede the living prophets. Chapel Mormons believe that the living prophets supersede the scriptures.
- Internet Mormons believe that a prophet's words may not apply to at least some of the people he's addressing. Chapel Mormons tend to believe that a prophet's words apply to everyone he's addressing.
- Internet Mormons believe that a prophet is not necessarily any better than his societal average. Chapel Mormons believe that a prophet is a foreordained man of the highest moral caliber.

"Whenever a Mormon is confronted with controversial and contradictory historical information which he or she can no longer simply ignore," continues Gallentine, "he or she has one of two choices: Either apostatize or convert to Internet Mormonism. As Internet Mormonism progressively claims a greater and greater percentage of Mormonism as a whole, it will be interesting to see how Mormon culture changes—and how the LDS hierarchy reacts thereto."[4]

Gallentine notes that most people who leave Mormonism were Chapel Mormons. It is not possible to document how many Chapel Mormons have left the Church because of information they read on the Internet. Nor is it possible to document how many people have been similarly *prevented* from joining the LDS Church.

The LDS Church in Japan, though, provides a microcosm that demonstrates the power of the Internet, which LDS author Jiro Numano says "changed the scene radically" when Church members (who previously had only limited, sanitized Church literature) gained access to web-based information. Apparently dozens of members left, including a respected bishop, a returned missionary, Relief Society officers, and others, when they were horrified to learn of what Numano calls "alternative histories." These included Joseph Smith's many marriages, the problems with the Book of Abraham, and *Book of Mormon* historicity. In response, an LDS apologetic site was launched with counter information.

However, says Numano, "Those who leave tend to be inquisitive and intelligent, thus, the Church in Japan has been losing significant human resources."[5] With a total Church membership in Japan of about 120,000, only 25,000 of whom are active members, such attrition is devastating, though as Numano believes, slowing. He notes that once seasoned members learn to avoid sites critical of Mormonism, the danger is primarily to new members.

Numano's strategy to counter the Internet problem is a threefold one that is probably mirroring what is happening in the US Mormon Church: (1) Church leaders, says Numano, must "confront" the accessibility of anti-Mormon materials online; (2) leaders must themselves become acquainted with LDS history issues, and release additional information to Japanese Mormons; and (3) neutral points of view must be provided. (However, I have observed that in the United States such a neutral point of view has often taken the form of the absolute denial of past doctrines, characterizing them in true "Internet Mormon" fashion as simply the opinions of past leaders.)[6]

ISSUE #2: MORMONISM IN THE NEWS AND THE PUBLIC EYE

Closely associated with the challenge posed by the Internet is the publicity of events and conditions which have brought unwelcome international attention to the LDS Church. What follows is a listing of such events that have occurred during, or slightly before, my lifetime. Some of them will be covered in more detail in subsequent listings. In somewhat chronological order, they are not all equal in the impact that they had on Mormons or those outside Utah, but each is significant.[7]

- 1945: The publication of *No Man Knows My History* by respected historian Fawn McKay Brodie, niece of David O. McKay (who would subsequently become prophet of the LDS Church). This biography of Joseph Smith, "warts and all," shocks the "Chapel Mormons" of the day and is even now a foundational work of LDS history.
- 1950: Membership of the LDS Church reaches over a million members.
- 1950: LDS historian Juanita Brooks publishes *The Mountain Meadows Massacre.*
- 1958: LDS member Wilford C. Wood self-publishes a photographic reproduction of the 1830 first edition of the *Book of Mormon* under the title *Joseph Smith Begins His Work, Vol. I.* Glaring differences between this printing and current editions arouse attention.
- 1962: LDS Church-owned Deseret Printing Company publishes Wood's second book, *Joseph Smith Begins His Work, Vol. II,* which was a reprint of the 1833 *Book of Commandments.* Though initially not opposed by the Church, it is later suppressed when the Mormon-owned Deseret Bookstore is ordered to no longer sell it.
- 1964: In downtown Salt Lake City, ex-Mormons Jerald and Sandra Tanner begin publishing *The Salt Lake City Messenger.* About this time they gain access to information about a "strange" unpublished account of Joseph Smith's first vision. Thus begins a love-hate relationship between the persistent couple who publicized information and photo-reprints of LDS documents through their Modern Microfilm Co., and the frustrated LDS scholars who often had no other access to such documents because the LDS Church either denied their existence or refused to publish them.
- 1967: New York's Metropolitan Museum of Art presents to the LDS Church the collection of papyrus manuscripts identified as the source of the Book of Abraham. Without exception, all non-LDS scholars identify the papyri as pagan texts having nothing to do with Mormonism.
- 1971: Researcher Wesley P. Walters discovers an 1826 document detailing the legal hearing against "Joseph Smith The Glass Looker," providing proof of Smith's involvement in

magic during the time that he was supposedly being prepared by Moroni to receive the *Book of Mormon.*

- 1972: Jerald and Sandra Tanner release *Mormonism—Shadow or Reality?* probably the most influential and foundational book ever to document inconsistencies in LDS doctrine and official history. Over 60,000 copies are sold; and a condensed, popularized version, *The Changing World of Mormonism* (Moody Press), goes on to sell about 26,000 copies.
- 1976: Thomas Stuart Ferguson, founder of the New World Archaeology Association (LDS archaeology apologist organization) reveals in private correspondence that he believes the *Book of Mormon* to be "fictional."[8]
- October 1976: President Spencer W. Kimball calls "theory" the repeated teachings of Brigham Young that are referred to as "the Adam-God doctrine," saying that they are "false doctrine."
- 1978: "Official Declaration—2" is added to LDS scripture, declaring that men of black ancestry can receive ordination to the LDS priesthood and are permitted to enter temples for the first time.
- 1979: A previously unknown manuscript by LDS historian B. H. Roberts surfaces in which he identifies the *Book of Mormon* as "merely of human origin."[9]
- Early 1980s: Forger Mark Hofmann produces forged "antique" documents, several of which cast doubt on LDS "faithful history." Forty-eight such documents are eventually acquired by the LDS Church, which attempts to suppress them.
- 1981: A new edition of the *Book of Mormon* changes the promise that in the latter days Native American Indians would become "white and delightsome" (2 Nephi 30:6) to a new reading of "pure and delightsome."
- 1985: Hofmann's bombings to cover his forgeries result in two deaths and his own serious injury. In 1986 he is charged with two counts of first-degree homicide and twenty-six counts of fraud and forgery in a highly publicized case.
- 1987: Hoffmann confesses the homicides and forgeries and enters into a plea bargain for prison time instead of a death sentence. This leads to public questions about the "inspiration" of LDS leaders who were deceived by the forgeries.

- 1989: George P. Lee, the only Native American General Authority of the LDS Church, is excommunicated for apostasy after he publicly accuses the Church of racism.
- 1990: Newspapers across the US report that LDS temple ceremonies have dropped the symbolic hand-motion representations of violence from vows and other aspects of the rituals.
- 1990: Helvecio Martins becomes the first black General Authority in the LDS Church. (He is later honorably released in 1995, and no other man of color has since become a General Authority.)
- 1991: Very popular General Authority and prolific author Paul H. Dunn publicly admits that he "had not always been accurate"[10] in his colorful stories about his military and professional baseball careers, and had participated in other activities not approved by the Church.
- 1992: The Mormon Alliance is formed to deal with "spiritual and ecclesiastical abuse in the Church and to protect the Church against defamatory actions."
- 1993: "The September Six," prominent LDS intellectuals and scholars, are publicly rebuked. Five are excommunicated for apostasy regarding their writing and speaking about LDS subjects and one is disfellowshipped.
- 1993: Pulitzer Prize–winning LDS cartoonist Steve Benson (eldest grandson of Ezra Taft Benson, who was then prophet of the Mormon Church) and his wife resign from the Church, citing the incompetence and intolerance of Church leadership.
- 1995: *Deseret News* describes and documents cases of ritual child abuse by Mormons.[11]
- 1996: President Gordon B. Hinckley is interviewed on television show *60 Minutes.*
- 1997: Christian Craig L. Blomberg and LDS Stephen E. Robinson publish *How Wide the Divide? A Mormon and an Evangelical in Conversation* (InterVarsity).
- 1997: President Gordon B. Hinckley, when interviewed by the *San Francisco Chronicle* and asked if God was once a man, answers, "I wouldn't say that. There was a little couplet coined, 'As man is, God once was. As God is, man may become.' Now that's more of a couplet than anything else. That gets into some pretty deep theology that we don't know very much about."[12]

- 1998: Members of the International Olympic Committee are accused of taking bribes from the Salt Lake Organizing Committee to persuade them to place the 2002 Winter Olympics in Utah.
- 1998: The *Larry King Live* television program interviews Gordon B. Hinckley, president of the LDS Church.
- 1999: The Tanners and their Utah Lighthouse Ministry are sued by the LDS Church for printing materials from the LDS *Church Handbook of Instructions*, a secret handbook outlining procedures for disciplinary matters. This was covered in the *New York Times*, and ironically quadrupled the number of people visiting the Tanners' website. The matter is settled in an agreement whereby the Tanners limit use of the Handbook but do not admit wrongdoing, and the injunction is dropped by the LDS Church.
- 1999: LDS President Gordon B. Hinckley dedicates a monument at the site of the Mountain Meadows Massacre and in his remarks states that the LDS Church still accepts no legal responsibility for the massacre.
- 2001: Modern polygamist Tom Green, who has publicly spoken of his practices on television, is sentenced to prison.
- 2002: Retired LDS Institute of Religion director Grant Palmer publishes *An Insider's View of Mormon Origins*, a well-documented and authoritative denial of the translating abilities of Joseph Smith, written for a nonscholarly audience.
- 2002: Jerald and Sandra Tanner launch online resources at utlm.org.
- 2003: Best-selling author Jon Krakauer's book *Under the Banner of Heaven: A Story of Violent Faith* describes Mormon Fundamentalist murders.
- 2003: Kidnapped Mormon girl, Elizabeth Smart, is rescued from polygamist Brian David Mitchell in a highly publicized case.
- 2003: Ex-Mormon evangelical Greg Johnson and LDS author Robert Millet begin public dialogues in Christian churches. Millet publishes several books as apologist for the LDS Church beginning in 1999.
- 2004: At a Johnson-Millet "Evening of Friendship" event in Salt Lake City, Dr. Richard Mouw, president of Fuller Seminary,

publicly accuses Christians of "bearing false witness"[13] and tells Mormons, "We evangelicals have sinned against you."[14]

- 2004: President Gordon B. Hinckley interviewed on CNN's *Larry King Live.*
- 2004: Molecular biologist Simon Southerton publishes *Losing a Lost Tribe: Native Americans, DNA, and the Book of Mormon,* which documents that DNA data for American Indians does not support the *Book of Mormon* story. Though already inactive in the Church for seven years, Southerton is excommunicated for adultery.
- 2004: Publisher Doubleday releases a bookstore-marketed edition of the *Book of Mormon* priced at $24.95. (Free copies published by the Church are still available from Mormon members.)
- 2004: An Illinois delegation including the lieutenant governor apologizes to the LDS Church for the 1844 murder of Joseph Smith.
- 2005: The cover story of *Newsweek* commemorates the 200th anniversary of the birth of Joseph Smith.
- 2006: Number of LDS temples dedicated worldwide (124) doubles since 1999.
- 2006: Fundamentalist Mormon polygamist Warren Jeffs, on the FBI's Most Wanted List, is captured.
- 2007: PBS *American Experience* program "The Mormons" airs.
- 2007: The *Book of Mormon* is again edited. The preface's previous text states that Lamanites were the "principal ancestors" of American Indians. It is now changed to read that Lamanites are "among the ancestors of the American Indians."
- 2007: 150th anniversary of the Mountain Meadows Massacre receives national attention with a ceremony and movies and books based on the event.
- 2007: LDS Mitt Romney announces his bid to be the Republican presidential candidate, bringing a national spotlight onto Mormon history, doctrines, and practices.
- 2007: LDS Church issues a statement: "Doctrine resides in the four 'standard works' of scripture (the Holy Bible, the *Book of Mormon*, the *Doctrine and Covenants* and the *Pearl of Great Price*), official declarations and proclamations, and the Articles of Faith."

- 2008: Official LDS Church membership reaches thirteen million.
- 2008: Texas authorities raid fundamentalist compound and take into protective custody hundreds of women and children, who are later returned to the Yearning For Zion Ranch and their polygamous lifestyle.

Besides Mitt Romney, in recent years many Mormons have been quite visible in public life. They include authors Stephen R. Covey, Stephenie Meyer, and Orson Scott Card; news commentator Glenn Beck; entertainers Donnie and Marie Osmond, Gladys Knight, Rick Schroeder, Ryan Gosling, and Jon Heder; football coaches Andy Reid, Mike Holmgren, and Norm Chow; athletes Golden Richards, Steve Young, Johnny Miller, and Torah Bright; politicians Harry Reid, Orrin Hatch, Bob Bennett, Gordon Smith, Mike Crapo, and Jon Huntsman; CEOs Bill Marriot (Marriot), Kevin Rollins (Dell Computers), Nolan Archibald (Black and Decker), Gary Baughman (Fisher-Price), Gary Crittenden (American Express), Nolan Bushnell (founder, Atari), and David Neeleman (Jet Blue); businessman Jon Huntsman (reportedly the wealthiest Mormon with an estimated net worth of $3.9 billion); scientist (and LDS apostle) Henry Eyring; space shuttle program director Ron Dittemore and space shuttle *Columbia* astronaut Richard Seafross; game show host Ray Combs and game show megawinner Ken Jennings; and of course the award-winning Mormon Tabernacle Choir.

The Church's public image of clean-cut youngsters and responsible, productive, patriotic adults is based on fact. Faithful Mormons work very hard at authentically fulfilling that image, and their lifestyle attracts many converts. The official Church website, lds.org, touts its humanitarian aid, resources for strengthening families, and statistics about its growth. Secular magazines such as *US News and World Report* characterize it as "growing by leaps and bounds."[15]

While wanting to be known for its moral lifestyle, the LDS Church also yearns for acceptance. "We're normal, everyday people," said Mormon journalist Jeff Benedict, author of *The Mormon Way of Doing Business.*[16] Some of that yearning is seen in LDS movies, like *Baptists at Our Barbecue,*[17] and in the surge of recently released books promoting dialogue between Mormons and evangelicals.

Yet the LDS population, like all large groups of people, has public relations challenges. Martha Nibley Beck, daughter of famed LDS scholar Hugh Nibley, not only revealed her own experience of alleged abuse by her father in her book *Leaving the Saints: How I Lost the Mormons and Found My Faith*

(Crown/Random House, 1995), but as an ex-Mormon she continues to document and counsel others of LDS background with similar experiences.[18]

A 2003 study entitled "Mormon Women, Prozac® and Therapy"[19] by LDS author Kent Ponder, PhD, describes the pressures on LDS women; and a national study by Express Scripts Inc., a pharmacy benefits management company, found that "antidepressant drugs are prescribed in Utah more often than in any other state at a rate nearly twice the national average."[20] The reasons for this are not hard to understand: Imagine a culture in which women are supposed to participate fully in all LDS meetings, give birth to multiple children, maintain a two-year supply of food and supplies properly rotated, keep themselves cheerful and sexually attractive to their husbands, and perform temple ordinances—all the while looking forward to an eternity of the same ramped up to the extreme: bearing children, this time entire populations of them, and comanaging planetary systems.

Nor is despair the exclusive province of women in the state of Utah, which is 70 percent Mormon. According to the *Deseret Morning News*, Utah leads the nation in suicides among men aged fifteen to twenty-four.[21] While the LDS lifestyle is unquestionably comforting, ennobling, nurturing, and communal to many, it can have quite a different effect on other individuals.[22]

The unfortunate fact is that many Americans don't like, and don't trust, Mormons. A 2007 Pew Research poll of 3,000 Americans found that while 53 percent viewed Mormonism positively, 27 percent did not, and only 23 percent used a positive word to describe Mormonism.[23] About the time that Mitt Romney suspended his presidential candidacy, a *Wall Street Journal/NBC News* poll revealed that while 81 percent of Americans could be "enthusiastic" or "comfortable" with an African-American president, and 76 percent would feel similarly about a woman president, over 50 percent of Americans said that they would have reservations or be "very uncomfortable" with the idea of a Mormon president.[24]

Political personalities and issues aside, secular-minded people might cite as reasons for their uneasiness the reputation of clannishness and the Church's strange history. But characterizing a group as large as the LDS Church is difficult: No group of thirteen million individuals can form a collective that is completely homogenous. While Church leadership would promote and desire the "Molly Mormon" image, relatively few maintain that ideal. Another social group has emerged, that of "cultural Mormons," who may be compared with cultural Jews, those who celebrate Jewish holidays and think of themselves as Jewish without a particularly religious fervor.

Cultural Mormons may have had a Mormon upbringing and still maintain membership in the LDS Church and support many of the Church's ideals, such as its lifestyle and associations. Many resemble LDS author and scholar Thomas Stuart Ferguson, who near the end of his life saw no validity in the claims of Joseph Smith nor the *Book of Mormon*, but who spoke of the satisfaction of singing in an LDS Church choir in the Mormonism he described as "probably the best conceived myth-fraternity to which one can belong."[25] In recent years many LDS scholars and intellectuals have joined his club.

Others maintain Church membership because to exit it requires a great deal of effort and often results in a "bishop's court" that brings shame to family members and friends. Still others know that the cost of doing business, especially small business, in Utah is LDS Church membership and at least the appearance of compliance with its ideals.

A "Jack Mormon," on the other hand, is one who might be described as a lapsed member, one who's heavy on the "Latter-day" and light on the "Saint" parts. Generally a Jack Mormon is self-identified as such, and is often characterized by smoking and the drinking of liquor, tea, and coffee. Usually they do not attend Church meetings nor make any other pretense of LDS lifestyle.

Because of today's Mormon's trusting and unquestioning nature and emphasis on financial success, says author John L. Brooke, Utah is well-known as the "scam capital of the United States,"[26] especially vulnerable to ponzi and pyramid schemes. A more dramatic example of a wolf in sheep's clothing in the Mormon flock is the highly publicized case of Mark Hofmann, the masterful forger of early LDS documents. Brooke believes that being the son of a plural wife in Mexico, Hofmann harbored deep resentment against the Church which encouraged polygamy in principle and then abandoned those who practiced it.[27] Others speculate that he truly believed he was filling in missing puzzle pieces of true Church history. But whatever his motives, Hofmann understood LDS leadership psychology very, very well, and made a fortune off the fears of those in high position who knew the Church already owned—and kept buried in its archive vaults—documents that would embarrass the Church if they surfaced. Hofmann capitalized on those fears and sold the LDS Church one "newly discovered" document after another. The money came from nearly limitless coffers—the resources of well-heeled members who would then donate the documents to the Church. In a sense, the purchase price had been laundered to keep the skirts of the LDS Church clean.

Hofmann met several times with Spencer W. Kimball, who was "prophet, seer and revelator" of a Church founded on texts that once purported to be newly discovered documents (the *Book of Mormon* and the Book of Abraham). Photographs of the presentation of the forged documents show Hofmann looking over the shoulder of Kimball, who learned the truth only later, along with the rest of the world, after two people lost their lives in Hofmann's bombings.

One of Kimball's titles was that of an elder in the Church, a title he shared with his two counselors and twelve apostles, none of whom apparently had the ability to see the fraud in Hofmann's documents, in spite of what LDS scripture teaches:

> And unto the bishop of the Church, and unto such as God shall appoint and ordain to watch over the Church and to be elders unto the Church, are to have it given unto them to discern all those gifts lest there shall be any among you professing and yet be not of God.[28]

The Hofmann affair was very public—at least five major mainstream books and countless articles and television shows were based on it. But for Mormons of the twenty-first century, the implications of the Hofmann forgeries are grave. In the words of the late Jerald Tanner,

> The inability of the Mormon leaders to detect the religious fraud perpetrated upon them raises a question as to their testimony with regard to the *Book of Mormon.* After all, if they could not determine that Hofmann's documents—which were only 150 years old—were forgeries, how can we trust their judgment with regard to a record which is supposed to be ten times as old? They have seen and inspected Mark Hofmann's documents, but they have never seen the gold plates the *Book of Mormon* was translated from. While it could be possible that Joseph Smith really had some kind of metal plates, how would the present leaders of the Mormon Church know if they were genuine or fabricated?[29]

Many people, and I am among them, see the LDS Church as a church that claims history, but only the parts it likes. It has taken its most flamboyant and charismatic leaders of the past, say journalists Richard and Joan Ostling, and rendered them "almost colorless," and thus acceptable for the twenty-first century.[30] Any denials of this insipid history is the very atmosphere, like Prohibition, that creates the black markets in which the

Hofmanns of Mormonism will always flourish, and for which the cottage industry of "spin" and crisis management of earlier days must be cranked up to ever-higher levels.

ISSUE #3: RACE

I think it would be fair to say that the LDS Church in the twenty-first century bends over backwards to try to present itself as having completely fair policies regarding race. No ethnicity nor mixture of ethnicities would today exclude a man from membership nor priesthood in the LDS Church. However, events within my own memory have pointed up the Church's problems regarding four ethnicities: Native Americans, Blacks, Jews, and Hispanics.

Bruce R. McConkie was a prominent and respected LDS leader and author of the book *Mormon Doctrine.* I was among the millions of Mormons who regarded his book as authoritative, since the author was an apostle and his often-quoted book purported to accurately represent, after all, Mormon *doctrine.* He stated unambiguously what Mormons understood about race. According to McConkie, God himself sent individuals to earth with racial markings—not just the differentiation of color and other bodily characteristics—but in what McConkie called "a caste system of his [God's] own, a system of segregation of races and people."[31]

Thus the long-standing LDS attitudes toward all non-white races had a well-defined doctrinal base. In LDS teaching, having a dark skin while on earth was an indicator of the person's actions in the preexistence. If he or she was not faithful—on the side with God and Jesus in the battle against Lucifer—he or she would be sent to earth in a dark skin. In the case of the Lamanites, their earthly rebellion against the teachings of God's prophets caused their skin to become dark.[32] The skin color of the Lamanites, however, was only temporary and could be changed—that is, lightened—if they would simply accept the Mormon gospel. To me, and to most Mormons, there was a sense of fairness and justice about it all.

This understanding also provided a framework within which a faithful Mormon could act compassionately despite the stigma of the dark skin/sin issue. The LDS Social Service began a program in 1947 called the Indian Student Placement Program. Through ISPP, Native American parents could send their children to LDS homes during the school year with the hope of a better education and other opportunities—and also be assimilated into Mormon culture. Many LDS families participated by taking in Indian children. I knew many Native American students at BYU who had lived with non-Indian LDS families through the program.

In spite of the fact that Spencer W. Kimball, who would later become the LDS prophet, claimed that children in the ISPP were in the very process of "turning white and delightsome" and that they were "often lighter than their brothers and sisters in the hogans on the reservations,"[33] no one else saw such changes. Since the *Book of Mormon* claimed that a change of skin color would accompany conversion but such never happened, the LDS Church responded to gathering concerns by cavalierly changing the wording of their own scripture (changing the wording of their own scripture! of "the most correct book on earth"!) so that it no longer read "white and delightsome" in 2 Nephi 30:6 but rather "pure and delightsome."[34]

The ISPP continued on, but it soon garnered sharp criticism from those who believed it eroded the heritage and identity of Native Americans. This criticism became national news in 1987 when Elder George P. Lee of the First Council of the Seventy (the group which reports directly to the LDS apostles) said that the LDS Church was "slowly causing a silent and subtle scriptural and spiritual slaughter of the Indians and other Lamanites."[35] Lee, the first Native American General Authority of the Mormon Church and himself a product of the ISPP, was escorted out of his office within mere minutes[36] of sending his superiors a letter accusing them of "superior race, white supremacy, racist attitude, pride, arrogance,"[37] and other sins.

Lee was later publicly accused, and convicted in a court of law, of the crime of child molestation; and some people speculate that this contributed as much to his excommunication from the LDS Church as did his public criticism. Lee reportedly returned to his Native American religion and served jail time for his crime. The ISPP was discontinued in 1996.

In 2002 LDS scholar Thomas W. Murphy published an article in a book, detailing what he saw as racism in LDS scriptures, specifically the teaching that American Indians descended from ancient Jewish roots. Murphy cited numerous scientists who said that not only were "virtually all" American Indians tested of Asian, not Hebraic, extraction,[38] but also that Polynesians and other island peoples (which Mormons once claimed to be Lamanite as well[39]) were similarly of Asiatic extraction.[40]

Murphy's findings were corroborated by LDS geneticist Simon Southerton. This former Mormon bishop's book, *Losing a Lost Tribe: Native Americans, DNA, and the Mormon Church*, utterly devastated the LDS claim that American Indians were descended from Israelites. Southerton also routed the modern LDS contention that former prophets had been mistaken and that the events of the *Book of Mormon* did not take place all over the Western Hemisphere as previously taught, but only in a small area of Central America.

Since Southerton's book, Mormon apologists have scrambled for explanations, including such far-fetched ones as "God transformed the Lamanites' DNA," "Nobody has a sample of Lehi's DNA so we couldn't match it," and other such explanations.[41]

The Church itself squelched some of the criticisms by changing the introduction to the *Book of Mormon*. For years it had stated, "After thousands of years all were destroyed except the Lamanites, and they are the principal ancestors of the American Indians." In present editions this sentence reads, "they are *among* the ancestors of the American Indians" (italics added).

This tiny change in wording made national news. But Bob Rees, a retired UCLA literature professor and former editor of a Mormon magazine, echoed the thoughts of many modern Mormons, as an Associated Press article showed: " 'A central tenet of Latter-day Saint beliefs includes the principle of continuing revelation and an open religious canon, so change should be expected,' Rees said."[42]

While the issue of the LDS Church's doctrinal relationship to American Indians and other natives of this hemisphere continues to be an active one, such is apparently not the case with what was once a tinderbox: blacks and the LDS Church. Though (for now) the verses (*Pearl of Great Price*, Abraham 1:22–27) that once supported the ban on blacks in the LDS priesthood remains in the canon, nonetheless the visibility of Mormon entertainer Gladys Knight, the calling of a black man as a General Authority in 1990, and the election of the first black as student body president at BYU in 2002 show that the face of the LDS Church is changing. "The Black Mormon Homepage" says that there are 200,000 black Mormons, 150,000 of whom live in Africa; and another unofficial website, www.blacklds.org, gives a timeline and provides a community for a growing number of blacks both in the United States and abroad.[43] In defending Mormonism's long history of banning blacks from the priesthood, such groups emphasize the antislavery stance of Mormon leaders in history, and the faithful membership of blacks from the time of Joseph Smith. However, they also compare the LDS ban to Protestant groups who supported slavery in the nineteenth century—a comparison that does not hold well when one considers that Christians used their own (unwarranted) interpretations of Scripture to support slavery, while Mormons (who claim direct, daily, linguistic guidance of their prophets) have no such defense of "opinion" for the scripture-based racist doctrines of such perpetuity in their Church.

A third ethnic group which has done public battle with the LDS Church is Judaism. According to Richard and Joan Ostling, in the mid-1990s Mormons performed proxy baptisms for about 380,000 deceased Jews in various LDS temples.[44] They included Sigmund Freud, David Ben-Gurion, Ba'al Shem Tov (founder of the Hasidic Jewish movement), and many Jews who died in Nazi concentration camps, including Anne Frank.[45] Adding insult to injury, zealous Mormons also stood in proxy for Adolf Hitler's and Eva Braun's baptisms and "eternal" marriage.[46]

If the prospect of meeting Hitler as a god in eternity rankles the sensitivities of most non-Mormons, imagine the impact of such an idea on a Jew. While they, like many Christians, would put little credence in the eternal effect of such temple ordinances, the idea of proxy Mormonism is reprehensible to them, as voiced by Aaron Breitbart, senior researcher for the Simon Weisenthal Center based in Los Angeles: "These people were born Jews, they lived as Jews, and many of them died because they were Jews.... They would not have chosen to be baptized Mormons in life, and there is no reason they would want to be baptized by proxy in death."[47]

In 1995 the LDS Church agreed to remove all such names from their databases and to stop baptizing any deceased Jew unless he or she is an ancestor of a living Mormon; or, alternately, the Church obtains written permission from all living members of the Jew's family.[48] Researcher Helen Radkey estimates, however, that over a million Jews have had proxy temple ordinances performed *after* the agreement of the LDS Church to cease performing vicarious baptisms for Jews.[49]

Finally, the LDS Church is well through the first decade of the twenty-first century without a single apostle of color, or of any identifiable non-European or non-American ethnicity. Thus the Mormon Church at its highest apostolic levels is comprised exclusively of old, white men. That is of particular interest considering the fact that over half of the Mormon Church's thirteen million members are now in countries outside North America, and more than a third (4.25 million) are Latin Americans.[50]

ISSUE #4: GENDER

LDS controversies over the last few decades regarding gender have centered in three areas: the idea of a Heavenly Mother (or mothers), women's role in the LDS Church, and same-sex issues.

LDS author Linda P. Wilcox, in her essay, "The Mormon Concept of a Mother in Heaven," describes a Mormon cartoon in which a woman asks her husband, "What do you think Heavenly Mother thinks about polygamy?" To which her husband replies: "Which Heavenly Mother?"[51] This cartoon indicates a ripening of the LDS doctrines about God's spouse (or spouses), but at a grassroots—not male-leadership—level among people in the LDS Church. Wilcox notes, "At present, the nineteenth-century generalized image of a female counterpart to a literal male father-god is receiving increased attention and expansion and is becoming more personalized and individualized."[52] Other writers describe the doctrine of a Heavenly Mother as "mainstream"—though forbidden in discourse—in the LDS Church.[53] Also at the forefront in the minds of Mormon feminists (and yes, absolutely, there are Mormon feminists) are issues such as those raised by Melodie Moench Charles, who believes that in a church based on changes in revelations, there is hope that "the time will come when opportunities for service in the Church will be based on talents rather than gender."[54] (Actually, one of Mormonism's finest scholars, D. Michael Quinn, contends that Mormon women have held priesthood since the days of Joseph Smith, and gives evidence to prove this assertion.[55])

But in a practical sense the time that Charles looks to has not yet come. According to Margaret Merrill Toscano, a formidable and articulate feminist in the LDS tradition (though she was excommunicated from the Church), the quest for gender equality in a Church that accepts male-only leadership as God's will—and whose women members do not feel subordinate and are, in the main, content with their roles—means no real change is in the offing.

After all, the Church isn't facing the kind of public outcry over feminist issues from outsiders such as it experienced over racial issues, at least not since Sonia Johnson's time. She was the founder of Mormons for the ERA and author of *From Housewife to Heretic*.[56] And the Church has made some concessions in recent years. In 1978 women were first permitted to pray in Sacrament meetings and to go to the temple without their husbands, and in 1990 the temple ceremony that once required women to swear to "obey" their husbands was changed to speak of wives following their husbands' "counsel." And President Hinckley's 1995 "The Family: Proclamation to the World"[57] actually spoke of equality of fathers and mothers in childrearing.

Feminists in and out of the Church are quietly pushing for such things as an independent Relief Society (women's organization), for more deference to women's opinions in policymaking, and for joint leadership of men and their wives in some priesthood positions. Yet Toscano argues that feminist issues will continue to smolder without any real flame of change. "In a hierarchical structure such as the Church's, every man is a 'girl' to the men above him in the priesthood pipeline," says Toscano. "Every doctrine is capable of becoming taboo like the Heavenly Mother, not on the basis of truth or logic or even popular disregard, but if it is pronounced such by those with the power to make it unspeakable."[58]

Though Mother-god controversies and feminism have been hot issues within Mormonism, there is no more visible way that I have seen the LDS Church change in regard to gender issues than in the area of same-sex relationships. In the first edition of this book, I made the statement that I had never met a Mormon homosexual. In hindsight, what would have been more accurate would have been to say that I didn't know that a few Mormons I had met were homosexuals. An example of this was when I attended the Mormon Arts Festival at BYU and admired the paintings of a faculty member, Trevor Southey. Though homosexual, he had been advised by his priesthood leaders to marry to overcome his sexual orientation. He later "came out" and was excommunicated from the LDS Church. Another prominent gay LDS man who was later excommunicated is Dr. D. Michael Quinn, who was a former professor at BYU, Church Historian's Office employee, and author. In his writing Quinn identified gay Mormons of the past, including Assistant Church President John C. Bennett[59] and former Church Patriarch Joseph F. Smith[60] (not to be confused with his relatives of the same name who served as presidents of the LDS Church). Gay Mormons of the present and recent past include authors Pat Califa and Martha Beck; and the late Leonard Matlovich (whose sexual orientation first brought national attention to the issue of gays in the military).

According to Affirmation, a group for homosexual, lesbian, transgender, and bisexual Mormons with over thirty-five national and international chapters, LDS history is full of people who would have been candidates for Affirmation membership, including the aforementioned patriarch of the Church, former lesbian-lover heads of the Primary (children's) organization, and a son of Brigham Young who performed in drag.[61] Other unsavory elements of LDS history that this organization recounts are the apparently brutal electric shock treatments administered to men with homosexual tendencies and/or feelings—the so-called "aversion therapy" experiments at BYU during the 1970s. However, Affirmation's website has a wide variety of materials, not just the shocking ones, and often evinces a sense of humor. To me, that is a sign that the organization is thriving and comfortable in its own skin, so to speak—and apparently, here to stay.

Though officially not affiliated with the Mormon Church, an organization under its aegis entitled Evergreen International offers resources for LDS people who experience same-sex attraction, with the aim of helping them "diminish their attractions and overcome homosexual behavior."[62] However, many gay Latter-day Saints believe that Evergreen International does not support the gay lifestyle and practices. At least six other organizations have websites of resources for LDS people with gender issues. There are even splinter-group church assemblies primarily for gays, lesbians, transgenders, and bisexuals such as the Restoration Church of Jesus Christ, with congregations in Utah and California[63] that teach many traditional LDS doctrines and even perform "sealings" of couples of the same sex in their own temples.

In the twenty-first century the LDS Church has backed away from its prior blanket characterization of homosexuality as a sin and instead identified homosexual actions—not feelings nor inclinations, which the Church calls "same-gender attraction"—as sin. An indication of the Church's proactive approach to information about its stance on same-gender attraction is a lengthy article and other materials on the subject on its official website.[64] This has not satisfied Affirmation members, who have requested face-to-face meetings with the newest Mormon president, Thomas S. Monson. At issue here is the fact that even though the LDS Church has excommunicated many Affirmation members, they still regard themselves as Mormons and seek official recognition—and changes—from the LDS Church.

ISSUE #5: VISIBILITY OF POLYGAMY AND SPLINTER GROUPS

Polygamy, the long-hidden stepchild of Mormon doctrine, has similarly burst out of its closet in recent years. The LDS Church has paid an enormous price for this doctrine—some people believe that Joseph Smith's denials that he was bedding and marrying the wives and daughters of his friends led to his death; others say that the Mountain Meadows Massacre was instigated by those who wanted to protect the practice, and almost anyone would agree that misunderstanding—and understanding too well—"eternal marriage" has separated Smith's followers from the outside world and each other for nearly two centuries. "He figured out how to commit adultery, and to do it sacramentally,"[65] says Mark Scherer, Church historian for the Community of Christ (formerly known as the RLDS Church). For better or for worse, plural marriage in the United States will forever be identified with Joseph Smith and the churches that claim him as prophet.

But for members of the Church of Jesus Christ of Latter-day Saints, it's not about the nineteenth-century caricatures nor the twenty-first century splinter group aberrations. For the LDS Church, it is eternal doctrine, and it is certainly affirmed by Church leaders who have made public statements affirming eternal polygamy and some who have married second wives in temple ceremonies after the death of their first wives.[66] For many younger

Mormons, the idea of polygamy in heaven may not be as active an issue, but the tiny sterling silver temple I wore on a chain around my neck at BYU meant that I was preparing to be one of many wives in eternity.

Seeing polygamy as an illegal and forbidden earthly practice brings an ethical issue to the fore for Mormons: They must condemn those who practice it while defending the doctrines that underlie it, and simultaneously believe they will someday themselves practice it on a greater scale than any earthly person now jailed for it. But meanwhile here on earth, the LDS Church just can't keep polygamy out of the news — not with the murders committed by the cold-blooded LeBaron clan and the killings perpetrated by the Lafferty brothers, not with the kidnapping of Elizabeth Smart, not with the FBI-Most-Wanted manhunt and capture of Warren Jeffs.

And the LDS Church can't keep polygamy out of literature[67] — from Sir Arthur Conan Doyle's first novel, *A Study in Scarlet*, to Zane Grey's *Riders of the Purple Sage*, to Jon Krakauer's *Under the Banner of Heaven*, to my own novel, *Latter-day Cipher (*Moody, 2009).

And the LDS Church can't keep polygamy out of popular entertainment — as witness the countless crime shows that focus on LDS splinter groups with multiple wives, and the HBO series *Big Love*.

Nor will they be able to escape the connection with what many people see as the inevitable successor to legalized same-sex marriage: the legalization of plural marriage, which many people are calling "the next civil rights battle." In the words of polygamist Owen Allred, "The man who wants several women to be his sexual partners can have children by them, and the state will support those children. He remains free of any legal accusation — until he marries more than one wife. Marry them, and he becomes a criminal. It is the marriage that becomes the crime."[68]

An Internet search reveals that this civil rights issue is being pushed by many groups outside the Latter-day Saint tradition. Ironically, perhaps only with the prospect of legalization of polygamy in both its incarnations as polygyny (men with multiple wives) and polyandry (women with multiple husbands) will Americans begin to identify plural marriage with non-Mormons.

I wonder what the LDS Church will do if, like same-sex marriage, polygamy becomes legal. Will the "prophet" reverse Wilford Woodruff's Manifesto? Or will Mormons and Christians be the only Americans whose doctrines will forbid them to have multiple wives?

Chapter 10

ISSUES AND CHALLENGES FACING MORMONISM IN THE TWENTY-FIRST CENTURY — PART 2

> *[Steve Benson] now refers to his former Church as "Red Square on Temple Square," a reference to the Mormon Temple in Salt Lake City. The Church is going through "a totalitarian mode," he said. "I wanted to be a good Mormon, but at the same time, I wanted to be truthful, I wanted to be honest and I wanted to be a good journalist. I found over time I could not be a good Mormon and an honest individual. I kinda had to make a choice."*
>
> —Walt Jayroe[1]

ISSUE #6: MORMONS AND POLITICS

Mitt Romney aside, Mormons have been involved in politics through the Church's history, as witness the self-declaration of Joseph Smith as king and candidate for president of the United States, the unofficial but vitriolic declaration of war of Brigham Young against the US government (an outgrowth of which was the bloody Mountain Meadows Massacre), the Reed Smoot hearings of the early 1900s in which the illegal persistence of LDS Church leaders in polygamy was revealed, and the appointment of John

Birch Society member, anticommunist Ezra Taft Benson (later a Mormon prophet) as Eisenhower's secretary of agriculture.

Janis Hutchinson was a faithful Mormon for thirty-four years, and she shared her concerns about the role of Mormons in politics on her website[2] when Mitt Romney's campaign was in full swing. Though she had no questions about Romney's morality or character traits, she had grave concerns about what she, and others, term a "secret agenda" of the LDS Church regarding politics: a public face and a private one, so to speak.

Hutchinson is not alone in her appraisal of two agendas. A 2008 article entitled "What Is It about Mormonism?" in the *New York Times* by Noah Feldman, a Harvard professor of law and adjunct senior fellow at the Council on Foreign Relations, points at one cause for this seemingly schizophrenic public image:

> What began as a strategy of secrecy to avoid persecution has become over the course of the 20th century a strategy of minimizing discussion of the content of theology in order to avoid being treated as religious pariahs. As a result, Mormons have not developed a series of easily expressed and easily swallowed statements summarizing the content of their theology in ways that might arguably be accepted by mainline Protestants. To put it bluntly, the combination of secret mysteries and resistance in the face of oppression has made it increasingly difficult for Mormons to talk openly and successfully with outsiders about their religious beliefs.[3]

Hutchinson documents from LDS and former LDS historians an organization formed by Mormon leadership under Joseph Smith called The Kingdom of God (or, alternately, The Government of God) that was to be ruled by a Council of Fifty who were sworn to secrecy about the organization and its aims and very existence.[4] This council ordained Joseph Smith as king over all the earth, and after Smith's death similarly ordained as kings subsequent LDS prophets up at least through Lorenzo Snow (who died in 1901). The express aim of the organization was the takeover of the United States government, not by violence, but by the grooming of Mormons to run for and win political office. In sufficient numbers, such lawmakers and policymakers would transition the government from a democracy to a theocracy.

Brigham Young had even more far-reaching plans for "the complete overthrow of the nation, and not only of this nation, but the nations of Europe."[5] The aim of the subsequent one-world government would be to prepare the world for the second coming of Christ and a thousand-year, literally theocratic kingdom. At one point LDS leaders were quite open about this agenda, as evidenced by a so-called "Political Manifesto" reported a century ago in the *Deseret News*, in which any LDS priesthood holder seeking political office was required to first garner permission from Church authorities.[6] As recently as the late 1960s, Mormon historian Klaus J. Hansen said of the Council of Fifty that Church leaders of his time were not likely to do away with it.[7] And as late as 1985, LDS authors Heinerman and Shupe claimed that "though the ceremony of coronation continues to this day, it is not publicized outside the Church," and they describe private rituals attended only by the highest-ranking Church officials.[8]

Janis Hutchinson recalls her own distress and that of her fellow Mormons when the Church ceased public endorsements by Church leadership of political candidates. "We *wanted* our prophet to tell us who to vote for," recounts Hutchinson. "We believed he was a recipient of heavenly revelation and would naturally know which candidate God approved of."[9]

Another disturbing, and well-documented, element of what Feldman called the "strategy of secrecy" is the blood oaths that were part of the LDS temple ceremony up until at least 1927. In these oaths, temple ordinance participants swore enmity to the United States government and promised to avenge the blood of LDS persons who died in conflict with the government. While there is no evidence that any man in current LDS leadership took that oath, its effect was intended to be ongoing, as noted by author Richard Abanes: "It required Mormons to promise that they would teach their children, grandchildren, and great-grandchildren to take vengeance on 'this nation.' "[10] (Did current LDS leadership teach this to their children and grandchildren? The fact that their own fathers would have sworn that oath gives reason for pause.)

In addition to these elements of LDS history—of which I knew nothing when I was a Mormon—was something I and fellow students at BYU *did* often openly and enthusiastically discuss, which was the firm belief in a prophecy of a future date in which the US Constitution would be in serious trouble, and only saved by the LDS Church.[11] As a people, it was our aim to produce as many LDS lawmakers, judges, politicians, and legal experts as we possibly could, so as to fulfill and satisfy that prophecy.[12]

Any faithful "temple Mormon" politician has a dilemma to which Mitt Romney responded in his well-publicized speech about his loyalties. The issue wasn't just in the minds of potential voters; it is a real dilemma for an LDS politician. If Romney, for instance, were to be elected president of the United States, he would be asked to swear a solemn oath to protect the Constitution of the United States as a priority over any other loyalties to any other earthly entity. However, when Mitt Romney "took out his endowments" (participated in a secret rite in an LDS temple prior to going on his LDS mission and later before being married in such a temple), he swore another oath before God and witnesses. With arms to the square, he and his wife swore to keep the "Law of Consecration": a vow to consecrate time, energy, talents, and material possessions to the Church for the purpose of "building up of the Kingdom of God on the earth and for the establishment of Zion."[13] In addition, Romney's "calling" to be a bishop in the Mormon Church required that he render absolute loyalty to the LDS Church and its prophet.

So what's the problem? I have no questions about any other "hidden" elements of Romney's character or past. (In fact, my freshman yearbook from BYU has a picture of him in it. As far as I know he was, and is, a nice guy.) But here is what I can envision, and fear:

New federal hate crime laws do not protect someone speaking against the religion of another person. When I critique Mormonism, I and all others who teach against pseudo-Christian cults, violent Islam, or any other unbiblical religious group, I'm in a "gray" legal area, one that has been exploited as a "hate crime" in other countries. Author and Templeton Prize–winner Chuck Colson points out this danger (specifically regarding speaking about the biblical prohibition of homosexual behavior). In an excellent article, Colson says that "in places where hate crimes laws have been passed, hate crimes have been defined to include verbal attacks—and even peaceful speech. The Thought Police have already prosecuted Christians under hate crimes laws in England, Sweden, Canada, and even in some places in the United States."[14]

Here's a scenario—what if my ministry is seen as a hate crime? What if someone decided to prosecute me for telling the truth about Mormonism? Where would Mitt Romney's allegiances lie? He'd be sworn to uphold the Constitution. But he has already sworn absolute loyalty to the LDS Church and its earthly prophet.[15] It's like swearing to be absolutely faithful to one wife. And then swearing to be absolutely faithful to another wife. (Oops. That's polygamy.)

What if all this information about secret councils and coronations and blood oaths is simply part of the distant past? What if they're not about the Mormonism of today, as its apologists would certainly assert. Why would people not want a Mormon-led government, one that would be held in its rightful place by the checks and balances of our national laws?

What would a Mormon government look like? Look at Utah, the "quasi-democracy" described by James E. Shelledy, editor of the *Salt Lake Tribune*.

"Eighty percent of officeholders are of a single party, ninety percent of a single religion, ninety-nine percent of a single race, and eighty-five percent of one gender."[16] An article published in *Washington Monthly* by Stephanie Mencimer, who grew up "Gentile" in Salt Lake City, gives some insight about how a Mormon theocracy works in practical terms. After describing an LDS-owned plaza in downtown Salt Lake City in which *only* Mormons can legally proselytize and "keep out those it found undesirable," Mencimer concluded: "It's no small irony that the Mormons came to Utah for religious freedom, only to create a culture as repressive as the one they were fleeing."[17]

ISSUE #7: LDS ACADEMICS AND INTELLECTUALS

In 1946 Fawn McKay Brodie, niece of David O. McKay (who became president of the LDS Church in 1951), was publicly ousted for her critically acclaimed biography of Joseph Smith, one that carefully documented a portrait of a multifaceted and often untrustworthy man caught up in his own stories. For years thereafter LDS scholars wrestled with the requirements of what the Church called "faithful history," the written representation of Mormon people and events which highlighted elements that might be considered "testimony building" and downplayed that which was not—even if by so doing, the facts of history had to be ignored or re-represented. Finally, the frustration of academics boiled over.

In 1993, LDS scholar and former editor of the official Church publication entitled the *Ensign,* Lavina Fielding Anderson, published an article that detailed how for years she and her fellow authors, teachers, speakers, and scholars in the Church had their membership records "tagged"; and they were threatened, edited without consent, censored, fired, and shunned.[18] In response to Anderson's chronicle of such a history, she was excommunicated, along with four other LDS intellectuals and scholars. Among them was Paul Toscano, a man I loved and respected when I was at Brigham Young University. He was my editor in 1970–71 when I wrote for the school's award-winning weekly news magazine, *Monday Magazine.*

The crackdown on the LDS Church's brain trust—honest researchers—gained the attention of those outside the Church as well. Salt Lake City newspapers began in the early 1990s to report on the LDS Church's attempts to stifle research by faithful Mormons who were unearthing information it considered harmful to its members. Documentation of Joseph Smith's involvement in folk magic and his many marriages especially to women who were already married, early Church teachings about a Heavenly Mother and the granting of priesthood to women by Joseph Smith, and post-

Manifesto polygamous marriages by Church leaders and other matters—all such things threatened the stability and image of the Church. Those who had been honored with teaching positions were suddenly in danger if they did not promote what the Church today calls "faithful history." The "Mormon Purge" had begun.[19] Other high-profile BYU professors and thinkers were dismissed from teaching and from the Church over the next few years, including the late Deborah Laake, who authored *Secret Ceremonies: A Mormon Woman's Intimate Diary of Marriage and Beyond*[20] and who like me was one of six staff writers for BYU's *Vantage Point* magazine in 1972 (her name then was Deborah Legler).

Boyd K. Packer, head of the Quorum of the Twelve, went so far as to publicly state that the greatest dangers facing Mormonism at that time were feminists, homosexuals, and intellectuals.[21] The Church instituted an organization—more of a practice, really—called the "Strengthening the Church Members Committee," which it publicly billed as a newspaper clipping service[22] but which in reality was a spy organization that encouraged members to report to their priesthood authorities the activities of members "who, however well-meaning, may hinder the progress of the church through public criticism."[23] It monitored, therefore, what the Church would regard as suspicious speeches and writings of its own members.

Such practices had gone on for years before the formation of this committee. When I was researching to write the first edition of this book, before I was excommunicated from the LDS Church, a man named Steven Mayfield who was employed at the LDS Church Office Building assumed an alias, and wrote letters to me pretending to be an ex-Mormon so he could "spy" on me because he learned I was writing a book detailing my experiences in Mormonism.[24]

Such "spying" only annoyed me, but it was devastating and disorienting to the dismayed scholars and teachers still active in Mormonism who regarded themselves as intellectually honest and yet lovers of their Church. An example of this was Dr. D. Michael Quinn, one of the "September Six." This author and scholar (his PhD in history was from Yale University, and he was an enormously popular professor of American Social History at BYU), still believed that Joseph Smith and Ezra Taft Benson (the LDS president when Quinn was excommunicated) were true prophets even when the Church booted him out. (However, he stated, "I vowed I would never again participate in a process which was designed to punish me for being the messenger of unwanted historical evidence and to intimidate me from further work in Mormon history."[25])

Quinn was unique among LDS scholars in his thirty years of research in Mormon documents, fifteen years of which he had access to materials no one outside the General Authorities had. After his excommunication, Quinn sardonically remarked, "BYU is an Auschwitz of the mind."[26] One would think that his credentials of six groundbreaking scholarly books—and academic courage—would make him a sought-after professor today, but that is not the case. Though at least three non-LDS universities have or plan professorships in the emerging field known as Mormon Studies, Quinn in 2006 declared himself "unhireable."[27] That's apparently because such professorships depend on funding from private donors with an interest in Mormonism (that is, well-heeled Mormons), who shy away from an excommunicated scholar like Quinn (who also subsequent to his excommunication revealed that he is gay).

Other LDS thinkers and writers, such as Paul and Margaret Toscano and Lavina Fielding Anderson who were also excommunicated, have continued to write, examine, and support the elements of Mormonism they continue to love. Ten years after her excommunication, Anderson, for example, still attended church at her local ward and played piano at the Relief Society meetings.[28]

Recent years have seen the flourishing of two magazines that deal with "envelope-pushing" LDS issues. *Dialogue: A Journal of Mormon Thought* and *Sunstone* both publish penetrating looks at LDS history and culture in both print and online editions. Likewise, maverick publishing companies such as Signature Books give voice to LDS authors with a commitment to historical investigation unfettered by, yet sympathetic to and derivative of, the LDS Church. The clashes continue between the monolithic Church and Mormons who criticize policies.[29]

As the events of 1993 showed, though, a Mormon who publishes materials critical of the Church engages in a kind of cautious blindfolded tango with a partner that can either dance with you or cut your legs off at will.

ISSUE #8: DEALING WITH "ANTIS" OR OPPOSITIONAL MEDIA

Published criticism of Mormon doctrine and practices (so-called "anti-Mormon literature") has been a thorn in the side of the Mormon Church for decades. For many years the official stance of the LDS Church was simply to ignore pamphlets and books, but in the 1990s organized and well-funded response groups sprang up. So-called "anti-anti" champions took a new tack: *Emphasize the victimization of Mormons and their doctrines by their aggressive opponents.*

In an online article entitled "Are Anti-Mormons Christians?" (the article's answer is "a clear and resounding no"), LDS author Russell McGregor asks, "Can anyone imagine a group of Latter-day Saints picketing, say, a Methodist Church? Of course not." That would be un-Christian, he says. Elsewhere he states: "Never mind that there is no book or pamphlet published by the Church that attacks, denigrates, undermines, or belittles the beliefs of any other church; we are attacking them simply by believing such 'ideas' as the First Vision."[30]

When I was a Mormon, I believed just as McGregor apparently does — I could not understand why anyone would oppose an organization that did so many good things for people. However, I never considered the implications of the very document to which McGregor specifically refers, in an early anti-Christian book published by the LDS Church, the one in which Joseph Smith said he was told about all Christian churches: "I was answered that I must join none of them, for they were all wrong ... all their creeds were an abomination in his sight, that those professors were all corrupt."[31] That of course is standard Mormon doctrine from the official version of the first vision itself in the *Pearl of Great Price*, firing the first shot in this battle directly at the *character and doctrines* of Christians.

> By name it [the LDS Church] has attacked all the major denominations at some point in time. The following is a summary of the statements made by the Mormon church and Mormon leaders through the years: all churches are wrong; Satan sits at the head of Christian churches; none of the Christian churches have authority to act in God's name; none is inspired; none can save souls; marriages performed by them are illegal and children by those marriages are illegitimate; the Roman Catholic Church is the mother of harlots; the Protestants are the harlot's daughter and apostate; the churches are the "whore of Babylon"; the Bible has parts removed or is mistranslated; the false Christian gods bear the same name as the true Gods of the Bible — Beyond this they have little resemblance (to true Christianity).[32]

"Abomination," "corrupt" — not merely the language of the nineteenth century. The defense of historical Christianity against Mormon claims was characterized by one General Authority as "theological pornography that is damaging to the spirit."[33] This man, Vaughn J. Featherstone, advised as do many LDS officials that members refuse to read materials critical of the Church.

Do some anti-Mormon materials deserve the label of "pornography"? Some, unfortunately, do deserve that characterization—not because they dealt with sexual themes but because they, like trashy demeaning pictures, put unsubstantiated or exaggerated disturbing images into the mind. Some of the anti-Mormon materials of the 1980s in particular (I'll call them "gasoline literature"; others have called it "New Age Anti-Mormonism" because of emphasis on a link between the LDS Church and satantic forces), which used overstatement, took words out of context, and did not properly document their claims could qualify for that label. Like pornography, some were sensationalistic; and even worse, they encouraged a kind of cocksure and superior attitude in their readers. Such things make me cringe. They represent the extreme end of the spectrum.[34] Others are characterized by being merely jarring and confrontational. (However, in spite of their excesses, some of the most unrestrained still have brought conviction to the hearts of some LDS readers.)[35]

The "middle ground" of literature critiquing Mormon doctrine and practices is honorably exemplified by the work of Sandra Tanner and her late husband, Jerald.[36] Though their frustrations with people and things Mormon sometimes show through in their writing (emotions also shown, I may add, in the epistles of the apostle Paul), they are scrupulous in the documentation of their claims. They were integral in my own exit from Mormonism. They have been rigorous not only in their research, but also in turning a spotlight on the writings of others who out of enthusiasm, sloppiness, pride, or other motives have not been accurate in their own claims against Mormonism.

A third group of people who interact with Mormon doctrine reflect an increased desire to depict and examine Mormonism *only as they say the everyday Mormon would describe it today to a non-Mormon.* Examples of Christians whose writing and speaking interact in this way are Craig Blomberg (who wrote with LDS author Stephen E. Robinson *How Wide the Divide?: A Mormon and an Evangelical in Conversation*[37]); and Gregory C. V. Johnson, who interacted with LDS author Robert L. Millet in *Bridging the Divide: The Continuing Conversation Between a Mormon and an Evangelical.*[38] On the positive side, such interchanges are marked by civility and deference to one another. However, Bill McKeever and Eric Johnson, seasoned ministry workers in Utah, believe that often such dialogues do not reflect accurately the Mormon-in-the-pew understandings of many basic doctrines (nor, indeed, many time-obscured foundational doctrines) and therefore can be misleading.[39]

Recently *Sunstone*, an independent Mormon studies magazine, announced its Mapping Mormon Issues Project, which aims to make available in multiple formats (including online) scholarship on controversial subjects. It lists topics such as polygamy, blacks and the priesthood, folk magic, the translation of the *Pearl of Great Price*, Mormonism and Freemasonry, among others. It aims to provide "fair, reliable, and comprehensive windows into these issues," charting a course between LDS apologist sites and those critical of Mormonism.[40]

A fourth approach to dealing with Mormon doctrine is that which mirrors the postmodern Christian church: Either minimize all differences in the name of religious unity; or, in some extreme examples, use the "pander/slander"[41] approach in which Mormons are courted at the expense and shaming of those who oppose their doctrine.

So how does the LDS Church in the twenty-first century respond to these four approaches of what it calls anti-Mormon teaching? Of course it has no battle with the postmodern Christian church. Its apologists such as Robinson and Millet adamantly redefine terminology so that it seems that Christians and Mormons have more in common than Christians previously thought (and therefore, little or no battle is necessary). In responding to the "gasoline literature," Mormons have only to point to hyperbole to discredit entire documents and their writers.

It is with the "middle ground" writers and speakers who critique Mormonism that the LDS Church pitches battle, those who point out how LDS doctrine is inconsistent with the Bible and with its own past. Here LDS supporters and apologists use several methods:

1. *Discredit the author or organization.* In my own case, after the "investigation" by Steven Mayfield of which I was quite unaware, the local LDS leadership in my area attempted to stymie my request for excommunication from the Church. "We don't have any record that you were ever a Mormon," said a bishop, and only when I produced my baptismal document and my temple recommend did the bishop's excommunication court proceed. I have also read on the Internet that I left the LDS Church because of a bitter breakup with an LDS boyfriend.[42]

2. *Methods for personal defense.* An article by Michael R. Ash in the LDS magazine *Meridian* lists the following motivations a person might have for writing/speaking against Mormonism: bitterness due to being offended by a Mormon, being surprised by the human side of LDS leaders, pride, trying to hide one's own sins, being led by the "spirit of the adversary," desire to help deluded Mormons, loss of belief, or desire for vengeance from being

duped.[43] Ash's advice is to (a) build a firm foundation of testimony of LDS doctrines, (b) avoid what Ash calls a "fundamentalist" approach to the LDS scriptures and prophets (that is, an approach based on the Bible), and (c) seek help from LDS apologists.

3. *Online resources*. The apologists of whom Ash speaks include local leaders and approved LDS books, but by far the most accessible source of LDS apologetics is their online resources. Most prominent and extensive is the Neal A. Maxwell Institute for Religious Scholarship (formerly known as FARMS—The Foundation for Ancient Research and Mormon Studies). Full-time LDS apologists at Brigham Young University gather and produce materials to counter anti-Mormon literature. The well-funded Institute produces books, two magazines, a newsletter, and symposia in addition to its replete website. FAIR (The Foundation for Apologetic Information and Research) is a nonprofit apologetics organization, which, because it is not tied directly to the LDS Church as is FARMS, I believe to be more aggressive and nonconciliatory in its answers and approaches. It provides short articles and brochures and has a bookstore. MormonFortress.com is essentially Ash's one-man operation but has extensive "rebuttal" materials and satires. A site called SHIELDS (Scholarly and Historic Information Exchange for Latter-day Saints) and the sites of individuals such as Jeff Lindsay are highly visible in Internet search results. They often employ sarcasm in their presentations.[44] While Mormons would portray themselves as defenders on these sites, even fellow Mormons deplore some of their tactics and have characterized the worst of them as hostile, scornful, misleading, and angry; and of portraying Christian apologists as stupid, mendacious, and people known for "fleeing the scene" when they are unable to answer the LDS assertions.[45] One "anti-anti" named Englund "may be most well known for creating 'mirror sites' that rebut or satirize anti-Mormon websites (replicating the look of each anti-Mormon site but replacing the content)."[46] Like the leadership of the LDS church, almost all "polemic" LDS apologists are male.[47]

BYU's Maxwell Institute also oversees institutes that specialize in the preservation of ancient documents and a research technology group as well. Such activities should dispel the erroneous assumption that there are no real biblical scholars in the LDS Church. Quite to the contrary, as Carl Mosser and Paul Owen (two evangelical theologians) point out. In their article, "Mormon Scholarship, Apologetics, and Evangelical Neglect: Losing the Battle and Not Knowing It?"[48] these two authors cite competent work done in Dead Sea Scroll and other ancient document research by LDS scholars. While saluting the excellence of Mormon academicians in these areas,

Mosser and Owen call for Christian scholar-specialists in such areas to stay abreast of the work of their LDS colleagues so that conclusions they draw can be properly evaluated. Otherwise, Christian thinkers could unknowingly build upon Mormon-doctrine-tinged research. Further, Mosser and Owen challenge Christian scholars to address many of the seemingly pro-Mormon issues raised by such LDS scholars.

One book that I believe meets that challenge and does a good job of addressing specifically whether or not the early Christian fathers taught LDS doctrines is Matthew A. Paulson's *Breaking the Mormon Code: A Critique of Mormon Scholarship Regarding Classical Theology and the Book of Mormon.*[49] Paulson shows how LDS scholars have selectively quoted—and sometimes misquoted—ancient writers with the aim of making it seem that Mormonism restores the original, doctrinally pure gospel.

Other scholars outside the LDS faith see the efforts of some FARMS (now Neal A. Maxwell Institute) apologists who write for Mormons who might be doubting their Church, as subpar in some areas.[50] Dr. Simon Southerton found little substantial:

> I was amazed at the lengths that FARMS went to in order to prop up faith in the *Book of Mormon*. I felt that the only way I could be satisfied with FARMS explanations was to stop thinking . . . The explanations of the FARMS researchers stretched the bounds of credibility to the breaking point on almost every critical issue.[51]

Are these materials and resources, though, effective in many cases? If such had existed, and had I accessed them when I was reading materials by the Tanners and others and trying to decide if Mormonism were true, I fear I would not have had the analytical skills to see through some of the untenable premises which they use as foundation. My desire to believe the Mormonism I loved was so strong, I am afraid I would have been swayed by them, at least for a while. Make no mistake about it, some of their materials are very, very persuasive.

Here's an example. In the previously quoted article by Ash, he makes the point that LDS critics often cite startling materials from the *Journal of Discourses*. Since in the 1800s most sermons were extemporaneous, says Ash, those speakers shouldn't be held accountable for the content (such as the Adam-God doctrine) that ended up in the *Journal of Discourses*.

(Now, that explanation of the unreliability of the *Journal of Discourses* would have had little effect on me, since when I left the LDS Church I had just taken a class at BYU entitled "Teachings of the Living Prophets" in which we were told to regard the statements of General Authorities when they spoke in Conference as being equal to any written scripture, and Brigham Young himself had said that he'd never preached a sermon that couldn't be sent out and regarded as scripture.[52])

But Ash's alibi for early LDS General Authorities speaking in their official capacities sounds reasonable to the average Mormon today who probably wouldn't know that Brigham Young, near the end of his life, also said Adam was God in his own Church-controlled newspaper.[53] If such a Mormon took Ash's advice to avoid the *Journal of Discourses* and not seek further information on the matter from any non-Mormon source, Ash's argument would be quite convincing.

ISSUE #9: EX-MORMONS

How many ex-Mormons are there? Richard Packham, a retired attorney and atheist ex-Mormon, compares US Census figures to LDS Church statistics and has concluded that in the United States there are about an equal number of Mormons and ex-Mormons. He cites an LDS sociologist's statistic that 75 percent of LDS converts in third world countries become inactive after a year (making them, in effect, ex-Mormons). Therefore, Packham concludes, there are more ex-Mormons than Mormons. (I had no trouble following Packham's figures but do not believe he accounted for deaths.) He also estimates the number from 1990 to 2001 who requested their names be removed from Church rolls or who were excommunicated to be 640,000 people.[54] A 2001 study by the Graduate Center of the City University of New York (CUNY) identified the LDS church's growth rate at 0 percent when it documented that approximately the same number of people left the LDS Church annually as joined it.[55]

What happens when a faithful Mormon is first confronted with evidence that the Church is not what he or she thought it was? I cannot speak for all Mormons, but when I had been a Mormon for about three years, someone gave me a booklet called "Mormon Claims Examined" by Larry Jonas. What I read there upset me so much that I gave the booklet back and resolved to forget what it said. And I *did* forget it. I managed to avoid or throw away unread all other such literature that came my way for seven years.

Wallace Turner noted that "to be a Mormon is to be born with a second nationality. The duties to maintain this connection are at least as demanding as those of the American citizen, and perhaps more demanding."[56] For a faithful Mormon, leaving this way of life is as hard as trying to accustom oneself to life in a foreign country. One man who lived and worked among

Mormons much of his life noted that this pressure is best analyzed in the cases where Christians marry LDS spouses. Thirty-nine times out of forty, he estimated, the Christian partner will become a Mormon. From social, economic, and emotional viewpoints, it is infinitely easier to become a Mormon than to become an ex-Mormon.

In my book *Why We Left Mormonism*, I profiled eight ex-Mormons. Three of these—Sandra Tanner, Thelma "Granny" Geer, and I—went on to write and teach against Mormonism. The other five had less visible ministries but provided fascinating insights on what it meant to leave Mormonism. Each had a "point of departure"—that event or understanding which broke the hold that Mormonism had on his or her mind. Amazingly, the precipitating event for each was completely different: a coworker's book on a desk, watching Mormon friends brawl, a pamphlet long forgotten in a pocket, an invitation to a Bible study, a Christian tract in the mail, a "burning in the bosom" while attending a Protestant church, reading an early edition of the *Doctrine and Covenants*, noticing that Joseph Smith had labeled as a man the figure of a woman in a woodcut.

Many times, Mormons who show signs of "losing their testimonies" are assigned extra jobs by their leaders. The thought behind this apparently is that the busier a person is, the less likely he or she is to dwell on controversial issues, that the act of service will kick in good endorphins and satisfaction. Years ago an ex-Mormon from my hometown, Gloria Pace, told me that one of her jobs when she was a Mormon was to drive missionaries to the local library to check out all the "anti" books. Of course, today the equivalent of thousands of such books are available in the privacy of one's home with a click of the mouse. Thus the doubter who voices concerns is often warned against anything other than official, "faith-building" sites to answer the kinds of questions for which many bishops and missionaries are unprepared.

Harold B. Lee, the eleventh president of the Church, demonstrated another tool commonly used by LDS leaders to discourage apostasy. Lee once stated that no one who left Mormonism ever had any influence in his or her community thereafter.[57] This is paralleled in the statement of my BYU bishop who told me that if I left Mormonism I would never be happy again.

Apostasy from Mormonism is no new thing, but most Mormons believe it is a rarity. Most don't know that of the eleven "witnesses" to the *Book of Mormon*, over half apostatized permanently, some after receiving their own revelations telling them that Mormonism was false.

Why do people today leave the Mormon Church? Mormons have their answers: "McConkie and Millet [LDS apologists] encourage the Saints to view critics in terms provided by LDS orthodoxy: as deceitful persecutors, self-justifying apostates, or misguided people blinded by false traditions."[58] One LDS writer wrote patronizingly of "the stages of grief" of ex-Mormons, noting their "strong sense of betrayal" and that people like Jerald and Sandra Tanner "appear to have never been able to move beyond the anger and frustration stage."[59] However, a poll on a former-Mormons website revealed some very concrete reasons. The greatest response—67 percent—said, "I found out about Mormon history," a history that poll respondents called "whitewashed." Second was "I never thought it was true" or "Mormon culture made me uncomfortable" (10 percent). And third was "I disagreed with leaders' ethics," a reflection of disillusionment with the way respondents believe that leaders such as Gordon B. Hinckley lied to secular media about Church doctrines on polygamy and godhood.[60]

Of course, many Mormons have in conscience "left" Mormonism while still remaining on Church rolls. Some do not want to hurt relatives with the public scandal of excommunication. Others, especially in Utah, want to preserve business connections. Still others who no longer recognize the authority of LDS leaders over them have seen no need to instigate formal excommunication procedures, which in itself could be a frustrating and harrowing experience. Others deal with cognitive dissonance between the virtues of LDS culture and some of its teachings by simply not dealing with them. "We have what we call some 'shelf doctrines'—things we put aside for the time being," says LDS apologist Robert Millet.[61] An example of a group that exchanges troubling information about the Mormon experience by individuals who have made a conscious decision to remain members of the Mormon Church are the so-called "New Order Mormons."[62]

There are many, many ex-Mormons who are serving Christ. Unfortunately, there are also many ex-Mormons who have been so disillusioned by Mormonism that they have vowed never to be tricked again by "religion." These live without God, preferring no salvation at all to the lies of Mormonism. When I was a Mormon, I thought that godlessness and gloom were the fate of all who left the LDS Church. However, some, such as the vocal and articulate atheist Richard Packham, seem actually to relish it.[63]

It is interesting to note that almost every vocal ex-Mormon Christian of today started out by trying to disprove the claims of those who wrote or spoke against Mormonism. One of the founders of a group called Ex-Mormons for Jesus, Melaine Layton, looked into Mormonism's past to investigate charges against her Church and found more questions than answers. Jerald Tanner too tried to defend the LDS Church against charges made by one of its first apostates, and along with his wife, Sandra, became the most influential apostates of all time. Among the most powerful witnesses to the falseness of Mormonism, in my opinion, are the people God is leading out of Mormonism right now, the ones who are today struggling with the issues of twenty-first-century Mormonism and will be able to speak to a new generation.

Not everyone who was once a Latter-day Saint would call himself or herself an ex-Mormon, former Mormon, or post-Mormon (though these are common terms). And yet as a group, these hundreds of thousands of people have managed to find an identity and fellowship through the Internet. While I had been a Christian for three isolated years before I met an ex-Mormon Christian in person, today's ex-Mormons have created a community in cyberspace. They have their own inside jokes and language (referring to the LDS Church as "the MORG," of mindless believers as "Mobots," and the aggressive researchers who defend LDS doctrine online as "the FARMS boys"). They rant about the experience of trying to leave Mormonism quietly:

> Can I just leave? Can you? Whatever group you belong to, whether a church, a club, a lodge, whatever—Can you just leave? Or will you be shunned, humiliated, defamed, excommunicated, or otherwise defrocked? Will you suffer loss of reputation? Will you be badgered and hounded to your dying day? Or can you just exercise your right to pack up and go somewhere else? It is an extremely critical question. And the answer in Mormonism is an emphatic NO. That in itself is sufficient reason to bail![64]

Another ex-Mormon describes his feelings:

> But instead of feeling **sad** at the loss of Mormonism, I felt ***angry***. I was furious that they had lied to me, lied to my family, fooled us all for so long, and continued to have such a hold over my family that they would not (and still won't) listen to me. I was mad that everything I believed in was a lie. I was upset that I had been manipulated to believe it all.
>
> I was so mad, that—although I still believed the Bible to be true (a minor miracle in itself after being born and raised in Mormonism)—I would not trust any religion for a long time. I refused to go to any church, since I felt that they were all man-made and would find some way of manipulating me, just as Mormonism had.

> But now that I look back, I think that may have been just an excuse I used. The real reason was that I was afraid because I was not sure what to believe. All I ever knew was Mormonism and Mormon doctrine. What was I supposed to believe about God, heaven, hell, salvation? And how do you go into a church as an adult and admit that you have no clue? A few people that I knew recommended some good books to read about foundational Christian beliefs. I started reading books by John MacArthur and David Jeremiah, and once I felt I had enough of a base to go on, I started looking for a good church.
>
> That was discouraging in itself, because now I was examining the doctrinal statements of all these churches I was visiting and was finding problems in many of them. But eventually I did find a good one, and God was faithful to continue teaching me the truth.[65]

Some organizations/sites offer FAQs about how to get one's name removed from LDS Church rolls.[66] The Tanners' Utah Lighthouse Ministry website, utlm.org, gets over 25,000 hits a day on its searchable database even without interactive features like blogs. The Mormon Curtain (www.mormoncurtain.com) bills itself as "the largest repository of Ex-Mormon materials in the world" with 3,103 articles on nearly two hundred topics, and interactive features. Others provide message boards on hundreds of other topics with thousands of posts a day having to do with the experience they share.[67] An Associated Press article[68] cited "word of mouse" as the factor that drives sites like exmormon.org (185,000 hits a day in 2007).[69] Another site, postmormon.org, grew from 50 hits a day in 2002 to 120,000 hits a day in 2007, and has its own magazines, local chapters, and even rents billboards in Utah communities with the website address and the message, "You are *not* alone."

Indeed, we are many, and we are not alone.

Chapter 11

CONCLUSION

It was not my idea to write about my own personal experiences in the original first chapter of *The Mormon Mirage*. Couldn't people accept the documentation and reasons for leaving—did they need to know about me? I asked the editors. I instinctively knew that no individual's experience is normative, though I didn't have the language to express that concept at that time. But the editors answered that such decisions need a face, so to speak, a human behind the facts. I reluctantly wrote chapter one.

Now I find myself concluding this edition of the book years later, bookending it with personal experience. I recognize that I stand in a unique position, straddling two generations, with a foot in the Mormonism of the twentieth century and trailing my toes in the Mormonism of this one.

I was there! And I believed!

About two months ago I sat at a restaurant with a college student who had grown up Mormon as she recounted to me her growing doubts about Mormonism. I shared that when I was an LDS college student, I also had to make some decisions about Mormonism. But things were very different, because the Church's doctrines had changed so much—what with the retraction of the ban on black men in the priesthood, the fact that all American Indians were no longer considered Lamanites ...

Her face went completely blank. "What do you mean, about blacks and priesthood?"

She had grown up her whole life a Mormon and never knew.

Her skepticism of my account was patent, even when I told her, "I was there. I believed."

At the close of World War II, General Eisenhower toured the Nazi death camps and insisted that photojournalists record the piles of emaciated bodies. He knew that the day would come when people would deny such things ever happened. As Mormon Hugh Nibley said in quite a different context, "People underestimate the capacity of things to disappear."[1] What my experience with the LDS college student demonstrated is that less than one generation can change history. First-person history, after all, is the representations of individuals who experienced events; and if those representations are edited, amended, or deleted, history changes. When "history" changes, our perceptions of reality itself change.

The Mormonism of my experience, I learned with jarring shock in 1973, bore little resemblance to the Mormonism of Joseph and Brigham; and now, the Mormonism of my own early adulthood resembles less and less the Mormonism of today. It is not just because my representations have changed; the religion itself has changed. Mormonism, I believe, aspires to be the greatest editor of reality in the religious world today.

Thus it is with greatest personal reluctance that I resume this role of straddler of histories and testifier of changes. I am not your typical "anti-Mormon writer" caricatured by Mormon apologists. I wrote several books decades ago on Mormonism and a couple of articles ten years ago, and have been interviewed here and there. I'm hardly the rabid dog snapping at the heels of Mormons and their doctrine. And, true to all the suspicions of Mormons, I lead the wild life of the apostate—except I never drank or smoked or used drugs, and I've only slept with one man in my life. I have attended the same church for thirty-five years, and my husband and children are likewise responsible members of our community and church.

A BACKSTORY

When people ask me why I became a Mormon, I tell them that I wanted to please God, and I believed that I could do that in Mormonism. No ulterior motives, no grand plan, just simplicity and the literal faith of a child. I (like the Baptist I was) had a great respect for Scripture and a love for my Creator, and Mormonism gave me the chance to expand and act on that love while learning more about God and his mysteries than I'd ever dreamed.

I found it incomprehensible then that everyone would not want this expanded, updated, self-correcting, and plenary version of Christianity. It seemed all very black and white to me. My senior year of high school, an English teacher had all her students write themselves letters, which she would mail to each of us after five years. I with eighteen-year-old sobriety spent the entire letter scolding my twenty-three-year-old future self for any minor infraction or distraction that would take me away from my wholehearted devotion to the Mormon Church. I congratulated her for staying faithful, for either going on a mission or being married in the temple, for beginning to fulfill the patriarchal blessing which promised me influence in the Church and in my community.

The next fall I went away to BYU, where I was gloriously happy. I took English, Spanish, writing, and religion classes on the *Book of Mormon*, the *Doctrine and Covenants*, "Teachings of the Living Prophets," and "The Gospel in Principle and Practice." I studied, believed, and lived Mormonism *as it wanted to be understood.*

My yearbooks show pictures of a relaxed, smiling, clear-eyed young woman, across the pages from Mitt Romney and my friends Deborah Legler and Paul Toscano.

When the Provo LDS temple was dedicated, I was in the crowd with a white handkerchief, waving it with the solemn "Hosanna shout." I honored the prophet and my leaders as personal heroes. I was there. I believed.

I worked hard, putting myself through school without any outside help other than writing scholarships and earned good grades and loved, just loved, being a Mormon. I participated in every ward function and continued to write and be published in BYU's publications and to read voraciously.

Of everything I read or studied at BYU, one work stands out in my memory above all others. In a literature class I was required to read Nathaniel Hawthorne's short story, "Young Goodman Brown." It is a highly symbolic story about a man who has a traumatic experience that causes him to lose what I would have then called "his testimony." The closing lines of the story read:

> Often, waking suddenly at midnight, he shrank from the bosom of [his wife] Faith; and at morning or eventide, when the family knelt down at prayer, he scowled and muttered to himself, and gazed sternly at his wife, and turned away. And when he had lived long, and was borne to his grave a hoary corpse, followed by Faith, an aged woman, and children and grandchildren, a goodly procession, besides neighbors not a few, *they carved no hopeful verse upon his tombstone, for his dying hour was gloom.* (italics added)

Why was that story so terrifying? Because I could not think of anything more dreadful than the loss of beloved belief. I do not believe that Christians understand the concept of perdition—utter loss—as it is taught in Mormonism. Our children grow up with such persuasive teachings about the grace and forgiveness of God that many do not truly fear him, I believe. In the Evangelical world, children go from a preaccountable state to cured culpability within the blink of an eye—whether by invocation or immersion—and from that moment trust in a last moment of reversal if necessary, when all can be forgiven. We have successfully assured them that a God of love will remember his Son's blood, or reward good intentions. Thus lostness as a heartfelt conviction is often at most momentary, something that exists only as a remote and, we assure them, nearly impossible, possibility.

But for a Mormon, you're either in or out. You're either a child or potential Mormon Gentile; or a post-baptism "confirmed" Mormon; or a member of a third class too horrible to contemplate. Consciously and permanently leaving the Mormon Church takes one beyond any hope. Apostasy from Mormonism—the idea of becoming what is called a son of perdition—is that of the sealed fate of a creature past redemption, a being of utter loss, beyond any spiritual lifeline or resuscitation, dead to God yet still living, a walking corpse of dismay to anyone who sees his or her spiritual condition.

Someone with no hopeful verse on his tombstone, someone for whom her dying hour would be gloom. Such were the rushing fears of the person who in May of 1975, two years after leaving Mormonism, read the letter she'd written herself five years before in high school, saying that Mormonism was the only source of happiness, that it was worth dying for.

"Never be happy again ..."

I had been there. I believed.

The process of coming back to faith—in anything—was a difficult one, yet one whose steps I can recount. Though it sounds simple, this process was agonizing.

First of all, I looked around me at the beauty and diversity of nature, and concluded that such order and creativity indicated the existence of a Creator. But power and ability to create do not necessarily imply goodness—look at the bloodthirsty Hindu goddess Kali, for example. I looked again at nature and decided that whoever made all that was both complicated and good. If he created all of nature, and I was part of nature, he had created me. If he created me and all humankind, I concluded that surely he would want to communicate with us. Since I had seen the danger of unfettered "personal revelation," I supposed that there would have to be a type of communication that would be beyond human contrivances, something truly reliable.

And that's where the true leap of faith was—to believe the Bible was the inviolate communication of this good, relationship-seeking, Creator God. I couldn't trust anyone or anything else on earth but that Book. But sometimes it was almost too painful to read, and I shrank from his touch.

Fellowship was not enough. Here is a truth my Christian friends probably don't want to hear. In spite of having the Bible, and in the presence of a loving husband and a congregation of accepting and nurturing people, for years I felt desiccated inside. I wept in secret for what I had lost in Mormonism. My Christian friends had put me to work teaching "cradle roll" and children's worship and running a church bus program, but no one knew how to teach me. In fact, they couldn't know how empty I felt even as they invited us over for dinner or hugged me with genuine affection and shared their lives with me. I responded the best way I knew: I was there every time the church doors opened and first on the list to take food to the sick, babysit, help at church camp, cleanup.

But the Sunday school classes and devotional books and even the Bible seemed strangely colorless beside the exciting old stories of handcart pioneers and the prospect of living the United Order. Regardless of its truthfulness, nothing Christianity has to offer, after all, can top the possibility of being a god-in-progress, participating in a religious revolution. But around me, the big issues seemed to be squabbles over dancing or divorce or the Holy Spirit. Nobody talked (to me, at least) about fasting or spiritual disciplines or direct guidance from God in personal decisions. I guess they assumed that I knew what I was doing.

My church took egalitarianism, the one-level priesthood of believers, and the practical aspects of the Christian life of service and good citizenship and Bible knowledge to such a level that it seemed impolite to intrude with anything that might be construed as portraying oneself as holier than the thous of them.

And yet I knew God had put me in this group of people.

I began *The Mormon Mirage* to explain to myself as much as to anyone why I had made the decision to abandon the single most satisfying and soul-healing thing in my life. Of course, the head decision was reaffirmed constantly. I was startled over and over by the contrast between what I'd been taught in my BYU classes and what Mormon history really was like. The *Book of Mormon* continued to crumble before my eyes, unredeemed even by its quaintness and platitudes. Again and again the glaring difference between Bible doctrine and LDS doctrine disquieted me as if I'd never seen it before—new every morning.

But still I wanted to believe the best about Mormons themselves and was genuinely, continuously surprised by their actions as well. I didn't want to believe that people would lie about an apostate who left for doctrinal reasons, until another woman who left the Church learned that it had been announced in Relief Society meeting that she—who had always been faithful to her husband—was excommunicated for adultery.

I didn't want to believe that my own local LDS leadership could be deceptive until I asked to be excommunicated from the LDS Church several months before *The Mormon Mirage* was to be published. (Unbeknownst to me, a Mormon who was a self-appointed mole in ex-Mormon organizations was corresponding with me under the pretext that he had left the Church too and apparently had been reporting my research to Church leaders.) When the new bishop of my hometown ward told me that I couldn't be excommunicated because they had no record I had ever been a Mormon, only the existence of my baptismal certificate and temple recommend made the procedure go forward. (And the legitimacy of writing this book thus was rescued.)

A similar situation happened when I requested repeatedly that my official college transcript be sent from BYU to UNM so I could finish my degree. Until a UNM registrar intervened with the documentation I had in my possession, I did not officially exist.

Why, knowing that Mormonism could not possibly be "the true church," did I not at first feel satisfaction in a Bible-believing, faithful, and generous group of people? Nobody knew how to address the needs of a heart broken by a church.

The unarticulated and untargeted sense of betrayal I felt became the permanent inner garment of my soul. Charles Spurgeon articulated it best: "If God be thy portion, then there is no loss in all the world that lies so hard and so heavy upon thee as the loss of thy God."[2] I have tried to describe the state in which I lived for years after leaving Mormonism by comparing it to the aftermath of the discovery that your "forever" lover has left you and will never come back.

When Christians ask me how it felt, I ask them to consider how it would feel to wake up tomorrow morning and know beyond a shadow of a doubt that the God of the Bible did not exist. How, I ask, would one assess all the hours of church attendance, all the vulnerabilities of prayer and fasting and secret sacrifice, all the people whose lives changed because of persuasion and diligence and risking of relationships just to get them lovingly wrangled into serving that God?[3] How utter the sense of loss, how unrecoverable the hours and years, how foolishly squandered the hopes.

Who do you blame when you have been duped by a church?

For me, I couldn't find anyone to blame. Not my Mormon friends. I knew their good hearts. Not Church leadership. At that time I found it incomprehensible that people I knew—my bishops, stake presidents, regional representatives—could be aware of what I had found out. But how far up the chain of command would I look to find the ones who did know these things and had hidden them? Could it be possible they were unaware too? I had no way of knowing where the line of inner-sanctum complicity began.

I couldn't blame myself, though the responsibility surely lay there. I wanted to reproach myself for being suckered—but how could I hold responsible the trusting eleven-year-old? The trusting teenager? The trusting college student?

If there is no loss as great as the loss of one's god, there are few tasks to compare with setting out to learn to serve another one. If you've been burned by a god, how do you learn to trust another one? Make no mistake about it, I knew I needed what only he could provide: forgiveness of sins, eternal life, church and community based on truth, not beloved fictions.

I knew I had been bested by a superior, One who held all the cards, and I wrote this poem to describe the type of battle I fought almost daily.

The Match

Like Jacob and the angel
We face each other warily
Our eyes never releasing their vision-lock
What soundless circling,
Sliding of bared feet
Upon the mat of my life
I have heard the bell
For the opening of the match:
It rings even now in my brain
Insistent, insistent,
Sounded by
My divine Opponent
And I sigh
Because I do not know if I have the strength
I do not know the outcome
(For he with whom I joust
Is also judge)
My crowded consciousness chants:
"Though he slay me
Yet will I hope in him"
The wrestling match
Begins

I knew from the beginning that I would walk with a spiritual limp the rest of my life, the price I paid for being there, and believing. From this I have learned a truth that those who hope to bring faithful Mormons out of Mormonism must acknowledge and somehow negotiate: The power of its sociology—its cultures, its traditions, its people—is of such intensity and persistent power for those who love it, that doctrine can pale in significance unless truth is more important than any other thing.

I came to a time when I hung on only by my fingernails and Scripture passages. The summer of 1983 I hungered so desperately for the ability to trust and be vulnerable to God that I asked him to take my life if I could not experience that. In 1984, in spiritual beggary, I read completely through the Bible eight times, fasted, prayed, and learned every synonym in English, Spanish, and German for the verb "plead." God brought extraordinary friendship, spiritual companionship, into my life. Ten years after leaving Mormonism, I began to recover from it.

In my writing I explored biblical themes in book-length projects on hospitality, agape love, stewardship, crisis, Bible marriage customs. I earned a master's degree from Trinity Theological Seminary and School of the Bible (Newburgh, Indiana, and Liverpool, Great Britain) and my PhD from Trinity Southwest University, a small, onsite and distance-education university in Albuquerque.[4] In addition, I wrote *Why We Left Mormonism*, interviewing seven other ex-Mormons including Sandra Tanner, to show that there is no single factor that causes someone to begin to wrench free from LDS lifestyle, teachings, and community.

Everywhere I go, fraught people come to me and ask what they can do to help their beloved Mormon child, spouse, friend, neighbor, coworker. If there were a single answer and it could be sold, its originator would be the wealthiest person on earth, for I know people who would sell all they have for that one solution. But there is no magic bullet to get someone out of Mormonism.

I knew that my ministry is writing, not one-on-one ministry, yet I also saw an enormous need to minister to ex-Mormons. The mad-as-hell-and-not-going-to-take-it-anymore, hurt apostate has very different emotional needs than someone who had loved Mormonism, yet all need a way to think about truth and find a way to set pylons for the building of faith.[5] So I set out to provide a resource to help Christians teach ex-Mormons so that they would not have the same kind of experience I had as a new Christian, and wrote another book, *After Mormonism, What? Reclaiming the Ex-Mormon's Worldview for Christ.*[6] In it, I used the "worldview" categories of James W. Sire[7] to help a Christian assess and deal with the usually unarticulated assumptions of someone who has left the LDS Church.

I have often compared the holding of doctrines in one's mind to filling up a bucket with water. One builds on what's already there, and the liquid conforms to all the space inside. If a bubble forms, its surroundings rush in to fill the holes. When one leaves an all-encompassing and comprehensive doctrinal system such as Mormonism, one does not just dump out the contents of the bucket. Only when resilient solids of biblical doctrine and understanding are placed in the bucket are some of the contents displaced; and only after a settling into order of those solids can the last vestiges of old ways be identified and dealt with. (All in all, if my experience is any indicator, it can take a long, long time and much of one's spiritual and emotional resources for the task. Perhaps it never ends—recently I found myself, over thirty years out of Mormonism, admonishing a flagging colleague to "magnify his calling").[8]

But as years passed and my writing interests turned away from the Mormon Church to the Bible, people continued to write to me mostly about Mormonism. When *The Mormon Mirage* went out of print, a stranger (who later became a researcher for this book), Bruce MacArthur, wrote to me requesting permission to enter the text of the book onto his computer's hard drive in order to create his own, searchable database. Friends Gary and Marie Smith disassembled a copy of the book and scanned it page by page so that I could put a copy of the book onto the Internet as a free resource. People I didn't know wrote reviews of my out-of-print book, using superlatives and urging that it be reprinted.

I began to revise it, thinking that just updating sources and statistics would be the biggest task. But the LDS Church had made changes I thought I'd never see—the retreat from doctrines about blacks, the retreat from doctrines about American Indians as Lamanites, the retreat from traditional pan-American *Book of Mormon* geography into a tiny slice of Mesoamerica, and most incomprehensible of all, the retreat from the distinctively Mormon doctrines about God himself. Mormonism had morphed before my eyes into syncretism and assimilation. With it, an entire well-financed culture of Mormon apologetics arose to muddy once-clear distinctives. My book updates took years, not months.

THE BOTTOM LINE: ELEMENTS OF DISPARITY

In a way, this book is my last will and testament about Mormonism. The first part of the book describes what factors caused me to make a decision to leave Mormonism. This second part describes why the rest of my life ratifies that decision. It can be quite simply stated: Mormonism is not biblical Christianity.

LDS apologists such as Robert Millet say those who critique Mormonism usually use a strawman approach: characterizing Mormonism in terms of obscure statements by long-dead men, and using disputed or fringe teachings to describe LDS doctrines. Even some Christian writers have made the same accusation.[9] Eric Johnson of Mormonism Research Ministry, however, has formulated a simple list of beliefs to which the vast majority of Mormons of the twenty-first century would agree:

1. The idea that "as man is, God once was; as God is, man may become."
2. The idea that temple work is essential to reaching the highest level of the celestial kingdom.
3. The idea that ultimate truth is to be found in the Standard Works[10] as well as the LDS prophet and apostles.
4. The idea that a person must be baptized in the Mormon Church to have an authentic baptismal experience.
5. The idea that Joseph Smith and succeeding Church leaders were given complete authority on earth.
6. The idea that the Mormon Church is the most trustworthy church in the world.[11]

To Johnson's list I would add the following:

1. The idea that a complete apostasy from Christ's teachings and Church began in the second century AD and necessitated a restoration instead of a reform.
2. The assertion that a personal, feelings-based "testimony" of events and doctrines outside of one's own personal experience (Joseph Smith's first vision, for instance) is a reliable arbiter and authenticator of truth claims.

This is the Mormonism of real Mormons today. And there's not a single statement there with which an evangelical Christian could agree, no matter how many friendly fireside chats are held between us. Just as they make Mormonism distinctive from traditional Christianity, these elements are also significant enough and powerful enough to disqualify Mormonism from categorization as Christianity.

In the previous two chapters I described nine issues that face the LDS Church in this century. Similarly, I would now like to address other less tangible issues and the conclusions to which I have come concerning them.

THE CONTROL OF LANGUAGE

One of the reasons that the Founding Fathers of the United States insisted upon freedom of the press is that they recognized that whoever controls language controls minds, and minds control circumstances. The distant history of the LDS Church shows a pattern of the attempt to control language, beginning with Joseph Smith's manipulative "revelations" to his wife Emma and the destruction of the *Nauvoo Expositor*; and in the more recent past in its retooling of the Church's logo to put "JESUS CHRIST" in the forefront. This trend has continued with the Church's official website asking journalists to emphasize "Latter-day Saints" and "the Church," a process of which Richard and Joan Ostling, professional journalists *par excellence*, said "is attempting to make water run uphill."[12]

Why do people still hold out against LDS terminologies? Christian journalists and others are understandably resistant to the full implications of calling Mormonism "the Church" with a capital C or, alternately, "the Church of Jesus Christ." Jan Shipps, a non-Mormon expert on the LDS Church, has also noted an "evolution" of language in which the word "Mormon" has gone from being a noun to an adjective, as in "Mormon Christian."[13]

A new genre of what I would term LDS "conciliatory" writings, characterized by the increasingly ubiquitous LDS apologist-for-the-masses, Robert Millet, demonstrates the technique of the redefinition of terms to create linguistic accord. An example of this is when he backs away from the historic LDS stance that it is the *only true church* to a statement that it alone has the fullness of truth.[14]

The problem is, most Mormons do heartily believe that they are indeed the only true church—and they get this doctrine from Joseph Smith's first vision in which he was supposedly told that all churches were wrong.

A friend at my church related how she tried to explain her faith to a Mormon neighbor who said, "We believe those things too." The problem is, her lifelong Mormon neighbor had to at least suspect that though they each used the same words, such as *God* and *salvation*, the concepts behind those words in each of their minds were very, very different.

The problem is, the redefinition of words and ideas is done only on Mormon terms. In no place is this more glaringly evident in the way that LDS apologists are re-representing the teachings of Brigham Young on blood atonement (which of course, was fleshed out in now-undeniable incidents such as the aftermath of the Mountain Meadows Massacre). Today LDS apologists call the polemic and incendiary language of Young and others "revival rhetoric,"[15] and say its purpose was solely to teach about the wages of sin. This bloody epoch of Utah history is something Mormons would like Christians and their own members to see as having commonality with Christianity, and so they have dubbed it the "Mormon Reformation." (Why, one might reasonably ask, would a church under constant, direct, divine, supervision need a reformation only thirty years after its founding?)

This is "spin" and "plausible deniability" as an art form. In my career as a secular journalist I often interviewed experts who offer crisis training to large corporations. In the case of an industrial accident or other such disaster that might be attributable to the corporation, the following protocols must be in place.[16] First, only one highly trained person or small group of persons can act as official spokesman and all other comments are disavowed if unfavorable or dissonant. Second, that spokesman is trained to do several things: to express distress over the situation and its victims without accepting responsibility, to parry questions which he or she cannot answer truthfully without accepting blame, and to skillfully turn questions and objections aside in favor of pointing out the positive aspects of the corporation and pointing to a future, though usually nonspecific, resolution to the problem. Here's the LDS version:

The highly trained small group that can renounce any other teachings: "Only the President of the Church, the Presiding High Priest, is sustained as Prophet, Seer and Revelator for the Church, and he alone has the right to receive revelations for the Church, either new or amendatory, or to give authoritative interpretations of scriptures that shall be binding on the Church, or change in any way the existing doctrines of the Church."[17] With such a structure in place, anyone, even someone as visible and supportive as Millet, can be disavowed; and any past doctrine no matter how fervently held by its adherents and Church leadership, can be repudiated.

An example of an official expression of distress without accepting blame: "That which we have done here must never be construed as an acknowledgment of the part of the church of any complicity in the occurrences of that fateful day."[18] (President Gordon B. Hinckley at the dedication of the monument at the site of the Mountain Meadows Massacre, September 11, 1999.)

An example of parrying questions that would bring blame or disfavor: "I don't know that we teach it. I don't know that we emphasize it ... I understand the philosophical background behind it, but I don't know a lot about it, and I don't think others know a lot about it."[19] (Response of President Gordon B. Hinckley when *Time* magazine asked him directly if the teachings of the LDS Church today were that God the Father was once a man.)

An example of turning questions aside in favor of pointing out positive aspects: "I never pay attention to the questions—that is, if the interviewer is antagonistic. If he doesn't ask the right questions, I give him the answers to the ones he should have asked," said LDS General Authority Henry D. Moyle.[20]

There seems, however, something shameful and un-Christlike about a prophet whose most-quoted responses to outsiders are variations on the theme of "I don't know," yet purports to be the earth's only authoritative spokesman for God; something just not right about a seer who cannot see.

Meanwhile, LDS apologists of the lower echelons, with a get-out-of-jail-free card for anything they say, often represent anyone who opposes the LDS Church's teachings as "heresy hunters" who "gang assault"[21] them. Of particular irritation to them are those like myself who characterize the LDS Church as a cult. Of course, the LDS Church of the past did everything possible to pursue and earn that label with its fiery condemnation of all other churches and its reclusive and clannish practices. (I was there. I believed.) However, the word *cult* (which according to the dictionary can have secular, business, sociological, and other meanings besides religious ones) is one that applies to several modern religious groups, including Jehovah's Witnesses, Christian Science, and others.

In fact, the word *cult* itself is becoming marginalized. "We are in danger of losing a perfectly good word to the forces of political correctness," says Los Angeles radio host Frank Pastore. "*'Cult' is in danger of becoming the new theological 'n-word.'*"[22]

When Christian writers use the word *cult*, they mean a religious group that represents itself as being Christian—while denying one or more of the essential doctrines of biblical Christianity. Such a group would humanize God, deify man, ostracize Scripture, and provide a different view of salvation. Cultists often obscure these distinctives by redefining the usage of traditional Christian words and phrases. (I outlined other prominent characteristics, such as charismatic leadership, exclusivity, etc. in my book *Why We Left a Cult*.)[23]

Here's where the Mormon blinders kick in—they do not understand that these four things, augmented by their attempt to control language, are just a few of many characteristics that continue to earn them the label of cult when outsiders assess their religion as a whole. Mormons are not unique in these characteristics. They are very much like the groups they too would agree are wrong, groups they would themselves probably call cults.

THE POWER OF REPRESENTATIONS

Probably one of the most useful concepts in my life that has helped me understand the authenticity of the Bible, and so to compare it to less-authentic systems of thought such as Mormonism, is an area of study about which I wrote in my dissertation. *Representational research* acknowledges the triadic nature of the things of God. God is triadic. A full understanding of reality shows it to be triadic, consisting of the invisible world of God, linked purposefully by the Holy Spirit to the visible world.[24] Even our own ability to process information about the outside world is triadic.[25] It is this relationship of facts (the things, events, conditions, etc.) to representations (images, language, other ways to "access" the facts) that has given me great insight into Mormonism, and buttressed my faith in the Bible at the same time.

The Bible is the mind of God in linguistic form.[26] In representational terms, he is the ultimate Fact, and the Bible is the exact representation of that mind in the same sense that Jesus Christ was the exact representation of his being.

(No confusion there—Jesus was, after all, the Word made flesh. This connection of the personality and ontology of Jesus to linguistic representations is one reason, apparently incomprehensible to many Mormons, that Christians take strong exception to the LDS belief in the insufficiency of the Word of God, the Bible. Such a deficit speaks by implication of a God too impotent to protect it, a Savior who abandoned its advocates, and a hell which could indeed prevail against them for 1,700 years.)

Mormonism and Christianity alike fall apart if, as many believe, the Bible is not a reliable document. The truthfulness of the Bible is presupposed by the nature of the God it represents. Such a God is entirely truthful and consistent. He is entirely able to protect that linguistic representation of himself—the Bible—from error. Likewise—and this assertion bears repeating—he is able to keep his commitments to protect the people who adopt those representations of reality (the mind of Christ) as their own thinking processes: The gates of hell, he promised, would not prevail against those people as a body, as the church.

Such people recognize that everything they know is accessed through representations and not through any direct contact with facts; and they choose biblical representations over the report of their own experiences, emotions, and senses. Just as those who celebrate the Passover in the twenty-first century say, "*I* was a slave in Egypt," so those who accept those representations of reality as articulated in the Bible consciously appropriate the facts of biblical history as if they happened to them personally. This was the kind of faith that Jesus congratulated—that which is based on the reliability of eternal truth, validated by someone who came back from the dead. Such "knowing" he himself contrasted to inferior, direct experience: You see and believe with your own senses, he conveyed to the doubting Thomas, but *blessed* are those who operate on authentic representations of truth, once removed, representationally speaking, from experience.

So what does that have to do with evaluating Mormonism? My first doubts about Mormonism came about when I saw that the depictions of early Mormonism given to me in Sunday school, seminary, and university classes were illegitimate representations of the facts as I could myself read them in early LDS documents (those written by Mormons sympathetic to their own cause—not detractors nor apostates).

Later when I sat looking at the woodcuts in the *Pearl of Great Price* and saw that Joseph Smith had labeled what was obviously a woman as a man, that was the jarring discovery of a representational deception. When I read of a flesh-and-bone, finite, space-bound God in a grove, I was seeing Prime Reality redefined, re-represented. When I read that Joseph Smith said that all churches were not only false but deliberately, maliciously so; and when I read the *Book of Mormon*'s description of the Bible as something that causes men to stumble and gives Satan power over them, I saw a re-representing of the facts of God-protected, traditional Christianity and the Bible on which it is based. I was witnessing the wresting of representational authority away from the Bible to be placed in the hands of a line of prophets *who themselves would be systematically denounced by their successors.*

I began to write about my findings and entitled my book *The Mormon Mirage*—and now, years later, I understand that a mirage is by definition a false representation of reality, one that not only deceives, but through its deception can mislead, disappoint, and possibly destroy by taking attention away from what is verifiably true and essential.

Thus I should not be surprised that the battleground marked out for our conflict with false religion is that of language. Words are the representations that are at stake. The way God chose to communicate with our minds, from eternity to our time-bound selves, is language (could he not have used downloads of nonverbal impressions, had he chosen, or other methods)? Words merely symbolize the facts they intend to depict in the mind.

Representational fraud is committed when one assigns new and privileged meanings to otherwise commonly understood words without informing the correspondent. This is what happens when Mormons tell Christians, "We worship the same God," or "Of course we believe you Christians will be saved" and speak thus because they want our approval or possible adherence more than they want representational truth. They have divested themselves not only of the shared meanings of linguistic symbols of Christianity, but even some of the precious iconic ones: There are no crosses anywhere in Mormonism. There is no wine in the Sacrament. A baptized person can remain dead.[27]

THE REPUDIATION OF HISTORY

When I was a Mormon, I carried in my purse a small pouch that contained three-by-five cards. In every church meeting I attended, I took detailed notes, and it was from those cards that, years later after leaving Mormonism, I checked myself to make sure that I accurately portrayed what I had heard and responded to as a faithful Mormon when I was there, and I believed. However, the circulation of such *ad hoc* notes from regional and stake conferences is no longer permitted: The First Presidency of the LDS Church in 2004 issued a statement, read to members in local wards, discouraging members from circulating their own accounts of such meetings. Because the precipitating incident was apparently an Idaho stake conference in which an apostle humorously characterized his fellow apostles, the unusual warning was interpreted by many as the triumph of a "sanitized" portrayal of their leaders. However, in this action LDS leadership has acknowledged an important representational principle: the representations, if not constrained by a sense of some ultimate authority beyond them, will become more powerful than the facts themselves—as Mormon history has continued to demonstrate.

The Mormon people have had a love-hate relationship with their own history, practically from the beginning. While espousing books that supposedly tied their religion to the history of the very ground they walked on—as garden of Eden, as home of the Lehites, as site for the second coming of Christ[28]—even the earliest of them had to overlook a bicameral history in the making from their new prophet. Joseph Smith created two narratives about his own marriages, formulated multiple narratives about the foundational vision that he said started it all, and pronounced repeatedly documented, thus-saith-the-Lord prophesies that just never came true.

And thus the parallel realities of "faithful history" began.

Entire books have been written documenting the multiplied thousands of changes in various editions of the *Book of Mormon*, the *Doctrine and Covenants*, and the *Pearl of Great Price*. The LDS *History of the Church* has undergone more than 62,000 words added or deleted, often leading to changes of meanings of the passages there.[29] (And they accuse early Christian scribal copyists of altering the Bible.)

Even today's LDS apologists would agree that the *Journal of Discourses* records grassroots-leadership theology run amok. Joseph Smith wrote the "Lectures on Faith," and prepared them for inclusion in the *Doctrine and Covenants*, where they were Scripture with a capital S (despite denials of that fact today) from 1835 to 1921. These lectures now lie in Mormonism's burgeoning theological dustbin of oddities. No one could have foreseen a day in which entire libraries of LDS history and doctrines would reside in the home of any person who could point and click to empty out those dustbins and wonder at their dissonant contents.

Though those who would characterize themselves as postmodern Christians would have no problem with the concept, other Christians are sobered by the trend in Mormonism to periodicize its own sacred words and to encourage the home-brewing of any theology's hemlock. When someone says that a teaching in the Bible is no longer relevant to our time, that person has periodicized the Bible; and Mormons rush after this bad example by distancing themselves from some of the teachings of their own prophets, seers, and revelators without even the excuse of thousands of years or antipodal cultures for their actions.

Making official history solely relevant to the present, as Mormonism now attempts to do, is a daunting, twofold task. The first is that of creating a history by acclamation, and through the threats and authority of leadership, getting people to accept that official, imposed representation of events and doctrines. But in the second place, they must convince people to posit historical truth in a single body of elderly men who, themselves, will be subject to revision after their deaths when they are replaced by new "living prophets."

One of the most striking demonstrations of this process appears in LDS apologist Millet's writings. If the LDS Church does what the Christian church might call "soft theology," then Millet is its dean. He tells in his book *Getting at the Truth: Responding to Difficult Questions about LDS Beliefs* of a Mormon woman who told him she'd heard for years that God the Father had sexual relations with Mary. Millet's response was to ask her if she'd ever read it in LDS scriptures or official Church curriculum or heard it taught in an official proclamation or general conference. The woman was greatly relieved when she could not recall any of those as the source of the story that had troubled her, and she thanked him fervently.

The misleading nature of Millet's response is not in the accuracy of the information his questions elicited: It is true that no current LDS scriptures nor official documents of the present teach this. But he wasn't honest with her. Millet allowed her to conclude that what she had heard was somehow the stuff of gossip and legends—that is, representations with no basis nor connection with any facts of history. The LDS Church asks of its members that they accept only the Church's current representations of all past facts in its history.

But of course there were times in the past that another nameless woman could have asked the same question of a fellow Mormon, and would have gotten the answer that this very doctrine was indeed then presently taught by a prophet of the Church and proclaimed in official publications.

When, all thinking Mormons should ask, did representations become the sole possession of the present, and the exclusive mental domain of a transient group of men?

Apparently a great many men high in LDS leadership espouse "neo-orthodox" Mormonism such as Millet espouses. But there are a considerable number of both writers and LDS members who believe the Millet camp is selling out.[30] It is not only anti-Mormon writers who continue to point out and appeal to the Mormonism of the past.

However, I believe the die is cast and the impetus too great as the LDS Church continues to put away as privily as a disgraced fiancée its own repudiated past. The age of the miraculous (if indeed the sparse and momentary existence of such a nineteenth-century phenomenon could even be hypothesized) in Mormonism is gone. The remnants of wonder are found in the often-awkward voyeurism of the temple ceremony, that repository of the last representational uniqueness of the religion; and it, like all other aspects of LDS history, morphs periodically into a whittled-down, more politically correct version of its many prior audacious selves.

TRUTH

The last major article I wrote about Mormonism has been republished online as much as anything I've ever written. Entitled "Mormonism and the Question of Truth," the article shows that the Mormon concept of, and approach to, the subject of truth is radically different from that of the Bible in at least nine ways.

A Mormon sees truth (1) as constantly changing; (2) as going, in culture and practice, far beyond written doctrine; (3) as determined by subjective feelings; and (4) as often divorced from its history. (5) The Mormon approach to truth is compromised by a heritage of deception as practiced by leaders from founder Joseph Smith to Elder Paul Dunn to current dissimulations. In addition, (6) truth to a Mormon is "layered" in the way that it is presented to prospective converts. And (7) the Church itself routinely edits both its own history and doctrine to make it seem consistent and palatable. In practice, therefore, (8) truth often yields to what the Church views as expedient. In the final analysis, (9) the Mormon concept of truth depends upon the character of its god, who as defined by LDS doctrine is constantly changing and himself ultimately human in nature.[31]

Nor is this assessment contradictory to what journalists Richard and Joan Ostling said of truth as Mormons would conceptualize it:

> For Mormons history—and truth, which is supposedly embedded in history—is dynamic and fluid.... As Mark P. Leone writes in *Roots of Modern Mormonism*, in Mormonism truth is not absolute or fixed; it is changeable, flexible, and additive. According to Leone, "it is no wonder that the church has discouraged any intellectual tradition that would interfere with disguising historical factors or with maintaining much of the social reality through the uncritical way lay history is done." Mormon teachers are required to present the currently acceptable, faith-promoting, official view of history, Apostle Boyd Packer said in a famous speech to the annual Church Educational System Religious Educator's Symposium in 1981.[32]

Such a view of truth has cornered today's Mormon apologists into astonishing statements that I—and an entire lecture hall of BYU students in my "Teachings of the Living Prophets" class—would have thought surely to be heresy. Millet now speaks of a Brigham Young who preached as a man in the morning but for the Lord in the afternoon[33] and concedes that any Mormon, including the prophet of the Church could "say something that simply isn't true."[34]

My concern is not so much that Mormon leaders of the past said things that do not agree with current LDS teaching. That is a given. Nor am I shocked, as I once was, by the fact that LDS leaders could make doctrinal pronouncements that were lies or false prophecies. I can even understand the exigencies that would cause the doctrinally encyclopedic Apostle Bruce R.

McConkie to plead with readers to forget everything he'd ever said—even as he had quoted his forebears as support—on the issue of the traditional LDS explanation for blackness of skin.[35]

But a representational understanding of truth demands clarification—is it the representation that has changed, or the fact on which the representation is based? What do Mormons mean when they say, "We don't believe that anymore"? Did representations change, or facts?

Consider several issues that are current Mormon doctrine:

When the ban on blacks and priesthood was lifted, that was a representational change. Did it imply that the "fact" of a state of unsuitability of all black males for priesthood changed on that calendar date?

When "eternal" ordinances in the temple were removed, altered, and added to, did that mean that the "fact" of the ideal temple ordinance in the mind of God changed too?

(Now, to be fair, Mormons and Christians alike might respond that these two events in Mormon history could be paralleled by precedents of which the same fact/representation questions could be asked: the revealing of the "mystery" in the New Testament that extended all gospel blessings to Gentiles; and the cessation of Old Testament temple worship and ordinances when their fulfillment was met in its permanent High Priest, Jesus Christ.)

But recent LDS events demonstrate something that has no biblical parallels.

When Mormonism's leaders can change its own time-hallowed and multiple-prophet-validated scripture—as in the change of wording of the *Book of Mormon* promise of "white and delightsome" skin for Native American Mormons—is that not the changing of the fact itself on which their decades of official doctrine, and statements by the prophet, was represented?

Surely, Mormons and Christians alike can see the serious ramifications of declaring scripture incorrect; or, alternately, as being in need of amendment or re-representation of any sort by anyone less than God on earth.[36] Theologically speaking, the "correcting" of one's own scriptures is a representational implosion.

Unfortunately, the LDS Church has chosen the equally counterproductive tack of bolstering its own legitimacy claims by denigrating the Bible. "The Bible is all they have," says LDS apologist and unofficial spokesman Robert Millet patronizingly; and he speaks of the way that Christians put an "impossible burden" on a book that is "poorly preserved."[37] (Only preserved, we must assure him, by the God who swore that his Word would never pass away.) He is an educated man who nonetheless speaks of the Bible as "copies of copies of copies," as if the Bible were passed a single copy at a time through history like Barney Fife's lone bullet, instead of what Millet must surely know of the many-branched manuscript families that have served as checks and balances on stray renegade scripts.

And this denigration of the document with the most manuscript attestation of any document from the ancient world,[38] the Bible, from a group that asks people to pray about the veracity of a book with the sole provenance of the assurances of one man; a church that presents to the world as divine the certifiably incongruent translations of ancient papyri; an organization that excises troublesome scripture passages as if they were tumors.

THE SHAMBLES OF A BELOVED FICTION

There is no more basic doctrine that defines a religion than that of its God—its bottom line, its prime number, its fact upon which all representations are based. One of the greatest struggles I have had in coming from faithful belief in the compartmentalized gods of Mormonism, is the lifelong task of apprehending the concept of a single, triune God in three Persons. I reject axiomatically the contention that since the Mormon concept of three separate gods is easier to understand, it must therefore be the right concept—because the God of the Bible attests that he is not like us and cannot be apprehended, in all the senses of that word, by any human being. The mysteries of Jesus' statement that he and the Father are one, for instance, still elude me in the sense of a plenary understanding, but I can still respect, love, honor, and seek to know him. After more than thirty-five years out of Mormonism and scores of readings of the Bible cover to cover, I have reached conclusions.

First, the Holy Spirit of the Bible is far more multifaceted, emotive, and powerful than the apocryphal, shadowy Holy Ghost of Mormonism. The biblical Holy Spirit fostered and protected the birth of Jesus. He is the spark and guardian of doctrine, breathing into holy men to give them new eyes that looked beyond fables and used only facts to produce Scripture. He brings truth to the minds of those who meditate on it, and comforts us in the absence of the Savior whose company we crave.

Second, I can at last articulate why I cannot (except in some points) find fellowship with Mormons on the subject of Jesus Christ. In the Bible, he promised that he would never leave or abandon us, which apparently the LDS Christ did for 1,700 years. In addition, the LDS version of Jesus Christ is body-bound to a location; however, LDS doctrine would allow his "Spirit" to be with us, and with that I can find some doctrinal agreement. But the following anecdote demonstrates why this touchpoint is an anomaly.

Recently my husband and I discovered that a woman had printed up checks with a fictitious name and address but containing our bank routing number. Unbeknownst to us, this woman had used these checks and a false identification to drain our bank account of thousands of dollars in just a few days. She had appropriated our resources, which represented hours of work and sacrifice, and used them as if she had earned them.

This incident helped me understand and articulate to others a truth about Mormon doctrine. The LDS Jesus does indeed have important points of correspondence with the Jesus of the Bible, just as our bank routing number and the money in the bank were a commonality between me and the woman who wrote those checks. But histories that have only commonalities diverge at some point. The Jesus Christ of the Bible, for instance, did not visit Nephites nor appear in a grove to Joseph Smith to set him on a course to prove that the Bible—the prior record of his ministry—was defective and misleading.

Nor is the LDS Jesus our "elder brother" whose history intersects with ours in a mythical preexistence with common parents. Christians love Jesus because he emptied himself of what he *was* to become one of us—not because he was inherently and ontologically a sibling. His Father adopts us; we can claim no prior relation.

Now, I am greatly heartened by the LDS Church's attempt to bring attention to Jesus Christ through emphasis on his name. That was not the case when I was a Mormon—though his name was most often uttered at the end of a prayer, his teachings usually took a backseat to those of latter-day leaders.

My observation of the current LDS temple ceremony is that he is hardly the focal point there, at the secret heart of Mormonism. The incidental Jesus of the temple ceremony does not resemble what God the Father intended for his only Son to be for humanity when he vested all his own authority and power in Jesus. Look at every sermon in the book of Acts. The point of every single discourse there was not the establishment of a church or the steps to salvation. The point was the fact—on which every subsequent representation was to be based—of an unprecedented and inimitable event: God came to earth and died and was resurrected.

That indeed was history enough; and only at the point of intersection with representational truth in the Bible is the Mormon Christ, therefore, "true."

Third, I affirm my conscious and repeated decision not to embrace the Mormon God the Father. Perhaps the most thoughtful and effective expression of my reasons for this resolution was articulated by Francis J. Beckwith in his article, "Philosophical Problems with the Mormon Concept of God."[39] Beckwith demonstrates that our God is personal and incorporeal versus the Mormon deity which is personal and corporeal or embodied; omnipotent versus limited in power; omniscient versus limited in knowledge; omnipresent in being versus localized in space; immutable and eternal versus mutable and not eternal (as God); both the necessary and the only God versus contingent and one of many gods.

A significant insight from Beckwith is the conclusion that the Mormon god is a contingent being. That is, he originated from another source and is dependent in some ways on factors outside himself. He's not a standalone God, for the Mormon god is subject to the prior existence and restrictions of laws of nature, one who can manipulate those laws but never dominate them. He is more a craftsman than a creator,[40] with his creativity merely variations on themes worked out an infinite number of times in similar processes by other, older, gods in a sequential eternity.

In representational terms, there is a vast difference between an organizer of ancient spirits and elements, and a God whose verbal representations precede and call into first-being the facts of every other single thing that would ever exist. Our God spoke, and all became.

Because of his uniqueness, God is very jealous of his identity: No other so-called gods were ever to compete with him in the minds and affections of his followers. He didn't want his history intersecting with any false ideas. When the Israelites made a golden calf and said, "Here are the gods that led us out of Egypt," he was incensed because he couldn't abide the idea of having his miracles attributed to a cow. Likewise, he won't suffer all his biblical deeds of power, his history, to be attributed to a mythical once-human said to dwell near Kolob.

Eventually after leaving Mormonism, I ceased to mourn the loss of its gods of the misrepresentations of reality, to miss the shambles of the beloved fiction. The shambles were, after all the tears, only shambles.

Now more than ever, the goal of progressing toward that fiction, to aspire to become a deity to be worshipped by my own creations, seems more presumptuous and unnatural than ever before. I can scarcely believe I could ever have been convinced to want it. My divorce from all that is Mormon godness, I sense, is final.

OF SEAGULLS AND HOSANNA SHOUTS

Of ex-Mormons it is often said, "They can leave Mormonism, but they can't leave it alone." Of course many can and do and never give it a backward glance, but they are the minority, I think.

Some can remain publicly silent about their experiences as I did for most of the last fourteen years. With many of us there is the residual and often resurgent illogic of the scam victim who is too ashamed to admit a loss; and the greater the loss, the greater the shame. Those who loved it and left it haul its sorrow ingloriously, just as Paul bore all his life his unresolved grief for the stubbornness of his own resistant people, the Jews.

Theologically speaking, Mormonism was my first love; and it broke my heart. At the very beginning, it left me without hope for anything other than a knuckling under to a Conqueror I couldn't begin to know how to trust. Nothing about leaving Mormonism seemed courageous nor noble at the time: It was pure spiritual survival, the escape from the burning building into the arms of strangers.

Some of us go still-singed into atheism, or simmer in anger, or distract ourselves with other things. Some pick at their own wounds. Some choose to still sing in the choir. We are millions, we are variegated. If some of the statistics are right, we may even outnumber the ones who stayed behind.

Some of us, through the grace of God, learn to love him. Often that one act can be the greatest sacrifice of will in our lives, to respond and surrender to his love for us. This is dearly bought relationship, extravagantly expensive union, and it rewards us with a clear-eyed and settled appraisal of where we've been.

We were there. We believed.

Just as LDS apologists tell the Christian world that Mormons must never allow someone not of their faith to "instruct" them in what they believe,[41] I cannot let the Mormon Church deny what it taught and believed when I was a Mormon, when I was there, and believed. There is no seamlessness in Mormon doctrine but rips and patches and raw selvage and fraying edges. The LDS Church has become more mosaic than monolith, and its struggle is to maintain control and coherence of an image within itself as much as the one it portrays to the world. It is not yet a postmodern entity, but beyond question it caters to a postmodern audience for whom, as well, truth is fluid and personal.

What can be said about a Church that is as much corporation as minster? What can we intuit regarding divine messages that went from "Thus saith the Lord" to "To whom it may concern"? What can we conclude from seeing a prophet who dodges questions in the media? I ask myself if I do not see a Church that is losing its nerve, and ponder the implications.

During the last five years I have been researching to update this book, I have sometimes been assailed by self-doubt. Have I taken heed that I be not deceived? Am I indeed their gainsayer? Do I lie in wait to deceive? Will I make the innocent offenders for a word?[42]

I had to know. In the summer of 2005 I went alone to a city out of state and attended a local LDS ward there where no one knew me. I was not looking for ammunition but dispassion. The meetings I attended were just as I remembered, as if time had stood still.

I found that I slipped back into that culture as smoothly as an expert diver parts the waveless water. It was seamless, without a ripple. It was home. I saw the relaxed and congenial banter of people comfortable with each other, the half-hearted singing, the formulaic prayers delivered by shy people who looked as if they would faint from the exertion but were proud of what they did. I saw all around me the fervency and sincerity of my own lost days, the cheerful supportiveness of an audience toward lay speakers who spoke of missions and food storage and told stories about the lives of twentieth-century prophets.

After I left the meeting I shuttered myself for five days and read the 1966 edition of *Mormon Doctrine*, the definitional book of my college days at BYU, cover to cover. I remembered exactly how I thought and how I felt, when I was there, when I believed.

The whole experience was disconcerting and dismaying. I felt homesick for a place of my memories that no longer existed. But through the sickness of heart I was able to representationally reenter the world that I would have to portray fairly in this book.

I have found that I am still reluctant to charge with any wrongdoing the individuals of the Mormon Church. I prefer to believe that they are as I was, sincere and unknowingly devoted to a false representation of reality. When they lose a part of their history of faith, I feel it too.

I felt a sense of personal loss, for instance, when I learned recently that the famous "miracle" of the seagulls in Utah was apparently not a miracle at all, at least not in the opinion of the people who witnessed it. According to Mormon lore, in 1848 the Utah pioneers had abundant, hard-earned crops, but a horde of crickets began eating the crops—until a great flock of seagulls miraculously appeared and ate all the crickets. But an examination of the diaries of the people who witnessed the event firsthand shows that most didn't even mention any seagulls, and the official First Presidency report that year said the gulls were "helpers but certainly not rescuers" of the harvest. In the words of journalists Richard and Joan Ostling, the story just kept growing far past the facts, an example of what they call Mormon "ritualized history."[43] It was one of the first stories I ever heard about the Mormon pioneers, and I cherished it even until a few months ago and only relinquished it with sadness and great regret.

Those birds, like many of the elements I so loved about Mormonism, simply were never what the Church said they were.

Mormon apologists want people to believe that we ex-Mormons who write about our experiences and assess Mormonism's doctrinal failings are territorial separatists, like willful children who don't want Mormons in our clubhouse because some of them misbehaved in the past. So, they imply, we will exaggerate and caricature them and so prejudice others against them.

But Mormon history is what it is. When its past prophets spoke, they were the "true and living" ones whose words were supposed to accurately represent the God they said guided them. Their voices are the warp and woof of all of Mormonism.

This book is no more perfect than I am, because it is a representation of my own mind—my experiences, my processing of repeated readings of the Bible, my reactions to the deceptions and changes in Mormon doctrine and those who administer it, even my faults and prejudices. For those failings I apologize.

Please, Mormons, do not follow your leaders of the past and shoot the concerned messengers who bring you warnings. Your house is burning down around your ears. How will you explain the fall of the set of linguistic representations you now defend as absolute truth, when you tell your children, "We don't believe that anymore"?

It is the spokespeople of the Mormon Church—leadership and unofficial apologists alike—that I challenge. They are presenting as crucial the wrong questions to their people. The central question is not what Joseph Smith may or may not have seen in a grove. Such a question becomes moot if one can correctly answer what is indeed the most vital question of all time: Was Jesus Christ resurrected from the dead?

If he was resurrected, he is the Son of God who has the power to enforce his promise that the gates of hell would not prevail against his own blood-bought church.

The supposed complete apostasy of the Christian church never happened; it is a Mormon fiction. Christ's own possession, his church, never ceased to exist, in spite of its own history as the victim of repression, persecution, genocide, and internal struggles. No restoration was necessary: We, and he, have been here all along. We extend to you fellowship on the basis of shared facts of Bible truths, not on the basis of words alone. Nothing would please me more than to see a true Mormon Reformation: to have Mormons come to him, and to him alone, divesting themselves of all the myths of Mormonism, throwing over their shoulders all its contingent doctrines, all its temporary prophets.

The meaning of the word *Hosanna* is not "praise" as some suppose. It is actually an urgent word, one that pleads for immediate action: "Save!" or even "Save now!"

This book echoes that urgent plea before the true and living God, as the final and ongoing "hosanna shout" of my life.

More than anything, it is a symbolic representation of the actions of the waving of a white handkerchief before the Lord, as I ask him again and again through liberating truth[44] to save those people who are as I once was, when I was there, and I believed.

Addendum

EVANGELIZING MORMONS IN THE TWENTY-FIRST CENTURY

Although I have no statistics to prove it, I believe it is nearly impossible to convert a Mormon missionary to Christianity while he or she is on a mission. There are several reasons for this. First, he is called on constantly to "bear testimony" of his Church. Many missionaries will admit frankly that they had no real "testimony" of their religion before going on a mission. Lewis Price noted, "Testimonies exercise a kind of thought control, sometimes even a hypnosis over him. He is a victim of his own propaganda."[1]

Even if a missionary were to begin to doubt Mormonism, his companion would surely notice, and duty-bound, report it to his leaders in weekly meetings. The wavering missionary would be transferred to another district before he knew what was happening to him. I have heard countless stories from Christians who felt like they were "making progress" in their discussions with missionaries, only to find that one or both were suddenly transferred to a distant town.

With chances so slim of converting a missionary, what should a Christian do with the fresh-faced young men who knock at his door? The Bible tells us that we are under no obligation to receive any person who does not teach true doctrine (2 John 10; 1 Tim. 1:3). Don't feel guilty for not opening the door if you are unprepared! Many churchgoers have done so, and are now sitting in Mormon pews each Sunday, singing, "We Thank Thee O God for a Prophet." If, though, you feel prepared to witness to them, consider that you may only have one shot at making one or two strong doctrinal points. Don't shotgun; aim with those points.

One thought-provoking one-shot tack I've used—though I didn't invent it[2]—is to question a missionary (or any Mormon) about the importance of the *Book of Mormon* and why it is so necessary. Give him plenty of time to talk about its doctrinal importance. Then ask about his concept of God. He will (probably reluctantly) respond that God is anthropomorphic, eternally progressing; he was once a man, etc. Then ask this Mormon to find substantiation for these concepts in the *Book of Mormon.* (There is none.) Then ask how that book could be the "fullness of the everlasting gospel."

Bob Witte's book *Witnessing to Mormons* is a good tool too and has an excellent handbook of original documents that can be used to show doctrinal inconsistencies.[3] On the Utah Lighthouse Ministry website (www.utlm.org) many books are available to help you try to share the true gospel with Mormons. Jerry Benson and Diana Benson in their book *How to Witness to a Mormon*[4] suggest scenarios in which a Christian can courteously ask a Mormon to contrast current Mormon beliefs with Bible passages—not to start a debate, but to spark questions.

Another excellent, very detailed book is Janis Hutchinson's *The Mormon Missionaries: An Inside Look at their Real Message and Methods.*[5] It gives useful and well-documented information about the missionary lessons.

Those of us who are "old hands" know that dedicated, contented Mormons are not won to Christ in one sitting. That rarely happens. First Corinthians 1:18 tells us to expect this, for "the preaching of the cross is to them that perish foolishness."

However, there is a single weapon that every devoted Christian possesses. It can be used effectively because of a misconception that Mormons have. When I was a Mormon, I believed that the only way to peace and joy was through Mormonism. When I knocked on the door of a Christian to invite him or her to church and that person slammed the door, or had a sour facial expression, or said something insulting, this just reinforced my belief—shared by every Mormon—that Christians are unhappy and incomplete without the Mormon gospel.

So what is the tool? It is your ability to tell them that your relationship with a living Savior Jesus Christ, and the fellowship of your Christian brothers and sisters is completely satisfying to you. That the Bible is complete, and enough. That you know Jesus, and love him, and know that he loves you.[6]

Though some of the most extreme LDS teachings of the past and present are the greatest witness to a Christian of the false nature of Mormon doctrine, often such are unknown (or if known, not a bit disturbing) to the LDS listener. Enough controversy exists even within Mormonism, and friction between LDS scholars and Church leadership as well, that there is little profit in debates based on doctrines that are disputed even among them.

However, the Bible does command us to confront wrong teachings about God. According to Bill McKeever and Eric Johnson, "The word 'confrontation' has been given a bad connotation. It is inaccurate to assume that those who actively share their faith without building a long-term relationship automatically exhibit a lack of love for the Mormon people. Many times we have seen Latter-day Saints lovingly 'confronted' with challenging information that has led *to* long-term relationships and even conversions."[7] (I myself, of course, am proof that the results of what some might term confrontational literature can indeed be effective and long-lasting.)

What do I do when I have the rare opportunity to share my faith with a Mormon? I must admit that it is a painful thing for me, since I am empathetic and know the cost of the kind of decision I'd like to lead them to. When missionaries show up at my door (they're not supposed to come to anyone's home who has been excommunicated, but they sometimes do, apparently by accident), I tell them that I am an ex-Mormon and that I made my decision to leave the Church when I was about their age. I offer to buy them each the biggest steak in town at any restaurant they want, and arrange to meet them there. I assure them that I will not force any information on them, that they will be able to leave if they are uncomfortable, and that I will try to answer any questions they might have about my life and my decision.

Once at the restaurant I keep the conversation light and enjoy asking each about his hometown, family, and plans after the mission. They always eat as if they are famished. Usually they are waiting for me to "spring" something on them or attack LDS doctrine, but I don't. They soon begin hesitantly asking me about why I left the Church, but I am gentle and retrospective in my answers. I tell them how much I loved the Church—its doctrines and its practices and its people.

I tell them I was there, and I believed.

I describe to them how difficult my decision was, but how it has been worth it for the sake of truth. Toward the end of the dinner I show them two genuine first-century oil lamps from Israel and tell them of my interest in archaeology. I remind them of the story of the wise and foolish virgins and show them how the larger lamp with a large reservoir for oil was for a home, and the smaller one was a type of ancient "flashlight," holding just enough oil for a short trip. They are always genuinely excited to hold something from the time of Christ, and I am excited to share it with them. Gently I remind them that artifacts that support the existence of the Israelites and their biblical culture are all over Palestine—so common that even I could own some of them. But artifacts that reflect the hundreds of years of uniquely Nephite and Lamanite culture—as described in the *Book of Mormon*—don't exist, except as "possible" links in museums. I ask them to keep that in mind, and to think about it, maybe later when their missions are over.

FOR FURTHER READING

Books listed here are in print, as of the writing of this book.

Abanes, Richard. *Becoming Gods.* Eugene, Ore.: Harvest House, 2004.

____________. *One Nation Under Gods: A History of the Mormon Church.* New York: Four Walls Eight Windows, 2003.

Anderson, Robert D. *Inside the Mind of Joseph Smith—Psychobiography and the Book of Mormon.* Salt Lake City: Signature Books, 1999.

Beck, Martha. *Leaving the Saints: How I Lost the Mormons and Found My Faith.* New York: Crown, 2005.

Beckwith, Francis J., Paul Owen, and Carl Mosser, eds. *The New Mormon Challenge: Responding to the Latest Defenses of a Fast-Growing Movement.* Grand Rapids, Mich.: Zondervan, 2002.

Beecher, Maureen Ursenbach and Lavina Fielding Anderson, eds. *Sisters in Spirit: Mormon Women in Historical and Cultural Perspective.* Champaign, Ill.: University of Illinois Press, 1992.

Blomberg, Craig L. and Stephen E. Robinson. *How Wide the Divide? A Mormon and an Evangelical in Conversation.* Downers Grove, Ill.: InterVarsity, 1997.

Brodie, Fawn McKay. *No Man Knows My History.* New York: Alfred A. Knopf, 1946. Subsequent editions still being published; this remains the most widely read and authoritative biography of Joseph Smith.

Brooke, John L. *The Refiner's Fire: The Making of Mormon Cosmology, 1644–1844.* New York: Cambridge University Press, 1994.

Buerger, David John. *The Mysteries of Godliness: A History of Mormon Temple Worship.* Salt Lake City: Signature Books, 1994.

Bushman, Richard L. [Lyman]. *Joseph Smith and the Beginnings of Mormonism.* Champaign, Ill.: University of Illinois Press, 1984.

Bushman, Richard Lyman. *Joseph Smith: Rough Stone Rolling.* New York: Knopf, 2005.

Carlson, Ron and Ed Decker. *Fast Facts on False Teachings.* Eugene, Ore.: Harvest House, 2003.

Compton, Todd. *In Sacred Loneliness: The Plural Wives of Joseph Smith.* Salt Lake City: Signature Books, 1997.

Cowan, Marvin. *What Every Mormon Should Ask.* Eugene, Ore.: Harvest House, 2000.

Cowdrey, Wayne L., Howard A. Davis, and Arthur Varnick. *Who Really Wrote the Book of Mormon? The Spaulding Enigma.* St. Louis, Mo.: Concordia, 2005.

Crane, Charles and Steven Crane. *Ashamed of Joseph: Mormon Foundations Crumble.* Joplin, Mo.: College Press, 1993.

Enroth, Ronald, ed. *A Guide to New Religious Movements.* Downers Grove, Ill.: InterVarsity, 2005.

Flake, Kathleen. *The Politics of American Religious Identity: The Seating of Senator Reed Smoot, Mormon Apostle.* Chapel Hill, N.C.: University of North Carolina Press, 2004.

Gruss, Edmond C. and Lane A. Thuet. *What Every Mormon (and Non-Mormon) Should Know.* n.p.: Xulon Press, 2006.

Hanks, Maxine, ed. *Women and Authority: Re-emerging Mormon Feminism.* Salt Lake City: Signature Books, 1992.

Hansen, Klaus J. *Quest for Empire.* Lincoln, Neb.: University of Nebraska Press, 1967.

Heinerman, John and Anson Shupe. *The Mormon Corporate Empire.* Boston: Beacon Press, 1985.

Hutchinson, Janis. *The Mormon Missionaries: An Inside Look at Their Real Message and Methods.* Grand Rapids, Mich.: Kregel, 1995.

Krakauer, Jon. *Under the Banner of Heaven.* New York: Doubleday, 2003.

Larson, Charles M. *By His Own Hand upon Papyrus: A New Look at the Joseph Smith Papyri.* Grand Rapids, Mich.: Institute for Religious Research, 1992.

LDS Classics CD-ROM, 2nd edition. Research Applications International, 1998.

Lewis, Gordon R. *Confronting the Cults.* Phillipsburg, N.J.: P&R, 1987.

Ludlow, Daniel H., ed. *Encyclopedia of Mormonism.* New York: MacMillan, 1992. Available in searchable form at www.lib.byu.edu/Macmillan/.

Marquardt, H. Michael and Wesley P. Walters. *Inventing Mormonism: Traditional and the Historical Record.* Salt Lake City: Signature Books, 1998.

Martin, Walter R. *The Kingdom of the Cults*, rev. ed. Bloomington, Minn.: Bethany House, 2003.

McConkie, Bruce R. *Mormon Doctrine.* Salt Lake City: Deseret Book, various editions, esp. 1966 and 1979.

McKeever, Bill. *Answering Mormons' Questions.* Bloomington, Minn.: Bethany House, 1991.

McKeever, Bill and Eric Johnson. *Mormonism 101: Examining the Religion of the Latter-day Saints.* Grand Rapids, Mich.: Baker, 2000.

Metcalfe, Brent Lee, ed. *New Approaches to the Book of Mormon: Explorations in Critical Methodology.* Salt Lake City: Signature Books, 1993.

Millet, Robert. *Getting at the Truth: Responding to Different Questions about LDS Beliefs.* Salt Lake City: Deseret Book, 2004.

Mulder, William and A. Russell Mortensen, eds. *Among the Mormons: Historic Accounts by Contemporary Observers.* Salt Lake City: Western Epics, 1994.

Naifeh, Stephen and Gregory White Smith. *The Mormon Murders.* New York: St. Martin's Press, 2005.

Newell, Linda King and Valeen Tippets Avery. *Mormon Enigma: Emma Hale Smith.* Champaign, Ill.: University of Illinois Press, 1994.

New Mormon Studies CD-ROM: A Comprehensive Resource Library. Folio Infobase (dual Windows & Macintosh). Salt Lake City: Signature Books, 1998. (970 Works.)

Ostling, Richard N. and Joan K. Ostling. *Mormon America: The Power and the Promise.* San Francisco: HarperSanFrancisco, 1999.

Palmer, Grant. *An Insider's View of Mormon Origins.* Salt Lake City: Signature Books, 2002.

Paulson, Matthew A. *Breaking the Mormon Code: A Critique of Mormon Scholarship Regarding Classical Christian Theology and the Book of Mormon.* Livermore, Calif.: Wingspan Press, 2006.

Petersen, LaMar. *Creation of the Book of Mormon: A Historical Inquiry.* Salt Lake City: Freethinker Press, 2000.

Quinn, D. Michael. *Early Mormonism and the Magic World View*, rev. ed. Salt Lake City: Signature Books, 1998.

______________. *The Mormon Hierarchy—Extensions of Power.* Salt Lake City: Signature Books, 1997.

______________. *The Mormon Hierarchy—Origins of Power.* Salt Lake City: Signature Books, 1994.

Remini, Robert V. *Joseph Smith.* New York: Viking Penguin, 2002.

Richards, LeGrand. *A Marvelous Work and a Wonder.* Salt Lake City: Deseret Book, 1993.

Roberts, R. Philip. *Mormonism Unmasked: Confronting the Contradictions between Mormon Beliefs and True Christianity.* Nashville: Broadman, 1998.

Robertson, Judy. *Out of Mormonism: A Woman's True Story.* Bloomington, Minn.: Bethany House, 2004.

Sire, James W. *The Universe Next Door: A Basic Worldview Catalog.* Downers Grove, Ill.: InterVarsity, 2004.

Solomon, Dorothy Allred. *Predators, Prey, and Other Kinfolk: Growing Up in Polygamy.* New York: W. W. Norton, 2003.

Southerton, Simon G. *Losing a Lost Tribe: Native Americans, DNA, and the Mormon Church.* Salt Lake City: Signature Books, 2004.

Spencer, Irene. *Shattered Dreams: My Life as a Polygamist's Wife.* New York: Center Street, 2007.

Tanner, Jerald and Sandra. Their publishing company, formerly called Modern Microfilm, Inc., is now called Utah Lighthouse Ministry (Box 1884, Salt Lake City, UT 84110). The following books can be ordered from them. In addition, they publish photo reprints of important Mormon documents and provide a wealth of online information. All are highly recommended.

______________. *3,913 Changes in the Book of Mormon.*

______________. *A Critical Look—A Study of the Overstreet "Confession" and the Cowdery "Defense."*

______________. *A Look at Christianity.*

______________. *Answering Dr. Clandestine.*

______________. *Archaeology and the Book of Mormon.*

______________. *Book of Mormon "Caractors" Found!*

______________. *Can the Browns Save Joseph Smith?*

_____________. *Changes in Joseph Smith's History.*
_____________. *Changes in the Key to Theology.*
_____________. *Did Spalding Write the Book of Mormon?*
_____________. *Falsification of Joseph Smith's History.*
_____________. *Joseph Smith and Money Digging.*
_____________. *Joseph Smith and Polygamy.*
_____________. *Joseph Smith's Successor.*
_____________. *Mormon Scriptures and the Bible.*
_____________. *Mormon Spies, Hughes, and the CIA.*
_____________. *Mormonism Like Watergate?*
_____________. *Mormonism, Magic and Masonry.*
_____________. *Mormons and Negroes.*
_____________. *Mormonism—Shadow or Reality?*
_____________. *The Bible and Mormon Doctrine.*
_____________. *The Case against Mormonism*, vols. 1, 2, 3.
_____________. *The Changing World of Mormonism* (Moody Press)
_____________. *The Mormon Kingdom*, vols. 1 & 2.
_____________. *The Tanners on Trial.*
_____________. *Tracking the White Salamander* (about Mark Hofmann and the forging of documents).
_____________. *Unmasking a Mormon Spy.*
Vogel, Dan. *Indian Origins and the Book of Mormon: Religious Solutions from Columbus to Joseph Smith.* Salt Lake City: Signature Books, 2004.
_____________. *Joseph Smith: The Making of a Prophet (A Biography).* Salt Lake City: Signature Books, 2004.
Vogel, Dan and Brent Metcalfe, eds. *American Apocrypha: Essays on the Book of Mormon.* Salt Lake City: Signature Books, 2002.
Walters, Wesley P. *New Light on Mormon Origins.* Draper, Utah: Mormonism Research Ministry, 1997.
Witte, Bob, comp. *Where Does It Say That?* Grand Rapids, Mich.: Gospel Truths, n.d.

You will also want to search for Latayne.com, which contains a blog, a comprehensive list of information-rich websites on Mormonism, a section entitled "365 Reason Why I Won't Return to Mormonism," book reviews of Mormon-themed fiction entitled "Cult Fiction," and many more resources for the reader. In addition, any errata from this book and new information about Mormonism will be updated frequently.

NOTES

PREFACE: FROM MIRAGE TO REALITY

1. Rodney Stark as quoted by Carl Mosser, "And the Saints Go Marching On," in *The New Mormon Challenge: Responding to the Latest Defenses of a Fast-Growing Movement*, ed. Francis Beckwith, Carl Mosser, and Paul Owen (Grand Rapids, Mich.: Zondervan, 2002), 62.

CHAPTER 1: A GENTLE APOSTASY

1. I no longer believe this statement. But when I wrote the first edition of this book, I believed it. I have left it in the book because it accurately reflects the feelings of most Latter-day Saints and of many who have recently left the LDS Church.
2. The missionary and I did end our relationship, but for reasons unrelated to the events that were happening in my life. Today (2008) he is one of the General Authorities of the LDS Church.

CHAPTER 2: THE JOSEPH SMITH STORY

1. This song, by William W. Phelps, is still in LDS hymnbooks. Here is the first verse and chorus.

   Praise to the man who communed with Jehovah!
   Jesus anointed "that Prophet and Seer"
   Blessed to open the last dispensation;
   Kings shall extol him, and nations revere.
   Hail to the Prophet, ascended to heaven!
   Traitors and tyrants now fight him in vain;
   Mingling with Gods, he can plan for his brethren,
   Death cannot conquer the hero again.

2. *Journal of Discourses* 7:289. *Journal of Discourses* is a twenty-six-volume work, authorized first by Brigham Young, to record sermons and other statements that were recognized at the time as doctrinal. It is available in print, on CD-ROM, online at *Journal of Discourses*, www.journalofdiscourses.org and Mormon Literature Database, mormonlit.lib.byu.edu/lit_work.php?w_id=8000.
3. *Journal of Discourses* 8:321.

4. *Journal of Discourses* 3:212.
5. *Journal of Discourses* 8:176.
6. Joseph Fielding Smith, *Doctrines of Salvation* (Salt Lake City: Bookcraft, 1954–56), 1:188.
7. Grant H. Palmer, *An Insider's View of Mormon Origins* (Salt Lake City: Signature Books, 2002).
8. From an 1853 account by the mother of Joseph Smith, Lucy Mack Smith, *Biographical Sketches of Joseph Smith the Prophet and His Progenitors for Many Generations* (Liverpool, England: 1853), 62–65. An online excerpt is available at Utah Lighthouse Ministry, www.utlm.org/newsletters/no99.htm.
9. William D. Morain, MD, *The Sword of Laban: Joseph Smith, Jr. and the Disassociated Mind* (Arlington, Va.: American Psychiatric Press, Inc., 1998), xx.
10. Joseph Smith, *Pearl of Great Price*, History 1:5–10.
11. Wesley P. Walters, *New Light on Mormon Origins* (Draper, Utah: Mormonism Research Ministry, 1997).
12. See Richard Abanes, *One Nation Under Gods: A History of the Mormon Church* (New York: Four Walls Eight Windows, 2002), 84; also Palmer, *An Insider's View of Mormon Origins.*
13. Smith, *Pearl of Great Price*, History 1:21–25.
14. View the document at Utah Lighthouse Ministry, www.utlm.org/onlineresources/jshandwriting.htm.
15. See it online, with documentation, at Nauvoo Christian Visitors Center, www.nauvoochristian.org/topics/The%20First%20Vision%20Quilt.htm.
16. Edmond C. Gruss and Lane A. Thuet, *What Every Mormon (and Non-Mormon) Should Know* (n.p.: Xulon Press, 2006), 38–46.
17. Abanes, *One Nation Under Gods*, 16–17. See Sandra Tanner's assessment at Utah Lighthouse Ministry, www.utlm.org/onlineresources/firstvision.htm.
18. Dan Vogel, "James Colin Brewster: The Boy Prophet Who Challenged Mormon Authority," *Differing Visions: Dissenters in Mormon History*, ed. Roger D. Launius and Linda Thatcher (Champaign, Ill.: University of Illinois Press, 1994), 120–39.
19. This is covered in great detail in the book by Jerald and Sandra Tanner, *Mormonism, Magic, and Masonry* (Salt Lake City: Utah Lighthouse Ministry, 1988), and in the book by D. Michael Quinn, *Early Mormonism and the Magic World View* (Salt Lake City: Signature Books, 1998).
20. Donna Hill, *Joseph Smith: The First Mormon* (Salt Lake City: Signature Books, 1999), 61.
21. Hugh Nibley, *The Myth Makers* (Salt Lake City: Bookcraft, 1961), 142.
22. These documents were donated to the LDS Church in 2005.
23. However, folk magic and money digging were not Smith's exclusive province. Robert V. Remini, *Joseph Smith* (New York: Penguin Putnam, 2002) documents the fact that people of this geographical area and time claimed visions and believed in what we would call folk magic. In addition, over five hundred of them, "respectable men," admitted to being money diggers (10–11).
24. Fielding Smith, *Doctrines of Salvation* 3:225. This was reaffirmed in 1994 by LDS author Richard S. Van Wagoner in *Sidney Rigdon: A Portrait of Religious Excess* (Salt Lake City: Signature Books, 1994), 57.

25. But the cat is out of the bag, so to speak. A good example of a recent biography by a still-faithful Mormon historian is Richard Lyman Bushman's recent biography, *Joseph Smith: Rough Stone Rolling* (New York: Knopf, 2005), which cautiously mentions many formerly ignored elements of this complex man's life.
26. Remini, *Joseph Smith*, 42.
27. Linda King Newell and Valeen Tippetts Avery, *Mormon Enigma: Emma Hale Smith* (Garden City, N.Y.: Doubleday, 1984), 26.
28. Mack Smith, *Biographical Sketches*, 85.
29. Roberts was also convinced that Joseph Smith had "sufficiently vivid and creative imagination" to produce the *Book of Mormon*, as Roberts demonstrated in an essay in *Studies of the Book of Mormon* (Champaign, Ill.: University of Illinois Press, 1985), 243, quoted by Abanes, *One Nation Under Gods*, 515.
30. Wayne L. Cowdery, Howard A. Davis, and Arthur Vanick, *Who Really Wrote the Book of Mormon? The Spaulding Enigma* (St. Louis, Mo.: Concordia, 2005).
31. Fawn McKay Brodie, *No Man Knows My History: The Life of Joseph Smith* (New York: Alfred A. Knopf, 1946), 43.
32. As quoted by E. D. Howe, *Mormonism Unveiled* (1834), 270–72. Utah Lighthouse Ministry, www.utlm.org/newsletters/no107.htm.
33. Scott C. Dunn, "Automacity and the Dictation of the *Book of Mormon*," in *American Apocrypha: Essays on the Book of Mormon*, ed. Dan Vogel and Brent Lee Metcalf (Salt Lake City: Signature Books, 2002), 17–46. In this essay, Dunn cites *Jane Eyre* and *A Course in Miracles* as precedents.
34. *Journal of Discourses* 7:164.
35. Another reference to the apostasy of the *Book of Mormon* witnesses is found in the *Journal of Discourses* 7:114–15.
36. All but McLellin were witnesses to the *Book of Mormon*. Joseph Smith Jr., *History of the Church*, 3:232. This book is Smith's own record of early LDS Church history, originally titled *History of Joseph Smith*, and is called variously *History of the Church* (HC), *Documentary History of the Church* (DHC), and *History of the Church of Jesus Christ of Latter-day Saints*.
37. John A. Widtsoe, *Joseph Smith: Seeker After Truth, Prophet of God* (Salt Lake City: Bookcraft, 1951), 58. See also *Doctrine and Covenants* 28:11.
38. From a sworn affidavit by G. J. Keen in Seneca, Ohio, quoted by Jerald Tanner and Sandra Tanner, *Mormonism—Shadow or Reality?* (Salt Lake City: Modem Microfilm Co., 1972), 54–55. Utah Lighthouse Ministry, www.utlm.org/newsletters/no82.htm.
39. *Doctrine and Covenants* 3:12; 10:7.
40. Dan Vogel, "The Validity of the Witnesses' Testimony," in *American Apocrypha*, ed. Vogel and Metcalfe, 108.
41. Abanes, *One Nation Under Gods*, 53.
42. Remini, *Joseph Smith*, 66–67.
43. Newell and Avery, *Mormon Enigma*, 25.
44. Tanner and Tanner, *Mormonism—Shadow or Reality?* 162.
45. Brodie, *No Man Knows My History*, 60.
46. Francis J. Kirkham, *A New Witness for Christ in America: The Book of Mormon* (Independence, Mo.: Zion's Printing and Publishing Company, 1951), 1:200–201.

47. Smith, *History of the Church*, 4:461.
48. LaMar Petersen, *Creation of the Book of Mormon: A Historical Inquiry* (Salt Lake City: Freethinker Press, 2000).
49. Edmond C. Gruss and Lane A. Thuet offer an excellent and detailed discussion concerning the historical inconsistencies regarding, and biblical teachings countering, LDS priesthood claims. *What Every Mormon*, 315–31.
50. Newell and Avery, *Mormon Enigma*, 75.
51. As quoted from Ezra Booth by Brodie, *No Man Knows My History*, 111ff.
52. *Doctrine and Covenants* 45:69.
53. *Doctrine and Covenants* 87:3.
54. *Journal of Discourses* 12:344.
55. Several documents online show that the US Civil War was not prophesied by Joseph Smith. Here is one: Utah Lighthouse Ministry, www.utlm.org/onlinebooks/mclaims5.htm#Prophecies%20in%20the%20Doctrine%20and%20Covenants.
56. Gruss and Thuet, *What Every Mormon*, 177–205.
57. Bushman, *Joseph Smith: Rough Stone Rolling*, 353–54.
58. *Doctrine and Covenants*, section 103.
59. When I was a Mormon, I believed that the Ten Lost Tribes of Israel were not scattered and absorbed by the other nations of the world, but were instead in a "land northward." This is corroborated and documented by Brodie, *No Man Knows My History*, which described that land as "continguous to the North Pole, separated from the rest of the world by impassable mountains of ice and snow" (111).
60. Tanner and Tanner, *Mormonism—Shadow or Reality?* 407.
61. *Journal of Discourses* 2:214.
62. Todd Compton, *In Sacred Loneliness: The Plural Wives of Joseph Smith* (Salt Lake City: Signature Books, 1997), 25.
63. *Times and Seasons*, 5:614–17. *Times and Seasons* was a monthly LDS publication, 1839–46. *Times and Seasons*, www.centerplace.org/history/ts/.
64. Smith, *History of the Church*, 2:497.
65. Brodie, *No Man Knows My History*, 198.
66. Smith, *History of the Church*, 3:180.
67. William E. Berrett, *The Restored Church* (Salt Lake City: Deseret Book, 1956), 146.
68. Joseph Smith quoted by George Hinkle, James B. Turner, and John D. Lee in Brodie, *No Man Knows My History*, 230–31.
69. Brodie, *No Man Knows My History*, 280.
70. LDS author Reed Durham noted, "I believe there are few significant developments in the Church, that occurred after March 15, 1842, which did not have some Masonic interdependence.... There is absolutely no question in my mind that the Mormon ceremony which came to be known as the Endowment ... had an immediate inspiration from Masonry" (as quoted by Abanes, *One Nation Under Gods*, 38).
71. *Doctrine and Covenants* 124:56.

72. Charlotte Haven as quoted by Jerald Tanner and Sandra Tanner, online on pages 455–56 at Utah Lighthouse Ministry, www.utlm.org/onlinebooks/changech17.htm.
73. Gary Dean Guthrie, "Joseph Smith as an Administrator" (master's thesis, Brigham Young University, May 1969), 161. As quoted by Jerald Tanner and Sandra Tanner, online on page 31 at Utah Lighthouse Ministry, www.utlm.org/onlinebooks/changech2.htm.
74. D. Michael Quinn described Smith as someone who "physically assaulted both Mormons and non-Mormons for insulting him." *The Mormon Hierarchy: Origins of Power* (Salt Lake City: Signature Books, 1994), 261–62.
75. Klaus J. Hansen, quoted in Tanner, *Mormonism—Shadow or Reality?* 415. Additional testimonies: Utah Lighthouse Ministry, www.utlm.org/onlinebooks/changech17.htm, 456–57.
76. Remini, *Joseph Smith*, 42.
77. Compton, *In Sacred Loneliness*, 11.
78. Ibid., 15–16.
79. Newell and Avery, *Mormon Enigma*, 164–65.
80. Several cases are documented by Compton, *In Sacred Loneliness*, 12–13.
81. Emma Smith's LDS biographers Newell and Avery (*Mormon Enigma*, 64–65) document that Joseph Smith began hinting at polygamy as early as 1831, with a direct commandment of the practice in July 1841. Apparently Smith forced his attentions upon a sixteen-year-old girl, Nancy Marinda Johnson, whose family's outrage led to an incident in which Joseph Smith was tarred and feathered.
82. Brodie, *No Man Knows My History*, 336. Compton, however, says the youngest was fourteen.
83. Newell and Avery, *Mormon Enigma*, 143.
84. Ibid., 147.
85. Smith, *History of the Church*, 5:372. This statement was apparently taken originally from the journal of William Clayton, Smith's personal secretary, who reported Smith's words and then inserted them into Smith's own writings. Additional information at Utah Lighthouse Ministry, www.utlm.org/onlineresources/kinderhookplates.htm.
86. From the out-of-print book by James D. Bales, *The Book of Mormon?* Quoted by Tanner and Tanner, Utah Lighthouse Ministry, www.utlm.org/onlineresources/kinderhookplates.htm.
87. Remini, *Joseph Smith*, 167.

CHAPTER 3: THE *BOOK OF MORMON*: "THE MOST CORRECT OF ANY BOOK"?

1. Smith, *History of the Church*, 4:461.
2. 1 Nephi 19:10; Helaman 8:19–20.
3. 1 Nephi 13:34.
4. R.A. Torrey, *The Divine Origin of the Bible* (Chicago: Fleming H. Revell, 1899), 60.
5. John Taylor called the Christianity of the nineteenth century "a perfect pack of nonsense," which had been "apostate for generations past." *Journal of Discourses* 6:167.

6. Perhaps I should specify that I do not include as Christians all the heretical writers of whom we have record, nor as doctrinal all the speculations of those who were Christians. Matthew A. Paulson's *Breaking the Mormon Code: A Critique of Mormon Scholarship Regarding Classical Christian Theology and the Book of Mormon* (Livermore, Calif.: Wingspan Press, 2006) demonstrates the increasing inclination of LDS scholars to try to make the Christian Fathers and others of their era "say" that they believed Mormon doctrine.
7. According to LDS doctrine, each human existed first as pure intelligence, then as a soul with a spirit body, and then came to earth to be clothed with a physical body.
8. In other words, merited levels of heaven.
9. Bob Witte, compiler, *Where Does It Say That?* (Safety Harbor, Fla.: Ex-Mormons for Jesus, n.d.), 4. This is a very useful and compact compilation of photo-reprints of LDS documents and other materials. It has various other printing dates and places of publication.
10. Edmond C. Gruss and Lane A. Thuet offer an excellent and detailed discussion concerning the historical inconsistencies regarding, and biblical teachings countering, LDS priesthood claims. *What Every Mormon*, 96–97.
11. Joseph Fielding Smith, *Answers to Gospel Questions* (Salt Lake City: Deseret Book, 1957–66), 3:96, as quoted in Daniel H. Ludlow, *A Companion to Your Study of the Book of Mormon* (Salt Lake City: Deseret Book, 1976), 163.
12. In 1979 the LDS Church copyrighted its own King James Version with textual notes and cross-references to the other LDS "standard works"—*Book of Mormon, Doctrine and Covenants*, and *Pearl of Great Price.*
13. *Journal of Discourses* 6:5.
14. See also LeGrand Richards, *A Marvelous Work and a Wonder* (Salt Lake City: Deseret Book, 1950, revised 1963), 66–68.
15. Ibid., 69.
16. However, as Dr. D. Michael Quinn's book *Early Mormonism and the Magic World View* repletely demonstrated, magic and occultic practices were very much a part of the fabric of the life of Joseph Smith and his church.
17. Mosiah 28:11–13.
18. George Reynolds and Jann Sjodahl, *Commentary on the Book of Mormon* (Salt Lake City: Deseret Book, 1961), 6:87, quoted in Ludlow, *A Companion to Your Study*, 185.
19. Joseph Smith, *Pearl of Great Price*, History 1:35.
20. Examples of these: John Sorenson, *Rediscovering the Book of Mormon*; John Welch, ed., *Reexploring the Book of Mormon*; and Noel Reynolds, ed., *Book of Mormon Authorship Revisited: The Evidence for Ancient Origins.*
21. For additional information written on a more scholarly level regarding linguistic forms, consult the excellent work in Francis J. Beckwith, Carl Mosser, and Paul Owen, eds., *The New Mormon Challenge* (Grand Rapids, Mich.: Zondervan, 2002).
22. See a list of Spauldings *Book of Mormon* parallels at *Book of Mormon Studies*, mormonstudies.com/spaldg1.htm. *Manuscript Story* itself is at The Anti-Mormon Preservation Society, antimormon.8m.com/spauldingindex.html.

23. Craig Criddle believes that Sidney Rigdon's use of Spaulding's materials contributed significantly to the *Book of Mormon. Sidney Rigdon: Creating the Book of Mormon. Book of Mormon Studies*, www.mormonstudies.com/criddle/rigdon.htm.
24. Matthew A. Paulson, *Breaking the Mormon Code* (Livermore, Calif.: Wingspan Press, 2006), 219. Also LDS author H. Clay Gorton in *Language of the Lord—New Discoveries of Chiasma in the Doctrine and Covenants* (Bountiful, Utah: Horizon, 1992) demonstrates 220 examples. Also see Sandra Tanner, "Chiasmus and the *Book of Mormon*," Utah Lighthouse Ministry, www.utlm.org/onlineresources/chiasmusandthebom.htm.
25. Hussein Abdul-Raof, *Quran Translation: Discourse, Texture and Exegesis* (London: Routledge, 2001), 116.
26. *Book of Mormon* 9:32–34. No non-LDS archaeologist or philologist gives any credence to the existence of such a language, nor have any examples of it been produced in multiplied decades of New World archaeology.
27. Quoted in Ludlow, *A Companion to Your Study*, 1.
28. Joseph Smith once wrote a letter addressing the criticism that he had used Greek terms in the *Book of Mormon.* "There was no Greek or Latin upon the plates from which I, through the grace of God, translated the *Book of Mormon.*" *Times and Seasons*, 4:194, as quoted by Jerald Tanner and Sandra Tanner, *Mormonism—Shadow or Reality?* 81.
29. Tanner, *Mormonism—Shadow or Reality?* 95.
30. A recently published book, *Farewell to Eden: Coming to Terms with Mormonism and Science* by Duwayne R. Anderson (n.p.: Arborhouse, 2003), contains another interesting point about the linguistic contents of the *Book of Mormon.* Anderson presents, in his own words, "a short analysis of the statistical distribution of month dates in the *Book of Mormon* that strongly suggest it is a fabrication."
31. Dr. Ross T. Christianson, *University Archaeological Society Newsletter*, no. 64, January 30, 1960, 5–6.
32. Ex-Mormon Craig Criddle's online document, "Sidney Rigdon: Creating the *Book of Mormon*," *Book of Mormon Studies*, www.mormonstudies.com/criddle/rigdon.htm provides convincing evidence of the concentration of what he calls "Rigdon-like theology" at the beginning of the *Book of Mormon* (when Rigdon would have helped Joseph replace the 116 manuscript pages lost—or disposed of—by the wife of Martin Harris) and at the end of Smith's collaborative opus (in the book entitled *Mormon within the Book of Mormon*).
33. Quoted in Ludlow, *A Companion to Your Study*, 179.
34. Ether 3:6–20.
35. Ether 2:1–2; 6:4.
36. Ether 8:18–26.
37. This person is not mentioned in the Bible.
38. This struggle caused Fawn Brodie to identify fratricide as a major theme of the *Book of Mormon* (*No Man Knows My History*, 413–16).
39. Elsewhere in the *Book of Mormon*, in 2 Nephi 30:6, the descendants of the Lamanites were promised that they too would become "white and delightsome"

if they turned to the Mormon gospel. This was true in all editions for the first 151 years the *Book of Mormon* was in print. That is what my own personal copy, which I used in seminary classes and *Book of Mormon* classes at Brigham Young University, stated. It was the promise on which all my Native American LDS friends based their hopes of receiving a change in skin color to signal God's approval of their turning to him. In 1981 the LDS Church leadership decided to replace that phrase with the wording "pure and delightsome." LDS officials say this is a correction of an early printing error, but the earliest extant handwritten copy of this passage by Smith says "white," as Jerald Tanner and Sandra Tanner point out online in the *Salt Lake City Messenger*, www.utlm.org/newsletters/no46.htm. The question remains: How did this error go undetected for 150 years with twelve prophets—including Joseph Smith, who examined the 1837 edition personally, as its preface states—all claiming the *Book of Mormon* was "the most correct of any book on earth"?

40. According to researcher Bruce MacArthur, *Strong's Exhaustive Concordance of the Bible* cites fifteen usages (in the KJV Old Testament) of the word *black* and seven different Hebrew words behind those renderings. The same reference volume cites some thirty-nine usages of the word *dark* and fifteen different Hebrew words. However, only one of those Hebrew words (6937 *qadar*) is translated both as "black" (four times) and as "dark" (four times) so twenty-one additional Hebrew words are translated *either* as "dark" or as "black," but *not* by both words.
41. Note the many references in the *Doctrine and Covenants* to Lamanites, which obviously referred to Native Americans: 3:18, 20; 10:48; 19:27; 28:8; 30:6; 32:2; 49:24; 54:8; and the introduction to section 57.
42. Regarding Native Americans and Polynesians who were supposedly descended from Lamanites: To show how completely ubiquitous this understanding was, consider this quote from my 1972 Brigham Young University annual yearbook, the *Banyan*, which I have in my possession. It describes the Brigham Young University club (still in existence) for Native Americans called "Tribe of Many Feathers": "Through weekly meetings ... Indian students learned about their people and themselves, and how to cope with the problems of University life. They added to the single Navajo or Apache or Cherokee feather that adorned individual headdresses, the 'many feathers' of the greater Lamanite family" (419). In addition, the club's singing representatives were called "The Lamanite Generation." Their recordings are still available for sale under that name; however, the group is now known as "Living Legends."
43. Southerton says the LDS officials summoned him to a hearing after the book was published, to excommunicate him on charges of adultery. The charge was later reduced to the charge of an inappropriate relationship with another woman (while he and his wife were temporarily separated), and the Church refused to let him speak of the DNA issue. *The Mormon Curtain*, www.mormoncurtain.com/topic_simonsoutherton.html. This is reminiscent of my personal experience in talking to other ex-Mormons and doubting Mormons whose bishops threatened them with excommunication on the grounds of sexual misconduct

when, as in Southerton's case, the accused person wanted to focus upon his or her theological reasons for leaving the LDS Church.

44. For an example of this, see William Lobdell, "Bedrock of a Faith Is Jolted," *Los Angeles Times*, February 16, 2006.
45. This quote is from Southerton's response to LDS websites such as FAIR and FARMS who criticized his findings. You may read his entire detailed response on his publisher's website: Signature Books, signaturebooks.com/excerpts/Losing2.htm.
46. 3 Nephi 2:11–16.
47. Mark Twain as quoted by Remini, *Joseph Smith*, 74.
48. 1 Nephi 4:13b.
49. "Under Christ Adam yet stands at our head.... Adam fell, but he fell in the right direction. He fell toward the goal.... Adam fell, but he fell upward." *Deseret News*, Church Section, July 31, 1965.
50. Some have seen in the *Book of Mormon*'s stance on the unity of the Godhead a view that is "tainted" with modalism, which "teaches that the Trinity is not three persons in one God but one divine person in three different roles or expressions," each of which modalism would say did not coexist eternally but rather consecutively, one at a time. Ronald V. Huggins of Utah Lighthouse Ministry, for instance, cites 3 Nephi 1:14 as an example of modalism. *Salt Lake City Messenger*, May 2007, 9.
51. 2 Nephi chapter 31.
52. Alma 34:31–35.
53. Ludlow, *A Companion to Your Study*, 103.
54. Tanner and Tanner, *Mormonism—Shadow or Reality?* 63–72.
55. Ibid., 88.
56. Hector Lee, *The Three Nephites: The Substance and Significance of the Legend in Folklore*, doctoral dissertation (Albuquerque, N.M.: University of New Mexico Press, 1949). Later published under the same title (n.p.: Ayer Company, 1977). Unfortunately this valuable book is out of print.
57. Ibid., 36.
58. Ibid., 33. See also Bruce E. Dana, *The Three Nephites and Other Translated Beings* (Springville, Utah: Bonneville Books, 2003).
59. At this point in the original printing of this book I mentioned that we had no evidence of the barley mentioned in the *Book of Mormon*, but Mormon apologists have documented the discovery of a type of barley in the New World. Maxwell Institute, http://maxwellinstitute.byu.edu/display.php?table=transcripts&id=126. Score one for Joseph Smith.
60. Joseph Fielding Smith, who became prophet of the LDS Church just before I left it, stated that "both the Nephite and Jaredite civilizations fought their final great wars of extinction at and near the Hill Cumorah (or Ramah as the Jaredites termed it), which hill is located between Palmyra and Manchester in the western part of New York." Quoted in Bruce R. McConkie, *Mormon Doctrine* (Salt Lake City: Bookcraft, 1966), 175. Only in the ensuing years since Smith's writing, with the continuing dearth of any archaeological evidence for those great wars of extinction, have LDS apologists begun to aggressively advance

their fallback theories that there must have been another hill named Cumorah in Central America. For an example of an online discussion of these issues, see *Book of Mormon Studies*, www.mormonstudies.com/geo1.htm.

61. An excellent online article "Does Archaeology Support the *Book of Mormon*?" can be found at Mormons in Transition, www.irr.org/mit/bomarch2.html.
62. Daniel C. Peterson, "Is the *Book of Mormon* True?: Notes on the Debate," maxwellinstitute.byu.edu/publications/bookschapter.php?bookid=&chapid=185.
63. Tolkien stands as an example of how a single man could in detail imagine and write about entire populations and physical sites which never existed.
64. Dan Vogel and Brent Lee Metcalfe, "Editors' Introduction," *American Apocrypha*, ed. Vogel and Metcalfe, vii-xvii. I strongly urge anyone who is swayed by the arguments of some supposed experts on *Book of Mormon* archaeology to read this essay, and Thomas Murphy, "Simply Implausible: DNA and the Mesoamerican Setting for the *Book of Mormon*," *Dialogue: A Journal of Mormon Thought* (Winter 2003): 109–32.
65. Brigham H. Roberts, *Studies of the Book of Mormon* (Salt Lake City: Signature Books, 1992), 271.
66. Jerald Tanner and Sandra Tanner, *Ferguson's Manuscript Unveiled* (Salt Lake City: Utah Lighthouse Ministry, 1988).
67. Palmer, *An Insider's View of Mormon Origins*, 261.
68. Hugh Nibley, *An Approach to the Book of Mormon* (Salt Lake City: Deseret News Press, 1957), 373.
69. For a more complete list, see Tanner and Tanner's book, *Ferguson's Manuscript Unveiled*, Utah Lighthouse Ministry, www.utlm.org.
70. Because of their thick lips, broad noses, and slanting eyes, observers have said they look either Asian or possibly African.
71. Stela 5, Izapa, found in the late 1950s. Former Mormon Lane Thuet has an excellent article online regarding it at Mormonism Research Ministry, www.mrm.org/topics/book-mormon/stela–5-and-lehis-vision-tree-life. Thuet's article quotes others within the LDS community who assert that, in order to make it seem to support a vision recorded in the *Book of Mormon*, M. Wells Jakeman, chairman of the Department of Archaeology at Brigham Young University, actually inaccurately drew pictures of the carving and even altered a plaster cast made from a mold of the carving "after his own interpretation" (in the words of professional archaeologist Dee Green, as quoted by Thuet).
72. Alma 11:4–19.
73. Brigham Young University's official Maxwell Institute site points to a horse found in Florida carbon-dated to 100 BC at maxwellinstitute.byu.edu/faq.php?id=6&table=questions. However, in private correspondence I asked Dr. Bruce J. MacFadden, the University of Florida's Florida Museum of Natural History's Curator of Vertebrate Paleontology: "What is the latest, pre-Columbian date for which we have carbon-dated proof of the existence of horses in the Americas? Does your research lead you to believe that horses were common in the three thousand years before Columbus?" He responded: "About ten thousand years ago. There is no evidence of horses the three thousand years before Columbus" (email to the author, dated 3/17/08). When told that he had been quoted in support of

pre-Columbian horses in Florida, MacFadden responded, "That is not an idea that I support" (email to the author, dated 3/17/08).

74. Ether 9:19.
75. See *Wheel*, www.mormonfortress.com/wheel4.html.
76. Alma 50:34 and numerous other places.
77. Mormon 6:2, 6; 8:2.
78. Alma 4:4; 22:29; 43:22; Mormon 1:10.
79. *Deseret News*, Church Section, February 27, 1954, 2–3.
80. The Tanners have excellent online materials on the Kinderhook plates at Utah Lighthouse Ministry, www.googlesyndicatedsearch.com/u/utlm?hl=en&ie=ISO–8859–1&q=kinderhook&btnG=Search. In addition, LDS author Grant Palmer cites the Kinderhook plates and other documents that Joseph Smith claimed to be able to translate but did not (*An Insider's View of Mormon Origins*, 36).
81. Fielding Smith, *Doctrines of Salvation*, 2:107.
82. 3 Nephi 8:19–23.
83. 3 Nephi 8:5–19.
84. 3 Nephi 9:2–12.
85. Gordon H. Fraser, *What Does the Book of Mormon Teach?* (Chicago: Moody Press, 1964), 84.
86. Mosiah 18:17.
87. Gruss and Thuet, *What Every Mormon*, 333–54.
88. Ether 12:26–27.

CHAPTER 4: ONE BIBLE, TWO BOOKS OF COMMANDMENTS, AND UNLIMITED WIVES

1. 1 Nephi 13:29.
2. Fielding Smith, *Doctrines of Salvation*, 2:107. See also Alma 45:19.
3. LDS apologist Robert Millet, in describing the so-called "Great Apostasy" that Mormon doctrine says was responsible for taking essential doctrinal elements out of the Bible, provides a comprehensive list of those elements in his book *Getting at the Truth: Responding to Difficult Questions about LDS Beliefs* (Salt Lake City: Deseret Book, 2004), 18. Unfortunately, not a single item on his list was restored by the *Book of Mormon*.
4. For further reading, I highly recommend F. F. Bruce, *The New Testamtent Documents: Are They Reliable?* (Grand Rapids, Mich.: Eerdmans, 2003).
5. James D. Bales, *The Book of Mormon?* (Rosemead, Calif.: Old Paths Book Club, 1958), 32.
6. In fact, the late LeGrand Richards, on whose classic *A Marvelous Work and a Wonder* (Salt Lake City: Deseret Book, 1958) I along with millions of other LDS depended for a concise and readable rendering of LDS doctrines, actually stated that "the everlasting gospel [i.e., Mormonism] could not be discovered through reading the Bible alone ... This is the only Christian church in the world that did not have to rely upon the Bible for its organization and government ... if we had no Bible, we would still have all the needed direction and

information through the revelations of the Lord 'to his servants the prophets' in these latter days" (41).

7. Known as "the Authorized Version," this LDS version uses the text of the King James but has distinctive notes that tie it to other LDS writings. It also includes excerpts from the "Joseph Smith Translation"—which is of course not a translation at all but rather a paraphrase.
8. Fielding Smith, *Answers to Gospel Questions*, 2:207.
9. Smith claimed he spent over three years in what he called translating the Bible, but apparently had no training at that time in either Greek or Hebrew. Acknowledging that reality, some Mormons now speak of it as a "revision" or commentary, despite Smith's own assertion that it was a translation.
10. Consider the logic that would explain the removal of such an item about Joseph Smith from the Bible. Only someone with complete knowledge of the future would do such a thing. Who has such knowledge? Any ungodly man? Not even LDS doctrine would concede that Lucifer has such omniscience.
11. Smith, *History of the Church*, 1:368.
12. *Doctrine and Covenants* 107:91–92 states that the prophet of the LDS Church is also a translator.
13. Millet quoted in Peter Scarlet, "Smith's Bible Translation Called Inspired," *Salt Lake Tribune* (January 21, 1995).
14. Millet, *Getting at the Truth*, 88.
15. Ibid., 81–82.
16. Joseph Smith, *Pearl of Great Price*, History 1:18–19.
17. As Gruss and Thuet point out in *What Every Mormon (and Non-Mormon) Should Know*, 346–49, the Bible tells us specifically that our feelings cannot be trusted. The authors cite Genesis 6:5, 8:21; Proverbs 14:12; Ecclesiastes 9:3; Jeremiah 11:7–8; 17:9; Matthew 13:15; Mark 7:21–23.
18. Of course some of Joseph Smith's writings within the *Pearl of Great Price* are also modern.
19. See present-day *Doctrine and Covenants*, section 1:6. Note also that chapters are now called sections.
20. Sidney B. Sperry, *Doctrine and Covenants Compendium* (Salt Lake City: Bookcraft, Inc., 1960), 763 footnote.
21. As quoted by Jerald Tanner and Sandra Tanner, *The Case Against Mormonism* (Salt Lake City: Utah Lighthouse Ministry, 1967), 1:188.
22. Charles A. Crane, *Christianity and Mormonism: From Bondage to Freedom* (Webb City, Mo.: Covenant Publishing, 2002), 115.
23. The variable LDS god, as we will see in a subsequent chapter, is perhaps variable because of an identity crisis: the *Book of Mormon* depicts him as one, a spirit (2 Nephi 31:21, Alma 18:2–5); the *Doctrine and Covenants* says he has a body of flesh and bones (130:22); and the *Pearl of Great Price* speaks of many "Gods" (Abraham 4).
24. B. H. Roberts, *A Comprehensive History of the Church of Jesus Christ of Latter-day Saints* (Provo, Utah: Brigham Young University Press, 1957), 2:176.
25. Sperry, *Doctrine and Covenants Compendium*, 66.
26. Smith, *History of the Church*, 1:176 footnote.

27. Richard Abanes states that such names were used to conceal the fact that Smith, in moving away from communal ownership of property, began assigning yet more strange names to such things as tanneries and print shops so that he could covertly distribute the assets to his friends in church leadership. Abanes, *One Nation Under Gods*, 128.
28. *Journal of Discourses* 12:158.
29. *Journal of Discourses* 12:221.
30. Sperry, *Doctrine and Covenants Compendium*, 451.
31. As documented by Tanner and Tanner, *Mormonism—Shadow or Reality?* 406–12.
32. According to an editorial in the *Salt Lake Tribune* (July 14, 1908), as quoted by Tanner and Tanner in *The Changing World of Mormonism*, www.utlm.org/onlinebooks/changech18.htm (page 482).
33. *Conference Report*, April 1898, 11.
34. See also *Doctrine and Covenants* 124:29–42.
35. Todd Compton, *In Sacred Loneliness—The Plural Wives of Joseph Smith* (Salt Lake City: Signature Books, 1997), 10.
36. Tanner and Tanner, *Mormonism—Shadow or Reality?* Photo-reprint, 202.
37. Isaac Sheen, *True Latter-day Saints Herald* 1, no. 1, p. 27. This publication, 1860–1863, is at Latter Day Truth Ministries, www.latterdaytruth.org/publications.html.
38. An interesting website that gives the dates of the marriages and biographical information about the wives is Remembering the Wives of Joseph Smith, www.wivesofjosephsmith.org/.
39. Joseph Fielding Smith, quoted in Tanner and Tanner, *Mormonism—Shadow or Reality?* 211.
40. Compton, *In Sacred Loneliness*, 487.
41. Jacob chapter 2, especially v. 27.
42. Brodie, *No Man Knows My History*, 336.
43. The Tanners have documented a witness who claimed that Joseph Smith "demanded the wives of all the twelve apostles that were at home then in Nauvoo." *Joseph Smith and Polygamy* (Salt Lake City: Utah Lighthouse Ministry, n.d.), 49.
44. *Journal of Discourses* 13:207, 317.
45. Ibid., 11:128.
46. T. Edgar Lyon, as quoted by Tanner and Tanner in *Mormonism—Shadow or Reality?* 225. The Tanners also document the research done by LDS writer Stanley S. Ivins who in *Western Humanities Review* 10:230 wrote an article called "Notes on Mormon Polygamy," in which he estimated the number to be 15 to 20 percent.
47. John A. Widtsoe, *Evidences and Reconciliations* (Salt Lake City: Bookcraft, 1960), 391.
48. *Journal of Discourses* 6:256.
49. See statement by Heber C. Kimball in *Journal of Discourses* 11:211.
50. *Doctrine and Covenants*, "Official Declaration—1," paragraph 4.
51. *Journal of Discourses* 4:55–57.

52. See the heartbreaking story of modern polygamous wife Irene Spencer in *Shattered Dreams* (New York: Center Street, 2007), married at age sixteen as a second wife.
53. *Journal of Discourses* 11:269–70.
54. Ibid., 17:224–25.
55. Ibid., 25:21.
56. John J. Stewart, *Brigham Young and His Wives* (Salt Lake City: Mercury Publishing, 1961), 29–30, as quoted by Tanner and Tanner in *Mormonism—Shadow or Reality?* 234.
57. Besides Smith, dozens of top LDS leaders continued to live in polygamy after the 1890 Manifesto, as documented by B. Carmon Hardy in his book *Solemn Covenant: The Mormon Polygamous Passage* (Champaign, Ill.: University of Illinois Press, 1992), as well as by D. Michael Quinn, "LDS Authority and New Plural Marriages 1890–1904," *Dialogue: A Journal of Mormon Thought* (Spring 1985): 9–105. The latter is at *Dialogue*, content.lib.utah.edu/cdm4/browse.php?CISOROOT=/dialogue&CISOSTART=1,61.
58. Many pro-polygamy websites assert that polygamy is the next civil rights battle.
59. Millet, *Getting at the Truth*, 149. Despite Millet and others who speak of God's role in rescinding the command to practice polygamy, the name of God does not appear in the Manifesto, which reads more like a press release than a revelation.

CHAPTER 5: THE PERILS OF THE *PEARL*

1. Parley P. Pratt, *Millennial Star*, July 1, 1842.
2. In April 1976 the LDS Church authorized the inclusion of two items into the *Pearl of Great Price*. One was the record of a vision Joseph Smith said he received in January of 1836. The second was the record of a 1918 vision of Joseph F. Smith, sixth president of the LDS Church. Both were later transferred to the *Doctrine and Covenants.*
3. Smith, *History of the Church*, 2:235.
4. The words of Josiah Quincy, who visited Joseph Smith at Nauvoo. From William Mulder and Russell Mortensen, ed., *Among the Mormons* (New York: Knopf, 1958), 136–37, as quoted by Tanner and Tanner, *Mormonism—Shadow or Reality?* 298.
5. Keith C. Terry and Walter Whipple, *From the Dust of Decades, A Saga of the Papyri and Mummies* (Salt Lake City: Bookcraft, 1968), 76.
6. As cited by Tanner and Tanner, *Mormonism—Shadow or Reality?* 363.
7. *Journal of Discourses* 6:5. In addition, see 6:4 for Smith's discussion of the Hebrew word.
8. Ludlow, *A Companion to Your Study*, 35.
9. Ibid., 131.
10. Dr. Sidney Sperry, *Ancient Records Testify in Papyrus and Stone* (Salt Lake City: Bookcraft, 1938), 81.
11. UTLM offers a publication entitled *Why Egyptologists Reject the Book of Abraham*. It consists of photo-reprints of *Joseph Smith, Jr. as a Translator* by Rev. F.

S. Spaulding, DD, and *Joseph Smith as an Interpreter and Translator of Egyptian* by the eminent Egyptologist Samuel A. B. Mercer, PhD.

12. An interview with Dr. Henry G. Fischer, *Dialogue: A Journal of Mormon Thought* (Winter 1967): 56–58, as quoted by Tanner and Tanner, *Mormonism—Shadow or Reality?* 302ff.
13. Terry and Whipple, *From the Dust of Decades*, 113.
14. *Daily Universe*, December 1, 1967.
15. *Doctrine and Covenants* 107:91–92.
16. Jerald Tanner and Sandra Tanner, *The Case Against Mormonism* (Salt Lake City: UTLM, 1968), 2:140.
17. This impression was shared by then-LDS author Grant H. Palmer. He noted that Nibley's articles ignored the writing around the facsimiles "and instead focused on Egyptian temple ritual, assembling culturally and spatially unrelated Abrahamic legends over several thousand years of history to demonstrate that the Book of Abraham had the support of some ancient traditions." Palmer, *An Insider's View of Mormon Origins*, 16.
18. Reverend Henry Caswell, *City of the Mormons; or, Three Days at Nauvoo* (London: 1842), 22–23.
19. Millett, *Getting at the Truth*, 103.
20. The color photographs of the papyri as printed in the book *By His Own Hand Upon Papyrus: A New Look at the Joseph Smith Papyri* (Grand Rapids, Mich.: Institute for Religious Research, 1992) definitely show red writing. Author Charles Larson, though, says that the portions with red ink were identified by Joseph Smith as "the writings of Joseph of Egypt" (85–86) and not the Book of Abraham. Larson's entire book—including the photographs—can be downloaded from the Internet at no cost at the Institute for Religious Research—www.irr.org/mit/Book-of-Abraham-page.html.
21. That the papyri were "linked to Joseph Smith" is demonstrated by Larson (op. cit.), who said the backing paper on which they were attached contained drawings of the LDS community of Kirtland, Ohio, and its temple.
22. Photocopies of *The Egyptian Alphabet and Grammar* are available from UTLM.
23. Nibley admitted that the LDS Church kept the document "hidden and suppressed" for 130 years. Hugh Nibley, "Prolegomena to Any Study of the Book of Abraham," *BYU Studies* 8, no. 2 (1968): 171–90.
24. Fawn McKay Brodie, *No Man Knows My History* (New York: Alfred A. Knopf, 1946), 292.
25. Wesley P. Walters, "Joseph Smith Among the Egyptians," *The Journal of the Evangelical Theological Society* 16, no. 1 (Winter, 1973). As reprinted by Modern Microfilm—now UTLM—in 1973.
26. Jerald Tanner and Sandra Tanner, *The Case Against Mormonism* (Salt Lake City: Utah Lighthouse Ministry, 1968), 2:163.
27. As stated in the heading to the Book of Abraham (in the *Pearl of Great Price*).
28. Tanner and Tanner, *Mormonism—Shadow or Reality?* 321.
29. Also cited in *History of the Church*, 2:235–36, 348–51.
30. Tanner and Tanner, *Mormonism—Shadow or Reality?* 323. *Fall of the Book of Abraham*, www.utlm.org/onlinebooks/changech11a.htm.

31. Ibid., 324.
32. Tanner and Tanner, *Changing World of Mormonism*, 343.
33. As quoted by McConkie, *Mormon Doctrine*, 818. Smith claimed that any later references to the presence of this instrument were either "errors" or misidentification with seer stones.
34. *Newsletter and Proceedings of the Society for Early Historic Archaeology* (Brigham Young University, October 25, 1968), 1–4. As quoted by Tanner and Tanner, *Mormonism—Shadow or Reality?* 328.
35. Klaus Baer translation, quoted in Tanner and Tanner, *Mormonism—Shadow or Reality?* 317. Baer's translation has been ratified by Robert K. Ritner, former teacher at Yale and the University of Chicago. Robert K. Ritner, "The 'Breathing Permit of Hor': Thirty-Four Years Later," *Dialogue* 4, no. 33 (Winter 2000). *Dialogue*, content.lib.utah.edu/cdm4/document.php?CISOROOT=/dialogue&CISOPTR=8716&CISOSHOW=8519&REC=6.
36. Smith, *History of the Church*, 4:519.
37. Tanner and Tanner, *Mormonism—Shadow or Reality?* 338–39.
38. *Latter-day Saints Messenger and Advocate* 2, no. 7 (April 1836): 299. This publication, 1834–36, is at *Messenger and Advocate*, www.centerplace.org/history/ma/.
39. *Journal of Discourses* 7:290.
40. Address by Brigham Young, as recorded in *Wilford Woodruff's Journal, 1833–1898*, vol. 4, typescript, edited by Scott G. Kenney (Salt Lake City: Signature Books, 1983), 97.
41. Mark E. Petersen, "Race Problems as They Affect the Church" (address, Convention of Teachers of Religion on the College Level, Brigham Young University, Provo, Utah, August 27, 1954). As quoted by Tanner and Tanner, *Mormonism—Shadow or Reality?* 279.
42. *Journal of Discourses* 10:110.
43. Quoted in Tanner and Tanner, *The Case Against Mormonism*, 2:171.
44. Tanner and Tanner, *Mormonism—Shadow or Reality?* (1976 edition), 15. See *Curse of Cain*, www.utlm.org/onlinebooks/curseofcain_part2.htm.
45. *Journal of Discourses* 22:304.
46. Grant H. Palmer, in his book *An Insider's View of Mormon Origins*, 16–17, argues convincingly that many of these ideas could have come from Joseph Smith's readings of *Antiquities of the Jews* by Flavius Josephus.
47. Joseph Fielding Smith, comp., *Teachings of the Prophet Joseph Smith* (Salt Lake City: Deseret News Press, 1956), 270.
48. Woodruff quoted Young as cited by Jerald Tanner and Sandra Tanner, *Mormonism Like Watergate* (Salt Lake City: Modern Microfilm [now Utah Lighthouse Ministry], 1974), 15.
49. *Juvenile Instructor*, 3:157. This was first an unofficial, then official publication of the LDS Church from the 1860s to 1930, at which time it was renamed *The Instructor*.
50. Joseph Fielding Smith, *Way to Perfection*, 101, quoted in Jerald Tanner and Sandra Tanner, *Mormons and Negroes* (Salt Lake City: Modern Microfilm [now Utah Lighthouse Ministry], 1974), 2.

51. *Look* (October 22, 1963), 79.
52. As quoted by Tanner and Tanner, *Changing World of Mormonism*, 306. Utah Lighthouse Ministry, www.utlm.org/onlinebooks/changech10a.htm.
53. Fielding Smith, *Answers to Gospel Questions*, 2:186.
54. McConkie, *Mormon Doctrine*, 476. This has been removed from subsequent editions.
55. B. H. Roberts, *The Contributor*, 6:296–97, as quoted by Jerald Tanner and Sandra Tanner in their online version of *The Changing World of Mormonism*, 293. Utah Lighthouse Ministry, www.utlm.org/onlinebooks/changech10a.htm.
56. John J. Stewart and William E. Berrett, *Mormonism and the Negro* (Orem, Utah: Bookmark, 1960, 1967), 51, as quoted by Jerald Tanner and Sandra Tanner, *Mormons and Negroes* (Salt Lake City: Utah Lighthouse Ministry, 1987), 6.
57. This according to President Joseph F. Smith in "Excerpts from the Weekly Council Meetings of the Quorum of the Twelve Apostles," as documented by Jerald Tanner and Sandra Tanner, *The Changing World of Mormonism*, 305. The Tanners' entire book, though out of print, is available in a free online edition at www.utlm.org/onlinebooks/changecontents.htm.
58. Tanner and Tanner, *Mormons and Negroes* (Salt Lake City: Utah Lighthouse Ministry, n.d.), 11.
59. Lester Bush, *Dialogue: A Journal of Mormon Thought* (Spring 1973): 45.
60. Tanner and Tanner, *Mormonism—Shadow or Reality?* 290, quoting David O. McKay.
61. 2 Nephi 10:20–21.
62. *Time* (June 18, 1965), 56.
63. *Newsweek* (June 17, 1963), 60.
64. As quoted by Tanner and Tanner, *Mormonism—Shadow or Reality?* 290.
65. *Journal of Discourses* 11:272.
66. Ibid., 2:143.
67. Fielding Smith, *Answers to Gospel Questions*, 2:188 (1958 edition).
68. The exact wording of "Official Declaration—2" states: "Accordingly, all worthy male members of the Church may be ordained to the priesthood without regard for race or color."
69. *Bob Jones University v. United States*, 461 U.S. 574 (1983). *Findlaw*, caselaw.lp.findlaw.com/cgi-bin/getcase.pl?court=US&vol=461&invol=574.
70. The examples of factors that may have influenced the LDS Church's decision to grant its priesthood to blacks is covered in much more detail and with greater documentation by the Tanners in various books. However, the most accessible to the average reader is the online version of Tanner and Tanner, *The Changing World of Mormonism*.
71. Current figures of Brazilian population show that nearly half its citizens are black or mulatto (mixed white and black). Central Intelligence Agency, www.cia.gov/library/publications/the-world-factbook/geos/br.html#People.
72. Armand L. Mauss, "Dispelling the Curse of Cain: Or, How to Explain the Old Priesthood Ban Without Looking Ridiculous," *Sunstone* (October 2004): 57.

CHAPTER 6: THE PRECARIOUS SUMMIT OF CONTINUING REVELATION

1. As documented by Community of Christ (formerly RLDS) writer Stephen L. Shields in *Divergent Paths of the Restoration* (Independence, Mo.: Herald House, 2001).
2. Quinn, *The Mormon Hierarchy: Origins of Power*, 227. A supporting online document by Quinn resides at *Some Interesting Notes on Succession at Nauvoo in 1844*, www.xmission.com/~research/about/successi.htm.
3. Ibid., 226.
4. Shields, *Divergent Paths of the Restoration*, 65–66.
5. Jason Szep, "Fundamental Mormons Seek Recognition for Polygamy," Reuters, June 12, 2007. *NHNE*, www.nhne.org/news/NewsArticlesArchive/tabid/400/articleType/ArticleView/articleId/3207/Default.aspx.
6. Richard Ostling and Joan K. Ostling, *Mormon America: The Power and the Promise* (San Francisco: HarperSanFrancisco, 1999), 56.
7. Dorothy Allred Solomon, *Predators, Prey, and Other Kinfolk* (New York: W. W. Norton, 2003), 394.
8. Interview with a polygamist in the *New York Times*, December 27, 1965.
9. Stanley S. Ivins, quoted in Tanner and Tanner, *Mormonism—Shadow or Reality?* 237.
10. Samuel Taylor, *I Have Six Wives* (New York: Greenburgh, 1956), 13.
11. Lowell L. Bennion, *An Introduction to the Gospel* (teacher's supplement) (Salt Lake City: Deseret Sunday School Union Board, 1964), 28–29.
12. Marie Felt, *What It Means to Be a Latter-day Saint* (Salt Lake City: Deseret Sunday School Union Board, 1963), 254.
13. Anonymous, *Jerald and Sandra Tanner's Distorted View of Mormonism: A Response to Mormonism—Shadow or Reality?* (Salt Lake City: n.p., 1977), 3. At the time of publication this was written anonymously, but it was later revealed that the author was LDS historian D. Michael Quinn, who himself was later excommunicated from the LDS Church.
14. Sperry, *Doctrine and Covenants Compendium*, 17.
15. "Search the scriptures; for in them ye think ye have eternal life: and they are they which testify of me" (John 5:39).
16. Orson Pratt, an apostle of the LDS Church, said: "Jesus made his appearance on the earth in the meridian of time, and he established his kingdom on the earth. But to fulfill ancient prophecies, the Lord suffered that Kingdom to be uprooted ... the kingdoms of this world made war against the kingdom of God, established eighteen centuries ago, and they prevailed against it, and the kingdom ceased to exist." *Journal of Discourses* 12:125.
17. Fielding Smith, *Doctrines of Salvation*, 1:170.
18. *Journal of Discourses* 13:95.
19. Quoting James E. Talmadge, *The Articles of Faith* (Salt Lake City: The Church of Jesus Christ of Latter-day Saints, 1968), 7.
20. J. Reuben Clark, as quoted in *Ensign* (September 2005): 17.
21. Clyde Williams, comp., *Teachings of Lorenzo Snow* (Salt Lake City: Bookcraft, 1984), 2.

22. Reed Smoot Case, 1:99, quoted in Tanner and Tanner, *Mormonism—Shadow or Reality?* 184.
23. Heidi Swinton, *In the Company of Prophets* (Salt Lake City: Deseret Book, 1993), 21.
24. For more details, consult Abanes, *One Nation Under Gods*, 386–89.
25. *Teachings of the Living Prophets: Student Manual Religion 333* (Salt Lake City: Church Educational System, 1982), 32. The process is detailed at www.lds.org, newsroom.lds.org/ldsnewsroom/eng/news-releases-stories/succession-in-the-presidency-of-the-church-of-jesus-christ-of-latter-day-saints.
26. Harold B. Lee, "The Place of the Living Prophet, Seer and Revelator" (address to Seminaries and Institutes faculty, Brigham Young University, Provo, Utah, July 8, 1964), 14.
27. Smith, *History of the Church*, 5:265 (1958 edition).
28. Lee, "The Place of the Living Prophet," 14.
29. Ezra Taft Benson stated in a widely publicized speech at Brigham Young University on February 6, 1980, that: *Anything* a prophet says should be regarded as coming from the mouth of the Lord, that a living prophet "is more important than any scripture or past prophet," that a prophet can speak for the Lord on temporal and political matters as well as spiritual ones, and that there is no need for a prophet to say, "Thus saith the Lord," for his words to be scripture. The full text of this speech is at Fourteen Fundamentals in Following the Prophet, www.lds-mormon.com/fourteen.shtml.
30. Sophfronia Scott Gregory, Anne Palmer Donohoe, and Richard N. Ostling, "Saints Preserve Us," *Time* (June 13, 1994): 65.
31. Steve Benson and Mary Ann Benson, "It's Becoming Red Square on Temple Square," *Arizona Republic*, May 22, 1994.
32. Of course the Lord gives himself the merciful option to relent and not bring about destruction he has previously announced when people repent, and the right to punish disobedience in those he has promised to bless (see Jeremiah 18:5–10).
33. 1 Nephi 13:12.
34. 1 Nephi 15:17–19.
35. For much more detail on the Civil War prophecy, see Abanes, *One Nation Under Gods*, 255–79. The Tanners also have an abundance of information on this subject online—just perform a search for "Civil War prophecy" at www.utlm.org.
36. Smith, *History of the Church*, 3:171.
37. Joseph Smith, quoted in N. B. Lundwall, comp., *Inspired Prophetic Warnings*, 6th ed. (Salt Lake City: Publishers Press, n.d.), 59.
38. Smith, *History of the Church*, 1:176; 2:188, 191.
39. Ibid., 2:182.
40. *Journal of Discourses* 10:250.
41. Ibid., 5:219.
42. *The Young Women's Journal* (1892): 263–64. A photocopy of this document is available in some editions of *Where Does It Say That* and the text is quoted at www.utlm.org/onlinebooks/mclaims5.htm.

43. *Journal of Discourses* 13:271.
44. Abanes, *One Nation Under Gods*, 143.

CHAPTER 7: THE MORMON PANTHEON

1. *Journal of Discourses* 10:5.
2. Ibid., 6:6.
3. McConkie, *Mormon Doctrine*, 750.
4. *Doctrine and Covenants* 131:7–8.
5. Lyrics by Eliza R. Snow.
6. Abraham H. Cannon, his journal, quoted by Tanner and Tanner, *Mormonism—Shadow or Reality?* 165.
7. Fielding Smith, *Answers to Gospel Questions*, 5:3, 142.
8. As quoted in R. Clayton Brough, comp., *Teachings of the Prophets—Statements of LDS Leaders on Contemporary Issues* (Bountiful, Utah: Horizon, n.d.), 120. This book, an earlier version of which I used when I took "Teachings of the Living Prophets" at Brigham Young University, in recent editions contains additional quotations from recent LDS leaders about the doctrine of a mother in heaven.
9. Orson Pratt, *The Seer* (March 1852): 37. Mormons note that this publication, though published by an apostle of the Church, was repudiated by the Church. This periodical at Brigham Young University, http://contentdm.lib.byu.edu/cdm4/document.php?CISOROOT=/NCMP1847–1877&CISOPTR=2915.
10. See Grethe Peterson's response to an article by Linda Wilcox in the pro-LDS publication *Sunstone* (September-October 1980): 17. "And the sticky question of whether there is more than one Heavenly Mother ... If that is the case, how does one relate to one, or to many, for that matter?"
11. John A. Widtsoe, *Discourses of Brigham Young* (Salt Lake City: Deseret Book, 1925), 50. *Questia*, www.questia.com/P.M..qst?a=o&d=9270729.
12. *Pearl of Great Price*, Moses 3:1–9. See also Fielding Smith, *Doctrines of Salvation*, 1:62–64.
13. Pratt, *The Seer*, 21; see also *Journal of Discourses* 16:333–34.
14. Richards stated the same in an article found at LDS Library, http://search.ldslibrary.com/article/view/3082043.
15. It is true that the word *trinity* does not appear in the Hebrew, Greek, or Aramaic of our Bible; nor does Scripture contain an explicit doctrine of the Trinity. However, in the words of Christian author Alister E. McGrath, "Scripture bears witness to a God who demands to be understood in a Trinitarian manner," *Christian Theology: An Introduction* (Oxford: Blackwell, 2001), 320. I also recommend Robert M. Bowman Jr., *Why You Should Believe in the Trinity* (Grand Rapids, Mich.: Baker, 1989), even though it deals specifically with Jehovah's Witness teaching; and Royce G. Gruenler, *The Trinity in the Gospel of John* (Eugene, Ore.: Wipf and Stock, 2004).
16. Fielding Smith, comp., *Teachings of the Prophet Joseph Smith*, 370, 372.
17. *Dialogue: A Journal of Mormon Thought* (Autumn 1966): 40.
18. Palmer, *An Insider's View of Mormon Origins*, 240. He concluded that "when he [Joseph Smith] rewrote his history in 1838, he reinterpreted his experience to satisfy institutional needs."

19. "*Book of Mormon* theology is generally modalistic," says LDS scholar Melodie Moensch Charles, "*Book of Mormon* Christology," in *New Approaches to the Book of Mormon: Explorations in Critical Methodology*, ed. Brent Lee Metcalf (Salt Lake City: Signature, 1993), 110.
20. See also Alma 11:26–31, 38–39, 44; Mosiah 15:1–5; Mormon 7:7.
21. Joseph Smith, "Lectures on Faith," Lecture Five (1833). The fact that these lectures did not square with later teachings about God's physical body was, I believe, the primary reason that the "Lectures on Faith" were finally dropped from the *Doctrine and Covenants.*
22. Palmer, *An Insider's View of Mormon Origins*, 21.
23. Robert Millet calls it "a divine presidency." *Getting at the Truth*, 117.
24. Apostle Erastus Snow, *Journal of Discourses* 26:214.
25. "President Packer Interview Transcript from PBS Documentary," lds.org, http://newsroom.lds.org/ldsnewsroom/eng/news-releases-stories/president-packer-interview-transcript-from-pbs-documentary.
26. "Elder Oaks Interview Transcript from PBS Documentary," lds.org, http://newsroom.lds.org/ldsnewsroom/eng/news-releases-stories/elder-oaks-interview-transcript-from-pbs-documentary.
27. Martha Beck, *Leaving the Saints: How I Lost the Mormons and Found My Faith* (New York: Crown, 2005), 86.
28. John Taylor in *Mediation and Atonement* (Salt Lake City: Deseret News Company, 1882), 160–61. (An exact reproduction exists, dated 1975 and reissued in 2007.) As quoted by McConkie in *Mormon Doctrine*, 248.
29. Millet, *Getting at the Truth*, 110–11.
30. *Journal of Discourses* 9:286.
31. This term is from the teachings of Brigham Young, *Journal of Discourses* 13:271. Also used by Fielding Smith, *Doctrines of Salvation*, 1:89.
32. Pratt, *The Seer*, 132.
33. Spencer W. Kimball, *The Miracle of Forgiveness* (Salt Lake City: Bookcraft, 1969), 286.
34. Several examples of LDS attempts to make the early Christian fathers "look Mormon" are delineated—and demolished—by Matthew A. Paulson, *Breaking the Mormon Code* (Livermore, Calif.: Wingspan Press, 2006).
35. His audience was, after all, people who wanted to stone him for blasphemy.
36. The exact wording of this couplet was first attributed to LDS prophet Lorenzo Snow and was reaffirmed in the LDS book *The Gospel Through the Ages* by Milton R. Hunter (Salt Lake City: Deseret Book, 1958), 105–6. See also Heidi Swinton, *In the Company of Prophets* (Salt Lake City: Deseret Book, 1993), 21. The quote is at the official LDS website, LDS.org, www.lds.org/ldsorg/v/index.jsp?vgnextoid=637e1b08f338c010VgnVCM1000004d82620aRCRD&locale=0&sourceId=6032f48fa2d20110VgnVCM100000176f620a____&hideNav=1.
37. *Ensign* (November 1975): 80.
38. *Journal of Discourses* 6:120. This was also affirmed by Orson Hyde in *Journal of Discourses* 1:123.
39. Fielding Smith, *Doctrines of Salvation*, 1:5–10; see also McConkie, *Mormon Doctrine*, 238–39.

40. Francis J. Beckwith, "Philosophical Problems with the Mormon Concept of God," *Christian Research Institute Journal*, www.iclnet.org/pub/resources/text/cri/cri-jrnl/web/crj0100a.html.
41. LDS apologist Robert Millet says that God's influence can be everywhere via "His Holy Spirit," affirming the LDS doctrine that the Holy Spirit is a separate entity/person from "the Holy Ghost" of Mormon doctrine (Millet, *Getting at the Truth*, 107).
42. 1 Timothy 6:16.
43. *Doctrine and Covenants* 107:53–55. Notice the inherent theological problem: Since Mormons say angels are resurrected beings, how could Adam have been an archangel in the *preexistence*?
44. *Journal of Discourses* 1:50.
45. "It is not clear, historically, that Brigham Young would have identified Elohim as the father and Jesus as Jehovah," said Sandra Tanner to the author in private correspondence, citing *Journal of Discourses* 12:99, where Young equated Eloheim [sic] with Jehovah. Tanner continues, "[Joseph] Smith seemed to identify Jehovah with God the Father." Other teachings indicate Elohim could have been a higher god above Jehovah, who in turn was a higher god than Adam, who is our father in heaven. See also LDS-Mormon.com, www.lds-mormon.com/jehovah.shtml and "Buerger: The Adam-God Doctrine," http://content.lib.utah.edu/cdm4/document.php?CISOROOT=/dialogue&CISOPTR=20104&CISOSHOW=19920&REC=3.
46. "When the Virgin Mary conceived the child Jesus, the Father had begotten him in his own likeness. He was not begotten by the Holy Ghost. And who is the Father? He is the first of the human family." *Journal of Discourses* 1:50.
47. As per LDS writer and Assistant to the Twelve Apostles, Sterling W. Sill, *Deseret News*, July 31, 1965, as documented by Tanner and Tanner, *Mormonism—Shadow or Reality?* 173.
48. *Deseret News*, October 9, 1976.
49. Brigham Young, *Deseret Weekly News* (June 18, 1873); *Deseret Evening News* (June 14, 1873).
50. Scanned images of each page of all twenty-six volumes are at *Journal of Discourses*, http://patriot.lib.byu.edu/cdm4/browse.php?CISOROOT=%2FJournalOfDiscourses3.
51. Darrick T. Evenson, *The Gainsayers* (Springville, Utah: Cedar Fort Inc., 1998), 174. This book, by a man who later left the LDS Church, is a bottom-of-the-barrel example of LDS writings against critics of Mormonism.
52. Rodney Turner, "The Position of Adam in Latter-day Saint Scriptures and Theology" (master's thesis, Brigham Young University, August 1953), 58.
53. *Journal of Discourses* 2:345.
54. Steven W. Gibson, *One Minute Answers* (Bountiful, Utah: Horizon, 2005), 146. (Italics appear in original.) Also at *One-Minute Answers by Stephen R. Gibson*, www.lightplanet.com/response/answers/contents.htm.
55. McConkie, *Mormon Doctrine*, 129.
56. *Journal of Discourses* 2:342.
57. 3 Nephi 9:15; Ether 4:7.

58. Mosiah 5:7; 15:10–13; Ether 3.
59. An example of this is found in *Doctrine and Covenants* 29:1, 41–46, where critics of Mormonism see only Joseph Smith's confusion of speakers.
60. "Our particular earth, the one to which Christ was sent to work out the infinite and eternal atonement, has seen greater wickedness among her inhabitants than has been the case on any other earth." McConkie, *Mormon Doctrine*, 213; see also *Pearl of Great Price*, Moses 7:29–36.
61. McConkie, *Mormon Doctrine*, 65.
62. 1 Nephi 11:13–18; Alma 7:10.
63. *Journal of Discourses* 1:51. Also affirmed by other, more recent LDS "prophets" such as Joseph F. Smith, *Family Home Evening Manual* (1972), 125–26; Ezra Taft Benson, *Teachings of Ezra Taft Benson* (Salt Lake City: Bookcraft, 1988), 7; and by such past codifiers of LDS doctrine as McConkie, *Mormon Doctrine*, 546–47, 742.
64. Fielding Smith, *Doctrines of Salvation*, 1:18–19.
65. An excellent source of quotes concerning this subject is Sandra Tanner, "LDS Leaders Define Their Concept of Jesus Christ, " Utah Lighthouse Ministry, www.utlm.org/onlineresources/ldsleadersconceptofjesus.htm.
66. *Deseret News*, October 10, 1866.
67. Pratt, *The Seer* 1, no. 10 (October 1853): 158. As noted in a previous chapter, this publication was repudiated by the LDS Church even though Pratt was a faithful Mormon apostle at the time.
68. *Journal of Discourses* 1:50.
69. Gibson, *One Minute Answers*, 131: "The opinion that Jesus was married, although held by several General Authorities, has not been accepted as doctrine, nor is it taught as doctrine by Church leaders today."
70. John chapter 2; for the Mormon interpretation of this see *Journal of Discourses* 2:81–82, 210; 4:259–60; Pratt, *The Seer*, 1:158–59.
71. *Journal of Discourses* 2:210.
72. Ibid., 1:346.
73. Evenson, *The Gainsayers*, 154–55; 197–99.
74. Ibid., 198–99.
75. I'm hardly an expert on Bible marriage customs, though I did cowrite a book with expert Dr. Glenn Greenwood on the subject: *Shout of the Bridegroom* (Joplin, Mo.: Covenant, 2002).
76. *Doctrine and Covenants* 107:53–54; Moses, chapter 7.
77. The sermon in which McConkie said this is available in printed form from Utah Lighthouse Ministry under the title, "Our Relationship with the Lord."
78. As quoted in Daniel C. Peterson and Stephen D. Ricks, *Offenders for a Word* (Provo, Utah: Foundation for Ancient Research and Mormon Studies, 1998), 71.
79. As reported in *Deseret News*, June 20, 1998.
80. McConkie, *Mormon Doctrine*, 359.
81. *Journal of Discourses* 5:179.
82. McConkie, *Mormon Doctrine*, 359.
83. *Doctrine and Covenants* 84:44–46.

84. Moroni 10:4–5.
85. Smith, *History of the Church*, 3:380–81.
86. *Journal of Discourses* 1:51. Bracketed material added for clarity.
87. Ibid.
88. Apostle George Q. Cannon (March 11, 1894), Brian H. Stuy, *Collected Discourses* (Burbank, Calif. and Woodland Hills, Utah: B.H.S. Publishing, 1987), 4:23; as quoted by Sandra Tanner, "LDS Leaders Define Their Concept of Jesus Christ," Utah Lighthouse Ministry, www.utlm.org/onlineresources/ldsleaders conceptofjesus.htm.
89. James R. Harris, "Pearl of Great Price: A Unique Scripture," *Ensign* (December 1972): 28.
90. John Taylor, *The Government of God* (Liverpool, England: S. W. Richards, 1852), 81.
91. LaMar Petersen, *The Creation of the Book of Mormon—A Historical Inquiry* (Salt Lake City: Freethinker Press, 2000), 161.
92. Ibid.
93. "Many of the Mormon kids on my [swim] team honestly believed that if they swam on Sunday, the devil would create an undertow that would drown them." Stephanie Mencimer, "Theocracy in America: What Gentile Life in Mormon Utah Can Teach Us about Church and State," *Washington Monthly* (April 2001), www.washingtonmonthly.com/features/2001/0104.mencimer.html. In addition, researcher Bruce MacArthur asks a logical question: If water is the domain of Satan, why would it be used for both baptism and the LDS Sacrament?
94. Orson F. Whitney, *Life of Heber C. Kimball* (Salt Lake City: Bookcraft, 1992), 144–46.
95. Wilford Woodruff, as quoted by Brian H. Stuy, *Collected Discourses* (Burbank, Calif. and Woodland Hills, Utah: B.H.S. Publishing, 1987), 1:243.
96. Parley P. Pratt, *The Key to Theology* (Liverpool, England: J. H. Smith, 1883), 117.
97. McConkie, *Mormon Doctrine*, 196.
98. *Times and Seasons*, 3:747. Times and Seasons was a monthly LDS publication, 1839–1846. *Times and Seasons*, www.centerplace.org/history/ts/.
99. *Journal of Discourses* 5:164.
100. Ibid.
101. Peterson and Ricks in *Offenders for a Word* say that logic demands a choice between the thought that God has a wayward son named Lucifer (Mormonism), or that God created a murderous robot (what they say Christianity would demand). But the Bible allows a third choice which these two authors ignore: God is the *Creator* of a being who by choice *became* wayward.
102. Hebrews chapters 1 and 2. I do acknowledge an exception to this hierarchy, a "special case" in Scripture, that of "the Angel of the Lord," whom I believe to be the preincarnate Jesus.
103. Pratt, *The Key to Theology*, 112.
104. Fielding Smith, comp., *Teachings of the Prophet Joseph Smith*, 170.
105. *Doctrine and Covenants* 130:7.

106. They do have the ability to physically interact with humans. See 2 Kings 19:35, where one angel killed 185,000 enemy soldiers in one night; and Acts 12:7, where an angel struck the sleeping Peter on the side to awaken him.
107. Interestingly enough, LDS apologists Peterson and Ricks identify "apostate Christianity, including fundamentalist Protestantism" as the different gospel of Galatians 1. *Offenders for a Word*, 152.
108. *Journal of Discourses* 1:50.
109. *Doctrine and Covenants* 27:11.
110. *Journal of Discourses* 1:50–51.
111. James E. Talmadge, *A Study of the Articles of Faith* (Salt Lake City: The Church of Jesus Christ of Latter-day Saints, 1968), 42.
112. Heber C. Kimball, *Journal of Discourses* 4:164–181.
113. Smith, *History of the Church*, 3:380–81.
114. McConkie, *Mormon Doctrine*, 754.
115. *Doctrine and Covenants* 136:21–22.
116. Ron Rhodes shows that God the Father, Jesus Christ, and the Holy Spirit each have the attributes of God (omniscience, omnipresence, omnipotence, holiness, eternality; are described as "truth"; and are called "Lord," "almighty," "everlasting," and "powerful") in *The 10 Most Important Things You Can Say to a Mormon* (Eugene, Ore.: Harvest House, 2001), 58.

CHAPTER 8: SALVATION AND EXALTATION

1. Daniel H. Ludlow, ed., *Encyclopedia of Mormonism* (New York: Macmillan, 1992), 542, as quoted by Sandra Tanner at www.utlm.org/onlineresources/gethsemaneandchristsbloodinldsreferences.htm. However, perhaps there is a recent softening in this stance. LDS apologist of the "kindler and gentler" Mormonism of the twenty-first century, Robert Millet, asserts that the atonement took place in the garden *and* on the cross, quoting LDS prophet Ezra Taft Benson. *A Different Jesus? The Christ of the Latter-day Saints* (Grand Rapids, Mich.: Eerdmans, 2005), 93.
2. In fact, an entire chapter was entitled "Fundamental Differences Between Salvation and Exaltation" in LeGrand Richards's foundational book, which I, like many Mormons, carried with me right along with my Mormon scriptures—*A Marvelous Work and a Wonder* (Salt Lake City: Deseret Book, 1950).
3. *Pearl of Great Price*, Moses 7:35; McConkie, *Mormon Doctrine*, 233–34.
4. Cleon Skousen, *The First 2000 Years* (Salt Lake City: Bookcraft, 1980), 69.
5. McConkie, *Mormon Doctrine*, 339.
6. George Romney as quoted by Wallace Turner, *The Mormon Establishment* (Boston: Houghton Mifflin, 1966), 72.
7. LeGrand Richards, "Heaven Doesn't Matter" (speech, Brigham Young University, 1973). *Speeches*, speeches.byu.edu/reader/reader.php?id=6094.
8. Alma chapter 1.
9. As exemplified by Millet, *Getting at the Truth*, 130.
10. Wallace Bennett, *Why I Am a Mormon* (New York: Thomas Nelson, 1958), 191.
11. Smith, *History of the Church*, 3:380.

12. *Pearl of Great Price,* Moses 6:55.
13. *Book of Mormon,* Mosiah 3:19.
14. *Doctrine and Covenants* 68:27.
15. This is quite in contrast to the Bible's clear teachings that our genealogies have nothing to do with our approval by God—in fact, just the opposite. See 1 Timothy 1:4 and Titus 3:9.
16. Tanner and Tanner, *Mormonism—Shadow or Reality?* 453.
17. *Doctrine and Covenants* 103:9–10.
18. *Journal of Discourses* 6:163.
19. Austin Fife and Alta Fife, *Saints of Sage and Saddle* (Bloomington, Ind.: Indiana University Press, 1956), 226. Unfortunately this book is out of print.
20. Smith, *History of the Church,* 4:231.
21. Before the dedication in 1993 of the San Diego LDS temple, local LDS families received a booklet of materials that included several pages chronicling experiences of temple attendees who had experiences with dead relatives and others while in the temple. Other such experiences are described in Mormon writer Joseph Heinerman's book, *Temple Manifestations—Heavenly Manifestations in Temples Built by the Church of Latter-day Saints 1836–1930* (Salt Lake City: Joseph Lyon and Associates, 2006). Another similar booklet is *Spirit World Experiences* (Dugway, Utah: Pioneer Press, n.d.), no author or compiler listed.
22. Although today females serve as proxies for females and males for males in baptisms for the dead, this was not always the case. For instance, Emma Smith, wife of Joseph Smith, was baptized in proxy on behalf of her deceased father and another dead male relative. Newell and Avery, *Mormon Enigma,* 104.
23. *Journal of Discourses* 19:229.
24. Ostling and Ostling, *Mormon America,* 190.
25. James Edward Talmage, Gustave O. Larson, and T. Edgar Lyon, *Principles of the Gospel* (Salt Lake City: Deseret Sunday School Union Board, 1943), 47–48.
26. Peterson and Ricks, *Offenders for a Word* is a paradigmatic example of anti-anti-Mormon literature. In it, the authors go to great lengths (111–13) to try to "prove" that early Christians engaged in secret rites, ignoring the reality that even assembly and worship were impossible for the persecuted early saints without secrecy—as exemplified by furtive meetings in the catacombs. In most cases, such "secret" meetings were only meant to exclude those who would kill them for their allegiance to Christ.
27. Alma 34:32–35.
28. Moroni 8:22.
29. Ostling and Ostling, *Mormon America,* 190.
30. Abigail Radoszkowicz, "Overzealous Mormons Continue to Baptize Jews," *Jerusalem Post,* July 1, 2004. Online at Rick A. Ross Institute, www.rickross.com/reference/mormon/mormon173.html.
31. Martin Wishnatsky, *Mormonism: A Latter Day Deception* (n.p.: Xulon Press, 2003). *Mormonism: A Latter-day Deception,* www.goodmorals.org/mormons/index.asp?poetlist=ChapterSix.htm.
32. Utah Lighthouse Ministry, www.utlm.org/onlineresources/hitlertemplework.htm.

33. *Dialogue: A Journal of Mormon Thought* (Spring 1983): 21, as quoted by the Tanners in www.utlm.org/newsletters/no98.htm#Second%20Anointing.
34. The website www.lds-mormon.com seems reliable to me and has this account, with nineteenth-century sources, *The Ordinance of Second Anointings*, lds-mormon.com/second_anointing.shtml.
35. Martha Beck (the daughter of acclaimed LDS apologist Dr. Hugh Nibley) writes of people she knew "freaking out" after their first temple endowment, but says that she was able to maintain some personal equilibrium in her first endowment by thinking of it as a cultural initiation ceremony: in *Leaving the Saints* (New York: Random House, 2005), 14. Deborah Laake in *Secret Ceremonies* (New York: Random House, 1993) remembers being mesmerized and calmed by the washing and anointing segment but unnerved by the prospect of having to wear the temple garments for the rest of her life (73–90).
36. Prior to 1990, the person would leave the dressing room wearing only the shield, which was open at the sides so that the washer/anointer could reach inside. In 2005 the shield's design was changed so that the sides were stitched closed as well.
37. Anyone who participated in temple ordinances before 1990 will see an *enormous* difference in the twenty-first century temple washings and anointing. Previously, the initiate was naked under the shield, which had open sides, and the temple worker (always of the same sex as the endowee and usually elderly) touched the listed body parts (except the loins—here the hips were touched) with the water and oil on the worker's fingertip. The garment was not donned until after the washings and anointings. "Also, the 'garment' used to be held open for the patron to step into as a symbolic gesture that it was being 'placed upon' their body. Now, the patron puts the garment on themselves," says former Mormon Lane Thuet. "When I went through the temple, this was the case—it was held open for me to step into, and I was specifically told that it was thus being 'placed upon' me. There are also numerous references to where LDS leaders mention that this was the intent, to have the garment placed upon them." See online information: *Mormonism 201: Chapter 15—The Temple*, www.mrm.org/topics/rebuttals-rejoinders/mormonism–201/temple-mcguire.
38. That name is the one that the LDS husband will use later in the ceremony to call his wife "through the veil" to the Celestial Kingdom, symbolizing his function at the great Resurrection, when he will call her forth from the dead. Sandra Tanner, "How the LDS Husband Hopes to Resurrect His Wife According to the LDS Temple Ceremony," Utah Lighthouse Ministry, www.utlm.org/onlineresources/resurrectwife.htm.

    Even though this is supposed to be a secret part of the ceremony, I remember unmarried women like myself joking about having to be really good wives when we got married, or else our husbands would conveniently "forget" our temple names and we'd lie forgotten in the grave; or, being thus effectively declared unmarried, we'd be resurrected as a servant to married Mormons.
39. Sterling W. Sill's assertion that "Adam fell, but he fell upward," was a variant of the teaching of early LDS Apostle Orson F. Whitney, who maintained that "Adam fell downward, yet forward." (As quoted by Millet, *Getting at the Truth*, 107.)

40. Up until about 1990, at this point in the ceremony women were required to swear to obey their husbands, but this vow was eliminated in an attempt to "reflect sensitivity toward women." Vern Anderson, Associated Press writer, "LDS Leaders Revise Temple Endowment," *Salt Lake Tribune*, April 29, 1990.
41. Up until 1990 this "token" also had a "penalty" and corresponding pantomime for those who betray this secret: They would verbally agree to have their lives taken. Early in the twentieth century, the verbal oath was to have their tongues torn out by the roots, and their throats cut from ear to ear. The penalty was demonstrated by forming the "sign," quickly drawing the right thumb across the throat, then dropping both hands to the sides.
42. Up until 1990, he chanted something the temple identified as the "pure Adamic language," which sounds like "Pay Lay Ale." Reportedly, some objected to what sounded like "Pale ale, ale."
43. Before 1990, there was a section at this point when a sectarian preacher appeared, whom Lucifer hired to teach Adam. The preacher declared that no one can preach without knowing the dead languages and then claimed belief in such things as a god who sits on the top of a topless throne. The preacher asked for a miracle, like restoring a dismembered leg or arm. The endowees would often find this part humorous—which explains the legendary lack of respect that temple Mormons of the past have had for paid ministry, study of biblical languages, and Trinitarian doctrines.
44. Its penalty, pre-1990, was an agreement to give one's life rather than reveal its secrets. (Early twentieth-century versions of the penalty voiced a verbal agreement to have one's heart and vitals cut out and given to wild animals.) The penalty was demonstrated by temple attendees making a cutting motion across the chest with the right hand.
45. Pre-1990, the sign required the participant to draw the right hand from right to left across the stomach as if slitting it. Its penalty, like the others, was an agreement to have one's life taken if the secret is revealed. (The old penalty was to have one's body cut asunder so that the bowels would gush out.)
46. At this point in the ceremony in previous twentieth-century versions of the last embrace, the "five points of fellowship" of Masonic lore were enacted: inside of right foot by the side of right foot, knee to knee, breast to breast, hand to back, mouth to ear. Not surprisingly, this embrace coming soon after ritual washings of the naked body under a shield "seriously agitated" many females. Judy Robertson, author of *No Regrets: How I Found My Way Out of Mormonism* (Indianapolis: Light & Life Communications, 1997), recalls the feeling of embarrassment and violation from the "Five Points of Fellowship" embrace (no longer part of the endowment as of 1990) when a worker "Lord" held her too close and, she felt, too intimately (61). "This probably contributes significantly to the fact that less than ten percent of those Mormons who are eligible actually attend the temple regularly," reported ex-veil worker Chuck Sackett, "while nearly triple that number have been through this experience once." *What's Going On in There? The Verbatim Text of the Mormon Temple Rituals Annotated and Explained by a Former Temple Worker*, second edition (n.p.: Ministry to Mormons, 1982), 10.

47. Martin Wishnatsky (*Mormonism: A Latter-day Deception*) described his experience: "At last my own Elohim released me, parted the veil, and, taking my hand, pulled me behind the curtain. When I looked puzzled as to what celestial revelation might come next as the culmination and perhaps compensation for what had so far transpired, he gestured for me to walk on ... I did so and came into the 'Celestial Room,' a Louis XIV-style lobby with a beautiful chandelier, ornate stuffed furniture, and lush carpeting. Other endowees were present, sitting quietly or whispering softly and reverently to one another. 'I guess we wait here,' I thought, 'for the real pay-off. I sure hope it gets better.' 'How did you like it?' one of my Mormon friends asked. And it hit me. This is it; it's over. Looking at my stricken face, another friend said, 'Whatever you may think, Martin, I want you to know that God is very pleased with what you've done today.' We then went downstairs and ate lunch." *Mormonism: A Latter Day Deception*, www.goodmorals.org/mormons/index.asp?poetlist=Introduction.htm.
48. Thelma "Granny" Geer's father, for instance, lived as a "Jack Mormon" refusing to give up tea, coffee, and tobacco, and thus was denied temple rites. But after his death a family friend stood in proxy for him so that her grandmother could be "sealed" to him in eternal marriage. Latayne C. Scott, *Why We Left Mormonism* (Grand Rapids, Mich.: Baker, 1990), 59; also described in Geer's own book, *Mormonism, Mama and Me* (Tucson, Ariz.: Calvary Missionary Press, 1979).
49. As quoted in Latayne C. Scott, *Why We Left Mormonism* (Grand Rapids, Mich.: Baker, 1990), 41.
50. Smith, *History of the Church*, 4:552.
51. William J. Whalen, *The Latter-day Saints in the Modern-day World* (Chicago: University of Notre Dame Press, 1967), 204. Also documented by Quinn, *The Mormon Hierarchy: Extensions of Power* (Salt Lake City: Signature Books, 1997).
52. There are simply too many books written about the relationship of Mormonism to Masonry to list them. It is one of the most overdocumented issues in Mormonism. I recommend Jerald Tanner and Sandra Tanner, *Mormonism, Magic and Masonry* (Salt Lake City: Utah Lighthouse Ministry, 1988) as a good starting place. More information at Utah Lighthouse Ministry, www.utlm.org/onlineresources/masonicsymbolsandtheldstemple.htm and Signature Books, www.signaturebookslibrary.org/essays/mason.htm. Also: Tanners, *Evolution of the Mormon Temple Ceremony 1842–1990* (Salt Lake City: Utah Lighthouse Ministry, 1990, updated 2005) and David John Buerger, *The Mysteries of Godliness: A History of Mormon Temple Worship* (Salt Lake City: Signature Books, 1994).
53. Beck, *Leaving the Saints*, 14–15.
54. Fielding Smith, *Doctrines of Salvation*, 1:135–36.
55. *Journal of Discourses* 3:247.
56. Sidney Sperry, *Doctrine and Covenants Compendium* (Salt Lake City: Bookcraft, 1960), 101.
57. *Doctrine and Covenants* 76:31–37.
58. Ibid., 42:18; 64:7; 132:27.
59. McConkie, *Mormon Doctrine*, 817.

60. *Journal of Discourses* 3:247.
61. Ibid., 1:108–9.
62. Ibid., 10:110.
63. Ibid., 4:219–20.
64. *Journal of Hosea Stout*, 2:71. (Page 56 of typed copy at Utah State Historical Society. For additional information on Hosea Stout and his diary, including notes and comments, see Juanita Brooks, ed., *On The Mormon Frontier: The Diary of Hosea Stout 1844–61* (Salt Lake City: University of Utah Press, 1964). Also, Volume One (typescript) is available at no cost at *Diary of Hosea Stout (1810–89)*, www.boap.org/LDS/Early-Saints/HStout.html.
65. *Journal of Discourses* 4:49–51.
66. *Doctrine and Covenants* 42:25–26.
67. *Journal of Discourses* 4:51.
68. Ibid., 4:219.
69. Tanner and Tanner, *Mormonism—Shadow or Reality?* 398–404A, 428–50, 493–515.
70. John D. Lee, *Confessions of John D. Lee*. Photoreprint. As quoted by Jerald Tanner and Sandra Tanner, www.utlm.org/newsletters/no56.htm.
71. Fielding Smith, *Doctrines of Salvation*, 1:134–36, as quoted by the Tanners in *Mormon Claims Answered*, www.utlm.org/onlinebooks/mclaims10.htm.
72. Moses 7:35. In addition, Robert Millet asserts in *Getting at the Truth* that in both Greek and Hebrew the words for "eternity" always mean a measurable period of time, not timelessness. I assert that there are two problems with this point of view: First, trying to measure eternity by seconds, minutes, hours, days, years, etc., is logically impossible because eternity is, by definition, *not* time. Rather than the sequential nature of time, eternity is a state, an ontology. Second, the words of the rich man in Luke 16:19–25 demonstrate that both the states of blessedness and torment were permanent. The rich man's only hope was to spare his loved ones his own hopeless fate.
73. Quoted in LeGrand Richards, *A Marvelous Work and a Wonder* (Salt Lake City: Deseret Book, 1960), 334.
74. *Doctrine and Covenants* 29:23–25.
75. Ibid., 88:99.
76. *Journal of Discourses* 7:289.
77. *Doctrine and Covenants* 130:6–9.
78. Ibid., 130:6–11.
79. Ibid., 76:103; *Book of Mormon*, 2 Nephi 9:27–39; 26:10.
80. 2 Nephi 9:36.
81. *Doctrine and Covenants* 121:23.
82. 2 Nephi 28:15; Moroni 8:14, 21.
83. *Doctrine and Covenants* 104:18.
84. 3 Nephi 12:22.
85. *Doctrine and Covenants* 88:33–35.
86. Brigham Young said he doubted whether there were any females in hell (*Journal of Discourses* 8:222). I have been called by Mormons such things as Beelzebub,

Judas, and a son of perdition. My response has always been to ask how I'm a son of anything.

87. McConkie, *Mormon Doctrine*, 351.
88. Widtsoe, *Evidences and Reconciliations*, 213–14.
89. Widtsoe, *Joseph Smith: Seeker After Truth*, 178.
90. *Doctrine and Covenants* 63:32–34.
91. Fielding Smith, comp., *Teachings of the Prophet Joseph Smith*, 347.

CHAPTER 9: ISSUES AND CHALLENGES FACING MORMONISM IN THE TWENTY-FIRST CENTURY—PART 1

1. As quoted by Thomas W. Murphy, "Lamanite Genesis, Genealogy, and Genetics," in *American Apocrypha*, ed. Vogel and Metcalfe, 53.
2. Abanes, *One Nation Under Gods*, 321–22. Italics in original.
3. One example is *Mormon Archipelago*, www.ldsblogs.org/, which describes itself as "the gateway to the bloggernacle."
4. "Internet Mormonism Versus Chapel Mormonism," *Mormon Information*, www.mormoninformation.com/imvscm.htm.
5. Jiro Numano, "Perseverance Amid Paradox: The Struggle of the LDS Church in Japan Today," *Dialogue: A Journal of Mormon Thought* 39, no. 4 (2006): 138.
6. Another example of entire wards dissolving in "a wave of apostasy" over their members and leaders discovering documented LDS history is described in Jorg Dittberner, "One Hundred Eighteen Years of Attitude: The History of The Church of Jesus Christ of Latter-Day Saints in the Free and Hanseatic City of Bremen," *Dialogue: A Journal of Mormon Thought* 36, no. 2 (2003): 68.
7. Some of this chronological information was derived from the *Salt Lake City Messenger* 100 (March 2003).
8. Thomas Stuart Ferguson, letter to Mr. and Mrs. Harold W. Lawrence, February 20, 1976, University of Utah as quoted in Stan Larson, "The Odyssey of Thomas Stuart Ferguson," *Dialogue: A Journal of Mormon Thought* (Spring 1990): 79. Also, *Salt Lake City Messenger* 69 (September 1988). Utah Lighthouse Ministry, www.utlm.org/newsletters/no69.htm.
9. This manuscript is now available as B. H. Roberts, *Studies of the Book of Mormon* (Salt Lake City: Signature Books, 1985 and 1992).
10. Paul H. Dunn, "An Open Letter to Members of the Church," *Church News*, October 26, 1991.
11. More information and documentation about child abuse and ritual child abuse is available at Utah Lighthouse Ministry, www.utlm.org/newsletters/no91.htm#RITUAL%20ABUSE%20CONFIRMED.
12. *San Francisco Chronicle*, April 13, 1997.
13. *Christianity Today*, www.christianitytoday.com/ct/2004/novemberweb-only/11–15–11.0.html.
14. *Deseret Morning News*, November 15, 2004.
15. Jeffery L. Sheler, "The Mormon Movement: The Church of Latter-day Saints Grows by Leaps and Bounds," *US News and World Report* (November 12, 2000).

16. As quoted in "Mormon Story Opens Up," *USA Today*, April 24, 2007.
17. See others at LDS Film, www.ldsfilm.com/.
18. See her resources at www.leavingthesaints.com. Among Beck's listed resources is the constantly updated *Rick A. Ross Institute Site for Mormon Women*, www.rickross.com/groups/mormon.html#Mormon_Women.
19. Kent Ponder, "Mormon Women, Prozac® and Therapy," www.exmormon.org/mormon/mormon197.htm.
20. Julie Cart, "Study Finds Utah Leads Nation in Antidepressant Use: Some Point to the Pressures of Mormonism, Especially for Women, to Explain the Surprising Findings," *Los Angeles Times*, February 20, 2002.
21. Lucinda Dillon and Dennis Romboy, "Deadly Taboo: Youth Suicide an Epidemic That Many in Utah Prefer to Ignore," *Deseret Morning News*, April 24, 2006.
22. A source of many demographic statistics on Mormons: "Sampling of Latter-day Saint/Utah Demographics and Social Statistics from National Sources," *Adherents*, www.adherents.com/largecom/lds_dem.html.
23. "Many in Poll Know Little of LDS, Muslims," Associated Press and Cox News Service, *Deseret Morning News*, September 26, 2007.
24. Suzanne Sataline, "Tabernacle on Trial: Mormons Dismayed by Harsh Spotlight," *Wall Street Journal*, February 8, 2008.
25. Letter reproduced in Charles M. Larson, *By His Own Hand Upon Papyrus: A New Look at the Joseph Smith Papyri* (Grand Rapids, Mich.: Institute for Religious Research, 1992), 184.
26. John L. Brooke, *The Refiner's Fire: The Making of Mormon Cosmology 1644–1844* (New York: Cambridge University Press, 1994), 299.
27. Ibid., 300.
28. *Doctrine and Covenants* 46:27.
29. Jerald Tanner's entire book *Tracking the White Salamander: The Story of Mark Hofmann, Murder and Forged Mormon Documents* is at Utah Lighthouse Ministry, www.utlm.org/onlinebooks/trackingcontents.htm. This quote is from chapter 7.
30. Ostling and Ostling, *Mormon America*, 248.
31. McConkie, *Mormon Doctrine*, 114. This appeared in the edition of McConkie's book (1979) published two years *after* the LDS Church's change of policy regarding blacks. *This edition was directly supervised and approved by the then-current LDS leadership.*
32. Alma 3:6.
33. In official LDS magazine, *Improvement Era* (December 1960), 922–23.
34. The *Book of Mormon* still clearly teaches the connection between sin and dark skin in 1 Nephi 12:23, 2 Nephi 5:21, Jacob 3:8, and Alma 3:6. In addition, in 3 Nephi 2:15 we read this concerning some of the Lamanites: "And their curse was taken from them, and their skin became white like unto the Nephites."
35. *Salt Lake Tribune*, September 2, 1989.
36. *Salt Lake Tribune*, September 10, 1989.
37. *Salt Lake City Messenger* 73 (October 1989). Utah Lighthouse Ministry, www.utlm.org/newsletters/no73.htm.

38. Thomas Murphy, "Lamanite Genesis, Genealogy, and Genetics" in *American Apocrypha*, ed. Vogel and Metcalfe, 68.
39. In the official LDS magazine, *Ensign*, Spencer W. Kimball, who later became the LDS prophet, stated: "A Lamanite is a descendant of one Lehi who left Jerusalem six hundred years before Christ ... and landed in America. And Lehi and his family became the ancestors of all the Indian and Mestizo tribes in North and South and Central America and in the islands of the sea,... Now the Lamanites number about sixty million; they are in all the states of America from Tierra del Fuego all the way up to Point Barrows, and they are in nearly all the islands of the sea from Hawaii south to southern New Zealand." Spencer W. Kimball, "Of Royal Blood," *Ensign* (July 1971): 7.
40. Murphy, "Lamanite Genesis, Genealogy, and Genetics," 76, footnote 84.
41. Southerton addresses many of these issues on his publisher's website, Signature Books, www.signaturebooks.com/excerpts/Losing2.htm.
42. "Word Change in *Book of Mormon* Intro Causes Stir," *Lawton Constitution*, January 12, 2008.
43. Ostling and Ostling, *Mormon America*, 103–6, gives a detailed look at how black LDS members regard the past history of their Church.
44. Ibid., 189.
45. Abanes, *One Nation Under Gods*, 404, quoting Bob Mims, "LDS Try to End Unauthorized Work for Jews," *Salt Lake Tribune*, May 2, 2001. *LDS Try to End Unauthorized Work for Jews*, nowscape.com/mormon/hitler_temple_3.htm.
46. Ibid., 403, quoting Bob Mims.
47. Ibid., 404, a quote in article by Mims.
48. Ostling and Ostling, *Mormon America*, 190.
49. Helen Radkey, "Proxy Baptism of Jews: The Splash Goes On," Utah Lighthouse Ministry, www.utlm.org/onlineresources/hitlertemplework.htm.
50. These figures from *Deseret Morning News 2004 Church Almanac* as quoted in *Salt Lake City Messenger* 103 (November 2004). Utah Lighthouse Ministry, www.utlm.org/newsletters/no103.htm#Appoints.
51. Linda P. Wilcox, "The Mormon Concept of a Mother in Heaven," in *Sisters in Spirit: Mormon Women in Historical and Cultural Perspective*, ed. Maureen Ursenbach Beecher and Lavina Anderson (Champaign, Ill.: University of Illinois Press, 1992), 72.
52. Wilcox, *Sisters*, 74.
53. Margaret Merrill Toscano, "Is There a Place for Heavenly Mother in Mormon Theology? An Investigation into Discourses of Power," *Sunstone* (July 2004), 15. *Sunstone*, www.sunstoneonline.com/magazine/issues/133/133–14–22.pdf.
54. Melodie Moench Charles, "Precedents for Mormon Women from Scriptures," in *Sisters in Spirit*, ed. Beecher and Anderson, 59.
55. "Mormon Women Have Had the Priesthood Since 1843," in *Women and Authority: Re-emerging Mormon Feminism*, ed. Maxine Hanks (Salt Lake City: Signature Books, 1992). Signature Books, www.signaturebookslibrary.org/women/chapter17.htm#Woman.
56. Sonia Johnson, *From Housewife to Heretic* (New York: Doubleday, 1981).

57. *The Family: A Proclamation to the World*, www.lds.org/ldsorg/v/index.jsp?vgnextoid=e1fa5f74db46c010VgnVCM1000004d82620aRCRD&locale=0&sourceId=5fd30f9856c20110VgnVCM100000176f620a____&hideNav=1.
58. Toscano, "Is There a Place," 21.
59. Quinn, *The Mormon Hierarchy: Origins of Power*, 631.
60. Quinn, *The Mormon Hierarchy: Extensions of Power*, 128.
61. Affirmation, affirmation.org/learning/fourteen.shtml. An Affirmation article also links to Connell O'Donovan, www.connellodonovan.com/abom.html. See also gay, ex-Mormon scholar D. Michael Quinn's *Same-Sex Dynamics Among Nineteenth-Century Mormons: A Mormon Example* (Champaign, Ill.: University of Illinois Press, 2001).
62. Evergreen International, www.evergreeninternational.org.
63. Restoration Church of Jesus Christ, www.rcjc.org
64. http://newsroom.lds.org/ldsnewsroom/eng/public-issues/same-gender-attraction.
65. As quoted in "The Mormon Odyssey," *Newsweek* (October 17, 2005), *Newsweek*, www.newsweek.com/id/50728/page/1.
66. "LDS Leaders Still Believe There Will Be Polygamy in Heaven," Utah Lighthouse Ministry, www.utlm.org/onlineresources/ldsleadersbelievepolygamyinheaven.htm.
67. My website, www.latayne.com has a section entitled "Cult Fiction," which reviews novels about Mormonism.
68. As quoted by Lawrence Wright, "Lives of the Saints," *The New Yorker* (January 21, 2002). *Lawrence Wright*, www.lawrencewright.com/art-saints.html.

CHAPTER 10: ISSUES AND CHALLENGES FACING MORMONISM IN THE TWENTY-FIRST CENTURY—PART 2

1. Walt Jayroe, "Drawing the Line on Religion," *Editor & Publisher* (1994). *Mormon Curtain*, www.mormoncurtain.com/topic_stevebenson_section2.html#pub_1151491931.
2. Janis Hutchinson, www.janishutchinson.com.
3. Noah Feldman, "What Is It about Mormonism?" *New York Times*, January 6, 2008. *New York Times*, www.nytimes.com/2008/01/06/magazine/06mormonism-t.html?pagewanted=1&_r=2.
4. Quinn, *The Mormon Hierarchy: Origins of Power*, 128. This book has a very complete discussion of this subject.
5. *Journal of Discourses* 18:341.
6. *Deseret News* (April 6, 1896), as quoted in Tanner and Tanner, *Mormonism—Shadow or Reality?* 423.
7. Here Hutchinson cites Klaus J. Hansen, *Quest for Empire* (Lincoln, Neb.: University of Nebraska Press, 1967), 65.
8. John Heinerman and Anson Shupe, *The Mormon Corporate Empire* (Boston: Beacon Press, 1985), 20.
9. Janis Hutchinson, www.janishutchinson.com/.
10. Abanes, *One Nation Under Gods*, 335.

11. *Journal of Discourses* 7:15. Brigham Young, July 4, 1854: "Will the Constitution be destroyed? No: it will be held inviolate by this people; and, as Joseph Smith said, 'The time will come when the destiny of the nation will hang upon a single thread. At that critical juncture, this people will step forth and save it from the threatened destruction.' It will be so."
12. Wright, "Lives of the Saints." Wright noted that though Mormons in 2002 made up only 1.8 percent of the US population yet five of the one hundred US senators were Mormons.
13. Jerald Tanner and Sandra Tanner, *Evolution of the Mormon Temple Ceremony 1842–1990* (Salt Lake City: Utah Lighthouse Ministry, 1990, updated 2005), 133.
14. *Townhall.com*, www.townhall.com/columnists/ChuckColson/2007/05/01/what_the_hate_crimes_law_would_do.
15. The question might arise: How is a Mormon's oath of loyalty different than the allegiances of a Christian in politics? It is true that a Christian's loyalty to the Lord has to be paramount. However, there is a substantial difference between loyalty to God and loyalty to an earthly hierarchal group of people whose history includes the prophecy of a theocracy which the LDS Church would head.
16. As quoted by Wright, "Lives of the Saints."
17. Stephanie Mencimer, "Theocracy in America: What Gentile Life in Mormon Utah Can Teach Us about Church and State," *Washington Monthly* (April 2001). *Washington Monthly*, www.washingtonmonthly.com/features/2001/0104.mencimer.html.
18. Lavina Fielding Anderson, "The LDS Intellectual Community and Church Leadership: A Contemporary Chronology," *Dialogue: A Journal of Mormon Thought* 26, no. 1 (Spring 1993): 7–64. *Dialogue*, http://content.lib.utah.edu/cdm4/document.php?CISOROOT=/dialogue&CISOPTR=22860&REC=19&CISOSHOW=22674.
19. Jerald Tanner and Sandra Tanner, *The Mormon Purge* (Salt Lake City: Utah Lighthouse Ministry, 1993).
20. Deborah Laake, *Secret Ceremonies: A Mormon Woman's Intimate Diary of Marriage and Beyond* (New York: William Morrow, 1993).
21. *Salt Lake Tribune*, September 20, 1993; as quoted by Jerald Tanner and Sandra Tanner in *Salt Lake City Messenger* (November 1993). Utah Lighthouse Ministry, www.utlm.org/newsletters/no85.htm.
22. LDS Apostle Dallin Oaks quoted in *Arizona Republic*, October 10, 1993; as cited by Tanners, *Salt Lake City Messenger* (November 1993). Utah Lighthouse Ministry, www.utlm.org/newsletters/no85.htm.
23. Peter Steinfels, "Secret Files," *New York Times*, August 22, 1992. *New York Times*, http://query.nytimes.com/gst/fullpage.html?res=9E0CE4DD1E30F931A1575B.C.0A964958260.
24. See *Salt Lake City Messenger* (August 1991): "In October 1976 we [Jerald and Sandra Tanner] received a letter from a man known as 'Stan Fields.' He claimed he was an 'Ex-Mormon for Jesus, and would like to be added to your mailing list ... God's blessings on you as you do His work, Sincerely in Christ.' This

man spent a great deal of time spying on various people who were critical of the Mormon Church. We later learned that his real name was Steven Mayfield and that he was also working for the FBI at the time he sent us this letter. In 1980, we discovered his deceitful game and the fact that at that very time he was employed at the Mormon Church Office Building. We confronted him on the job and he confessed to his duplicity and consented to a tape-recorded interview (see our publication, *Unmasking a Mormon Spy*). During the time that Steven Mayfield was carrying out his nefarious operations, he went to great lengths to protect his 'cover.' In a letter to Latayne Covett *[sic]* Scott, Mr. Mayfield went so far as to say that the Mormon Church was inspired by the Devil: 'I read some of the Tanners' material and became thoroughly convinced that the Mormon cult the church of my youth, the church of my ancestors was wrong, false, and Satan inspired.' In the same letter, Mayfield went on to complain concerning 'the falseness of man-made religion (like Mormonism) which leads men to hell.' After he was exposed, Steven Mayfield admitted that these statements were only made in an attempt to gain the confidence of Mormon critics so that he could spy on them." Utah Lighthouse Ministry, www.utlm.org/newsletters/no79.htm.

25. As quoted by Jerald Tanner and Sandra Tanner, *Salt Lake City Messenger* (November 1993). Utah Lighthouse Ministry, www.utlm.org/newsletters/no85.htm.
26. "Ex-BYU Professor Claims Beliefs Led to Dismissal," *Salt Lake Tribune*, July 30, 1988.
27. Daniel Golden, "In Religion Studies, Universities Bend to Views of Faithful: Scholar of Mormon History, Expelled from Church, Hits a Wall in Job Search," *Wall Street Journal*, April 6, 2006.
28. Peggy Fletcher Stack, "Exiles in Zion," *Salt Lake Tribune*, August 16, 2003. *Rick Ross Institute*, www.rickross.com/reference/mormon/mormon116.html.
29. The September Six incident was preceded in 1987 by an incident in which a Brigham Young University professor was guaranteed continued employment in exchange for not publishing with UPI an article about the untruths publicly told by LDS Apostle Paul Dunn. *Salt Lake Tribune*, February 21, 1991, as quoted by Jerald Tanner and Sandra Tanner, Utah Lighthouse Ministry, www.utlm.org/newsletters/no78.htm. In 2006 a Brigham Young University adjunct professor, Jeffrey Nielsen, who criticized the LDS Church's opposition to gay marriages in an article he wrote for a Salt Lake City newspaper, was not fired, but was not rehired for the subsequent term.
30. Russell McGregor, "Are Anti-Mormons Christians?" *FAIR*, http://fairlds.org/Anti-Mormons/Are_Anti-Mormons_Christians.html.
31. *Pearl of Great Price*, Joseph Smith—History 1:19.
32. Ex-Mormon John R. Farkas quoted by Gruss and Thuet, *What Every Mormon*, 17. Farkas has footnoted each of these claims in the Gruss-Thuet book.
33. Vaughn J. Featherstone, "The Last Drop in the Chalice" (speech, Brigham Young University, September 24, 1985). *Speeches*, http://speeches.byu.edu/reader/reader.php?id=6988.
34. My observation, after spending some time on Internet message boards where ex-Mormons post about their experiences, is that even the vehemence of the

most extreme "anti-Mormon spokespersons" of the last two decades pales in comparison to the rage, resentment, and sense of betrayal expressed online by many "regular" *ex-Mormons* in speaking of the LDS Church.

35. Some people regard the work of Dr. Walter Martin as being too extreme, for instance, while others such as ex-Mormon Cindy Baer count him as one of the most positive influences on her. See my book *Why We Left Mormonism: Eight People Tell Their Stories* (Grand Rapids, Mich.: Baker Books, 1990), 140.
36. Thousands of pages of authoritative, documented information resides on their site at Utah Lighthouse Ministry, www.utlm.org.
37. Craig L. Blomberg and Stephen E. Robinson, *How Wide the Divide?: A Mormon and an Evangelical in Conversation* (Downers Grove, Ill.: InterVarsity, 1997). In their conclusion, responding to the titular question, Blomberg and Robinson list both items on which both Mormons and evangelicals can agree, but also a substantial number—most notably questions about godhood and heaven—about which there can be no agreement.
38. Gregory C. V. Johnson and Robert L. Millet, *Bridging the Divide: The Continuing Conversation Between a Mormon and an Evangelical* (Rhinebeck, N.Y.: Monkfish, 2007).
39. Bill McKeever and Eric Johnson, "The Bridge or the Beehive? Mormon Apologetics in a Postmodern Age," *Christian Research Journal* 30, no. 4 (2007).
40. "Sunstone Announces the Mapping Mormon Issues Project," *Sunstone*, www.sunstonemagazine.com/news-and-headlines/mapping-mormon-issues.html.
41. "'If you want to pander to the Mormon apologists not ready for real dialogue, the cost is going to be a willingness to slander the Christian brethren that went before you.' Anyone who has read *How Wide the Divide?* by Evangelical Craig Blomberg and Mormon Stephen Robinson, a project spurred on by Standing Together's Greg Johnson, will have noticed that Mormon scholar Stephen Robinson very quickly wraps himself in a cloak of victim privilege and makes sure Blomberg understands he is going to regard any challenges to his idiosyncratic expressions of Mormon doctrine as persecution. He acts in other words as a victim-bully." Ronald V. Huggins, ThD, "An Appeal for Authentic Evangelical-Mormon Dialogue," *Mormons in Transition*, http://irr.org/MIT/authentic-dialogue.html.
42. Book reviews of *The Mormon Mirage* on Amazon, www.amazon.com/review/product/0310389119/ref=cm_cr_dp_all_helpful?%5Fencoding=UTF8&coliid=&showViewpoints=1&colid=&sortBy=bySubmissionDateDescending.
43. Michael R. Ash, "Hard Questions and Keeping the Faith," *Meridian*, www.meridianmagazine.com/lineuponline/040318harquestions.html.
44. See ex-Mormon, Pulitzer Prize–winner Steve Benson's assessment at Mormon Curtain, www.mormoncurtain.com/topic_stevebenson_section4.html#pub_–1002160683.
45. John-Charles Duffy, "Defending the Kingdom, Rethinking the Faith: How Apologetics Is Reshaping Mormon Orthodoxy," sidebar article, "Hostility and Contempt in LDS Apologetics," *Sunstone* (May 2004): 26.
46. Ibid., 23.
47. Ibid., 27.

48. Carl Mosser and Paul Owen, "Mormon Scholarship, Apologetics, and Evangelical Neglect: Losing the Battle and Not Knowing It?" *Cephas Ministry*, www.cephasministry.com/mormon_apologetics_losing_battle.html.
49. Matthew A. Paulson, *Breaking the Mormon Code: A Critique of Mormon Scholarship Regarding Classical Theology and the Book of Mormon* (Livermore, Calif.: Wingspan, 2000) .
50. As does Duffy, *Defending the Kingdom.*
51. Simon Southerton, "DNA Genealogies of American Indians and the Book of Mormon on Mormonism," *Recovery from Mormonism*, www.exmormon.org/whylft125.htm.
52. *Journal of Discourses* 13:95.
53. "How much unbelief exists in the minds of Latter-day Saints in regard to one particular doctrine which I revealed to them, and which God revealed to me—namely that Adam is our father and God ... Then he said, 'I want my children who are in the spirit world to come and live here. I once dwelt upon an earth something like this, in a mortal state. I was faithful. I received my crown and exaltation ... I want my children that were born to me in the spirit world to come here and take tabernacles of flesh that their spirits may have a house, a tabernacle.'" Brigham Young, *Deseret Weekly News*, June 18, 1873, facsimile at Utah Lighthouse Ministry, www.utlm.org/onlinebooks/changech8.htm, p. 97.
54. Richard Packham, http://packham.n4m.org/morexmos.htm. In addition, John Dart, "Counting Mormons: Study Says LDS Numbers Inflated," *The Christian Century* (August 21, 2007), says if LDS membership rolls were accounted like Baptists or Presbyterians, they would have only about 3.2 million members in the United States and are losing members through "defection and apostasy" as fast as new converts are added. Only the extraordinarily high LDS birthrate, says Dart, accounts for three-fourths of the Church's US growth rate.
55. As quoted by Peggy Fletcher Stack, "Keeping Members a Challenge for LDS Church," *Salt Lake Tribune*, July 26, 2005.
56. Wallace Turner, *The Mormon Establishment* (Boston: Houghton Mifflin, 1966), 4.
57. Harold B. Lee, *Conference Reports* (October 1947): 67.
58. Duffy, *Defending the Kingdom*, 24.
59. Craig Foster, "Understanding the 'Stages of Grief' of Former Members Who Attack the Church," *Meridian*, www.meridianmagazine.com/articles/030627grief.html.
60. Scott Tracy, "Why They Leave," *NetXNews*, September 23, 2007. Though I am familiar with neither the author nor his polling methodologies, his results ring true from my own experience of corresponding with ex-Mormons for thirty-five years.
61. Quoted by Wright, "Lives of the Saints."
62. New Order Mormon, http://newordermormon.org/.
63. Richard Packham, http://packham.n4m.org/.
64. Ex-Mormon Jay Crosby, *The Black Sheep Roster*, www.salamandersociety.com/blacksheep.

65. Lane A. Thuet, volunteer researcher and writer for Mormonism Research Ministry, in private correspondence with the author.
66. An example: *Wayne and Dianne Simister's UTAH Information & Family Pages*, www.geocities.com/wsimister/remove.htm.
67. My website, www.latayne.com, has a list of links to organizations listed here.
68. Patty Henetz, "Websites Provide Confidential Community for Former and Wavering Mormons," Associated Press, June 26, 2003. *Rick Ross Institute*, http://rickross.com/reference/mormon/mormon109.html.
69. *Recovery from Mormonism*, http://exmormon.org.

CHAPTER 11: CONCLUSION

1. As quoted by Jerald Tanner and Sandra Tanner, *The Changing World of Mormonism*, www.utlm.org/onlinebooks/changech5c.htm.
2. "The Treasury of David, Psalm 30," *The Spurgeon Archive*, www.spurgeon.org/treasury/ps030.htm.
3. The only literary works I have read that approach the articulation of this sense of loss are C. S. Lewis's *A Grief Observed* and Paul L. Maier's *A Skeleton in God's Closet.*
4. Note to the FARMS boys and their cousins: No, the school is not accredited; and yes, I did years of research and teaching, and wrote a dissertation on a subject other than Mormonism.
5. Mormons in Transition, www.irr.org/mit/mentor.html, provides a mentoring service for people coming out of Mormonism. I cannot imagine how better my life would have been had such a service been available for me.
6. Latayne C. Scott, *After Mormonism, What? Reclaiming the Ex-Mormon's Worldview for Christ* (Grand Rapids, Mich.: Baker, 1994).
7. James W. Sire, *The Universe Next Door: A Basic Worldview Catalog* (Downers Grove, Ill.: InterVarsity, 2004).
8. A Mormon term for optimizing your service or responsibilities in the Church.
9. Beckwith, Mosser, and Owen, eds., *The New Mormon Challenge.* Mosser, one of the editors, levels the charge that "some evangelical apologists jealously guard the kind of Mormonism they don't believe in" (page 81).
10. "Standard works" of the LDS Church are its four books of scripture.
11. Review by Eric Johnson, "The New Mormon Challenge," Mormonism Research Ministry, www.mrm.org/topics/reviews/new-mormon-challenge-responding-latest-defenses-fast-growing-movement.
12. Ostling and Ostling, *Mormon America*, xii.
13. As quoted by Gustav Niebuhr, "Adapting 'Mormon' to Emphasize Christianity," *New York Times*, February 19, 2001.
14. Millet, *Getting at the Truth*, 138–39.
15. Ibid., 48.
16. Please note that I am not criticizing these protocols and procedures. I am, however, saying that such techniques reflect the mainstreaming and secularization of an organization which claims revelation as its foundation and divine approval its buttress.
17. J. Reuben Clark, as quoted in *Ensign* (September 2005): 17.

18. "President Gordon B. Hinckley Goes to Mountain Meadow, Denies Church Was Involved," *Idaho Statesman*, September 13, 1999.
19. David Van Biema, "Kingdom Come," *Time* (August 4, 1997): 56.
20. As quoted by Millet, *Getting at the Truth*, 78.
21. Peterson and Ricks, *Offenders for a Word*, 181.
22. Frank Pastore, "Mormonism: Religion, Denomination or Cult?" Quotation marks and italization are in original article. *Townhall.com*, www.townhall.com/columnists/FrankPastore/2007/04/28/mormonism__religion,_denomination,_or_cult.
23. I did not originate the list of characteristics of a cult. It originated with the Utah Christian Tract Society (which was absorbed at the retirement of its founder by Mormonism Research Ministry).
24. Actually, in the "Three-D Model of Reality," a gablelike teaching device formulated by my colleague and friend Dr. J. Michael Strawn, the unseen and seen realms are actually connected by a series of "stacked indices" or successive connectors. The Holy Spirit is foundational, and upon his agential actions are built revelation (in particular the Bible itself), faith, and finally our own disciplined thoughts, words, and actions which are atop—and grow out of—the previous layers.
25. As thinking beings, we are surrounded by facts—that is, physical objects, conditions, events, and so on. Yet we have no direct access to those facts without representations—the visual icons, sensory impressions, language, memories, and so forth—which we link in various ways—some conscious and deliberate, some seemingly automatic—to the facts. For instance, I see a mountain range outside my window. Even when I travel to another state, I can still access the image of that mountain in my head, because the mountain is only "there" because I brought it into my consciousness. For more details on these concepts, I refer readers to my dissertation, "A Definitional Study of Biblical Representational Research and Its Current Applications" (Albuquerque: Trinity Southwest University, 2003), to "The Logic of True Narrative Representations" by Drs. John W. Oller and Steven Collins, *Biblical Research Bulletin*, http://biblicalresearchbulletin.com/Biblical_Studies.html; to Drs. Collins and Oller, "Is the Bible a True Narrative Representation?" *Biblical Research Bulletin*, www.biblicalresearchbulletin.com/Biblical_Studies.html; and to Dr. John W. Oller, "Adding Abstract to Formal and Content Schemata: Results in Recent Work in Peircean Semiotics," *Arisbe: The Peirce Gateway*, www.cspeirce.com/menu/library/aboutcsp/oller/schemata.htm.
26. The Bible of course cannot contain the infinite mind of God, but does accurately represent what he wants us to know of that mind.
27. One of the ironies of vicarious baptism for the dead is that they stay dead; while Christian baptism is a death that raises one to new life.
28. *Doctrine and Covenants*, section 116.
29. Abanes, *One Nation Under Gods*, 407.
30. Carl Mosser, "And the Saints Go Marching On," in *The New Mormon Challenge*, Beckwith, Mosser, and Owen, eds., 81–82.
31. Originally published in *Christian Research Journal* (Summer 1992): 24. *Christian Research Journal*, www.iclnet.org/pub/resources/text/cri/cri-jrnl/web/crj0110a.html.

32. Ostling and Ostling, *Mormon America*, 249.
33. Millet, *Getting at the Truth*, 52–53.
34. Ibid., 51.
35. Bruce R. McConkie, "All Are Alike Unto God," *Speeches*, http://speeches.byu.edu/reader/reader.php?id=11017.
36. Eph. 2:11–16.
37. Millet, *Getting at the Truth*, 104.
38. F. F. Bruce, *The New Testament Documents: Are They Reliable?* (Grand Rapids, Mich.: Eerdmans, 1983), 14–17.
39. Francis J. Beckwith, "Philosophical Problems with the Mormon Concept of God," *Christian Research Journal* (Spring 1992). *Christian Research Institute*, www.equip.org/site/c.muI1LaMNJrE/b.2733561/k.B9AA/DM410.htm.
40. See Paul Copan and William Lane Craig, "Craftsman or Creator? An Examination of the Mormon Doctrine of Creation and a Defense of *Creatio ex Nihilo*," in *The New Mormon Challenge*, Beckwith, Mosser, and Owen, eds., 59–80.
41. Millet, *Getting at the Truth*, 50.
42. All these phrases are references to the titles of classic books written by Mormons about "anti-Mormons."
43. According to witnesses cited by the Ostlings, the historical accounts of the seagull incident show it was not at all the unique, supernatural event of Mormon lore. Ostling and Ostling, *Mormon America*, 241–42.
44. John 8:32.

ADDENDUM—EVANGELIZING MORMONS IN THE TWENTY-FIRST CENTURY

1. Lewis Price, "The Testimony of a Former Mormon Missionary" (n.p.: Utah Christian Tract Society, n.d.). Unfortunately this publication is long out of print.
2. Sandra Tanner, among others, suggests this. Her excellent and concise online guide for witnessing to Mormons is available at Utah Lighthouse Ministry, www.utlm.org/onlineresources/sharingyourfaithwithlds.htm.
3. Bob Witte, *Witnessing to Mormons* (Grand Rapids, Mich.: Gospel Truths, n.d.). Available in print from utlm.org or at Institute for Religious Research, www.irr.org/mit/WDIST/Where-Does-It-Say-That-Main.html.
4. Jerry Benson and Diana Benson, *How to Witness to a Mormon* (Chicago: Moody Press, 2000).
5. Janis Hutchinson, *The Mormon Missionaries: An Inside Look at Their Real Message and Methods* (Grand Rapids, Mich.: Kregel Resources, 1995).
6. Of course, that implies that you must indeed *have* such a relationship with the Lord yourself. If you do not, it is my respectful advice that you *not* try to convince Mormons to give up the satisfaction of their history and culture to join you in another superficial religious experience.
7. McKeever and Johnson, "The Bridge or the Beehive?"

SUBJECT INDEX

MORMON SCRIPTURE INDEX

SCRIPTURE INDEX

The Mormon Mirage

A Former Member Looks at the Mormon Church Today, Third and Expanded Ebook Edition

Latayne C. Scott

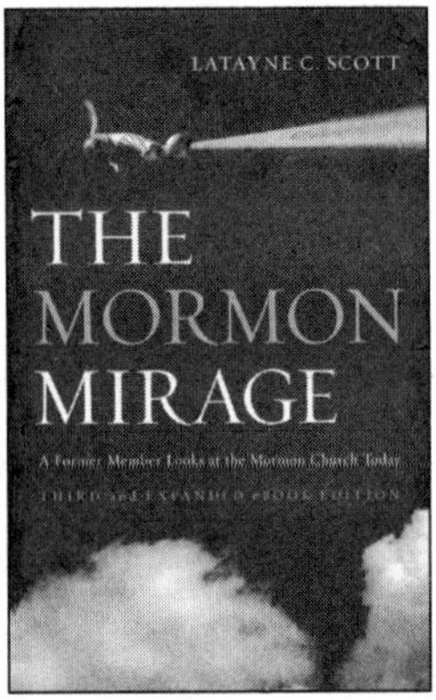

Latayne C. Scott's journey out of Mormonism is a remarkable testament of God's love and grace. For those interested in even more of her story, and additional formidable evidence against the claims of the LDS church, expanded ebook editions of the Mormon Mirage, 3rd ed. are available in these convenient formats:

- Sony eReader 978-0-310-29354-5
- Microsoft Reader 978-0-310-29355-2
- Adobe Reader 978-0-310-29356-9
- Palm Format 978-0-310-29357-6
- Kindle/Mobipocket 978-0-310-29358-3
- ePub 978-0-310-31310-6

With 150 additional pages, including extensive footnotes, the ebook is more than a riveting, insider's scrutiny of the Mormon faith—it is a testimony to the trustworthiness of Scripture and the grace of Jesus Christ.

Hardcover: 978-0-0310-29153-4

Pick up a copy today at Zondervan.com!

ZONDERVAN®
.com

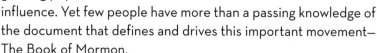

Encyclopedic Dictionary of Cults, Sects, and World Religions

Revised and Updated Edition

Larry A. Nichols, George A. Mather, and Alvin J. Schmidt

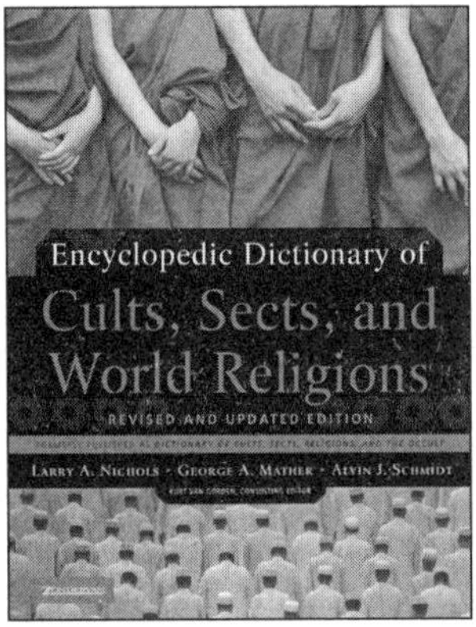

Up-to-date, well-documented, comprehensive coverage of cults, sects, and world religions, from the historical to the contemporary including: Jehovah's Witnesses, Mormons, Islam, and Baha'i and other groups with a significant North American influence.

REVISED, UPDATED, AND EXPANDED TO INCLUDE NEW ENTRIES AND NEW INFORMATION

- Updated information on Islam and its global impact
- New entries: the Branch Davidians, Native American religions, Heaven's Gate, Aum Supreme Truth, the Boston Movement, the Masonic Lodge, and many others
- Developments in the world of cults and the occult

Formerly titled *Dictionary of Cults, Sects, Religions, and the Occult,* this book provides reliable information on the history and beliefs of nearly every form of religion active today. This extensively revised edition includes new topics, updated information, and a brand-new format for a clearer, more organized approach. You'll also find group histories, numerous illustrations, charts, current statistics, websites, bibliographies, and other useful information.

Hardcover, Printed: 978-0-310-23954-3

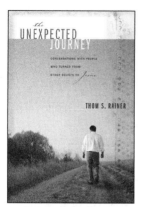